MONEY IN THE MEDIEVAL ENGLISH ECONOMY: 973–1489

Manchester University Press

MANCHESTER MEDIEVAL STUDIES

SERIES EDITOR Professor S. H. Rigby

The study of medieval Europe is being transformed as old orthodoxies are challenged, new methods embraced and fresh fields of inquiry opened up. The adoption of inter-disciplinary perspectives and the challenge of economic, social and cultural theory are forcing medievalists to ask new questions and to see familiar topics in a fresh light.

The aim of this series is to combine the scholarship traditionally associated with medieval studies with an awareness of more recent issues and approaches in a form accessible to the non-specialist reader.

ALREADY PUBLISHED IN THE SERIES

Pacemaking in the middle ages: Principles and practice
Jenny Benham

Reform and the papacy in the eleventh century
Kathleen G. Cushing

Picturing women in late medieval and Renaissance art
Christa Grössinger

The Vikings in England
D. M. Hadley

A sacred city: consecrating churches and reforming society in eleventh-century Italy
Louis I. Hamilton

The politics of carnival
Christopher Humphrey

Holy motherhood
Elizabeth L'Estrange

Music, scholasticism and reform: Salian Germany 1024–1125
T. J. H. McCarthy

Medieval law in context
Anthony Musson

The expansion of Europe, 1250–1500
Michael North

Medieval maidens
Kim M. Phillips

Gentry culture in late medieval England
Raluca Radulescu and Alison Truelove (eds)

Chaucer in context
S. H. Rigby

The life cycle in Western Europe, c.1300–c.1500
Deborah Youngs

M^{ANCHESTER} M^{EDIEVAL} S^{TUDIES}

MONEY IN THE MEDIEVAL ENGLISH ECONOMY, 973–1489

J. L. Bolton

Manchester University Press
Manchester and New York
distributed exclusively in the USA by Palgrave

Copyright © J. L. Bolton 2012

The right of J. L. Bolton to be identified as the author of this work has been asserted by him in accordance with the Copyright, Designs and Patents Act 1988.

Published by Manchester University Press
Oxford Road, Manchester M13 9NR, UK
and Room 400, 175 Fifth Avenue, New York, NY 10010, USA
www.manchesteruniversitypress.co.uk

Distributed in the United States exclusively by
Palgrave Macmillan, 175 Fifth Avenue, New York,
NY 10010, USA

Distributed in Canada exclusively by
UBC Press, University of British Columbia, 2029 West Mall,
Vancouver, BC, Canada V6T 1Z2

British Library Cataloguing-in-Publication Data
A catalogue record for this book is available from the British Library

Library of Congress Cataloging-in-Publication Data applied for

ISBN 978 0 7190 5039 8 hardback
ISBN 978 0 7190 5040 4 paperback

First published 2012

The publisher has no responsibility for the persistence or accuracy of URLs for any external or third-party internet websites referred to in this book, and does not guarantee that any content on such websites is, or will remain, accurate or appropriate.

Typeset in Monotype Bulmer
by Koinonia, Manchester
Printed in Great Britain
by Bell & Bain Ltd, Glasgow

DEDICATION

To Jack, Max and Tom, who make me laugh, and to the medical, nursing and auxiliary staff of the Gastroenterology Department at first Oldchurch Hospital and now at The Queen's Hospital, Romford, Essex, for the care they have given me since 1988.

CONTENTS

List of figures and tables	page xi
Visual references	xii
Acknowledgments	xiii
Abbreviations	xv

Part I Theories and problems

1 Modelling the medieval economy: the equation of exchange

Population and prices	3
The Fisher identity of equation of exchange: the theory	5
The Fisher identity or equation of exchange: the problems	8
Measuring monetisation and commercialisation	14

2 Money and the money economy

A definition of money	19
The emergence of a money economy	21
Population growth and the expansion of the market	22
The money supply	23
Reckoning, recording, accounting and amounts systems	28
The growth of government	31
Capitalism	37

3 Coinage and the bullion supply

The purchasing power of money	44
Coins in circulation	50
The silver coinage	50
The gold coinage	51
Moneys of account	52
Mints and minting	52
Estimating the volume of currency in circulation: coin-hoard and single-find evidence	57
The bullion supply	65
The mint price and seignorage	68
Bi-metallism, gold:silver ratios and bi-metallic flows	70
Credit and 'paper money'	71
Conclusion	74

Part II The coinage and the economy, 973–1489

A: A monetised economy

4 The coinage from the late tenth century to 1158

The coinage 973–1066
- The reform of 973 — 87
- *Renovatio monetae*: the theory — 89
- The geld and the coinage — 91
- *Renovatio monetae*: the debate — 93
- Weight standards — 96
- The geld, the bullion supply and the coinage — 98
- The coinage 973–1066: conclusions — 99

The coinage 1066–1158
- The new weight standard — 100
- The Norman coinage — 102
- The bullion supply — 103
- The end of *renovatio monetae* — 106
- Conclusion: the size of the circulating medium — 106

5 A monetised economy, 973–1158?
- Introduction — 113

The case for a money economy
- The use of money as a medium of exchange — 114
- Commercialisation, taxation and lordship — 117
- Reckoning, recording and accounting — 119
- Credit — 122

The case against a money economy
- The GDP and the velocity of circulation — 124
- Payments in kind — 128
- The flow of money to the countryside — 130
- Regional variation in the use of money — 131
- Conclusion: a monetised economy — 132

B: The emergence of a money economy, 1158–1351

6 The coinage 1158–1351
- Introduction
  - The flood of silver — 141
  - Mints and exchanges — 142
- The coinage 1158–1290
  - The Tealby coinage (cross/crosslets) 1158 — 145
  - The short-cross recoinage of 1180 and the partial recoinage of 1205 — 147

The outflow of coin 1154–1244	149
Silver imports 1154–1247	151
The long-cross coinage 1247–79	152
A failed experiment: gold in 1257	154
The recoinage of 1279–90	156
The circulating medium in 1290	159
Monetary instability 1290–1343: the crisis of silver	
1290–1300: pollards and crockards	159
The recoinage of 1300–2	161
Early fourteenth-century problems: monetary fluctuations	162
The revaluation of silver and the introduction of gold, 1343–51	167
Conclusion	169

7 The making of a money economy, 1158–1351

Introduction	174
Inflation in England, 1199–1247	176
Inflation in England, 1247–1351	182
Inflation 1180–1300: conclusion	184
Inflation, the direct management of estates and 'the crisis of the knights'	185
The emergence of a money economy	187
The coinage and the rural economy	188
Credit and the market economy	191
Loans and partnerships	193
The Jews and the Italians	196
Literacy and numeracy	199
The recovery of debts and the enforcement of contracts	202
Credit provision by the English: lay and ecclesiastical moneylenders	205
Credit provision by the English: the merchants	207
Credit provision by the English: village moneylenders	209
The money market	211

C: The money economy challenged, 1351–1489

8 The coinage 1351–1489

Introduction: infrequent recoinages	227
War and its consequences	229
Plague and depopulation	231
Famine and economic downturn	231
The bullion crises	232
The English coinage 1351–1489	236
The mints: the Tower and Calais	240
The volume of coin in circulation	241

CONTENTS

    Bullionism and the balance of trade   245
    The shortage of silver   250

9   Testing the money economy, 1351–1489
    Introduction: the nature of the evidence   258
    Modelling the late medieval economy   259
    'Stagnation tinged with gloom'   260
    Other models of the late medieval economy   261
    'Money answereth all things.'   263
    Monetary deflation, prices and wages   264
    'Wage stickiness'   268
    Credit and the money supply   268
    The shortage of coin   270
    Taxation and the coinage   272
    The credit market   274
    Assignment of debts   279
    The bond obligatory and the question of 'paper' money   280
    The law of debt   283
    Banks and bankers: credit in overseas trade   284
    Credit in internal trade   288
    Debasement: the advice of 1379 ignored   293
    Conclusion   295

10 **Conclusions**   304

Bibliography www.history.qmul.ac.uk/bolton/   310
Index   311

LIST OF FIGURES AND TABLES

Figures

2.1	Fluctuations in the money supply 1180–1351	24
6.1	The outflow of coin 1180–1250	150
7.1	Wheat and oxen sale prices 1160–1356	183
8.1	Calais mint output 1362–1450	242
9.1	Real wages of building workers in southern England 1350–1499	265
9.2	Carpenter's wages per day. 1350–1500, ten-year averages	267

Tables

2.1	Coinage per head of population 973–1158	25
2.2	Silver coinage per head of population 1180–1351	26
2.3	Coinage (silver and gold) per head of population 1351	27
3.1	The weight and fineness of the English silver coinage 1158–1526	48
3.2	Tower and Troy pounds in grains and grams	54
4.1	The ranking of Anglo-Saxon mints by output, 1066	95
4.2	Coinage per head of population in 1087: Dolley's estimates	107
8.1	Coinage and coinage per head of population 1290–1470	244
9.1	Borrowing by way of exchange, 1438–9	285
9.2	GDP and per capita GDP 1086–1470	295

VISUAL REFERENCES

Readers will find digital images of all the coins mentioned in this book, along with their numismatic classification, at the following websites:

973–1180. The Fitzwilliam Museum, Cambridge, EMC/SCBI websites, www.fitzmuseum.cam.ac.uk/coins/emc Left click on 'Search the Corpus' and follow the instructions on the search tools.

1180–1500. www/britishmuseum/org/collection takes you straight to The British Museum's Collection database. Under 'Search' enter 'coins' and the name of the king in whose reign the coins in which you are interested were minted. So: 'coins Henry III'. Then, under 'Date' enter 1216 and 1272 respectively, remembering to click on 'AD'. Click on the 'Search' button, and this will produce images of coins in the Museum's collection which date from his reign.

Alternatively, enter http://finds.org.uk/database/search/mednumismatics, click on 'Medieval numismatic search' in the left-hand column, and follow the instructions in the search tools. Images here are taken from the Museum's Portable Antiquities database.

My thanks to Dr Martin Allen of the Fitzwilliam Museum, Cambridge, and Dr Barrie Cook of the British Museum for their help in this matter.

ACKNOWLEDGEMENTS

It has taken more than twenty years to write this book. During that over-long time, much new research has been published on both coinage and economy and that has led to constant revision of all the chapters, as footnotes and bibliography will show. During that time I have also become involved in another project, on the ledgers of Filippo Borromei and company, a Milanese bank with branches in Bruges and London in the 1430s and 1440s. Working on the day-to-day records of two fifteenth-century banks has made me look at the whole problem of 'money' again and this has much influenced the first three and last two chapters of this book. Given the time scale, many debts and kindnesses have to be gladly and gratefully acknowledged here. First on the long list is to the School of History at Queen Mary, University of London which has generously funded my room and full internet and library services after the grant from the ESRC (Award no. R000239125) for the Borromei Bank Research Project expired in 2004-5. The help and support of successive Heads of School and of my colleagues has been boundless, as has that of the members of the Late Medieval Seminar at the Institute of Historical Research. They have endured years of my obsession with money, banking and credit with cheerful rudeness and have constantly passed on to me invaluable evidence for the book acquired as part of their own researches. It has been academic collaboration of the highest order and for that they deserve all the thanks I can give them. My colleague at the Borromei Bank Research Project, Dr Francesco Guidi Bruscoli of the University of Florence, has taught me much about money and international banking in the late Middle Ages. He has also held in check my tendency to pursue improbable theories, although his continued support for A.C.F. Fiorentina, *la viòla*, does make one wonder about his critical judgment. Dr Martin Allen of the Department of Coins and Medals at the Fitzwilliam Museum, Cambridge, has been a constant source of much-needed advice and encouragement, generously sending me copies of his many articles on the coinage and the money supply, often in advance of their publication. He also writes acerbic and very funny answers to daft questions sent him by email. Without his help, and that of Professor Stephen Rigby, the General Editor of this Series, this book would never have been finished. Professor Rigby, in particular, has generously and rigorously read and edited the first and second drafts of the text, both to shorten it and give it greater clarity. I am grateful to Martin Hargreaves for his efficient and speedy compilation of the index.

ACKNOWLEDGMENTS

Professor Paul Latimer of the University of Bilkent also gave me valuable advice on the twelfth- and thirteenth-century sections of the text. My debt to the many numismatists, historians and economists whose works I have used is great and I hope that they will not feel that I have misrepresented their ideas in any way. All errors are of my own making. My final thanks, as ever, go to Ann who has had to put up with this book for far too long and has done so with her usual forbearance and understanding. *Dux femina facti.*

Queen Mary, University of London, and Romford, Essex   Jim Bolton

ABBREVIATIONS

ABIB	Archivio Borromeo dell'Isola Bella
AgHR	*Agricultural History Review*
BNJ	*British Numismatic Journal*
EHD	*English historical documents*
EcHR	*Economic History Review*
EHR	*English Historical Review*
EL	*Economic Letters*
GDP	Gross Domestic Product
HR	*Historical Research*
JEEH	*Journal of European Economic History*
JEH	*Journal of Economic History*
JEMH	*Journal of Early Modern History*
JHG	*Journal of Historical Geography*
JHS	*Jewish Historical Studies*
LHR	*Law and History Review*
NC	*Numismatic Chronicle*
OED	*Oxford English Dictionary*
P&P	*Past and Present*
PRO	Public Record Office
PROME	Parliament Rolls of Medieval England (Digital Edition)
RP	*Rotuli Parliamentorum*
TNA	The National Archives
TRHS	*Transactions of the Royal Historical Society*
£	Pounds
s	Shillings
d	Pence

PART I

Theories and problems

1

Modelling the medieval economy: the equation of exchange

Population and prices

The idea that money in its various forms plays an important part in economic development is nothing new. There was a long-standing medieval tradition which saw society as a body with the stomach as its treasury. If it was not fed with money, then it would wither away and die. In the early seventeenth century Sir Francis Bacon put it more earthily: 'Money is like muck [manure], not good except it be spread', while the eighteenth-century Scottish philosopher David Hume likened it to oil which made the economic wheels go round. A late twentieth-century economics textbook takes his comparison even further. 'Money', its authors say, 'oils the wheels of commerce and debt funds growth in industrial capitalism. On these two generalizations economic historians are agreed. A complex market-based industrial economy cannot function without money and credit.'[1]

Therein lies our first problem. It could be argued that we, as modern historians, should not take our ideas of what causes growth in an industrialised economy and apply them to a largely agrarian medieval society which had no conception of an 'economy', be it national, regional or local, or of sustained economic policies, let alone the means to implement or enforce them. This would be a serious mistake on at least two grounds. In the first place it would deprive us of some useful analytical tools which can help us understand, measure and explain changes in the medieval economy. Secondly, we should never underestimate medieval man's ability to grasp the practicalities of any given situation and to see that there were some fundamental steps that could be taken to ensure general well-being. One such step was thought to be the maintenance of a sound coinage, a constant demand throughout the period. This meant that there should be in circulation coins with a high silver or gold content and not clipped or badly worn and therefore light in weight, which would affect their purchasing power.[2] As early as 1124 the Anglo-Saxon chronicler showed a clear understanding of the relationship between poor coinage and rising prices. 'In the course of the same year', he wrote,

> the weather in England was very bad for corn and all products, so that between Christmas and Candlemas (2 February) it was said that seed wheat for an acre ... went up to six shillings and barley ... went up to six shillings and oats ... to four shillings. That was because corn was scarce, and the penny so bad that if a man had a pound at the market he could not by any means get the value of twelve pence for it.[3]

Writing from Peterborough Abbey in the depths of the Fens, the first continuator of the Anglo-Saxon Chronicle showed remarkable prescience. He accepted that prices reflected both changes in the balance between supply and demand and in the purchasing power of money centuries before modern economists reached the same conclusion. Prices are now regarded are one of the most important variables in the economy. Tracking their movements over both short and long periods provides analysts with evidence of changes in the balance between supply and demand and in patterns of demand. In the much simpler economy of twelfth-century England, grain prices were clearly related to the quality of the harvest. National or local harvest failures would send them soaring, usually in the spring and early summer of the following year before the next harvest was brought in.

Long-run prices series, constructed so as to iron out short-term fluctuations due to unusual or temporary circumstances, are therefore one of the best ways of monitoring changes in living standards. They can also be used to explain investment decisions. For instance, it must have become obvious to many fifteenth-century English farmers that grain prices had fallen sharply and remained low over many years while prices for meat and dairy products were rising. Some did nothing, waiting hopefully and vainly for the good times to return. For others, however, grain had only been a profitable crop when prices were high. Their land was equally, and perhaps even better, suited to pastoral farming and a change to rearing cattle for the market began to look like an attractive option. But it required capital investment in hedging and enclosing fields and for the purchase of livestock and the extra feed needed for over-wintering more animals. Increased working capital would also be needed because of the long credit chains from the producer to the consumer who might be far away in London, the principal centre of consumption in the British Isles.

Prices, then, are a good guide to changing patterns of consumption, rising or falling standards of living and patterns of investment in the medieval as well as the modern world. They have been used by many if not most medieval historians as a central plank in what is known as the population and resources model of the economy. Hatcher and Bailey define it thus:

> Agriculture dominated the economy of medieval England and the great bulk of the country's resources were devoted to providing the basic subsistence needs of its inhabitants ... At the very least 80 per cent of the population lived in the countryside and were directly engaged in farming the land. Agricultural productivity relied on the muscle-power of the men and women who worked the soil and tended the livestock, assisted only by draught animals and basic equipment. Farming technology changed but slowly, and most farms were small and utilized little capital. Hence the relationship between the number of people and the amount of land available to support them was of overwhelming significance to the economy and the balance of this relationship was subject to dramatic change over time.[4]

What matters here is the size of the population. Slow, cumulative growth over a long period will push up demand for land, either to purchase or to rent, and the price of food, since production cannot easily be increased to meet demand, especially when the limits of cultivation have been reached. The reverse, of course, is that if the population falls dramatically, so will the price of both land and grain, the most important arable crop in medieval agriculture, while wages will rise because of shortages of labour.

This is a straightforward and elegant explanation of change in the medieval economy and it is easy to see why it has been widely adopted. Certainly, the long-run price series from the twelfth to the fifteenth century seem to support the argument. They show rising prices from the late twelfth to the early fourteenth centuries, when population began to reach the limits of its subsistence, and then falling prices after the 1370s as depopulation caused by recurrent outbreaks of plague began to have serious consequences for the agrarian economy. By the mid-fifteenth century the population had fallen to about half its level in 1300 and, outside London, recovery did not begin until well into the sixteenth century.[5]

The Fisher identity or equation of exchange: the theory

Not all historians accept that medieval prices rose and fell simply in response to increasing or decreasing population levels, however. For them, fluctuations in the money supply – that is, the physical amount of coin in

PART I: THEORIES AND PROBLEMS

circulation – are an equally if not more important variable. They are known as monetarist or monetary historians, not because they follow slavishly the theories of Milton Friedman and the Chicago School of economists, but because of their belief that variations in the stock of precious metals (silver and gold coins) of themselves affect prices, wages and investment policies and control the amount of credit extended in society generally.[6] The latter will be discussed at length in the final chapters: for the moment it is the problem of the consequences for prices of variations in the money supply that concerns us. Rigby, in his *English Society in the Later Middle Ages*, gives the clearest worked explanation of the theory that dominates monetarist arguments. It is known as the Fisher identity or equation of exchange, since it was developed by Irwin Fisher in his book, *The Purchasing Power of Money*, first published in New York in 1911.[7] Its simplest form is **MV = PT**, where **M** is the total amount of money in circulation, **V** the average number of times each coin changes hands or its velocity of circulation, **P** the average level of prices of all goods traded for money and **T** the total volume of monetary transactions taking place. By manipulating the equation mathematically **P** can be made to equal $\frac{MV}{T}$.

To non-mathematicians – alas, reprehensibly, most of us – that means little. It is here that Rigby's worked example is of the greatest value. He proposes an imaginary economy which produces only two commodities, grain and cloth. During the whole year twenty transactions take place, made up of ten sales of one unit of grain and ten sales of one unit of cloth. Each unit of grain costs £12 and each unit of cloth £8. The total value of goods sold in the twenty transactions, or **T**, is therefore £200 (£120 + £80) and the average price for each transaction, or **P**, is £10 (£200 ÷ £20). In this 'virtual' economy there are 100 coins in circulation, each worth £1, so that the money supply, **M**, amounts to £100. In order for there to be £200-worth of transactions, each coin must be used twice. The number of times each coin changes hands is known as its velocity of circulation, or **V**, which in this case is two (2). If the coin is used more than twice, in a greater number of transactions, then its velocity of circulation increases. Conversely, if it is hoarded away against a rainy day or simply to preserve wealth, then its velocity of circulation decreases. So, from Rigby's example, we can see that:

    P (price of an average unit)   = £10
    T (number of transactions)   = 20
    M (money supply)   = £100
    V (velocity of circulation)   = 2

Expressed arithmetically, 10 × 20 = 100 × 2, which must necessarily be the case, since the two sides of the equation are saying the same thing, that the total amount of money spent (average price × number of transactions) equals the total amount of money spent (money supply × number of times each coin is used).

It is this circularity which has led to the Fisher Identity being criticised as a truism, something that is a self-evident truth. As Rigby comments, truisms have a habit of being true and the equation is even more valuable because it can be manipulated so as to isolate P, or prices, by making

$$P = \frac{MV}{T}$$

In the example given above this would be:

$$\pounds 10 = \frac{100 \times 2}{20}$$

Any change in the values on the right hand side of the equation must mean an equivalent exchange in the product on the left. Fisher argued that **V** and **T** would be little affected by any increase or decrease in **M**, so that the critical factor in price movements is the quantity of money in circulation, or, to put it more formally, 'the value of money is inversely proportional to the quantity in circulation'.[8]

Taking Rigby's example again and arbitrarily increasing the money supply to £200 shows the immediate effect on **P**, which doubles from 10 to 20.

$$\pounds 20 = \frac{200 \times 2}{20}$$

Money is therefore like any other commodity. The more of it there is in circulation, the cheaper the value of each unit, or coin, becomes. A good harvest yields more grain, so the price per standard measure falls. At times of poor harvests or harvest failures, grain prices rise sharply unless the shortfall can be made good through imports.[9] In exactly the same way, if many more coins are put into circulation, then the price or value of the standard unit, which in England until 1351 was the silver penny, will fall. Where something offered for sale had earlier cost one penny, it would now cost two. This is known as monetary inflation and monetary historians believe that it was the sharp rise in prices between 1180 and 1220 caused by an influx of silver from Europe that kick-started the economic expansion of the long thirteenth century and not the steadily growing pressure of population upon resources.[10] The opposite, of course, is monetary deflation, where the amount of money in circulation falls rapidly and the value of each coin in terms of its purchasing power rises sharply. What had earlier cost two pence now cost only one and monetary historians argue that it was falling prices, caused by growing bullion shortages from the late 1370s onward, that created a downward spiral in the economy and the economic stagnation of the fifteenth century and not the depopulation brought about by successive waves of plague.[11]

The Fisher identity or equation of exchange: the problems

Fluctuations in the money supply and their consequences therefore offer a powerful alternative explanation of economic change in medieval England and a challenge to the population and resources model. But much of the case made by the monetarist historians depends on the validity of the Fisher Equation although at first sight the link between the money supply and prices seems unchallengeable. Closer inspection reveals difficulties and ambiguities, however. Defining what constituted the money supply in the medieval period is the first problem. Should it include not only the total amount of coin put into circulation but also some estimate of the value of deposits at banks and of credit extended by institutions or individuals? Today both are included in some versions of **M**, but as deposit banking was – supposedly – unknown in medieval England, it can be excluded for our present purposes. Credit presents a more difficult problem. In plain terms, if the supply of credit is limited in any way, then the economy suffers from a lack of investment to finance trade and industry or to stimulate consumer spending. Credit was essential to the medieval economy, although its importance became greater as towns, trade and industry developed. Monetarist historians also argue that in the Middle Ages all credit transactions eventually had to be repaid in coin which meant that the availability of credit was directly linked to fluctuations in the money supply.

There is a great deal of truth in their argument. When **A** lent money to **B** it might be only a short-term transaction, to tide **B** over until the harvest came in or the wool clip was sold. **B** would then be able repay **A** who would expect to receive his money back in cash in hand, in coin. Such a transaction might well not be recorded in writing and there would be no evidence of it unless something went wrong and the parties went to court to resolve their dispute. If the period of the loan went on for more than a few months, however, it became more and more necessary to record its terms, the day or days on which either instalments or the principal became due. How these written instruments acknowledging debt emerged is one of the most important themes in the following chapters, but a brief discussion of whether or not they could be transferred to a third party and so take on some of the characteristics of paper money is needed here. In the example given above, the assumption was made that all debts were contracted and had to be repaid in coin. In reality, this was not always the case. Services or goods could also be pledged against the loan of other services and goods, such as so many days' work in the fields or so many bushels of corn, to be completed or repaid in kind at a specified time. A money value was usually attached to the transaction, to ensure the equivalence of exchange, so that that which was returned was of the same value as that which had been lent. A might prefer to be repaid in cash, however, because the money could then be spent on other goods or used to pay rents or taxes, and credit and coin became almost inextricably linked. If money became tight – that is, in short supply – then lenders were more likely to hold on to their coins for their own use and far less willing to extend credit, for fear that they would not be repaid. Credit would dry up and that would directly affect consumers and producers in town and countryside alike, since the buying and selling of goods depended upon it. In this way, the monetarist historians argue, fluctuations in the money supply affected the availability of credit as well as prices. What they also argue is that written credit instruments were not transferable and could not be passed from hand to hand as a form of paper money, so increasing the money supply. For them **M** is to be seen only in terms of the amount of coin in circulation.

While this definition of **M** might hold good for the earlier part of our period, by the second half of the thirteenth century a significant change was under way. The written bond, eventually with a penalty clause in case of default, was being used to record both debt and other types of obligation. It was a short instrument where one party acknowledged that he or she was indebted to another in a specific sum that had to be repaid on a set day or days in the future. If the debtor defaulted, then the penalty clause could be invoked and an action for recovery of the penal sum could be taken at the common law. By the later fourteenth century, bonds had become a common way of ensuring performance of obligations, perhaps as a result of changing social conditions after the Black Death.[12] In the case of debt the key issue is whether these bonds were transferable and/or discountable. Creditors (lenders) were often themselves debtors (borrowers) to other parties and one fairly obvious way of paying their creditors would be to pass over a bond of debt owed to them by a third party for the same amount. They might even tempt their creditors to take up such an offer by making over a bond of, say, £12 repayable in three or six months' time in payment of a debt of £10 that was about to fall due and which would have to be repaid in coin. The person to whom the bill was made over took a

PART I: THEORIES AND PROBLEMS

risk. The original debtor might default and then there would the question of whether the debt could be recovered at law. If there was mutual trust between the parties, however, it could be a profitable transaction for the new creditor while the original debtor could temporarily avoid payment of his obligation 'in good and legal English money'. In these circumstances bonds became both transferable and to a certain extent discountable and became, at least for a short time, the equivalent of 'paper money', thus easing shortages in the money supply.[13]

If this is the case, then should some notional figure be added to **M** to allow for new forms of money, at least from the late fourteenth century onward when the use of the bond became widespread? Monetarist historians are quite emphatic on this point and their answer is 'No'. They argue that such transfers of written instruments were not protected by the common law and that debts could only be recovered by the creditor named in the original bond and so could not acquire any of the characteristics of 'paper money'. Consequently, even if a notional figure for the value of the bonds in 'circulation' could be calculated it should not be added to **M**, the money supply. Other historians disagree and argue that this strict definition of **M** takes no account of what was actually happening. They suggest a wider definition of **M**$_1$ which would alter our view of the problems caused by severe shortages of gold and especially of silver between 1370 and at least 1460.[14] This is an extremely important issue which will be discussed further and in greater detail in both Chapters 3 and 9, but it is only the first of several problems involved in trying to define what constituted the money supply.

The first is whether some estimate of bullion held in plate should be added to **M**? Gold and silver were much used for purposes of display, to demonstrate wealth and status and, in the Church, to glorify God. Foreign visitors, from the Vikings to the Italian diplomat who came to London in the late fifteenth century, were amazed by the amount of plate to be found in England and it obviously formed a reserve of wealth for which some allowance should be made. Its value would certainly be included in the simplest modern definition of the money supply, **M**$_0$ which consists of the amount of physical currency circulating, that is, notes and coins, and any assets held in a central bank that can quickly be converted into ready cash. There were no banks as such in medieval England but plate held by individuals or by corporations such as the Church and mercantile gilds and companies could be and often was taken and sold to the mint where it would be melted down for its bullion content and then struck into new coins. The proceeds of the sale went towards paying debts and taxes and financing new commercial enterprises and in this way the new coin passed into general circulation, so increasing the money supply. The monetarists argue that coins produced by the melting-down of plate have already been included in existing estimates of the money supply and that no allowance should be made for reserves of bullion when establishing a figure for **M**. That is partially true, but what their argument ignores is that not all plate was melted down, even at times of bullion famine. Substantial amounts of gold and silver were still held in the form of plate, whose quantity and quality so much impressed foreign visitors. For the moment, however, let us exclude this bullion reserve from the definition of **M**, which remains the amount of coin in circulation.[15]

The next problem is how to allow for barter. It is, by definition, a non-monetary form of exchange which contributes to economic activity without adding to the money supply. If it could be quantified, which seems an almost impossible task, then it should not be added to **M** but should be included in any estimates of the Gross Domestic Product (**GDP**), or the total money value of all goods and services provided in an economy over one year. Yet by its very existence barter allows the money supply to do more work than would otherwise be possible. The more there is of this simple form of exchange, the less the need for money, although some historians argue that by inhibiting the use of coin it slowed down the emergence of a money economy.[16] But, again, let us exclude it from **M** for the moment and turn instead to two further and more important difficulties. At times large quantities of foreign coins passed into circulation within England, in spite of vigorous attempts to exclude them. The late Anglo-Saxon kings had decreed that there should be but one coinage in the realm, that struck by their own mints. Merchants or other travellers coming to England with foreign coins were supposed to take them, until about the late twelfth century, to the moneyers in the boroughs and after that, from the early thirteenth century onwards, to specially appointed royal officials, the king's exchangers.[17] The purpose was the same in both cases. The foreign coins would be weighed and valued according to their bullion content which depended on their fineness, the percentage of pure silver and later gold they contained. They would then be melted down, refined and struck into new English coins, to be added to the general circulating medium. Those bringing bullion to the mint would be paid the agreed price for it in the new English coins. How mint prices for silver and gold were set is another important matter for further discussion. For the moment it is sufficient to say that unless they were pitched at the right level, bullion would not flow to any mints either in England or elsewhere in Europe.[18]

By imposing these restrictions, which remained in place throughout the medieval period, kings tried to ensure that only coins struck at their mints to a specified weight, fineness and design passed into general circulation within England. In practice, foreign coins could not always be kept out, most obviously when there were severe shortages in the money supply. Such was the case in the late thirteenth and early fourteenth centuries when imitations of English silver pennies known as crockards and pollards, struck at mints in the Low Countries, flooded into the country. Complaints to Edward I (1272–1307) about the state of the coinage were loud and long but, fortunately for us, it is fairly easy to estimate the amount of foreign currency in circulation and add its value to figures for the money supply calculated from coin hoard evidence and mint output figures.[19]

When foreign coin flowed in, it was often to replace the English silver and gold that had drained abroad, causing shortages of money in England and, on occasion, monetary deflation. This is often explained in terms of what is known as 'Gresham's Law' that bad money drives out good. In fact, the great Tudor merchant and royal financier formulated no such law: it was invented in his name by the nineteenth-century Scottish economist H.D. Macleod. What Gresham actually observed was that coins with a bullion content equal to or greater than their face value would be removed and melted down, leaving in circulation only those with a metal value lower than their face value. Gresham was saying nothing new when he included this warning in his letter to Queen Elizabeth I on her accession in 1558. The Polish astronomer and philosopher Nicolaus Copernicus had already made much the same point in his treatise *Monetae cudendae ratio* (Concerning the principle of coining money) of 1526, as had others before him, and it is a fact that coins with a high bullion content – higher than their face value, that is – were often melted down for the specie they contained. The problem for England was that throughout the Middle Ages its coins were maintained at a level of weight and fineness almost unknown elsewhere in Europe. They were sought after in the northern world simply because they could be sold to foreign mints at a considerable profit because of their bullion content and were replaced by inferior imitations such as the late thirteenth-century crockards and pollards.[20]

This was a constant problem, but what caused more substantial difficulties was the shipment abroad of large quantities of English coins to pay for warfare and ransoms. The Viking invaders were bought off with silver by Æthelræd II Unræd in the late tenth and early eleventh centuries, and the troops and allies necessary for William the Bastard's conquest in 1066 were paid for from the riches of his new kingdom. After 1066, the kings of England were frequently involved in campaigns either to defend or reconquer their continental possessions. As the costs of warfare rose and war itself became more continuous, so more and more English coin was shipped abroad.[21] At times, notably between 1290 and 1307 and in the opening stages of the Hundred Years War in the late 1330s and early 1340s, this led to shortages of coin in England and, in the 1340s, to severe monetary deflation.[22] Again, allowances can be made for this, but what it does show is that **M** could vary considerably over fairly short periods of time. It also shows that we need to focus on **M** as the probable amount of coin in circulation at any given time. Figures taken from the records of mint production are not on their own reliable indicators of the actual value of the circulating medium. Losses, hoarding, and the constant drain of money abroad mean that at times it was substantially less than they suggest.

The problems with the Fisher equation of exchange are not limited to the definition of **M**, however. In Chapter 8 of *The Purchasing Power of Money* he argued that changes in **V**, the velocity of circulation, would be matched by changes in **T**, the total volume of transactions. If the latter rose or fell rapidly, then so must the number of times each coin changed hands. That being so, **V** and **T** cancel each other out, leaving **P** always directly proportional to **M**. Yet that need not always be the case. A rise in **M**, taken here as the actual volume of coin in circulation, could cause a rise in **T** without there necessarily being a similar rise in **V**, the velocity of circulation. There are quite straightforward reasons why this should be so. More coin in circulation made it easier to trade and make money payments at all levels in society. The volume of transactions was likely to increase but, simply because the money supply had increased, the work that each coin had to do was less. Velocity of circulation was actually higher in cash-starved economies, where coins had to move rapidly from hand to hand if any trade was to be done, than in those with a much greater amount of coin per head of population. Substantial increases in the money supply will therefore allow the velocity of circulation to fall and even for cash balances to be accumulated and held by individuals to make future payments when needed.[23] Theoretically, that ought to mean no substantial rises in **P**, and the apparent contradiction of an increase in the money supply actually holding back prices. Similarly, when money is in short supply, the volume of transactions need not necessarily fall, as is sometimes argued. If, or rather when, the crown made increasing demands on its subjects for war, in the form of taxes, then men and women would be forced to trade, to raise the coin they needed to meet their dues. The volume of transactions, **T**, would therefore remain steady, while **V**, the velocity of circulation would rise, as money went abroad and each coin was made to work harder. Here **M** falls, **V** rises and **T** remains roughly constant so that there may not be any fall in prices to match the fall in **M**.

Measuring monetisation and commercialisation

None of these problems mean that the Fisher equation should be abandoned and along with it the strict monetarist interpretation of economic change. That would be foolish: it is far too useful an analytical tool for it to be entirely dismissed. Nevertheless it must be used carefully, accepting that it was not only changes in the money supply that affected prices in the Middle Ages, but also variations in **V** and **T**, sometimes in conjunction with and sometimes independently of fluctuations in **M**. Indeed, the attempt to measure **V** lies at the heart of one of the most interesting pieces of recent economic speculation: Nicholas Mayhew's 'Modelling medieval monetisation'. His aim is to determine whether the use of money in all forms of transactions was greater in 1300 than it had been in 1100. He first estimates and compares the volume of coin in circulation at both dates and then tries to determine the amount of work the currency was being asked to perform in the economy of those times, or its velocity of circulation. By defining this, he argues, it should be possible to see the extent to which the economy was monetised, monetisation being understood as an increase in the use of money for making payments in all types of transaction rather than simply as growth in the money supply, although the two could go hand in hand, as they certainly did between 1100 and 1300. The greater availability of coin permits both a rise in prices and a fall in the velocity of their circulation, **V**, since each coin would change hands fewer times, as has been argued above. This would facilitate commercial developments in both local markets and long-distance trade, and the buying and selling of all types of commodities, including labour. If the velocity of circulation can be measured, then it should indicate the extent to which society had become monetised and commercialised between 1100 and 1300. His argument has become all the more important since Langdon and Masschaele have recently argued that it was growing entrepreneurship and commercialisation that caused the growth in population between 1100 and the last quarter of the thirteenth century by providing more opportunities for employment in both the agrarian and urban sectors of the economy and thus encouraging an earlier age of marriage. They take no account of any growth in the money supply in their argument, which is surprising, since monetisation and commercialisation must go hand in hand.[24]

Even allowing for considerable problems, some already discussed, others to be considered, it is not too difficult to show that there was a 29-fold increase in the currency between 1100 and 1300, from perhaps about £20,000 (the highest of Allen's recent estimates) to at least £1,100,000, an increase which far outstripped the 2- to 3-fold increase in the population. But did this actually cause a corresponding fall in the velocity of circulation? This is the critical point. Mayhew seeks to show that it did, and that the increase can actually be measured, rather than guessed at, by adroit use of the Fisher equation in its basic form, **PT = MV**. Since **PT** 'neatly summarises the total number of transactions at current prices', then it is the equivalent of the Gross Domestic Product (**GDP**), a modern term meaning, as has been seen, the total money value of all goods and services produced within the economy in the space of one year. Economists now express this as **Y**, for convenience. So **MV = Y** and **V** can be isolated within this equation by expressing it thus:

$$V = \frac{Y}{M}$$

M can be estimated, but can **Y**? Mayhew argues that it can, using evidence from Domesday Book and from Dyer's work on social structure and standards of living in the later Middle Ages, and produces figures of c.£300,000 for 1086 and c.£5 million for 1300.[25] The equations then become:

$$1086 \quad V = \frac{£300,000}{£37,500} = 8 \quad [26]$$

$$1300 \quad V = \frac{£5,000,000}{£900,000} = 5.5 \quad [27]$$

Using the revised figures produced in 2008 by Campbell for **GDP** and by Allen in 2001 for **M** results in an even lower index for **V**:

$$1290 \quad V = \frac{£3,500,000}{£1,000,000} = 3.5 \quad [28]$$

So, according to Mayhew's calculations, there had been a significant decrease in the velocity of circulation between 1086 and 1300, even allowing for the substantial increase in population in the same period. The greater availability of coin, rising from about 4d per head to over 60–70d per head, reduced the need for non-money exchange (barter) so that the velocity of circulation declined, at first slowly and then much more rapidly after 1180.[29] The Fisher equation thus provides a very valuable tool to prove and, most importantly, to measure, the degree of monetisation and commercialisation in the economy. We would be foolish if we did not use this valuable tool in our attempts to make sense of the monetary history of medieval England.

PART I: THEORIES AND PROBLEMS

Notes

1 D. Wood, *Medieval Economic Thought* (Cambridge: Cambridge University Press, 2002), p. 70, citing John of Salisbury, Christine de Pisan and Poggio Bracciolini; Sir Francis Bacon, 'Of Seditions and Troubles', *Essays* (London: 1625); D. Hume, *Writings on economics*, edited and introduced by E. Rotwein (London: Nelson, 1955), p. 33; M. Mackintosh et al., *Economics and Changing Economies* (Milton Keynes: Open University, 1996), p. 20.
2 See below, pp. 35–6. 49–50, 133, 293–4, for further discussion of this issue.
3 *EHD*, vol. ii, *1042–1189*, ed. D.C. Douglas (London: Eyre and Spottiswoode, 1955), p. 191. The relationship between the intrinsic value of the bullion in coin and prices is discussed below, pp. 45–9.
4 J. Hatcher and M. Bailey, *Modelling the Middle Ages: The History & Theory of England's Economic Development* (Oxford: Oxford University Press, 2001), p. 2.
5 C. Dyer, *An Age of Transition? Economy and Society in England in the Late Middle Ages* (Oxford: Oxford University Press, 2005), p. 3, gives a population range of 2–2.5 million in 1100, rising to 5–6 million in 1300, falling to 2.5 million c.1450 and remaining there until 1540; B.M.S. Campbell, however, suggests a peak of 4.5 million in 1315, 'Benchmarking medieval economic development: England, Wales, Scotland, and Ireland, c.1290', *EcHR*, 2nd series, 61 (2008), 925–7.
6 See below, pp. 72–3, 122–4, 191–2, 261–4, 268–70.
7 S. Rigby, *English Society in the Later Middle Ages: Class, Status and Gender* (Basingstoke: Macmillan, 1995), pp. 95–7; I. Fisher, *The Purchasing Power of Money: Its Determination and Relation to Credit, Interest and Crises* (New York: Macmillan, 1911), pp. 29, 79, 149–50.
8 R.B. Outhwaite, *Inflation in Tudor and Early Stuart England* (London: Macmillan, 1969), p. 26.
9 See below, pp. 44–5, 177, 182–7, 231–2.
10 P.D.A. Harvey, 'The English inflation of 1180–1220', *P&P*, 61 (1973), 3–30; P. Spufford, *Money and its Use in Medieval Europe* (Cambridge: Cambridge University Press, 1986), Chapter 5, 'New silver c.1160–c.1330', pp. 109–131; J.L. Bolton, 'The English economy in the early thirteenth century', in S. Church (ed.), *The Reign of King John: New Interpretations* (Woodbridge: Boydell, 1999), pp. 27–40; P. Latimer, 'The English inflation of 1180–1220 reconsidered', *P&P*, 171 (2001), 3–29.
11 The case is clearly stated in W.C. Robinson, 'Money, population, and economic change in late-medieval Europe', *EcHR*, 2nd series, 12 (1959), 63–76.
12 See below, pp. 73–4, 195, 280–2.
13 See below, pp. 30–1, 72–4, 278–84.
14 See below, pp. 125, 128, 280–4.
15 N. Mayhew, 'Modelling medieval monetisation', in R. Britnell and B.M.S. Campbell (eds), *A Commercialising Economy: England 1086 to c.1300* (Manchester: Manchester University Press, 1995), pp. 65–6.
16 W.J. Baumol and A.S. Blinder, *Economics: Principles and Policy* (New York: Harcourt Brace Jovanovich, 5th edn, 1991), pp. 224–5, 355–6; barter is still a matter of debate among modern economists: see A. Marvasti and D.J. Smyth, 'The effect

16

of barter on demand for money: an empirical analysis', *EL*, 64 (1999), 73–80; see also below, pp. 22, 28, 117, 129, 132–4, for a further discussion of barter.
17 T.F. Reddaway, 'The king's mint and exchange in London 1343–1543', *EHR*, 82 (1967), 7–8; N.J. Mayhew, 'From regional to central minting, 1158–1464', in C. Challis (ed.), *A New History of the Royal Mint* (Cambridge: Cambridge University Press, 1992), pp. 87–97; and see below, p. 52–7, 142–4, 240–1.
18 See below, pp. 68–9.
19 See below, pp. 159–61.
20 See below, pp. 48–9 and Table 3.1.
21 D. Bates, 'Normandy and England after 1066', *EHR*, 104 (1989), 866–9.
22 See below, pp. 159–60, 162–6.
23 Mayhew 'Modelling medieval monetisation', pp. 68–76; see below, pp. 124–8, 179–84.
24 Mayhew, 'Modelling medieval monetisation', pp. 62–8; J. Langdon and J. Masschaele, 'Commercial activity and population growth in medieval England', *P&P*, 190 (2006), 41–2.
25 Mayhew, 'Modelling medieval monetisation', pp. 57–62.
26 Mayhew is using Dolley's estimates for the size of the coinage in 1087: see below, pp. 107 and Table 4.2.
27 Mayhew based his calculations upon there being £37,500 in circulation in 1100 and £900,000 in 1300. Allen's more recent estimates have suggested a total of £25,000 in 1100 and between £1,100,000 and £1,400,000 in 1299, including pollards and crockards. That would mean a higher V score of 12 in 1100 and between 4.5 and 3.8 in 1299, thus reinforcing Mayhew's argument. M. Allen, 'The volume of English currency 1158–1470', *EcHR*, 2nd series, 54 (2001), 603, Table 1; the calculations are mine.
28 Campbell 'Benchmarking', 925; Allen, 'Volume of the English currency, 973–1158', 603.
29 See Chapter 2, Table 2.2, p. 26.

2

Money and the money economy

So far, two important assumptions have been made: first, that money was coin and secondly, that a money economy actually existed throughout the period under discussion. But was this actually the case? Definitions are now essential. First and foremost, what money was in this period, what its functions were, what the term 'a full money economy' actually means must be discussed. We then need to examine the nature of the coinage: which silver and then gold coins were in circulation; how they were produced and put into circulation; and how, physically, they provide modern historians and numismatists with evidence in the shape of coin hoards and stray finds. The role of credit in the economy and the contentious issue of whether written credit instruments could or did circulate as forms of paper money, both of which can increase **M**, also have to be examined. Finally, it is vital to know how the bullion from which the coinage was struck was acquired. Some was mined in England and Wales and some was provided by melting down existing coins and re-coining them. But, because of wear and tear and losses, this was never enough, even to replace the existing money stock. Much of the precious metals needed first to make up the shortfall and to maintain the level and quality of the circulating medium after initial re-coinages had to come from abroad. The quantity of bullion available for minting was one of if not the chief determinant of how many coins could be produced and put into circulation, and thus of the size of **M**. Changes in the value of silver and gold on the international market, in response to fluctuating mining output and the balance of trade between Europe and the Near East also affected the intrinsic value of the precious metal in each coin, and thus its purchasing power. How were sufficient supplies of bullion to be won for England, and then kept within the country? Why, at times, were supplies abundant, but at others severely restricted, and what were the consequences in both cases? Together, these are the problems to be addressed in the next two chapters, which deal with money and the money economy and changes in the bullion supply.

A definition of money

Money is a medium through which exchange is effected, or, more simply, a means of payment.[1] It need not necessarily take the form of coin or notes or tokens. In primitive societies where there is only a limited market economy, commodity money is sometimes used. Cowrie shells, slabs of salt, whale and porpoise teeth, woodpecker scalps, giraffe tails and cattle have all been used as forms of primitive money in remote societies in the nineteenth and twentieth centuries.[2] But commodity money is an unsatisfactory medium of exchange. Cattle, or other animals,

> have serious disadvantages as money. All goats are not alike; if a man sells a piece of land for twenty goats, he may consider himself cheated when he receives the twenty skinniest and most diseased of the purchaser's flock. Goats have other disadvantages. An outbreak of disease may decimate a man's wealth. The breeding season will cause a plethora in the community's supply of money.[3]

Nor can cattle easily be cut up to allow for small purchases, and they are not transportable, they cannot be carried about on one's person, to be used when needed and they are not durable.

The step upward from the use of such primitive money in a non-market economy to the use of coinage, general purpose money, in a market economy, is a very substantial one. As W.S. Jevons argued in 1875, the advantages of coinage are that it can act as a common measure of value, as a medium of exchange and as a store of value, all at one and the same time. It is portable; indestructible (unlike goats or cattle); homogenous, that is, coins are of roughly equal weight and value; divisible into sub-units such as halfpennies and farthings (quarter pennies); stable in value; and cognisable, carrying a symbol or symbols that would guarantee its acceptance throughout a territory.[4] In all this Jevons, whether he knew it or not, was merely echoing the words of a fourteenth-century German Augustinian canon, Henry of Friemar (d. 1340) who in his *Commentaries upon Aristotle* produced his own list of the essential properties of money:

> The first is that it be of very small size, so that subtraction cannot be made from it without easy detection, which would not be the case if it were of large size and ample form. The second is that it be impressed with the stamp of some prince, for otherwise anybody might fabricate

and falsify money, by which equality in exchange would be done away with. The third is that it be of due weight, for otherwise a fixed price cannot be put on commodities by means of it. The fourth is that it endure long without corruption, for otherwise future demand cannot be provided for by means of it ... The fifth is that it be of precious material, like gold or silver, so that a price can be put on goods easily and promptly according to its value.[5]

Money in the form of coin is thus a store of value, unlike perishable goods such as cattle or fish. It can be stored away and hold its value while being stored, to be used for exchange at a later date. It also functions as a standard or measure of value, against which exchanges or other transactions could be measured. If, for example, a cart is to be exchanged for so many cattle or sheep or goats, then there has to be some understanding that there is equity within the exchange, that the cart is worth so many cattle and vice versa. If the cart and the cattle can be appraised as both being worth so many units of exchange, then the one can be sold for the other. No units of exchange need actually change hands. They are simply being used as a standard of value, to make sure that both sides of the sale are equal.

For units of exchange to act as both store and standard of value they have to be made of some substance which is both durable and regarded as valuable by geographically wide-ranging groups of people. As Crowther says, 'It is a comparatively early discovery in the history of money that metals are among the most suitable of all commodities to serve as money'. Most metals have been used as money, iron, copper and bronze particularly, but gold and silver became pre-eminent, in Western civilisation at least. Gold was too scarce and so too highly valued to serve as general purpose money in the early and central Middle Ages. Silver, by contrast, was 'precious, but not too precious'. Supplies were sufficient to make wide circulation of the coins struck from the metal possible, and so silver coins became the most commonly used units of exchange in the medieval Western world. Both gold and silver are light in weight and high in value. Coins struck from them can be carried around and stored fairly easily, unlike those made from iron or other heavier metals. It is not surprising, therefore, that from the earliest times coins were made from gold and silver.[6]

Yet the simple striking of a coin, not in itself a difficult technical problem,[7] might not involve its use as money. It could be a political action, with coins serving as prestige symbols, as they certainly did in the early Anglo-Saxon kingdoms in England. For coins to be useful as stores and standards of value and as units of exchange they required certain other attributes. They have to be in use for a substantial period of time. Defining money as a standard of value suggests that the units of exchange are in continuous use and hold their value over many years, so that they can be used both as a medium for deferred payments and as a store of value.[8] Coins must also have an agreed and accepted value. In practice that meant that they had to have a recognised weight and a known bullion content, and each coin in the series would have to meet those standards. How could users know that this was the case? The only practical way was for the coins to be validated in some way by 'the state'. They would have to bear the recognised mark or symbol of that state, usually a portrait of the ruler with his name on the obverse, and a design on the reverse, often to prevent clipping. In the case of English coins, the names of the mint at which the coin had been struck and of the moneyer who struck it were also put on the coin.[9] For the ruler, these symbols were important ways of disseminating propaganda and of asserting his authority widely through the population. They also gave him a means of checking the authenticity and quality of the standardised coinage circulating through his realm, which was often struck at some distance from the centre.[10] More importantly, to the customer, the user, they gave the coins *recognisable* legality and credibility, and so the confidence to use them.

Finally, coins had to have three other attributes to make them widely acceptable as units of exchange. First, they had to be portable, so that they could be carried from one place to another and then pass from hand to hand. Secondly, they also had to be of a size that would allow them to be stored easily. Finally, they had in some way to be divisible, with the subdivisions related to each other in terms of weight and bullion content. As will be seen, coins were often worth more than their face value because of the amount of gold or silver they contained, and that made them difficult to use for small purchases. It was therefore important, particularly as the market economy grew, either to have a main coin that could be physically subdivided into halves and quarters, or to strike lesser coins, halfpennies and farthings, again directly related in weight and value to the main coin. This would allow small purchases to be made either with one coin or a mixture of coins.[11]

The emergence of a money economy

General-purpose money that could be used in a whole range of transactions, both for goods and services and for payments to the state, had to have these attributes or functions. Its most convenient form was as a minted coin and in late Anglo-Saxon and Anglo-Norman England this meant the silver penny which became the national currency in the reign of King Edgar (959-975).[12] But the appearance and use of coins has led all too often to the assumption that a 'money economy' came into existence more or less simultaneously. The phrase 'a money economy' is used almost as indiscriminately as 'the rise of the middle class' and is nearly as meaningless. Small amounts of currency in circulation will lead only to a 'monetised' economy. Here money is used as a standard of value and in a limited way for exchange, in buying and selling and in the payment of rents and taxes. But self-sufficiency, payments in kind and barter for both goods and services persist on a wide scale. Land and the tenure of land in return for service, military or physical, in the form of labour services on a lord's estate, form the basic bonds in society. Wealth here is tied up in land and cannot easily be mobilised to provide cash incomes which can then be spent, so stimulating trade. Towns and markets certainly exist, but mainly to serve very local demand. The industrial sector is small and division of labour, a key to more efficient production, not common. Such an economy is the product of and suited to a largely self-sufficient society, where there is only a limited amount of coin in circulation. Its inefficiencies are obvious. Barter is a clumsy and time-consuming method of exchange. It involves one person having goods or produce to exchange finding another with precisely the goods he wants who also happens to need or desire what the first person has to offer. Far more effective is the adoption of some shared medium of exchange.

Population growth and the expansion of the market

Of itself, then, the use of coin cannot be taken as evidence for the existence of a money economy. Rather, for a money economy to emerge, there has to be a convergence of circumstances, a whole series of factors working together to enhance and accelerate the others and to create new mechanisms of accounting and new legal instruments and actions.[13] The first of these factors was a sustained growth in the population, which was accompanied or even caused by a rapid expansion of the market.[14] In a relatively underdeveloped economy, such as obtained in most of Europe throughout the Middle Ages, any such growth would upset the rough equilibrium between supply and demand that had hitherto existed. This is precisely what happened in Europe, north and south, from the late eleventh to the mid-thirteenth century, so much so that in some rural areas, and notably Tuscany, Flanders and the east Midlands in England, population densities were not to reach the same levels again until the nineteenth century.[15]

Demand for food soared. More and more land was brought into cultivation, but limited agricultural techniques meant that by the end of the century European farmers could barely feed a population that had increased at least two- and probably three-fold.[16] There was also a need for more tools, more basic consumer goods such as clothes, boots and shoes and pots and pans, for more houses and, as the upper ranks of society, benefiting from increased incomes from rents and the sale of produce from their estates, grew richer, for more luxury goods.

The result was a sustained expansion in the market and the rapid growth of an urban network. Existing towns and cities grew, new ones were founded and fairs and village markets proliferated. Growing demand for food, raw materials and manufactured goods had to be supplied, usually from local sources but quite often over long distances. There was substantial investment in roads and bridges and new land routes were opened, connecting northern and southern Europe via the Alpine passes and western Europe with the newly settled lands in the east. The Gough map of *c.*1360, based on an earlier map that no longer exists, shows well-developed road and river transport routes throughout England, but not the dense networks of local routes connecting towns to the villages that surrounded them or between the villages themselves. Developing these land routes would have been pointless unless more cost-effective means of transporting goods along them had been found. Most freight was moved by road and there were significant increases in carrying capacity thanks to the introduction of the horse collar and horse harness. Lumbering ox-drawn vehicles were replaced by horse-teams pulling two- or four-wheeled carts which could move bulk goods to market faster and at a lower cost. There were equally striking developments in ships, navigational techniques and port facilities which made possible the expansion of international trade along routes between the North Sea and the Baltic, within the Mediterranean and between the Mediterranean and the North Sea. Nor was international trade simply the icing on the economic cake. It stimulated the growth of routes to and from ports, of agrarian production for export markets, of manufacturing industries and, quite probably, of the coasting trade in the northern seas, which was itself important in the distribution and redistribution of bulk products.[17]

The money supply

A sustained growth in population thus stimulated demand. Markets grew to serve that demand and improvements in transport made supplying them quicker, easier and less expensive. Taken together, they are the first of the key factors in the emergence of a money economy, and of an importance that cannot be overemphasised. Yet it is doubtful whether this economic expansion could have been sustained without a second, further important development, the increasing availability and *use* of money. As Alexander Murray has felicitously put it, money facilitates exchanges, so reducing their costs as against other means of distributing property. A reduction in the costs of exchange, or transaction costs, as they are best called, increases the volume of exchange and that increase in volume made the market more fluid, reducing the preference for payment in kind. It raised the demand for money, and without that raised demand a money economy would probably not have emerged in large parts of Europe and particularly in England, as it did during the course of the thirteenth century.[18]

So, the next vital factor in this self-accelerating process had to be a massive increase in the money supply and this is what happened. If the European population grew two- or threefold between 1100 and 1300, then in the one country for which the money supply is measurable, England, it grew at an even greater rate, as Figure 2.1 and Tables 2.1, 2.2 and 2.3 show. In 1100 there were probably between two and four silver pennies per head of population. By 1205 that had risen to between 17d and 20d per head, according to whether one accepts the low or the high estimates of the volume of coin in circulation and of the size of the population, and by

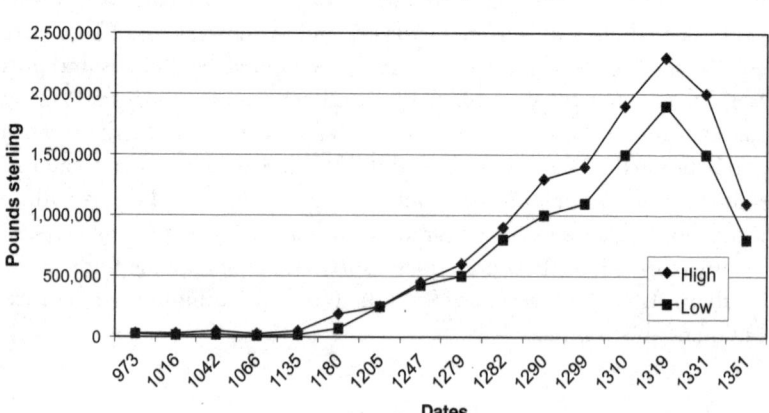

Figure 2.1 Fluctuations in the money supply 1180–1351.

Sources: M. Allen, 'The volume of the English currency, c. 973–1158' in B. Cook and G. Williams, *Coinage and history in the NorthSea world, c. 500–1250* (Leiden: Brill, 2005); M. Allen, 'The volume of English currency 1158-1470, *EcHR*, 54 (2001).

Table 2.1 Coinage per head of population, 973–1158

Dates	Volume of currency in £	Population Millions	Coin (silver pennies) per head
973–1016	25,000	1.5	4.00d
		2.0	3.00d
	30,000	1.5	4.80d
		2.0	3.60d
1016–42	15,000	1.5	2.40d
		2.0	1.80d
	30,000	1.5	4.80d
		2.0	3.60d
1042–66	20,000	1.5	3.20d
		2.0	2.40d
	50,000	1.5	8.00d
		2.0	6.00d
1066–1135	10,000	1.5	1.60d
		2.0	1.20d
		2.25	1.06d
	25,000	1.5	4.00d
		2.0	3.00d
		2.25	2.26d
1135–58	20,000	1.5	3.20d
		2.0	2.40d
		2.25	2.13d
		2.5	1.92d
	50,000	1.5	8.00d
		2.0	6.00d
		2.25	5.30d
		2.5	4.80d

Source: M. Allen, 'The volume of the English currency, c.973–1158', in B. Cook and G. Williams (eds), *Coinage and History in the North Sea World, c.500–1250* (Leiden: Brill, 2005), pp. 487–501.

Table 2.2 Silver coinage per head of population, 1180–1351

Year	Volume of currency in £	Population in millions	Coin (silver pennies) per head
1180	70,000	2.25	7.50
		2.5	6.70
		2.75	6.10
	190,000	2.25	20.3
		2.5	18.2
		2.75	16.6
1205	250,000	3	20.0
		3.5	17.1
1247	425,000	4	25.5
		4.5	22.7
	450,000	4	27.0
		4.5	24.0
1279	500,000	4.5	26.7
		4.75	25.3
	600,000	4.5	32.0
		4.75	30.3
1282	800,000	4.5	42.7
		4.75	40.4
	900,000	4.5	48.0
		4.75	45.5
1290	1,000,000	4.50	53.3
		5	48.0
		5.5	46.6
	1,300,000	4.5	69.3
		5	62.4
		5.5	56.7
1299	1,100,000	4.5	58.7
		5	52.8
		5.5	48.0
	1,400,000	4.5	74.7
		5	67.2
		5.5	61.1
1310	1,500,000	4.5	80.0
		5	72.0
		5.5	65.5
	1,900,000	4.5	101.3
		5	91.2
		5.5	82.9

Year	Volume of currency in £	Population in millions	Coin (silver pennies) per head
1319	1,900,000	4.5	101.3
		5	91.2
		5.5	82.9
	2,300,000	4.5	122.6
		5	110.4
		5.5	100.36
1331	1,500,000	4.5	80.0
		5	72.0
	2,000,000	4.5	106.6
		5	96.0
1351	700,000	3.5	48.0
		4	42.0
	(900,000	3.5	61.7
		4	54.0

Source: M. Allen, 'The volume of the English currency 1158-1470', *EcHR*, 54 (2001).

1290 to between 46d and 62d per head. The growth in the money supply, by a factor of at least 20, is quite staggering and the increase in the volume of coin in circulation had a profound effect upon the development of the market. By the mid-thirteenth century the concentrated money supply in England had probably reached the critical point that would allow coins to be used as the normal medium or agent of exchange. They could be used to buy and sell goods, to pay wages and other dues that peasants owed to lords. They could be collected as taxes and offered or demanded in lieu of feudal military service, and kings could now pay their much larger armies with coins. The feudal bond based on the tenure of land by service could be replaced by the bastard feudal bond based on an annual money retainer, while money payments could be substituted for feudal labour

Table 2.3 Coinage (silver and gold) per head of population, 1351

Year	Silver £	Gold £	Total £	Population in millions	Coinage per head
1351	700,000	100,000	800,000	3	64
				3.5	54.9
	900,000	200,000	1,100,000	3	88
				3.5	75.4

Source: M. Allen, 'The volume of the English currency 1158–1470', *EcHR*, 54 (2001).

rent. For the first time, society in England became thoroughly geared to buying and selling as a means of acquiring goods and services and, thanks to the incomes received, to making a whole range of payments to lords and to the state. A very substantial increase in the money supply, which occurred at the same time as but independently of population growth, allowed regular and regulated exchange to replace the informal practices of earlier centuries.[19]

Not completely, however, since barter, informal exchange, has never disappeared. The notion of a full money economy, where exchanges only take place in terms of coin or its written or electronic substitutes is probably a chimera. Even today there is some degree of barter. Baby-sitting or 'school-run' groups work in this way and academic book reviewers are paid in kind. They keep the books they receive for review. When builders work privately for each other, it is often a case of 'You do my brick laying and I'll do your plastering.' In the later Middle Ages, and especially when coin was in short supply, the many cases brought in manorial courts for goods not delivered or services not rendered as promised all point to some degree of non-money exchange.[20] A money economy contained and always will contain within it a substantial and generally unquantifiable amount of non-monetary payments. It should also be understood, however, that where barter was used, equality of exchange was normally established by the use of money as a standard of value.[21]

Reckoning, recording, accounting and amounts systems

What a money economy also needs are systems of reckoning, weights and measures and recording, without which it cannot function properly. Reckoning may sound simple enough when the basic unit of currency was the silver penny and its subdivisions, the halfpenny and the farthing. Small transactions – and most transactions were small – were easily reckonable. They could be done either in the head or with the use of counters such as stones, for simple addition or subtraction. Shepherds seem to be able to count their sheep and to remember them individually without the use of any form of written or mechanical record. Nor do literacy and numeracy necessarily go together. As late as 1387 the University of Florence thought it quite possible to have a treasurer who was both illiterate and innumerate.[22] But, in general, once the economy expands and trade becomes more common, then men and women are likely to be engaged in several transactions at the same time. Some will involve making or accepting deferred payments, at specified times in the future. When that happens, a record of the transaction becomes essential. It could take a written or, as will be seen, a physical form, a wooden tally stick notched according to an agreed system to record the sum owed.[23] New types of coins that made accounting more complicated were introduced, struck rather than cut halfpennies and farthings in the twelfth and thirteenth centuries, groats and half-groats (worth 4d and 2d respectively) from the late thirteenth and mid-fourteenth centuries, and then a gold coinage to run alongside the silver money, again from the mid-fourteenth century and with coins worth 1s 8d, 3s 4d and 6s 8d.[24] The mere fact that there were 240 pennies to the pound, twelve pence to the shilling and twenty shillings to the pound made addition and subtraction more difficult, as anyone who went to school in Britain before 1971 and the introduction of the decimal currency will testify. Here 'ghost moneys' and moneys or denominations of account had a part to play. There were no shilling or pound coins in medieval England before 1489. Rather, like the mark of 13s 4d, they were simply units of account that made the reckoning of large sums easier and all three became an essential part of the accounting system.[25]

Buying and selling using coins is best done within the framework of a standard set of weights and measures where precise amounts of the money unit were used to buy precise amounts of goods. A standard weight of bread or ale must be sold at a standard price, a length of cloth must be offered at so much per foot (12 inches), yard (36 inches) or ell (45 inches), a bushel of wheat or barley would be worth so many pence, rent would be so much per acre of land or its subdivisions or multiples.[26] Kings, however, by virtue of their office and ambitions, had a love of order and insisted that there should be one law code, one currency and one set of weights and measures within their realms, in order to bring unity to what were often loose collections of regions with separatist tendencies. It was also practical and sensible. A trader buying wheat at a distant market where it was plentiful in order to exploit a local scarcity at home will need to know that standard measures are being used. This makes it easier to calculate potential profits, quickens the whole process of buying and selling and helps to prevent fraud. Ptolemy of Lucca (d. *c.*1328), a pupil of the great theologian and philosopher Thomas Aquinas, argued that:

> weights and measures ... are as necessary as the coinage for preserving the government of any lordship, since they are used in the payment of tributes, since their use decreases quarrels and protects fidelity in purchases and sales, and finally, since they, like coins, are instruments of human life and, even more than coinage, imitate natural action ... it seems that weights and measures take their origin from nature more

than the coinage does, and therefore they are even more necessary in a republic or kingdom.

The idea that God was the standard of all things was a central theme in both the Old and the New Testaments of the Bible. As King Solomon says in Proverbs 16: 11, 'A just weight and balance are the Lord's: all the weights of the bag are his work' and this theme continues in Christ's Sermon on the Mount where he warned that 'With what judgment ye judge, ye shall be judged, and with what measure ye mete, it shall be measured to you again' (Matthew 7: 2). The concept of weighing and measuring was fundamental to the Christian faith, as it was to Judaism and Islam. Given this, it is not surprising that the Anglo-Saxon rulers of England, probably following the example of the great Frankish Emperor Charlemagne, sought to standardise weights and measures.[27] In his laws promulgated at Grately, near Andover (Hants) between $c.926$ and $c.930$ King Athelstan proclaimed that there should be one coinage over all his dominions, and King Edgar repeated this law $c.962$ and added another that there be one system of measurement, as at Winchester.[28] Standardising weights and measures was to prove far more difficult than issuing a uniform coinage for England, however. There was repeated legislation on the subject, which is usually a sign that existing rules and regulations were not being obeyed, and local and national variations in weights and measures persisted in England until the late nineteenth century. Nevertheless, what these and subsequent attempts at establishing national standards show is the importance of making goods measurable by money, so that money could be freely used within the market.[29]

Reckoning, then, has to be done in both money and amount: length, breadth, volume, weight and area all have to be added into the increasingly complex equation. It also has to be done over time. Deferred payments, for goods and services bartered or sold on credit terms, must always have existed, but the use of money made contracting and discharging debts that much easier. The more money was used, the more impetus or incentive there was to borrow it. Credit is essential in a market economy, since it extends the purchasing power of those to whom it is granted, and helps to quicken the process of exchange. Trade can be financed through credit. Money can be borrowed to meet obligations, to pay taxes, to live beyond one's means or just to survive, since distress borrowing at times of harvest failure was often essential, simply for survival. Bonds of lordship, so important at all levels in medieval society, were initially based on the tenure of land in return for service, military or manual. The process of replacing such obligations by money payments instead of being summoned, fully equipped, to join a war band or ploughing the fields and bringing in the harvest was long and complex and not explicable simply in terms of the growth of a money economy, as will be seen.[30] By the fourteenth and fifteenth centuries lords were paying or retaining men to fight for them, while for most, if not all peasants, labour rents had been replaced by money rents. Such payments required definition. They had to be made by a certain date, by instalments throughout the year or over a period of years. Here there was a strong customary element, with a cycle of known dates throughout the year, related to the rhythm of agriculture and the major feasts of the Church, on which payments were made. But in each case there was reckoning to be done, and reckoning over time, and the need to record such agreements so that payments could be enforced, eventually through legal processes and penal bonds.[31] Codere argues that if money, counting, measurement and time are taken together, then this taxes the capacities of the human mind beyond the holding powers of its memory and its computational powers. Written records therefore become essential, to record transactions, the amounts involved, the payments to be made and the times at which they are to be made. Without them, the exchange of goods, the making of payments, the performance of bonds, the fulfilling of agreements is hit or miss, unintegrated and ruled more by custom or by rule of thumb than by calculation.[32]

The growth of government

Records and accounts are therefore an essential element in a money economy. It was a long time before they were widely kept, and there is a lively debate as to the extent of record-keeping before the Norman Conquest. The later Anglo-Saxon kings certainly levied taxes, gelds, on the value of land. Each county had to be assessed, and liabilities and exemptions were recorded on rolls, such as that which has survived for post-Conquest Northamptonshire.[33] Landed estates were leased out by great lay nobles, cathedrals and monasteries looking for regular cash incomes from rent rather than the fluctuating profits from the sale of produce. The formal, written document granting the lease usually described the area of the estate, the period for which it was to be let, and the rent to be paid at specified dates. Landlords also began to make and keep surveys of their estates, noting in particular the rents and services owed by their peasant tenants, and one or two of these have survived, such as that of the Gloucestershire estate of Tidenham from the late tenth or early eleventh century.[34]

It seems unlikely that the Domesday Survey could have been drawn up as quickly as it was if a substantial corpus of surveys and rentals, tax rolls and other records, on which they could base their enquiries, had not already existed. Domesday Book itself is a monument to the recording of money, time and area, and to the way in which information from inquests made at a local level could be drawn together in a central statement of values and fiscal obligations.

The main impetus to accounting, as opposed to listing, undoubtedly came with the emergence of the royal Exchequer in the twelfth century. The Norman kings drew their revenues from a wide variety of sources. Some came from taxation, some from feudal dues and the royal right to the income from vacant archiepiscopal and episcopal sees. The largest single source was the farm of the counties, a composite sum paid yearly by the sheriff of each county, which was made up of the profits of justice, the revenues from the crown lands and from the royal boroughs, and of all other sources of revenue arising from the sheriff's area of jurisdiction. The king needed a financial bureau where all these revenues could be drawn together, audited, money in the form of coin paid over and debts and obligations recorded to ensure their future discharge. This bureau was the Exchequer, first mentioned in 1110. Much of the accounting was done orally before officials known as 'auditors' because they *heard* the evidence presented to them. Everything had to be thoroughly checked and the results recorded in writing. How this was done has been revealed to us by Richard Fitznigel in his *Dialogue or Course of the Exchequer*, written in 1177–8.[35] His father was Nigel, bishop of Ely, Henry I's Treasurer from the mid-1120s. At the beginning of his reign, in 1154, Henry II had to persuade Nigel to come out of retirement to re-establish Exchequer practices after the Anarchy of Stephen's reign (1134–54) and the king then appointed Nigel's son, Richard, as his Treasurer in 1160, a post that he was to hold for nearly 40 years.[36] When Richard wrote the *Dialogue*, he was drawing on his own and his father's first-hand experiences of Exchequer practices in the twelfth century. The key to the Exchequer's success was its use of an abacus, in the form of a chequer board, on which counters were moved around to compute sums ranging from pence to thousands of pounds. When this had been done, the payments and liabilities of named individuals were recorded on the pipe rolls, the first surviving example being that for the financial year Michaelmas (the Feast of St Michael and All Angels, 29 September) to Michaelmas 1129–30.[37] The Exchequer also used something with which the Anglo-Saxon kings may have been familiar, the notched stick or tally as a receipt for and an obligation to make payments.

The appropriate sums were shown on the tally by cuts or notches of varying width and depth made at certain intervals. The notched stick was then split down its length. The larger part, the stock, was used as a receipt, while the thinner part, the foil, was kept in the Exchequer. The name and business of the person concerned was written on it in ink, making the tally ' a sophisticated and practical record of numbers'. The tallies were more convenient to store than parchment rolls, less complex to make, and harder to forge, as the two halves had to match exactly.[38]

Domesday and the Pipe Rolls mark important stages in the development of recording and accounting. But they were only the first stages, and very much the product of the centre. Written evidence that recording and accounting had spread from the centre to the localities before the late twelfth century is sparse. In his absorbing study *From Memory to Written Record: England 1066–1307*, Clanchy addresses what he calls

> an archaeological fact which demands an explanation: that masses of writings survive from twelfth- and thirteenth-century England by comparison with the preceding Anglo-Saxon and Roman periods. Probably this was because more documents were made, as well as preserved.[39]

If the proliferation of record-keeping was inextricably linked to the growth of bureaucracy, to the spread of royal justice and administration, which forced people to become more literate, then it was the steady increase in the use of money as a medium of exchange that made them more numerate. As has been seen, there was a need to know what was due, a need to record agreements, and a need to enforce obligations, debts and contracts. Satisfying these needs took time, however, and one of the main themes of Chapters 4–9 is how both law and practice developed to meet them.[40] Clanchy has established a widely accepted chronology for the spread of literacy and record-keeping, with the real expansion in both coming in the reign of Edward I (1272–1307). The chief influences at work are seen to come from the development of political, legal and administrative institutions, and rightly so. Yet he makes virtually no mention of the increasing use of money, although his chronology more or less parallels that of the massive increase in the money supply.[41] Already, by 1187, the capacity to count money and to measure cloth was said to be the test of legal majority for a burgess's son,[42] and the ability to count, measure, record and account had to spread far beyond the towns into the countryside, as more and more of society was able to use or had to use money on a regular basis. Both literacy and numeracy had major parts to play in the emergence of a money economy.

To them we should add the growth of government and of the state. As has been seen, coins bore the image of the ruler as a guarantee of their weight and fineness. That image also, of itself, enhanced the ruler's sovereignty: the coin was a symbol of power and authority, and so engendered trust in the user, a trust that was vital if coins were to become widely acceptable as a means of exchange.[43] According to Piron, money also had an important role to play in the formation of national identity, both internally and externally. Establishing the sole right to issue coin was politically essential for the ruler of an emerging state, as in France, where authority was fragmented and royal power had to be asserted over semi-independent nobles, each issuing his or her own coins.[44] In England, exceptionally and from as early as the tenth century, both mints and coinage were firmly under the control of a single monarch.[45] This meant that coins bearing the king's head, irrespective of where they were struck, had to be accepted throughout the realm and the king, through his legislation, had to insist that they were, because it was essential that those using money should not distinguish between coins produced by different regional mints. Kings also had to act against counterfeiters and Æthelræd II's London laws of 978 set the pattern for the future when they specified that 'coiners who work in the woods, or who make similar things [coins] anywhere, are guilty for their lives'. Edward III's Statute of Treasons of 1352 merely confirmed that falsifying coining was a hanging matter[46]

The increasing use and issue of coinage and the growing authority and administrative competence of the state thus go hand in hand.[47] Hodges argues that there is a direct relationship between increasing political complexity (i.e., the growing power and authority of government) and the size and standardisation of individual coin issues; the development of unit variations – that is, of divisions and multiples of the basic coins, in the case of England pennies, halfpennies, farthings, groats and half groats; changes in the organisation of coin production; and in the use of coins as vehicles for propaganda. The more complex government becomes, the greater the control it seeks to assert over the coinage.[48] The more money is used, the more use the state can make of it. A plentiful supply of coins makes it possible to pay officials and soldiers, rather than rewarding them with land, while taxes and warfare are powerful stimuli to the growth of institutions and the circulation of coin. Similarly, the king's right to draw upon the resources of his subjects was of major importance to the development of the administrative process. The late Anglo-Saxon rulers did this through the geld, a tax levied throughout the shires (the counties) on units of assessment, in money payments. It was essentially a tax on land, with each county divided into variable units of area, such as the hide of between c.60 and c.120 acres. Special gelds at high rates could be levied for a standing army (the heregeld), for shipbuilding for the navy (shipgeld) or to buy off the Danish invaders, the infamous Danegeld.[49] By the late thirteenth century a sufficiency of coin allowed personal taxation on individual wealth in the form of moveable property – that is, grain, animals and other goods offered for sale. This all involved large numbers of officials, paid and unpaid, to assess, collect and account for the taxes and to pay them over to a central bureau, the Exchequer, and to keep records of all their transactions.[50] The taxes and the customs duties, levies on imports and exports, went to pay large armies, so that Edward I could request a force of 16,000 infantry for the Scottish campaign of 1300, even if only 9,000 men actually mustered at Carlisle. The rate of pay of an infantryman was 2d per day. Keeping a sizeable force in the field even for a limited period required a great deal of coin, provided chiefly through taxation.[51]

The relationship between the state and the coinage was not a one-way process, however. If the king insisted on his sole responsibility for the coinage, then his subjects looked to him to provide 'sound money'. This was an emotive phrase. It meant the maintenance of a coinage of good weight and fineness – that is, containing a high percentage of gold or silver – so that its purchasing power would not deteriorate. If it did not, then complaints were sure to follow, urging reform of the coinage. Those of the Anglo-Saxon Chronicler in 1124 have already been noted and in the late thirteenth century they had become commonplace at times of poor coinage or monetary instability in both England and France. Shortly before the English recoinage of 1279–81, the chronicler Thomas Wykes bemoaned that the coinage weighed only half what it should, and that the poor state of the currency had caused a rise in prices. Modern research tends to support his claims, since prices appear to have risen sharply in the 1270s, while in Cornwall it was said that the poor state of the coinage made the collection of taxes almost impossible.[52] In France, Philip IV's manipulation of the coinage in the late thirteenth and early fourteenth centuries produced what can only be called howls of rage, and demands for a return to the 'good' money of his saintly predecessor, Louis IX.[53] By the late fourteenth century Nicholas of Oresme, bishop of Lisieux in Normandy, argued in his treatise *De Moneta* (Concerning the mint) that money belonged to the community and to individuals and not to the prince alone, so that any alteration in the coinage should only be made with the agreement of the whole community. This argument had earlier been advanced by Jean Buridan, rector of the University of Paris (d.1358) and was part of an acrimonious

PART I: THEORIES AND PROBLEMS

debate taking place in France, against a background of debasement, over who controlled the currency, with both Pope Innocent III (1198-1216) and Thomas Aquinas (1225-74) arguing that this right belonged to the prince.

By the fourteenth century this view was being challenged both in France and in England. Edward I had already used parliament to legislate on the coinage, in the statute of Stepney of 1299. Now that body was increasingly offering a forum for voicing discontent, and worries about debasement were expressed in the parliament held at Stamford in 1309. Then in 1311, in the Ordinances of that year which sought to control the crown's independence of action, it was specifically stated that, because every time a change of coinage was made in the kingdom the whole people suffered greatly in many ways, the king should not [in future] change the coinage without the assent of the baronage, and that in parliament. As the very outspoken author of the *Mirror of Justices* put it, 'It was ordained that no king of this realm could change, impair or amend his money, nor make money of anything save silver, without the assent of all his earls.' This was the beginning of strong parliamentary opposition to any adjustment to or debasement of the coinage in fourteenth-century England. Edward III (1327-77) was to discover this in the 1340s, when in the face of huge costs for foreign war and a growing shortage of bullion in Europe, he debased the coinage. Much alarmed, the commons in the parliament of 1346 petitioned the king that the coinage should in future not be debased without parliamentary consent. The principle was never established but in the Statute of Purveyors of 1352 Edward had to promise not to alter either the weight or fineness (gold or silver content) of the current coinage and, indeed, in late medieval England there were only two further major recoinages when the weight but not the fineness of the coins was altered, the first some 60 years later, and the second after a further 50 years. Such was not the case in France or elsewhere in northern Europe, and Oresme wrote against a background of constant debasement. His treatise is often seen as a piece of special pleading on behalf of the landed classes, but both *De Moneta* and the English parliamentary legislation show us how central to perceptions of economic well-being the maintenance of a sound coinage had become.[54]

It was not an easy task for any ruler, lay or ecclesiastical. Kings and princes needed to keep tight control over their mints, over the moneyers who actually struck the coins, and over the exchangers who bought the bullion needed for the re-coinages. They had to enact laws to prevent counterfeiting and coin-clipping and, from the late thirteenth century onward, export controls, to stop the supposed flow of gold and silver from the land and other measures to ensure a regular flow of bullion to English mints.[55]

During the 'bullion crisis' of the late Middle Ages there was much debate in parliament on these issues, leading to a substantial body of legislation which is discussed at length below in Chapter 8.[56] Much of the legislation was repeated, in parliament after parliament, and this must raise doubts about its effectiveness and about the need for it, except in political terms, since it bought the support of merchants sitting in the Commons in Parliament. What it does show us, quite emphatically, however, is this, that it was seen as the king's duty to maintain both the quantity and the quality of money put into circulation by his mints.

Capitalism

The state and the money economy emerged almost simultaneously, then, although the state was always slightly in the lead since the money economy could not exist unless there was a strong framework of government to promote, defend and control it. What also emerged, again at near equal pace, were capitalist attitudes and structures. There is no one generally agreed definition of capitalism, but we can most usefully turn to the three definitions provided by Christopher Dyer as a good starting point for our future discussions.[57]

The first sees capitalism as a system of exchange relations, an economic system dominated by the market. Entrepreneurs are involved in specialised production and competition, and those who own capital use it to earn profits in the market place. Everything of utility can be bought or sold or, as the Wife of Bath has it in Chaucer's *Canterbury Tales*, 'ale [all] is for to selle'.[58] There is little difference here between capitalism and a basic market economy, with no account being taken of the development of capitalist ideas and attitudes. Hence Dyer proposes his second definition, based on the works of Max Weber and Werner Sombart, who stressed the mentality of capitalism.[59] Economic activity will be conducted in a rational spirit, with traders and producers learning to appreciate the disciplines of the market, and developing habits of thought that help them maximise profits. An acquisitive, thrifty and individualistic society appears but, again, with the market and its disciplines firmly at its centre. The third definition, based on the works of Karl Marx, switches the emphasis from the interplay of market forces to the question of the ownership of the means of production. Marx saw capitalism as a system of relationships in production, where the ownership of the means of production is concentrated in the hands of the entrepreneurs. They employ a free labour force, who have no ownership or control of the means of production, but are separated from it and so have to work for wages. Capitalists buy the labour of the workers. They sell the goods the workers produce, at a profit. Marx contrasted this with 'feudalism' where lords exercise non-economic powers of compulsion to extract rents, often in kind, and services from their peasant tenants. Those tenants had no need of lords economically, but were controlled by them. The lords extracted from them a share of their surplus product. Rents were not fixed by market forces, land was possessed, not owned since peasants were tenants, not proprietors. The peasant household was the basic unit of production and goods were made or grown for use, not for sale. The market was limited and its needs satisfied by small artisan producers through a limited urban sector.[60]

For Marx, the contrast was between a static, feudal economy, little touched by the market and a dynamic, thrusting economy where individuals engaged in the market or gained control of the means of production. There is no general agreement as to when or why the transition from feudalism to capitalism occurred, but for our immediate purposes one thing is very clear. If feudalism could exist either without or with only a limited use of money, capitalism could not. Money has a central role to play in each of Dyer's three definitions of capitalism, or in any mix of them. Markets function imperfectly without money to simplify and quicken exchange. Wealth static in land can be released by money rents or through mortgages, to be accumulated as a store of value, lent at interest, used to purchase more land or for trading enterprises. Partnerships could be formed between those with money and those with commercial expertise. Producers could employ wage labour at either daily, weekly or yearly rates, so allowing them to control the means of production, a control much emphasised by Marx. Money breeds money: it also breeds changed attitudes as to what constitutes wealth and to ways of creating wealth. In a society where the Church taught that the taking of interest was a sin, making money work in these ways was difficult but not impossible. There also had to be changed attitudes to the purposes of wealth, and a challenge to the idea that it was created simply for consumption, an idea firmly rooted in medieval society, rather than for investment. Yet, no matter which of the three definitions is adopted, and important though such changes were, the growing availability and use of money were essential for the development of capitalism. Similarly, to define a money economy without recognising that capitalism and capitalist ideas have a key role to play in it would be perverse.

So, a money economy was and is the sum of many parts. It did not appear fully fledged as soon as coins were first used in some exchange transactions. The interaction of a whole series of factors was necessary before it could operate effectively within the general market for all forms of goods and services. Reckoning, recording, accounting, amounts and legal systems were as essential to a money economy as the growth of the market and an abundant supply of coin in circulation. But in many ways, the key factors were changes in the money supply. If it expanded, prices would rise, according to the workings of the Fisher identity: if it contracted, they would fall. Much modern analysis of the workings of the medieval English economy has been tied to those two propositions, in terms of the rapid expansion due to monetary inflation in the late twelfth and thirteenth century and contraction due to monetary deflation in the fifteenth. Whether this analysis will stand closer examination will be discussed at length below.[61] What is immediately clear is that the quantity of money in circulation must be seen along with population growth and decline as one of the main variables in what, by the second half of the thirteenth century at least, was a money economy. But no ruler could ensure that sufficient quantities of coin of good weight and fineness were put into circulation unless there was an abundance of bullion, of silver and gold, from which they could be struck. 'Sound' money required such weight and fineness, and it is important now to know how coins were made, how their quality was controlled, and how they were taken out of and put into circulation. It is also important to have a full understanding of the problems of the bullion supply, of how it fluctuated in the medieval period, and how those fluctuations affected the purchasing power of money. Here we have to look far beyond England to the silver mines of central and southern Europe, to the gold fields of Hungary and the Sudan and to the question of the balance of trade and payments between Europe, the Near East and Asia. This will be the purpose of the next chapter.

Notes

1 F.C. Lane and R.C. Mueller, *Money and Banking in Medieval and Renaissance Venice: Coins and Money of Account* (Baltimore and London: Johns Hopkins, 1985), p. 4.
2 R. Hodges, *Dark Age Economics: The Origins of Towns and Trade, 600–1000* (London: Duckworth, 1982), pp. 104–5; Baumol and Blinder, *Economics: Principles and Policy*, pp. 226–7; W.S. Jevons, *Money and the Mechanism of Exchange* (London: Kegan Paul, Trench, Trübner & co.: 1875), pp. 24–35; P. Grierson, *The Origins of Money* (London: Athlone Press, 1977), p. 7; H. Codere, 'Money exchange systems and a theory of money', *Man*, 3 (1968), 560, 557.
3 G. Crowther, *An Outline of Money* (London: Nelson, 1948), p. 4; R. Hodges, *Primitive and Peasant Markets* (Oxford: Blackwell, 1988), pp. 104–5.
4 Jevons, *Money and the Mechanism of Exchange*, pp. 30–40.

PART I: THEORIES AND PROBLEMS

5 Wood, *Medieval Economic Thought*, pp. 87-8.
6 Crowther, *Outline of Money*, pp. 4-10.
7 See below, p. 52-5.
8 Lane and Mueller, *Money and Banking in Medieval and Renaissance Venice*, p. 5; Crowther, *Outline of Money*, pp. 3-4.
9 See below, pp. 65-6. This was not unique to English coins, of course.
10 Hodges *Primitive and Peasant Markets*, p. 112; S. Piron 'Monnaie et majesté royal dans la France du 14e siècle', *Annales, Histoire, Sciences Sociales*, 51-2 (1996), 324-54, *passim*.
11 Hodges, *Primitive and Peasant Markets*, pp. 103, 109; T.J. Sargent and F.R. Velde, *The Big Problem of Small Change* (Princeton: Princeton University Press, 2005), pp. 3-7 and Chapter 5, 'Medieval ideas about coins and money', pp. 69-99, *passim*.
12 See below, pp. 86-7.
13 The arguments concerning the importance of self-accelerating factors are taken from A. Murray, *Reason and Society in the Middle Ages* (Oxford: Clarendon, 1978), pp. 28-9.
14 See below, Chapter 4 *passim* and pp. 174-5, 182, 187-8.
15 D. Nicholas, *The Growth of the Medieval City: From Late Antiquity to the Early Fourteenth Century* (London: Longman, 1997), p. 275; P. Contamine, M. Bompaire, S. Lebecq and J-L. Sarrazin, *L'Économie médiévale* (Paris: Armand Colin, 1993), pp. 141-4; Campbell, 'Benchmarking', gives revised figures for English and Welsh towns in 1290, Table 4, 908.
16 See above, pp. 5, n.5, for population totals.
17 For a detailed discussion of the growth of the market in England, see below, pp. 174-6; Nicholas, *Growth of the Medieval City*, pp. 178-9, 211, 279; P. Nightingale, 'The growth of London in the medieval English economy', in R.H. Britnell and J. Hatcher (eds), *Progress and Problems in Medieval England* (Cambridge: Cambridge University Press, 1996), pp. 90, 96-7; Contamine et al., *L'économie médiévale*, pp. 234-47; M.M. Postan, 'The trade of medieval Europe: the north' in M.M. Postan and E. Miller (eds), *The Cambridge Economic History of Europe*, vol. ii, *Trade and Industry in the Middle Ages* (Cambridge: Cambridge University Press, 2nd edn, 1987), pp. 186-8; D. Abulafia (ed.), *The New Cambridge Medieval History, vol. v, c.1198-c.1300* (Cambridge: Cambridge University Press, 1999), pp. 53-6, 744-5; *Grosser Atlas zur Weltgeschichte* (Brunswick: Westermann, 1997), p. 84-5; N.J.G. Pounds, *An Economic History of Medieval Europe* (London: Longman, 1974), pp. 371-3; P. Spufford, *Power and Profit: The Merchant in Medieval Europe* (London: Thames & Hudson, 2003), pp. 55-6, 140, 144; D. Harrison, *The Bridges of Medieval England: Transport and Society 400-1800* (Oxford: Oxford University Press, 2004), pp. 35-56; D. Birkenholz, *The King's Two Maps: Cartography and Culture in Thirteenth-century England* (London: Routledge, 2004), pp. 113-48; the Gough Map itself can be studied in detail at http://143.117.60/website/GoughMap/viewer.html; J.F. Edwards and B.P. Hindle, 'The transportation system of medieval England and Wales', *JHG*, 17 (1991), 123-34; J. Langdon, 'The efficiency of inland water transport in medieval England', in J. Blair (ed.), *Waterways and Canal-building in Medieval England* (Oxford: Oxford Univer-

sity Press, 2007), pp. 110-30. Pounds, *Economic History of Medieval Europe*, p. 387; J. Langdon, *Horses, Oxen and Technological Innovation: The Use of Draught Animals in English Farming from 1066 to 1500* (Cambridge: Cambridge University Press, 1986), pp. 4-21 and *passim*; J. Masschaele, *Peasants, Merchants and Markets: Inland Trade in Medieval England 1150-1350* (Basingstoke: Macmillan, 1997), p. 43, and especially Chapter 9, *passim*; E. Miller and J. Hatcher, *Medieval England: Towns, Commerce and Crafts 1086-1348* (London: Longman, 1995), pp. 144-5; Contamine, *L'économie médievale*, p. 234. R.W. Unger, *The Ship in the Medieval Economy 600-1600* (London: Croom Helm, 1980), pp. 135-46, 161-7, 171-8.

18 Murray, *Reason and Society*, pp. 28-9.

19 The growth in the money supply was dependent upon a growth in the supply of bullion. This is discussed at length below, pp. 65-8. The growth of the market in England between 1180 and 1330 is analysed fully by R.H. Britnell, *The Commercialisation of English Society 1000-1500* (Cambridge: Cambridge University Press, 1993), Chapters 4 and 5 *passim*.

20 E. Clark, 'Debt litigation in a late medieval English vill', in J.A. Raftis (ed.), *Pathways to Medieval Peasants* (Toronto: Pontifical Institute, 1981), pp. 253-5, 261-2; C.C. Dyer, *Standards of Living in the Later Middle Ages: Social Change in England c.1200-1520* (Cambridge: Cambridge University Press, 1989), pp. 185-86; Dyer, *An Age of Transition?*, p. 175.

21 See below, pp. 132, 134, 187.

22 Murray, *Reason and Society*, pp. 190-1.

23 See below, pp. 32-3.

24 See below, pp. 167-8.

25 See below, pp. 120-1.

26 One inch equals 254 mm. A bushel was a dry measure for grain and other goods which was the equivalent of 2,150.42 cubic inches or 35.24 litres, according to the 'Winchester' standard. A modern acre of land equals 0.405 hectares, but its size varied considerably in the Middle Ages.

27 Wood, *Medieval Economic Thought*, pp. 88-99; Codere, 'Money exchange systems', 562.

28 II Athelstan, cl. 12; II and III Edgar, cl. 8, 8.1, *EHD, vol. i*, pp. 384, 397.

29 For attempts to regulate measures from 1196 onward see W. Stubbs (ed.), *Chronica Magistri Rogeri de Hovedene*, Vol. iv, Rolls Series (London: H.M.S.O., 1871), pp. 33-4; R.D. O'Connor, *The weights and measures of England* (London: H.M.S.O., 1987), pp. 90-1; *EHD, vol. iii*, pp. 230, 856-7; *Statutes of the Realm*, Vol. i, ed. A. Luders et al. (London: Record Commission, 1810, reprinted Dawsons of Pall Mall, 1963), pp. 204-5; Codere, 'Money exchange systems', 564.

30 See below, pp. 118-19, 212.

31 See below, pp. 72-4.

32 Codere, 'Money exchange systems', 564-5.

33 H. R. Loyn, *Anglo-Saxon England and the Norman Conquest* (London: Longman, 1962), pp. 175-9, 305-14; H.R. Loyn, *The Governance of Anglo-Saxon England, 500-1087* (London: Arnold, 1983), pp. 119-22; J. Campbell (ed.), *The Anglo Saxons* (Harmondsworth: Penguin, 1991), p. 243, illustration 208.

PART I: THEORIES AND PROBLEMS

34 For Anglo-Saxon leases and rentals see R.J. Faith, *The English Peasantry and the Growth of Lordship* (London: Leicester University Press, 1997), Chapter 6, *passim*; P.D.A. Harvey, 'Rectitudines singularum personarum and gerefa', *EHR*, 108 (1993), 1–22.

35 Richard Fitz Nigel, *Dialogus de scaccario*, ed. and trs. by C. Johnson, with corrections by F.E.L. Carter and D. Greenaway (Oxford: Oxford University Press, 1983). There is a new edition ed. and trs. by E. Amt (Oxford: Oxford University Press, 2007).

36 J. Hudson, *Oxford Dictionary of National Biography* (Oxford: Oxford University Press, 2004), Vol. 40, pp. 900–02, Vol. 46, pp. 746–8; see also Hudson, 'Administration, family and perception of the past in late twelfth-century England: Richard Fitz Nigel and the Dialogue of the Exchequer', in P. Magdalino (ed.), *The Perception of the Past in Twelfth-century Europe* (London: Hambledon Continuum, 1992), pp. 75–98.

37 For further discussion of and examples from Domesday and the pipe rolls, see below, pp. 120–1.

38 Clanchy, *Memory to Written Record*, pp. 65–6, 124, 136–8, and plate viii; Fitz Nigel, *Dialogus, passim*; W.L. Warren, *The Governance of Norman and Angevin England, 1086–1272* (London: Arnold, 1987), pp. 73–8; L.C. Hector, *The Handwriting of English Documents* (London, 1958), pp. 40–1.

39 M.T. Clanchy, *From Memory to Written Record: England, 1066–1307* (Oxford: Blackwell, 2nd edn, 1992), p. 21.

40 See below, pp. 72–4, 202–4, 274–84.

41 Clanchy, *Memory to Written Record*, p. 76; and see above, pp. 26–7 and Table 2.2, Chapter 6, *passim*, for increases in the money supply.

42 Ranulf de Glanvill, *The Treatise on the Laws and Customs of the Realm of England commonly called Glanvill*, ed. and trs. by G.D.G. Hall (Oxford: Oxford University Press, 1993), p. 82.

43 See above, pp. 19–21, for a fuller discussion of this point.

44 S. Piron, 'Monnaie et majesté royale', 325–7.

45 Lane and Mueller, *Money and Banking in Renaissance Venice*, p. 10.

46 See below, pp. 104–5; III Æthelræd II (978–1008), cl. 8, 8.1; IV Æthelræd II, cl. 5: *EHD, vol. i*, p. 404 and A.J. Robertson, *The Laws of the Kings of England from Edmund to Henry I* (Cambridge: Cambridge University Press, 1925), pp. 69, 71, 75, 77; P. Nightingale, 'The ora, the mark and the mancus: weight standards and the coinage in eleventh-century England', part two, *NC*, 144 (1984), 240; 25 Edward III, st. 5, c. 2, *RP, vol. ii*, p. 239a.

47 The complex administrative processes of simultaneously taking an existing coinage out of circulation, striking a new one, and putting that into circulation, are discussed below, pp. 52–7.

48 Hodges, *Primitive and Peasant Markets*, pp. 106–12.

49 Warren, *Governance of Norman and Angevin England*, p. 35; and see below, pp 98–100.

50 A.L. Brown, *The Governance of Late Medieval England, 1272–1461* (London: Arnold, 1989), pp. 70–1.

51 M. Prestwich, *Edward I* (London: Methuen, 1988), pp. 485–6; J.L. Bolton, 'Inflation, economics and politics in thirteenth-century England' in P.R. Coss and S. Lloyd (eds), *Thirteenth-century England IV* (Woodbridge: Boydell and Brewer, 1992), pp. 8–9; and see below, Chapter 7, pp. 191, 212.

52 T. Wykes, 'Chronicon vulgo dictum Chronicon Thomae Wykes, 1066–1289', in H.R. Luard (ed.), *Annales Monastici* (Rolls Series, 1864–69), iv, p. 278; Prestwich, *Edward I*, pp. 244–5 and fn. 44; and see below, p. 156.

53 J.R. Strayer, *The Reign of Philip the Fair* (Princeton, NJ: Princeton University Press, 1980), pp. 394–7; Spufford, *Money and its Use*, pp. 302–3.

54 C. Johnson (ed.), *The De Moneta of Nicholas Oresme and English Mint Documents* (London: Nelson, 1956), especially Chapter 6, pp. 10–11, and Chapter 24, pp. 39–42; *EHD, vol. ii*, p. 536; W.J. Whittaker (ed.), *The Mirror of Justices*, Selden Society, vii (London, 1895), pp. 10–11; J. Strachey (ed.), *Rotuli parliamentorum; ut et petitiones, et placita in parliamento, vol. ii* (London: Bowyer, 1767–77), pp. 160a, 240b: there is now a much revised digital version of this volume, edited by C. Given-Wilson et al., *The Parliament Rolls of Medieval England [PROME]* (Leicester: Scholarly Digital Editions, 2005); Spufford, *Money and its Use*, pp. 303–8; J.H.A. Munro, *Wool, Cloth and Gold: The Struggle for Bullion in Anglo-Burgundian Trade, 1340–1478* (Toronto: Toronto University Press, 1972), pp. 34–5; Lane and Mueller, *Money and Banking in Renaissance Venice*, p. 14; Piron, 'Monnaie et majéste royale', 353.

55 Mayhew, 'From regional to central minting', pp. 88, 93–7. Clipping was trimming the edges of coins to obtain small quantities of silver, which could then be sold or used for other purposes: see above, p. 21, and below, pp, 46, 87, 147, 156–7, 177, 238, 245–6.

56 See below, pp. 228–35, 244–8.

57 C. Dyer, 'Were there any capitalists in fifteenth-century England?' in J. Kermode (ed.), *Enterprise and Individuals in Fifteenth-century England* (Stroud: Sutton, 1991), pp. 1–10.

58 Wife of Bath's Prologue, line 414: the context here was the sale of sexual favours but the spirit of the money and market economy pervades the whole prologue.

59 M. Weber, *Die protestantische Ethik und der Geist des Kapitalismus*, Archiv für Sozialwissenschaft und Sozial Politik (1904–5); W. Sombart, *Der moderne Kapitalismus* (Munich and Leipzig: Duncker und Humblot, two vols, 1902). There are translations of both these works.

60 Rigby, *English Society in the Later Middle Ages*, pp. 49–52; S.H. Rigby, 'Historical materialism: social structure and social change in the Middle Ages', *Journal of Medieval and Early Modern Studies*, 34 (2004), 473–522, where the author discusses Marx's and Engels's definitions of capitalism and feudalism and their interpretations of the structure of medieval society.

61 See below, pp. 268–700.

3

Coinage and the bullion supply

The purchasing power of money

Money in the medieval period meant coins, although whether that was exclusively so remains a matter of debate.[1] Payments could also be made by ingots of nearly pure silver or gold, which were used by merchants and princes to transfer large sums of money, usually to another country. This is hardly surprising, given that transporting coins in bulk was a cumbersome business. In the thirteenth century £145 worth of English silver pennies weighed a modern hundredweight (112 lb) or 50.8 kilos. Shipping thousands of pounds to Scotland or Wales or abroad, to pay armies and allies, was difficult and expensive. Ingots were easier to handle than barrel-loads of silver pennies or, later, of gold nobles, yet the preferred method of making payments still seems to have been by coin. That made sense within the country where they were legal tender. Coins commanded a premium over bullion by virtue of their immediate portability, and because all the labour and other minting costs had already been paid. Curiously, however, even when other means of transferring sums abroad by written instruments had been developed, payments were still made in coin. Given the high silver, and later gold, content of English coins, they were in themselves a form of bullion. They could quickly be melted down and turned into local coins, to the profit both of those taking them to the mint and of the prince who controlled it.[2]

Small payments could not be made by ingot. A bushel of wheat, a length of cloth, a wey of cheese, all had to be paid for in coin. Similarly, the king required his taxes and the lord his rents in money that could be spent, even if it did mean that each time a county sheriff paid £100 into the Exchequer, 24,000 silver pennies had to be counted and recounted.[3] But it is important to understand that the value of a medieval coin was not a constant.

It changed, sometimes quite rapidly, due to immediate circumstances or, more gently, due to long-term depreciation. Each coin actually had two values, whether it was a silver penny or halfpenny, a groat or a gold noble. The first was its *face* or nominal value, the second its *intrinsic* value, which depended on the quantity and purity of the precious metal it contained. The king, by bringing the coinage under his control and placing his image on the coins, acted as a guarantor of its worth. So, it is argued, and rather like the modern coin, the nominal value of a silver penny was what mattered in term of internal trade, and not variations in its weight or fineness – that is, how much silver it contained and the purity of that metal. However, for external trade, both were of considerable importance, as will be seen.[4] But, internally, coins are held to have changed hands at face value: a penny was a penny, and would buy a penny's worth of goods. Prices for foodstuffs and manufactured goods rose and fell according to fluctuations in the quantity of money in circulation (**M**), in response to harvest crises or to changes in labour costs but not to changes in the value of the precious metal each coin contained or its intrinsic worth.

This is the theory: in practice it does not seem to have been the case. It was important for coins to have a guaranteed face value, simply to ensure that there were standard and related units of exchange.[5] But contemporaries realised only too well that what a coin could buy varied for several reasons. A good harvest always led to a fall in wheat prices. A bad harvest, or worse still a run of bad harvests, would send them through the roof. The chronicles are full of references to poor harvests and the high price of corn, and quite rapid short-term price fluctuations were part and parcel of medieval life. That is why modern economic historians trying to understand long-term price trends often use moving averages.[6] What the chroniclers also realised, as we have seen, was that high prices were not always the result of poor harvests but were, at times, related in some way to the state of the coinage. Why should this have been?

The most serious physical problem was constant wear and tear. The bullion content of each coin was very high.[7] Silver, in particular, is a soft metal which wears away quickly, as coins pass from hand to hand. Modern estimates suggest that losses were between 2 and 2¾ per cent of the total quantity of the silver in the coinage per decade. In the 1290s there were between 216,000,000 and 240,000,000 pennies in circulation, with a face value of between £900,000 and £1,000,000. Silver losses through wear and tear on a coinage of this size would have amounted to some seven tons over a decade. The silver was not stolen, hoarded, or lost: it just vanished into thin air. Consequently, new coins had to be struck and put into circulation each year simply to replace losses. Even when this was done, coins could still become very worn, to the extent that the design on them was all but obliterated. It was obvious that they contained less silver than newer and heavier coins and so they were discounted, that is to say, they were worth less than their face value in the market place. What sometimes made matters worse was the illegal but widespread practice of coin clipping. Shaving minute quantities from the edges of coins for their bullion content was all too common, and on occasion the subject of quite ferocious punishment.[8]

A coin therefore had both a *face value* and an *intrinsic value*, which varied according to the quantity of precious metal it contained. This was well understood. Exchequer officials were aware that the weight of a coin and the fineness and purity of the bullion it contained made a significant difference to its value. Henry I's need for good coined money to pay the mercenary troops used to suppress revolt in his continental possessions led to the end of payments in kind from royal manors. His officials gave the food renders a monetary value instead and then added a surcharge of sixpence in the pound to safeguard the king's income from currency depreciation. Even this was found to be insufficient, and so it was ordained that the coins be weighed and then that their actual silver content be established by assaying. This only reflected current practice. Flat rate surcharges, weighing and assaying are all to be found in Domesday Book (1086) as a means of safeguarding the value of payments, and the Pipe Roll of 1129–30 records payments being made at the Exchequer by the face value of the coin; in 'blanched' money; by 'tale' or 'numero'; or by weight. Blanching involved taking a random sample of the coins paid in by the county sheriff. Two hundred and forty pennies (which were supposed to weigh one pound) were then selected from that sample and handed over to the smelter who reduced them to bullion in order to purify the silver. When the smelter judged the silver to be sufficiently purified, he removed it from the fire and weighed the ingot against the Exchequer pound. If the scales balanced, then the silver and the coins from which it had been produced were judged to be of the correct fineness in terms of their silver content. That seldom happened and pennies from the original sample were added to the side of the scales holding the ingot until they balanced. It was then decided that the coins paid in by the sheriff would be discounted by the number of pennies added to the scales. He would have to make good the shortfall which could be substantial if the assay had shown the deficit was as much as seven pence in the pound.[9]

Blanching was a lengthy process and so payment by 'tale' or by 'numero' was accepted instead. The pennies were counted out and a deduction of 5 per cent (a shilling in the pound), made from their combined face value.[10] Again, this had to be made good by whoever was making their account, and everyone making payments into the Exchequer must have been aware of these deductions. What sheriffs or other officials paid over, however, was what had been collected from the population at large. It is beyond belief that similar adjustments were not made to the sums of silver pennies that had been handed over to them. Legal or not, institutions and individuals kept scales for weighing money, or had it weighed for them, so that 'light' coins could be rejected. In 1335 Salamon de Ripple at St Augustine's Abbey, Canterbury, forced debtors to pay anything between 3s 4d and 5s in the pound over face value by making them match their coins against the weight of his own chosen heavy coin. Sibston Abbey, Suffolk, paid eleven pence for two balances to weigh gold in 1363–64, and it cost Crowland Abbey in the Fens 16d to have a payment of 34s 8d weighed. But perhaps the best and non-anecdotal evidence for the clear understanding of the difference between the nominal or face value of a coin and what it was worth in the market place comes from the last two parliaments of Henry V's reign. In May 1421 the king had ordered the recoinage of the gold noble to ensure that each coin contained enough gold to make it worth 6s 8d, its face value. This recoinage was still in progress, with a completion date of November 1422, when in the next parliament in December 1421 Henry was granted a lay subsidy or tax for the defence of the realm. Collecting it proved a problem because there were so many worn gold coins still in circulation so the king conceded that a gold noble worth 5s 8d by weight would be accepted by the tax collectors at its face value of 6s 8d. He also agreed that 'good, lawful and true weights for the noble, half noble and gold farthing [quarter noble] should ... be sent in all possible haste to all the cities and towns in the counties of England ... so that people who need to can have recourse to them and have lawful knowledge of them ... so that they are not deceived by fraudulent counterfeiters and those who use false weights to cheat the people.'[11] Modern work on medieval prices has shown that they rose in the years immediately before partial or complete recoinages. One reason for this was that old and worn coins had lost some of their purchasing power and prices were adjusted accordingly. It now took two worn pennies to buy what a newer coin containing more silver had previously purchased – and contemporaries clearly realised this.[12]

The purchasing power of a coin also changed in response to another and not-so-obvious variable, however: the price or value of bullion on the open market. Precious metals were truly international commodities, in demand throughout Europe and well beyond its frontiers. European

PART I: THEORIES AND PROBLEMS

mining output could not always meet that demand. Between c.1160 and the early fourteenth century there was a boom in silver production, but by the late 1330s that had come to an end as existing seams were exhausted and no new ones came on stream. From the mid-fourteenth to the late-fifteenth century Europe was to suffer from increasing shortages of silver, the metal from which coins for mass circulation were struck. Bullion shortages were made worse generally by outflows of silver and gold from Europe to pay for the luxury goods imported from the Near East and Asia and, at a local level, by increasing competition between princes anxious to attract precious metals to their mints so that they could profit from recoinages. This competition was particularly intense in north-western Europe, where the introduction of bi-metallic currencies created an additional problem. Bi-metallic currencies worked smoothly provided that the ratio between the two metals that could be freely minted into coins (in our case, gold and silver) approximated to their values on international bullion markets. If these values diverged, and there was no adjustment in this gold:silver ratio, then the metal with the higher international market value would drain abroad to be replaced by the other. At times there could be substantial outflows of one or other of the precious metals, leading to serious shortages of either gold or, more frequently, silver.[13]

It is against this complex background that changes in the weight and fineness of the penny have to be set.

At first sight Table 3.1 seems to show the steady devaluation of the silver coinage over nearly three centuries. But column three shows that fineness was maintained at 92.5 per cent throughout the period, with no debase-

Table 3.1 The weight and fineness of the English silver coinage 1158–1526

Date	Weight in grams	Percentage fineness
1158–1279	1.46	0.925
1279	1.44	0.925
1335–44	1.44	0.833
1344	1.32	0.925
1345	1.31	0.925
1346	1.3	0.925
1351	1.17	0.925
1411	0.97	0.925
1464–1526	0.78	0.925

Source: C.E. Challis, *A New History of the Royal* Mint (Cambridge: Cambridge University Press, 1992), Appendix 2, pp. 699–717.

ment that would have seen this silver content of the coins reduced and the copper content increased. The weight reduction was a response to the falling output from the European mines from about 1330 onward. The international price of silver rose sharply, so that if the weight of the penny had been maintained at 1.46 grams its purchasing power would have been such as to make it difficult to use for day-to-day transactions. These weight adjustments eased the deflationary effects of the ever rising value of silver. Had they not been made, then prices would have fallen even further than they did in the late fourteenth and fifteenth centuries.[14] The English silver coinage remained, throughout the Middle Ages, one of the best in Europe.

Prices therefore responded to changes in the total volume of money in circulation, and in the fineness and weight of the coins themselves. But there was a further dimension to the problems caused by maintaining a high-value coinage, in relation to that of England's continental trading partners: it made exports dearer and imports much cheaper. The mint parity theory of exchange rates between two countries using currencies based on silver or gold argues that the rate is determined on a weight to weight basis of their respective currencies which, in the medieval period, would be tied to price of both metals on the international bullion market. If 240 pennies, or sterlings as they were known internationally, were struck from a known pound of silver, but 360 from the same pound in another hypothetical foreign currency, then any merchant exchanging his coins for sterlings, as he had to do when entering England, would lose heavily in the process. He would receive back from the English exchangers only two-thirds of the nominal or face value of his own coins, which would make it harder for him to buy English goods for export. In terms of his own currency he would have to pay far more for them than he might wish, which might well encourage him to seek alternative goods in a market in another country with more favourable exchange rates. Conversely, English merchants travelling to our hypothetical country would receive 360 pennies for their 240 sterlings and would be able to buy more foreign goods for import. Such goods could then be sold for lower prices than English manufactures, leading to import substitution which would damage English industry.[15]

Since it was through the balance of trade that bullion was won for English mints, this theory has important implications. It has been argued that in the Anglo-Saxon period the weight of the coinage was deliberately manipulated to boost exports and so obtain the silver needed to buy off the Danes. Later, in the fifteenth century, the high quality of the coinage, coupled with the rising value of precious metals, may have caused substantial problems for English cloth exporters. Contemporary public opinion demanded 'sound' money, and kings bowed before such pressure, but it might have been in the best interests of both consumers and exporters if they had not done so.[16]

Coins in circulation

Prices within England, then, responded to supply and demand, to the quantity of money in circulation, and to the changing value of gold and silver on the international market. The latter was related to mining output, to the mint policies of rulers in north-western Europe and to bi-metallic flows. However, none of these complex issues can be properly understood without relating them to the coins themselves. The silver coinage will be discussed first and then the introduction of a full gold coinage in the mid-fourteenth century and, briefly, its consequences. How coins were made, the reasons for partial and complete recoinages, and the quantity of bullion needed to strike a new coinage and maintain it in circulation will then be considered, before finally moving to the continual problem of how adequate supplies of silver and gold could be secured for the English mints.

The silver coinage

The workhorse of the medieval English coinage was the silver penny. It was introduced in the late eighth century by Offa, king of Mercia, with the first issues in south-east England coming in the 760s and 770s. A direct copy of the Carolingian silver denier, it was a broader and thinner coin than its predecessor which is sometimes but erroneously called a *sceatta*. Offa's mints struck pennies weighing about 1.46 grams (22.5 grains) from a pound of silver weighing approximately 12 ounces or 349 grams. All these weights are approximate, but the relationship between the pound of silver of 12 ounces, later called the Tower pound, and 240 pennies was established in Offa's reign, as was the fineness of the penny itself. At 95 per cent fine it was made of nearly pure silver and it could not be maintained at that high standard, soon falling to 92.5 per cent fine, around which level it fluctuated for the rest of the Middle Ages.[17]

As will be seen, Edgar made the silver penny the standard English coin from about 973 onward. It was a small coin, about the same size as a current five-pence piece and just over half its weight. The practical problem with it was that, given its high silver content, its purchasing power was surprisingly high. A gallon of ale (8 pints or 4.55 litres) could often be bought for a penny and not everyone wanted or could afford to buy so much. Peasants needed to buy and to sell in small quantities and for that small change, halfpennies and farthings (quarter pennies) were needed.[18] The simplest answer to this enduring problem of small change would have been to strike large numbers of these lesser-value coins but this was not done in earnest until 1279. Before that date the common solution to the problem was to cut pennies into halves and quarters using a hammer and a cold chisel, hence the differentiation numismatists make between 'cut' and 'struck' halfpennies and farthings.[19] Even putting struck small change into circulation from 1279 onward did not always satisfy demand and, at times, there never seemed to be enough small change in medieval England.[20] It was also in 1279 that a further silver coin was first introduced, the groat, worth four pence. At that point it was too valuable for everyday use, since it was worth more than twice the daily wage of the skilled labourer, and the coin failed. By the mid-fourteenth century, however, circumstances had changed. Wages were rising sharply and in 1351 the groat was successfully reissued, along with the half groat worth two pence.[21]

The gold coinage

The penny and its subdivisions, with the groat and half groat, were the basic silver coins of the Middle Ages. They were used to buy and sell wheat, cheese, boots, shoes, nails, lengths of cloth, pots of ales, or to pay rents and taxes, and until the mid-fourteenth century they were the only coins in general circulation, if one disregards the flood of foreign imitations entering the country in the late thirteenth and early fourteenth centuries. Then, in 1344, and finally succumbing to a movement that had been sweeping across Europe from south to north since the mid-thirteenth century, Edward III introduced a gold coinage, and bi-metallism. Henry III had tried to keep pace with his European rivals and in 1257 had issued a gold penny. It was probably intended mainly for alms-giving since it was grossly over-valued in terms of silver and, not surprisingly, it failed.[22] But by the mid-fourteenth century the demands of war and the complaints of the merchants forced Edward III to issue the first gold coins for general circulation in January 1344. They were the leopards, with their halves and quarters. The leopard was valued at 6s, the equivalent of two little florins of Florence, the half at 3s, the quarter at 1s 6d. Again, they were overvalued in terms of silver and were quickly replaced in 1344 by the noble, half noble and quarter noble, with face values of 6s 8d, 3s 4d and 1s 8d. They became the standard gold coins in circulation until 1464, when new nobles, with

PART I: THEORIES AND PROBLEMS

their halves and quarters, were issued, this time with face values of 8s 4d, 4s 2d and 2s 1d. Like the earlier leopards they too were unsuccessful because of their value in relation to that of the silver coinage, and in the next year were replaced by the noble ryal, or rose noble (10s), with halves and quarters, and the angel (6s 8d) and half angel (3s 4d).[23] From the mid-fourteenth century and particularly in the fifteenth century, gold became by far the more important of the two coinages, in terms of the value and weight of the precious metal struck into coins.

Moneys of account

There were pennies, groats, nobles and angels in circulation, then, but no shilling or pound coins. Such coins were not struck until the reign of Henry VII, the pound in 1489 and the shilling perhaps at the same time.[24] Until then, shillings and pounds were simply moneys of account to make reckoning easier.[25] They may have been introduced by Edgar, as part of his reform of the coinage in the late tenth century, to bring England into line with practice in the Carolingian dominions. Certainly, Domesday Book shows us a world where money was reckoned in pounds, shillings and pence, as well as in two other units of account, the mark and the ora. The mark was originally a unit of weight, with eight ore as its subdivisions. In the eleventh century the ora was valued at 16d but in Domesday there is also an ora of 20d, and the difference has been much discussed. The best explanation is that offered by Nightingale, namely that the change to the ora of 20d was linked to the introduction of a new heavier penny by William I in 1077, and to a new weight standard, the ora of 27 grams and the mark of 216 grams. If one ora was now equal to 20 of the heavier pennies, then a mark was worth 13s 4d, the simple arithmetic being:

27 grams × 8 = 216 grams = 1 mark by weight
20 pence = 1 ora: 1 ora × 8 = 160 pence = 13s 4d.

The ora disappeared: the mark did not. To the end of the Middle Ages it was a unit of account equal to 13s 4d.[26]

Mints and minting

Putting a substantial volume of coin into circulation and then maintaining it at or about the original level was a major undertaking. When a new design was introduced or a worn coinage had to be replaced, the old coins were called in and melted down, to provide much of the bullion for the new issue. Then, because of wear and tear, losses, hoarding and drain of coin abroad, regular 'topping-up' issues were needed, just to maintain the volume in circulation. The sheer quantity of coins that had to be struck is quite staggering. A coinage of about £37,500, the amount Dolley argued was in circulation in the Conqueror's reign, would have required the production of nine million pennies, all struck by hand. By Edward I's reign, at the end of the thirteenth century, the volume in circulation had risen to about £900,000. To maintain it at that level, in the twenty years between the recoinages of 1279 and 1299–1300 the total output from all mints was something like 280 or 290 million coins, of which nearly 50 millions were halfpennies and farthings.[27] That required a great deal of bullion. It also required a complex mint organisation, controlled by the crown, which at all times sought to exploit its rights over the coinage for its own legitimate profit. Isolating the various stages of production for purposes of discussion will probably give a false impression of instant efficiency. In fact, the issue of a new coinage always stretched over several years. It involved a whole range of people, from the king and his council down to the workers at the mints who actually struck, by hand, the millions of coins. To make it intelligible, the various stages of a hypothetical recoinage are described here. It is very much an idealised picture, and more applicable to the later Middle Ages than to the Anglo-Saxon period when, for example, the dies from which the coins were struck were not always supplied from one main centre. But it will serve as a model, as long as it is remembered that, in reality, nothing in the Middle Ages ever worked as smoothly as this.

The king and his council had first to decide on the design of the new coin. The frequent recoinages of the late tenth, eleventh and early twelfth centuries resulted in a variety of different portraits of kings on the obverse of the coins, and of different patterns on the reverse, crosses long and short, quatrefoils, circles, stars, lozenges, aimed at distinguishing the new coins from the old and defeating the counterfeiters and clippers. The steel dies for striking the coins then had to be engraved and sent, in sets, to the moneyers at the mints. As long as the crown controlled the manufacture and issue of the dies, it also controlled who struck the coins, and could thereby insist on uniformity of design. Decisions were also taken about the weight and fineness of the new coins, weight being controlled by ordering how many pennies were to be struck from the pound of pure or near pure metal.

Between the Norman Conquest and 1526, what came to be known as the Tower pound and not the better known Troy pound was used in England for weighing precious metals. The relationship between the two weight systems is shown in Table 3.2:

Table 3.2 Troy and Tower pounds in grains and grams

	Troy		Tower	
	Grains	Grams	Grains	Grams
Grain	1	0.065 gr	1	0.065 gr
Pennyweight (dwt)	24	1.56 gr	22.5	1.46 gr
Ounce (20 dwt)	480	31.1 gr	450	29.16 gr
Pound (240 dwt)	5760	373 gr	5400	350 gr
11.25 Troy ounces		=		1 Tower Pound

What can be seen in both cases is that there were 240 pennyweights to the pound. This meant that 240 pennies could be struck from the Tower pound of silver, hence the basis of the duodecimal system of 12 pennies to the shilling and 240 pence or 20 shillings to the monetary pound. Because the Troy system is the better known, coin weights throughout this book are given in metric grams and Troy grains, with 1.46 grams equalling 22.5 grains. Between 1158 and 1279 240 pennies were indeed struck from the Tower pound so that the average weight of the penny was or should have been 1.46 grams or 22.5 grains.[28] From 1279 to 1335, 243 pennies, 486 halfpennies, or 970 to 1,000 farthings were struck from the Tower pound, the one exception being 1285 when Edward I seems to have ordered 245 pence. In 1335, and in the face of growing shortages of silver, the rate went up to 252 and 254, although in fact only halfpennies and farthings were being struck at that point; then to 270 in 1346; to 300 between 1351 and 1412; to 360 between 1412 and 1461; and then 450 from 1464 onward. This was a steady fall in weight, for reasons already discussed, and not to be compared to the very rapid changes in both weight and fineness in the period before 1158.[29]

Fineness (92.5 per cent for silver and 99.5 per cent for gold) seems to have been controlled by assaying. A certain amount of alloy had to be added to silver in particular, to harden this soft metal, and then the moneyers who struck the coins were allowed to add more, at least an extra six pennyweights to the pound. In this way, more pennies could be struck from the Tower pound of silver, and the moneyers were allowed to keep the extra coins to defray their costs.[30] But the precise processes by which fineness was monitored and controlled are not at all clear. Craig argued that in the thirteenth century mints were issued with what were called trial plates. These were small, standard pieces of silver, one pure, the other of coin fineness, each of about two ounces in weight. Other, larger plates were kept at the Exchequer itself. Presumably, the fineness of the metal being used for the coinage would be compared with the silver from the trial plates by the process of assaying, and so the standard would be maintained. It is possible that from 1279 the official use of standards was replaced by improved specifications which, for the first time, expressed exactly the constituents of sterling silver, but standard plates for both silver and gold were still part of the equipment at the mint within the Tower of London in the late fifteenth century. The metal was assayed when it was brought in for coining. It seems to have been a troublesome and lengthy business, and as an alternative, for gold at least, the touchstone was used. This was a black, flint-like stone. A piece of silver or gold rubbed on its surface left a streak which differed in colour according to its quality. That could then be compared to other streaks made from needles of metal of a known fineness, and so the fineness of the metal on test could be established. Apparently, this was quite accurate for gold, but less so for silver, and in practice there were variations in the weight and fineness of the silver pennies from each issue. Standard quality control was impossible to maintain, and a degree of tolerance between narrow limits was thought acceptable.[31]

The crown also decided where the mints would be situated. The word 'mint' conjures up pictures of a purpose-built factory where coins were struck, in a highly organised production process. Little could be further from the truth in the Middle Ages, although minting did become more sophisticated as it became more centralised at the Tower of London in the thirteenth century. But, as Brand has pointed out, late Anglo-Saxon and Norman mints, sometimes as many as 70 of them, located throughout the country, were not establishments as they have been imagined. Rather, there would have been a moneyer, or moneyers, men of substance who bought in bullion in exchange for new coin but who then put out the work of striking the coins to lesser men at small forges within the town. Within these forges, the manufacturing process remained largely unchanged throughout the Middle Ages. Coins were made by inserting a silver or gold blank between a set of dies, and then striking the upper of the pair with a hand-held hammer, probably weighing somewhere around two pounds or one kilo. Up to 1279, the blanks were cut from flans of silver, created by forming sheets of metal of the requisite fineness, and then hammering them out to cover an area of approximately the right thickness for the penny. Square shaped blanks were then cut from these sheets, each being of roughly a penny weight. The blanks were placed between the dies, the coins struck, and then their corners cut off to make the round penny. After 1279, two new methods of making the blanks have been suggested. The precious metal may have been turned into small, square rods, of a cross section equal to the area of the intended coin. From them, slices were cut, slightly above the coin's weight, and these slices were rounded off by reheating and beating them. Next, they were trimmed and filed to the correct weight, heat-treated again to make them workable and then, finally, struck between the dies. Alternatively, it is now thought that after 1279 droplets of molten silver were poured on to a flat plate, to make the flans or blanks of approximately the right weight. They were then flattened by beating, annealed to make them more malleable, and passed on to the worker at the dies for striking.[32]

From at least the Conquest onward, and certainly on one occasion before, the dies were supplied centrally. By the mid-twelfth century they were cut, and then issued from the Exchequer at Westminster to the moneyers at the various mints. If the mint was at a distance from the central storehouse, as those at Durham and York were, then a local stock of dies would be kept at a royal castle, so that worn-out dies could easily be exchanged for new ones when necessary. The dies themselves were cylinders of iron, on one end of which the designs of either obverse or reverse of the coin were engraved, as reverse or mirror images. The bottom die, or pile, bearing the obverse, or king's head, was spiked, so that it could be driven into a block of wood, to give it stability. The upper die, or trussel, with the reverse design, was a cylinder long enough to be held by hand, so that it could be struck by the workman's hammer. The firmly-fixed obverse die lasted much longer than the upper die, which often cracked or split under repeated hammering. This explains why dies were often supplied in threes, two reverse, one obverse, and why obverse dies could be used to produce two or even three times more coins than reverse dies, a point further discussed below.[33]

Although by modern standards this was technology at a fairly low level, considerable care had to be exercised at all stages in the production of coin. Allowances were made for loss of metal 'in the fire', that is, during smelting, but they could not be exceeded without penalty. Assaying and weighing were both skilled arts, and all clippings and filings had to be collected carefully to avoid fraud and loss. The mint buildings themselves were often simple and little more than forges, especially in the tenth, eleventh and early twelfth centuries when, during the frequent recoinages, as many as 70 mints might be in operation. From then onward there began a period of contraction, so that by the fourteenth century production was concentrated first on the Tower mint at London and at Canterbury and then on the Tower and the mint at Calais, which was open between 1363 and 1440, with some local production at the archiepiscopal and episcopal mints at Canterbury, York and Durham. A central organisation gradually emerged, based on the mint at the Tower of London, with a hierarchy of officers, warden, master, comptroller and assayer, keeper of the exchange and, from 1279 onward, fixed contracts with one man, or a syndicate of men, who undertook to produce the coinage. This was a long process, and it was accompanied by changes in the ways in which the crown sought to profit from the coinage. The practice of taking fixed fees from the moneyers who struck the coins or from the towns in which the mints were located was abandoned in favour of what were, effectively, taxes on production. The moneyers were also deprived of their right to exchange old, worn and foreign coins for freshly-minted coins. That now passed to the king's exchanger and the crown took the considerable profits that had previously gone to the moneyers.[34]

Estimating the volume of currency in circulation: coin-hoard and single-find evidence

How the newly-struck coins were put into circulation after c.1180 remains something of a puzzle. Before the re-organisation and centralisation of the mints in the twelfth and thirteenth centuries it could be accomplished quite easily. Old coins were taken to the nearest mint and sold to the moneyer for their bullion content, payment being made in new coins to the face value of the price for the silver. At each recoinage extra mints were opened on a temporary basis in the major towns, allowing relatively easy access to them by anyone holding coins. Most of the exchanging in the countryside was probably done by merchants engaged in local, regional and national trade who collected the old coins from their customers in return for new. Although this is a largely speculative argument, it makes sense and perhaps there is no need to look further for alternative explanations. When regional minting was abandoned and production concentrated on a smaller number of mints, it becomes much more difficult to explain how coins passed into general circulation. Central minting also meant the opening of royal exchanges in London and at such provincial mints as were in operation during the less frequent recoinages, as has just been seen. This certainly happened in 1180-2, 1205-7, 1248-50, from 1280 to 1300 and in the 1330s and there were exchange tables at the major ports.[35] Coin-hoard evidence from the later Middle Ages suggests that currency issued at the various mints was thoroughly mixed together within a decade of the date of issue,

PART I: THEORIES AND PROBLEMS

but this is more evidence of active local and inter-regional trade than of how new issues passed into circulation in the remoter areas of north and south-west England, for example, both regions far away from mints and royal exchanges. Perhaps the growing commercialisation of society from the early thirteenth century onward provides part of the answer to the question as does the development of the state and of national taxation. Regular payments into and from the Exchequer offered ample opportunities for collecting old and issuing new coins, and the payment of wages to the large infantry forces raised for Edward I's Welsh and Scottish wars certainly helped the spread of monetisation in areas of England far from the main mints.[36]

If this question remains largely unresolved, so, in some ways, does the next: is it possible to estimate the size of the money supply with any degree of accuracy? There are three sources of data that can be used to make such estimates: recorded mint outputs; coin hoards; and the number of dies used to produce the coins. Taking these in order, the English mint accounts in the pipe rolls and other Exchequer records provide us with details of the quantities of bullion minted from the 1220s onward, with a few breaks, at London, Canterbury and Calais. There are also some records for minor royal mints but only from about 1300 onward. They cannot provide us with figures for all coin output, however. No evidence exists for production at the smaller royal mints between 1220 and 1300 and royal records ignore bullion struck into coins at the three ecclesiastical mints of Bury St Edmunds, Durham and York. These gaps in the evidence can be partially filled by using coin-hoard evidence from the period *after* 1220. If coins deposited by hoarders do represent a sample of coins produced at all English mints, then it is theoretically possible to calculate the ratio of those struck at the major royal mints to those struck at the minor royal and ecclesiastical mints. Assuming, hypothetically, that there were a hundred coins in a hoard dating from the 1220s and 80 of them were struck at the major royal mints and the other 20 at the other mints, then this would be a ratio of 4:1. If royal records show that output from the major mints had struck coins to the face value of £400,000 in the same period, then that would represent 80 per cent of output and 100 per cent would be £500,000.

All estimates contain inherent flaws. In this case it must always be remembered that mint output does not equal the volume of coin in circulation. Coins were lost, they drained abroad or were saved, since cash balances had to be accumulated to pay rents and other dues and debts and to make purchases of equipment and food. This could keep substantial and completely unquantifiable amounts of coin out of circulation for weeks, months or even years at a time, although they were likely to pass back into general use at some point. Conversely, it is by no means certain that all the old coins were demonetised when a new issue was struck. In theory they should have been taken out of circulation and melted down to provide much if not most of the bullion needed for the new coinage. In practice that did not always happen, most notably in the late tenth century and after the recoinage of 1205–7, while in the fifteenth century, some earlier Lancastrian gold and silver seems to have remained in use after the recoinage of 1411–12. At other times and, as has already been seen, especially in the late thirteenth century, large quantities of foreign coins passed into circulation, replacing English silver shipped abroad to pay for war in Flanders and Gascony.[37] Nevertheless, after about 1220, the written records do allow some fairly accurate estimates of the volume of coin in circulation to be made, and, of course, they also specify the types of coin struck, and their weight and fineness.

For nearly half the period considered in this book, however, namely the 247 years between 973 and 1220, the only evidence for the size of the circulating medium comes from coin hoards and from calculations based on the number of die pairs used to produce a given coinage. The theory runs thus: a coin hoard can provide us with a random sample of, say, 100 coins from a particular coinage. Each coin bears distinguishing marks from the pair of dies that struck it, given that the design on every die differed from that on others used to produce the same issue. If no die pairs at all were found in the sample, that is, no coins struck using the same set of dies, then it is impossible even to guess at the total number of dies used for the coinage as a whole. If all the coins were struck from the same set of dies, it is overwhelmingly possible that only one set of dies was used to produce the entire coinage, although this seems highly improbable. Where some duplication of dies occurs, however, numismatists believe it is possible to calculate the total number of die pairs used to produce a specific coinage, within a large margin of error. The next step is to estimate the average coin output per reverse die in the pair, remembering that this was the die that wore out first, and then multiply that by the number of reverse dies used, in order to arrive at a figure for the total volume of coinage produced. This method can produce widely differing estimates, however. Based on a hoard of about 350 late tenth-century coins ($c.985$) found at Iona in 1950, Metcalf calculated a die estimate for the whole coinage of 2,346 pairs ± 469. Using an average coin output per reverse die of 10,000 coins he concluded that there was a total coin population of between 19 and 28 million pennies, or £79,167 and £116,667. Applying the same techniques to the Chester Castle

Esplande hoard which contained 543 coins of c.970, 145 of them from Edgar's pre-reform coinage – that is, before 973 – results in an estimate of 6,252 pairs ± 1,332 and a coin population of 50 and 70 million pennies or between £208,334 and £291,667. That suggests a dramatic fall in the volume of the coinage in circulation between 970 and 985 and, as Grierson remarks, 'Both sets of figures cannot be correct.'[38]

There are, indeed, three major questions to be asked about the methodology based on coin-hoard evidence and die-pair output used by Metcalf and by other numismatists to estimate the size of the coinage between the late tenth and the early thirteenth centuries. The first is quite straightforward: can the coin hoards provide truly random samples of the coinage between 973 and 1220? The answer must be 'No', in all but a few cases. We have no idea of why the coins were collected together and then either lost or concealed, to be found many hundreds of years later. The most rational explanations for deliberate concealment are fear of disorder or of debasement, when old coins of a heavier weight would be worth more because of the bullion they contained. But rationality need not have been the determining factor in the decision to hide money away. A hoard could be savings hidden and for some reason not recovered; the treasures of a miser; or a night's winnings at dice put in a supposedly safe place. Since many of the hoards contain only a few coins, usually in their tens and twenties rather than in their hundreds and thousands, it is likely that most of them were the savings needed to meet dues and pay bills. The basis on which the coins were saved may have been entirely irrational, however. The hoarder may have selected pennies struck at a particular mint or by a particular moneyer or those that were shiny. If any degree of irrationality was involved in collecting the coins that were hidden away, that makes them less than completely random samples of the coinage.[39]

Nor can the problem of 'locality' be ignored. Anglo-Saxon and Anglo-Norman coins were struck at a large number of mints and although the mixed character of many hoards shows that circulation was less stagnant than might be supposed, there is nevertheless always a good deal of regional bias in those found in England. The Chester hoard may have contained 145 coins from Edgar's pre-reform coinage but 33 of them were struck at York and another 66 at various north-western mints. They provide some evidence of production at northern mints but not for the much busier mints in London and East Anglia and certainly not for the coinage as a whole.[40] This 'localisation' need not necessarily be of the place where the hoard was actually found. A traveller, possibly a trader, might bring with him – or, less likely, her – groups or parcels of coins collected as he passed from region to region. At some point, local disorder may have been such that he decided to hide his money away, without adding to it. The coins in such a hoard are representative only of the regions through which the traveller had already passed, not of the locality where it was concealed and certainly not of the entire country. Hoards buried when a new issue was in progress will also only give a picture up to the date of burial, not of the issue as a whole.[41] A process of selectivity by weight may also have been applied fairly continuously and not just when debasement was thought likely. Brand argues that in the late tenth century heavy pennies were deliberately selected and light coins ignored and he too is sceptical about hoards as a sample cross section of the currency generally in circulation, even at the point at which they were hidden.[42] The truth is that we simply do not and cannot know the motives behind the amassing of hoards. Projecting the admittedly valuable evidence from them in order to draw conclusions about the currency in general may well be dangerous.

If hoards are not completely random samples of the coinage at a certain date, neither are many of them statistically significant in terms of their size. Allen lists a total of 130 found in England containing coins dated between c.973 and 1158. Of these, 20 pose problems that make them difficult to use as evidence, leaving 110 on which to base estimates of the coinage over a period of 185 years. One or two of the hoards are numerically very large: more than 12,000 coins struck in William I's reign (1066–87) were found at Beauworth in Hampshire in 1833 and more recently, in 1993, 10,000 coins from Æthelræd II's and Cnut's reigns (979–1035) 'somewhere in the Cambridge area'. Most, however, are small. Fifty-nine of the hoards contain fewer than fifty coins and of that number thirty-eight contain fewer than ten. The practical consequences of this can be seen in Dolley and Metcalf's 1961 analysis of the coinage in Edgar's reign. They based their arguments on the evidence from twenty-eight hoards, eleven of which came from Ireland, seven from Scotland, and two each from Wales and the Isle of Man. Only six were found in England, all of them in the north of the country, with three being from a single place. The actual numbers of coins in these hoards is also a matter of concern. Only seven contained more than 120 pennies; there were twelve with between 20 and 120 and eight with fewer than 20 in all. This seems scant evidence on which to base even what they admit to be distorted views of Edgar's coinage.[43] The Cambridge hoard of c.10,000 coins seems to provide ample evidence for the reigns of Æthelræd II and Cnut (979–1035) but it is dwarfed in size by the huge hoards found in Scandinavia, Poland and Russia, containing in all between 60 and 70,000 English silver pennies struck between 991 and

PART I: THEORIES AND PROBLEMS

c.1020. This should be compared with a total of about 52,000 coins found in all 110 English hoards with coins dating from 973 to 1158. It might seem, therefore, that the one period where coin hoards can provide the evidence on which estimates of the volume of the English currency in circulation would be the late tenth and eleventh centuries. Unfortunately, the Scandinavian hoards present another major and unresolved problem: were the coins they contain ever intended for circulation in England, or were they struck specifically for the purpose of buying off the Danes?[44]

The hoard evidence from Henry I's reign illustrates a further difficulty. Between 1130 and 1135 there were fifteen issues of very variable quality and so far thirty-seven hoards containing coins from the period have been discovered. The majority of the surviving coins come from only four of them, however, two deposited towards the end of the reign, two during the opening years of his successor, King Stephen (1135–54). Little can be learnt from them about the coinage in the early part of the reign, so that Henry I's coinage is one of the least understood of any since Edgar's. One substantial find could radically alter the situation, and the case of the halfpenny shows how that might happen. In spite of there being a reference to a round halfpenny by the chronicler John of Worcester in 1131, the existence of this distinctive coin was always doubted, even when a specimen seemed to have been found in 1950. Then, in 1989, two new examples turned up on a site in London, another was found in Berkshire, and a fifth in Norfolk. All are of the same design, but were issued from five different mints. These stray finds, along with at least three others discovered since by the use of metal detectors, have led to a rapid revision of a long-held belief that no struck halfpennies, as opposed to those cut from whole pennies, existed before Edward I's reign.[45] What we do not know yet is whether these useful coins were struck in any quantities and, if so, how this would affect estimates of the volume of the currency in Henry I's reign.

Coin hoards, then, cannot provide us with entirely random samples of the coinage. The second problem in trying to estimate the volume of currency in circulation in this way is that the equation used to calculate the total number of die pairs used to strike a specific coinage has a wide margin of error. Originally developed by I.D. Brown for his study of the Elizabethan coinage, it relies on the proposition that

$$x = \frac{y(y-1)}{2p}$$

where **x** = the original total of die pairs, **y** = the sample of coins and **p** = the number of die pairs in the sample. Where **p** is smaller than 4 the equation cannot produce a useful solution to the problem. If, in a sample of 250 coins, 8 die pairs are discovered, then

$$x = \frac{250(250-1)}{2 \times 8}$$

or 3,890 die pairs. The statistical margin of error in this calculation is huge, however, being no less than ±1,376 die pairs, which gives a maximum possible number of 5,266 die pairs and a minimum of 2,514. As has already been seen, in any die pair the reverse produces less than the obverse so that estimates of the volume of coinage produced must be based on the number of coins that could, on average, be struck by a reverse die, and Metcalf estimates that to be 10,000, a figure that has been quoted before in this chapter. It is time to take a much closer look at this figure, since whether it can be regarded as in any way reliable is the third of the questions to be asked of the coin-hoard evidence.

Assuming that it is, and taking the example given above, the number of coins produced by 3,890 reverse dies is 38,890,000 silver pennies or £162,083. Allowing for the margin of error of ±1,376 dies, the maxim number of coins struck would be 52,660,000 or £219,417 and the minimum 25,140,000 or £104,750. The difference between the top and bottom of the range is 27,520,000 coins or £114,667, almost two thirds of the figure produced by using the estimate of 3,890 dies and 10,000 coins per reverse die. Equally worrying are the disagreements among numismatist about the number of coins that could be struck from a reverse die. In the tenth, eleventh and twelfth centuries a figure of 10,000 coins per die might be reasonable for busy mints like London, Norwich, York or Chester, but could hardly have been the case at the many smaller provincial mints, where dies would not have been used at full capacity simply because not enough bullion came to such mints to warrant constant production.[46] Taking this factor into account, the average figure for reverse-die production at all mints should be much lower, at something like 7,000 per die, and the consequences for the estimated volume of coin struck during a recoinage can be seen by substituting this figure for the 10,000 used in the calculations above. There were what seemed to be good reasons for the choice of 10,000 coins as an average for reverse die output. It was based on the evidence of die output at English mints in the late thirteenth and early fourteenth centuries when they were working at full capacity producing the largest silver coinage in the medieval period, ten or twenty times greater than any issue struck during the Anglo-Saxon or Anglo-Norman period. There was scarcely any slackening in their output and the dies would have been in constant use. The average number of coins struck by a reverse die may well have been between ten and twenty thousand coins but a recent study (2004) has drawn attention to the extreme variations in the reverse die output. These, says the author, demonstrate the folly of any attempt to use a single arbitrary figure for average die-output to estimate the size of a coinage.[47]

It is much easier to destroy arguments than to propose alternatives and numismatists would say that they have to work with the only evidence available to them and that speculation is not only inevitable but essential. They are certainly correct to do so. Without their meticulous analysis of hoard evidence there would be nothing on which to base estimates of the size of the currency between 973 and 1220, but we need to be fully aware that these estimates have very large margins of error indeed. Interestingly, in recent years, there has been much more focus on what single or stray finds can tell us. They have best been described as coins accidentally lost from general circulation and thrown up again after many centuries by ploughing, building excavations or, increasingly, discovered through the use of metal detectors.[48] When these finds are entered on a database and correlated, they can provide valuable information about the use, size and duration of individual issues. In 1977 Rigold argued that there was also a direct relationship between the number of modern single finds of a specific issue and the total amount of coin in general circulation in the Middle Ages. His argument seems to be broadly true, although there are some discrepancies between the written and the stray-find evidence. The latter suggests an elevenfold increase in the circulating medium between 1086 and 1300, compared with the twenty-fivefold increase indicated by the mint records. On the other hand, single finds have produced coins that are not found in the hoard evidence, most notably in Henry I's reign, thus adding considerably to our knowledge of the early twelfth-century coinage. However, if the relationship between single-find evidence and the size of the coinage is valid for the period after 1158, it should also be valid for the preceding period and it probably is. The stray-find database held at the Fitzwilliam Museum in Cambridge indicates that the volume of currency in circulation rose between c.973 and 1042 and 1042 and 1066, but then fell between 1066 and 1135. This is broadly in line with the estimates from the coin hoards although there is an apparent conflict with the die estimates for the reigns of Æthelræd II and Cnut (942–1035) which are much higher than stray finds would suggest. This can almost certainly be explained by the striking of more coins to pay the geld, which then appeared in the Scandinavian hoards.[49]

Between them, the die-estimates and the stray-find evidence can give us a broad idea of the possible minimum and maximum value of the currency in circulation in the Anglo-Saxon and Anglo-Norman periods. Accepting this, it must also be acknowledged that there is much else to be learnt from the coin hoards and stray finds. The very survival of large numbers of certain issues points to the volume of minting and of coin in circulation at specific times, even allowing for the difficulties already discussed. More importantly, until 1279 coins bore the name of the moneyer and the mint at which they were struck which makes it possible to determine the pattern of provincial minting in the Anglo-Saxon and Anglo-Norman periods, and to establish when the change to centralised production occurred, as well as the identity of the moneyers themselves. Up to 1180 the moneyers controlled both mints and exchanges and from the profits of both often became local providers of credit. Knowing their names helps us to confirm suspicions gleaned from the sparse written sources. Coin hoards can also show the actual use of coins in other ways. Their geographic distribution, along with analysis of their contents, as to type and date, provide some indicators of both when money was being used regionally within England, and of how general that use was. Along with the valuable evidence from stray finds, coins can also tell us about patterns of internal trade. The distances they travelled from the mint of their issue show local trading connections. If they were carried a long way, from Canterbury to the Midlands, say, or vice versa, then this is good evidence for the development of inter-regional trade, while English coins finds abroad can usually be linked to foreign trade or warfare. Scattered finds have also been used to indicate what were, apparently, quite dramatic changes in the types of coin in circulation. Rigold has shown that at one hundred sampled sites, the number of stray finds of small denomination coins, half-groats and below, from the period 1412-64, was only one-fifth of those found in the period 1279-1351. This points to a sharp decline in the amount of small change in circulation, and suggests that complaints in the fifteenth century about the shortage of silver coins and especially of halfpennies and farthings were not without some justification.[50] But at all times caution is needed when using evidence from both hoards and stray finds. It has much to tell us about the volume of coinage in circulation and how it was used, but sometimes not quite as much as we are led to believe.

The bullion supply

No coins could have been struck at all, however, had there not been adequate supplies of bullion. That may be stating the obvious but the question of the bullion supply became a very contentious issue in fourteenth- and fifteenth-century parliaments and is much debated by modern historians. Putting a large silver and gold coinage into circulation and then maintaining its quantity and quality over a number of years required substantial amounts of precious metal. As the coinage reached its peak, at the end of the thirteenth century, it has been estimated that the annual production of English mints amounted on average to over 30,000 pounds weight of silver, for a coinage of between £900,000 and £1,000,000 in silver pennies, halfpennies and farthings. Less was required in the Anglo-Saxon period, but less was probably available.[51]

The bullion came from three main sources. There existed at all times a stock of precious metal in the coinage itself. When there were major recoinages, the old coins could be called in, demonetised, melted down and struck into new coins. That would not necessarily have produced all the bullion needed. The old coins were often worn or clipped, and therefore light in weight, and there would have been significant losses from hoarding and the drain of coin abroad. Nor is it certain that all old coins were taken out of circulation when new issues were made. That certainly did not happen in the Anglo-Norman period and perhaps not earlier either, in Aethelræd II's reign.[52] Moreover, when, after 1156–57, frequent coinages were abandoned, and one main type or types remained in circulation for long periods, there was a constant need for topping-up issues, and for the bullion from which they could be struck. Some, again, would come from old and worn coins brought to the mint to exchange for new, but constant recycling of the existing coinage could never meet total needs, even during a complete recoinage.

A second potential source of gold and silver lay in the plate and jewellery held by individuals and institutions. Wealth in the Middle Ages had to be displayed, to confirm rank or status or to the greater glory of God. But plate and jewellery were also used as stores of wealth, to be broken up, melted down and exchanged for coin when needed to finance trade, war or land purchases, to pay taxes, or when there was an opportunity to profit from a recoinage. That this was done cannot be doubted. Plate was melted down to pay the geld in Æthelræd II's reign, while the Jews in the twelfth and thirteenth centuries acquired it from clients to sell it to the moneyers for striking into new coin. It seems unlikely, however, that plate and jewellery were ever major sources of bullion, even at the most desperate of times.[53]

What was needed was a constant flow of bullion from European mining output. Gold and, more importantly, silver were mined in England and Wales at various times, at Beer-Alston in Devonshire, in the Mendips, at

Alston Moor in Cumberland, and in Flintshire. Only Hodges seems to suggest that in the Anglo-Saxon period the English and Welsh mines produced significant amounts of silver for the coinage, while Blanchard's suggestion that the Cumbrian mines produced floods of silver in the twelfth century has been severely criticised. Probably the most productive silver mines were those discovered in Henry III's reign (1216–72), at Beer-Alston, and in Edward I's reign (1272–1307) strenuous efforts were made to increase their output. Between 1292 and 1296, the mines yielded an average of just over 700 pounds weight of silver a year, rising to 1,100 pounds in 1296–97, to 1,400 in 1299, and perhaps to 1,800 in 1305, at a time when English mints were actually coining on average over 30,000 pounds of silver per annum. By the end of the thirteenth century the costs of mining, refining, and shipping this silver to London actually outweighed the profits, and by 1347 only 70 pounds of silver were produced. By contrast the mines and refineries at Kutná Hora in Bohemia yielded as much as 25 tons of silver per annum in the late thirteenth and early fourteenth centuries. The contribution of English mines to the silver supply was insignificant and the inescapable conclusion is that the bullion needed both to increase and then maintain the volume of coin in circulation had to come from European mines.

It is generally agreed that the main way in which precious metals were acquired was through favourable trade balances. English exports, first of wool and then later of finished or semi-finished cloth brought the necessary silver and gold into the realm. The foreign coins or unminted bullion they earned were taken by native (or denizen) merchants to the moneyers or, later, the royal exchangers at the mints, to be changed for English coin, the only money allowed to circulate within the realm. Foreign merchants coming to buy exports had to do the same, and so the bullion supply was secured. Most numismatists and modern monetary historians take it as axiomatic that trade surpluses did serve this purpose. There is also an argument that in the eleventh century the currency was deliberately manipulated by devaluations and revaluations, to encourage exports and promote import substitution, in order to earn the silver needed to buy off the Danes, while there is not much doubt that in the late Middle Ages the wool export trade was made the vehicle for the acquisition of bullion, much to its detriment.[54]

This does not mean that England was never to be troubled by difficulties with the bullion supply. Nothing could be further from the truth. Europe *was* awash with silver between *c.*1160 and *c.*1330, and some of it did flow to England along well-established trade routes, but not always in the quantities sometimes assumed. Notions of floods of silver pouring into the country in the eleventh century and between 1180 and 1220 need to be treated with some caution, as will be seen. But it is broadly true that European mines and favourable trade balances provided the bullion from which the huge English silver coinage of the late thirteenth and early fourteenth centuries could be struck. Then, from the mid-fourteenth century onward, problems began to multiply. European mining output slumped. There were severe shortages of silver and, it has been argued, a 'Great Bullion Famine' in the late fourteenth and early fifteenth centuries, which had dire consequences for the European economy generally, while a second 'famine' is thought to have brought it to a grinding halt in the 1450s and 1460s from simple lack of coined money. Again, these are issues to be discussed fully and sceptically below, but the evidence for increasingly fierce competition for limited supplies of bullion between mints in north-western Europe cannot be ignored.[55]

Paradoxically, these 'bullion wars', as Munro has called them, were made worse by the introduction of gold coinages, running alongside the silver coinages already in circulation throughout Europe.[56] At first sight this may seem to make no sense. If there was a shortage of silver, then it could be made good by the introduction of gold coins. But their purchasing power was too high for daily use, and the introduction of bi-metallism seems only to have intensified the scramble for both gold and silver and, favourable trade balances or no, made the acquisition of bullion by English mints more difficult.[57] There were two reasons for this, the first being the mint price set for silver and gold not only in England but at competing mints across north-western Europe and most importantly by those in the Burgundian Netherlands where England's main export markets lay. The second was a direct consequence of bi-metallism itself. When two coinages, silver and gold, are in circulation at the same time there has to be a fairly exact relationship between the value of the metal each contains, in terms of the price of bullion on the international market. A noble must contain 6s 8d-worth of gold and 80 pennies must contain the same value, 6s 8d, in silver, to ensure parity between them. If this parity was not achieved then, as will shortly be seen, bi-metallic flows would result and either silver or gold would be drawn abroad to rival mints.

The mint price and seignorage

Bullion did not flow to any mint in England or in Europe unless a fair price was offered for it, and that price was set by the prince. All rulers, including the kings of England, expected to make a profit from their right to control the coinage. As has already been see, before about 1180 English kings had achieved this by direct taxation on the moneyers who struck the coins or on the towns in which the mints were located. From the late twelfth century onward the English crown began to bring mints and exchanges previously in private hands directly under its own control to maximise its revenues from both and began to levy a new duty on production called 'seignorage'.[58] This was based on the difference between the number of coins actually struck from the Tower pound and the number of new coins handed back to the merchant bringing silver or gold to the mint. One example from 1343/44 will show how this worked. For the recoinage of that year, the crown ordered that 22s 2d-worth of pennies (266 coins) should be struck from the Tower pound of silver. Of these, the minters took 8d to cover their costs and profits, which was known as mintage, and the king deducted 6d as his tax, seignorage. The merchant who brought silver to the exchange received back 21s 0d in pennies of lighter weight than the previous issue, but not necessarily of less value, because of the changing international price for silver. The mint price for silver was, in effect, the amount of new coin returned to the merchant after the deduction of seignorage and mintage. In this case the crown had misjudged the mint price. Silver did not flow to its mints in 1343/44 and Edward III was forced to increase the number of pennies to be struck from the Tower pound from 266 to 270, the extra four pence going to the merchants.[59]

Setting the right mint price was therefore of great importance. If either seignorage or mintage were too high, then the merchant who brought bullion to the exchange would not receive back sufficient new coins for it to be a profitable transaction and would take his silver or gold elsewhere. The temptations for needy kings to levy seignorage at a high rate were all too obvious. The complete recoinage of 1279–81 earned Edward I something like £25,000, at a time when he was embarking on the military conquest of Wales. Seignorage was levied at between 9d and 12d in the pound, which was clearly seen as reasonable, since large quantities of silver flowed to the mints. In the 1290s, however, Edward I refused to follow the widespread debasements taking place in France and the Low Countries, where mint prices were set at levels that would attract bullion. Silver flowed to those mints, and not to Canterbury, which had to close between 1296 and 1299, or to London, where mint output was reduced to a trickle. One of the consequences was that England was flooded with foreign imitations of the silver penny, the pollards and crockards, while sterling coins of high value drained abroad.[60]

Bi-metallism, gold:silver ratios and bi-metallic flows

Until the mid-fourteenth century successive English kings faced the difficult but not impossible task of managing recoinages and 'top-up' issues by setting mint prices for silver that reflected demand for the precious metal on the international market. Edward III's introduction of bi-metallism, gold coins to run concurrently with silver, made his and his successors' task much more difficult and it helps to explain why there were so many complaints about the bullion supply in the late fourteenth and throughout the fifteenth century.[61] Again, this can best be explained by a specific example. When Edward III issued his first gold coin in 1344 the ratio of gold:silver was set at 1:14. At that point gold was simply not worth fourteen-times its weight in silver on the open market, and the over-valued gold coins were simply rejected by the merchants. The coins had to be recalled, and a new issue struck at a ratio of 1:12. That was acceptable to the merchants and the new gold coins passed into circulation.[62] In part this was a consequence of the relative value of gold and silver on the open market at that time, but there was also the added problem of the mint prices being offered for both gold and silver by foreign mints.

Bi-metallic coinages were also inherently unstable. The relative values of both metals kept changing, so that their coinage could never be free and unhindered. Values changed in line with supply and demand. If gold was highly valued in one area, and an attractive mint price was set for it, then the metal would flow to that area, while silver would flow to other mints in regions where it was temporarily in demand. The reverse would happen if silver was over-valued in terms of gold and so there arose what are known as bi-metallic flows. These occurred within north-western Europe and between southern Europe and the Near and Far East where they were made much worse by the need to pay for luxury imports in specie. Within England's immediate trading zone, around the North Sea, frequent recoinages, with attractive mint prices set, could help overcome the shortage of one metal or the other, but the difficulty for England was that its high-quality coinage remained in circulation for long periods, without proper readjustment of the gold:silver ratio. The consequences can be seen in the early fifteenth century when the English gold:silver ratio had become completely out of line with those of its major trading partners in the Low Countries. As a result of the under-valuation of gold, English nobles left the country in vast quantities, while silver was so over-valued in England that large amounts flowed to the Calais mint, to be struck into huge issues of groats in the 1420s.[63]

English kings were at least partly to blame for the late medieval shortages of silver, however. Willingly or unwillingly, in the late fourteenth and fifteenth centuries they accepted mint policies that consistently favoured gold over silver and set their mint prices accordingly. As a direct result the weight of gold minted in England far exceeded that of silver and the lack of silver coins was as much a consequence of this preference for gold as it was of declining output from European silver mines. It is against this background of what might be called both local and international bullion flows, and the complex political issues of war and trade, that the fierce late medieval debates on bullionism and the restrictions on the export of gold and silver from the realm must be seen.[64] But, broadly speaking, the story of the coinage is one of limited silver supplies until the mid to late twelfth century, followed by an avalanche of silver until c.1330, and then of bi-metallism, international bullion shortages and increasing monetary problems from 1343/44 to 1489, with both mint prices and gold:silver ratios becoming vexatious issues.

Credit and 'paper money'

This contraction in the coinage has to be seen in the context of severe depopulation, however. By 1450, and as a result of successive outbreaks of plague, the population of England was probably only half what it had been in 1300. Less money but fewer people meant, in theory at least, more coin per head of population. In theory, yes, but in practice that need not necessarily have been the case, because of the lack of silver coins. Table 8.1 (p. 244 below) shows what can only be described as a collapse in the silver coinage from £1,000,000 in 1290 to £150,000 in 1422 and then a recovery to about £350,000 in 1470, which was still only 35 per cent of what it had been in 1300. Population decline did mean that there was a less dramatic fall in coinage per head, but it went down from a possible 56d per head in 1351 to 13d in 1422 and then up to about 30d per head in 1470. The silver penny and its fractions were the coins most commonly used by the mass of the population. The purchasing power of most of the gold coins in circulation was far too great for their day-to-day needs and what they mostly complained about was the lack of silver and above all the lack of small change. According to the Fisher equation, such a radical reduction in the money supply would cause a fall in prices, or monetary deflation, which, if it persisted, would in turn lead to general depression in the economy.[65] This is an issue still being vigorously debated by modern historians, with two of the key issues being whether a growing shortage of coin, and in particular of silver coin, could have been offset by the increasing use of credit and, more contentiously, whether written credit instruments came to act as forms of paper money.

Credit was a vital part of the money economy, always provided that it was widely available and that agreements were legally enforceable.[66] In its various forms, it offered a series of ways of extending the money supply. It made trading much easier. If merchants had had to pay cash down for all the goods they bought, then that would have limited the scale of their operations. By both accepting and offering sale credits, they could spread repayments for their purchases over a number of years and at the same time allow their customers time to pay. It also meant that they could engage in more than one transaction at a time, since there was no longer a need to realise profits from the sale of imports, say, before goods for export could be bought. This is to see credit in the context of foreign trade, but it was as widely used in the domestic market. Deferred payments, sale credits, whether for a bushel of wheat, a piece of land, a bale of wool, a bolt of cloth or for building works, were, or became, the norm. Loans at interest were made in various ways, whatever the Church might say about the sinfulness of usury. Then, as now, the rich could borrow more easily than the poor and at lower, commercial rates of about 5–10 per cent per annum rather than the 40 per cent charged for short-term distress borrowing. Medieval society also had its own ways of establishing credit ratings. Standing within the community, general trustworthiness and family connections were as important as known or perceived assets and the capacity to repay. The evidence for lending and borrowing at all levels in society in the late Middle Ages is compelling. Credit provided liquidity in the money economy. It freed trade from the limitations of the money supply, since there was never enough coin in circulation for all transactions to be made in cash.[67]

By implication, therefore, if credit was widely and increasingly available, it might have helped overcome the illiquidity resulting from a severe contraction in the money supply in the late fourteenth and fifteenth centuries. Monetary historians argue strongly against this theory, however. Their case is that loans were advanced in coin and both they and deferred sale credits had to be repaid in coin. Creditors had to be able to accumulate sufficient cash balances to allow them to lend money and wait for payments for goods sold while still being able to conduct their own day-to-day business affairs. If money was 'tight', that is, if coin was not readily and generally available for any reason, then none of this was possible. Those who before had been willing to lend would hold on to such money as they had for their own immediate use and would not extend credit because they feared that shortages of coin would prevent debtors honouring their obligations. The size of the credit market would therefore rise and fall in direct relation to the quantity of money in circulation, **M**. It follows that problems caused by bullion famines or bi-metallic flows could not have been solved by the increasing use of credit.[68]

This remains an unresolved argument and the subject of a vigorous debate which has one further important dimension.[69] Those who believe that the availability of credit was linked to fluctuations in the money supply also hold that debt was not transferable and negotiable and that written credit instruments could not and did not act as 'paper money'. By the later fourteenth century these written credit instruments took various forms. There were enrolled recognizances, debts recorded as part of a formal legal process under the statutes of Acton Burnell (1283), Merchants (1285) and most importantly, the statute of the Staple of 1353. These gave the creditor greater security against the debtor who would be liable to have his goods seized and the rents and profits from his lands collected by the creditor if he or she defaulted on the debt. There were letters, or bills, of exchange, used for the transfer of money to and from England, and for borrowing money in one currency and repaying it in another, in order to finance trade to and from England. More significantly, there was the written obligation, the bill of debt, also known as a bond, by which one party formally bound him- or herself to repay another a certain sum of money at a specified date.[70] Increasingly, penalty clauses were attached to these bonds, to be invoked if repayment was not made on time. These bills or bonds were regularly being used to pay debts to a third party not involved in the original transaction. So, **A** borrows £20 from **B**, entering into a written agreement to repay the sum on a specified date or by instalments, again at specified dates. **B** then finds that he owes £20 to **C**, and in payment passes on his bill of debt from **A** to pay **C**. In this way Niccolò di Giovanni of Lucca (**B**), an Italian merchant trading in London, used debts owed to him by a group of London vintners (**A**) to pay his own debts to John Higham, a London draper (**C**), in 1430.[71] Assignment of debt had become an accepted method of payment, and a form of paper money. Other financial instruments were also used in this way. The Company of the Staple, which controlled the wool-export trade in the fifteenth century, and acted as an organ of royal finance, took deposits from its members. It issued both certificates of debt and warrants for payment of debt, and these were frequently used as a means of paying other debts, as were debentures issued by the royal wardrobe.[72]

Writings obligatory and certificates of debt had acquired one of the first attributes of 'paper money', its 'fiduciary' or 'fiat' nature. Today we are accustomed to bank notes and coins that have no intrinsic value and retain their worth only because people have faith that the issuer, usually the state, will stand behind the notes or the coins and limit their production. In much the same way bills of debt only circulated freely when the creditworthiness of the debtors was known and accepted by all parties to the transfer.[73] This constituted, in a sense, a promise to pay, that the debt would be honoured. But for these written instruments to be fully negotiable in law, they would have had to be payable to the bearer, and not necessarily to the creditor named in the instrument itself, or to his attorney, his agent for the recovery of the debt. So, in the theoretical example given above, **C**, the bearer, to whom the bond had been assigned, would have been able to collect the debt directly from **A** and would be able to go to law to enforce the debt. **B** would have been replaced in the chain, as would **C** if he then assigned the bond to a fourth party, **D**. If these bonds became both negotiable and discountable – that is, given a specific money value less than their face value, to allow for the fact that they were not due to mature, or become payable, until some time in the future – then they would have circulated as paper money, and as a supplement to the coinage. As such, their value would have to be added to **M**, the money supply in the Fisher equation of exchange, and not to **V**, because assigned non-negotiable debts are held to increase only **V**, the velocity of circulation.[74] The argument is speculative and the evidence both sparse and obscure, as will be seen. But, if forms of paper money were being used in the later Middle Ages, then the consequences of dwindling bullion supplies may have been less severe than is currently being suggested.[75]

Conclusion

This chapter began by making a general assumption that money in the Middle Ages usually meant coin. It has ended by suggesting that this might not always be the case and that by the fifteenth century 'paper' money had begun to circulate, in response to shortages of coin and the need to maintain credit networks. Central to the whole argument has been the idea that the volume of the currency in circulation was directly linked to the bullion supply. The more silver there was, the more coins could be struck. This may be stating the obvious, but it is nonetheless true. It could also have been a coincidence that the output from the European silver mines reached its highest levels in the late thirteenth and early fourteenth centuries at exactly the same time as the European population reached its peak, but that seems highly unlikely. The two went together because demand for silver and then for gold from the mines in Hungary and the Sudan was stimulated by economic expansion and the increasing need for coined money to speed the process of exchange at all levels. In the first chapter the various models of the medieval economy were discussed and it was suggested that 'population and resources' was probably the most widely accepted, with main variable being the population. The purpose of the first part of this book has been to make the case for the money supply being factored into this model as one of the determinants of price levels and of the rate at which society could be commercialised. It was not the sole determining factor, as monetarist historians argue.[76] Money, coin, had to work within the framework of royal government, law, literacy and numeracy. Without that supporting framework a money economy would not have emerged in late thirteenth-century England. Without a money economy England would have been much worse placed to withstand the combined shocks of severe depopulation and shortages of coin in the century and a half after the arrival of the Black Death.

Money and its use must form one of the main themes to be followed in any analysis of the medieval English economy. Using the evidence provided by the coinage is much more difficult than it seems at first sight, however. Fisher's equation of exchange, beloved of monetarist historians, has its limitations, while estimating the volume of currency in circulation before the 1220s poses so many problems that it is safest never to give a specific figure for any one year or decade and to accept that reality lies somewhere between the highest and the lowest of the estimates. Relating the money supply to the population by calculating coin per head probably provides a better way of assessing the economic consequences of increases and decreases in the money supply. Its weakness lies in the generality of the figures it provides, since no account is taken of inequalities in wealth or of marked variations in regional levels of monetisation.

Historians always complain about the inadequacy of their sources, however, and it is now time for us to acknowledge their limitations and use the evidence drawn from cautiously, in the light of what we have learnt from these first three chapters and accepting that money does not answer all things.[77] In Chapters 4 and 5 it will be argued that between 973 and 1180 England had a 'monetised' rather than a 'money economy', with shortages of silver holding back its development. Chapters 5 and 6 discuss the consequences of the vast increase in the money supply in the second half of the thirteenth century and the first quarter of the fourteenth when the 'money economy' finally emerged. The final chapters see that money economy being challenged by the consequences of depopulation, bi-metallism, shortages of bullion and, possibly, monetary deflation; surviving these challenges; and even being strengthened by them, at least in terms of the credit market. This is not a story of a movement forward into broad, sunlit uplands. Poverty still existed and on a large scale in years of harvest failure. The problem of small change was as great in 1489 as it had been in the eleventh and twelfth centuries, perhaps more since there was now both a market and a money economy, with all levels of society accustomed to buying and selling in order to survive and, at times, to make profits. Wealth was still unequally distributed and life-expectancy actually seems to have fallen in the second half of the fifteenth century. In these circumstances, the question can reasonably be asked, what benefits, if any, did the growth of a money economy bring? Answering that question is one of the two purposes of the following chapters. The other has already been stated. It is to demonstrate that the consequences of changes in the money supply – that is, in the volume of coinage in circulation – must be fully included in any and all models of the medieval English economy. We must now turn to examining the consequences of changes in the money supply – that is, in the volume of coin in circulation – for the lives of the people of medieval England.

Notes

1 See above, pp. 19–20.
2 J.D. Brand, *The English Coinage 1180–1247* (Glasgow: British Numismatic Society, 1994), pp. 8, 14–15; Spufford, *Money and its Use*, pp. 209–24; Lane and Mueller, *Money and Banking in Medieval and R-enaissance Venice*, pp. 22, 24; J.H.A. Munro, 'Bullion flows and monetary contraction in late-medieval England and the Low Countries' in J. F. Richards (ed.), *Precious Metals in the Later Medieval and Early Modern Worlds* (Durham, NC: Carolina Academic Press, 1983), p. 109; J.B. Gillingham, *Richard the Lionheart* (London: Weidenfeld & Nicolson, 2nd edn, 1989), p. 373; and see below, pp. 70–1, 98–9, 149–51, 159–61, 163–4, 245–8.
3 Brand, *English Coinage*, p. 6.
4 R.H.M. Dolley and D.M. Metcalf, 'The reform of the English coinage under Eadgar', in R.H.M. Dolley (ed.), *Anglo-Saxon Coins: Studies presented to F.M. Stenton* (London: Methuen, 1961), p. 158; S.R.H. Jones, 'Devaluation and the balance of payments in eleventh-century England', *EcHR*, 2nd series, 44 (1991), 602; and see below, pp. 93, 293–5.
5 See above, pp. 19–21.
6 See above, pp. 19–21.
7 See above, Table 3.1, p. 48.
8 N. Mayhew, 'Numismatic evidence and falling prices in the fourteenth century', *EcHR*, 2nd series, 27 (1974), 3; Lane and Mueller *Money and Banking in Medieval and Renaissance Venice*, pp. 25–26 and fn.1; see below, pp. 147–156–7.

9 Richard fitzNigel, *Dialogus de Scaccario*, ed. and trs. by E. Amt (Oxford: Clarendon Press, 2007), pp. xxiv-v, 54-8.
10 These practices can be seen in operation in the extract from the pipe roll given below, Chapter 4, pp. 120-2.
11 J.A. Green, *The Government of England under Henry I* (Cambridge: Cambridge University Press, 1986), pp. 62-3; W.L. Warren, *Henry II* (London: Eyre Methuen, 1977), p. 26; Warren, *The Governance of Norman and Angevin England*, pp. 70-1; A.L. Poole, *From Domesday Book to Magna Carta* (Oxford: Oxford University Press, 2nd edn, 1955), pp. 414-15; Brand, *English Coinage*, pp. 58-69, discusses these practices in relation to the fineness of the coinage, 1180-1279; N.J. Mayhew 'The monetary background to the Yorkist recoinage of 1464-7', *BNJ*, 44 (1974), 64; Mayhew, 'Numismatic evidence and falling prices in the fourteenth century', 3; H. Miskimin, 'Money and money movements in England and France at the end of the Middle Ages', in Richards (ed.), *Precious Metals*, p. 84, argues that governments could not insist on face value, but that coins were weighed and more or less circulated as bullion. A.J. Rolnick, F.R. Velde and W.E. Weber, 'The debasement puzzle: an essay in medieval monetary history', *JEH*, 56 (1996), 790-3, agree, but Munro, 'Bullion flows, p. 109, insists that silver coins circulated by value and not weight. This seems unlikely in light of the parliamentary evidence: *RP, vol. iv*, pp. 130, 154-5; *PROME*, Introduction to the December parliament of 1421.
12 Prices movements and the state of coinage are discussed fully below, pp. 156, 161, 177, 182; Brand, *English Coinage*, pp. 16-17, summarises the problem neatly.
13 A.G. Kenwood and A.L. Loughead, *Growth of the International Economy 1820-2000* (London: Routledge, 4th edn 1999), p. 105; see below, pp. 70, 233-4.
14 Mayhew, 'Monetary background', 62; Spufford, *Money and its Use*, p. 317; Mayhew, 'From regional to central minting', pp. 144-5; C. Oman, *The Coinage of England* (Oxford: Clarendon Press, 1931), p. 168; J. Craig, *The Mint: A History of the London Mint from AD 287 to 1948* (Cambridge: Campbridge University Press, 1953), pp. 61-6; Spufford, *Money and its Use* p. 402; C.E. Challis, *A New History of the Royal Mint* (Cambridge: Cambridge University Press, 1992), Appendix 1, pp. 699-720; and see below, pp. 264-70. One grain = 0.0648 grams.
15 'Gold standard', in J. Eatwell, M. Millgate and P. Newman (eds), *The New Palgrave Dictionary of Economics*, Vol. ii (London and New York: Macmillan, 1987), pp. 539-40.
16 These issues are further discussed below, pp. 245-6, 293-4.
17 P. Grierson and M.A.S. Blackburn, *Medieval European Coinage, 5th to 10th Centuries*, (Cambridge: Cambridge University Press, 1986), Chapters 8 and 10, pp. 158-89, 267-325, *passim*; D. Chick, 'The coinage of Offa in the light of recent discoveries', in D. Hill and M. Worthington (eds), *Æthelbald and Offa; Two Eighth-century Kings of Mercia*, British archaeological reports, British series, 383 (Oxford: Archaeopress, 2005), 111-22.
18 C. Dyer, *Making a Living in the Middle Ages* (New Haven and London: Yale University Press, 2002), pp. 39-40; J.L. Bolton, *The Medieval English Economy, 1150-1500* (London: Dent, 1980), pp. 70-1, 76; Dyer, *Standards of Living*, pp. 134-5, and below pp. 189-90, 202 for peasant income and expenditure in the thirteenth century.

PART I: THEORIES AND PROBLEMS

19 [R.H.] M. Dolley, 'An introduction to the coinage of Aethelred II', in D. Hill (ed.), *Ethelred the Unready: Papers from the Millenary Conference, 1978* (Oxford: British archaeological reports, 59, 1978), p. 128; M. Blackburn, 'Coinage and currency under Henry I: a review', in M. Chibnall (ed.), *Proceedings of the Battle conference, 1990* (Woodbridge: Boydell Press, 1991), pp. 49, 63; Hodges, *Primitive and Peasant Markets*, p. 117; Sargent and Velde, *The Big Problem of Small Change*, pp. 48–50.
20 See below, pp. 65, 76, 105, 128, 157, 243–6.
21 Reddaway, 'The king's mint and exchange in London', 4, 16; Mayhew, 'Monetary background', 69–70; Oman, *Coinage of England*, pp. 236–7, 241; and see below, pp. 141, 157, 167.
22 See above, pp. 70–1 for an explanation of gold:silver ratios and Chapter 6, pp. 154–5 for Henry III's gold coinage.
23 Spufford, *Money and its Use*, p. 409; and see below, pp. 141, 157, 167, for further discussion of these coins.
24 Oman, *Coinage of England*, pp. 236–7, 241.
25 See above, pp. 64–5; Hector, *Handwriting of English Documents*, p. 41.
26 P. Nightingale, 'The ora, the mark and the mancus', parts i and ii, 248–57 and 234–48, *passim*; and see below, pp. 87–8, 101.
27 See below, p. 157.
28 Mayhew, 'From regional to central minting', p. 161 and fn. 253; Craig, *The Mint*, p. 6.
29 Spufford, *Money and its Use*, p. 127, n. 2; Mayhew 'From regional to central minting', pp. 84, 119 and nn. 119, 134 and table 3; Brand, *English Coinage*, appendix two, pp. 72–3; Craig, *The Mint*, p. 418; Challis (ed.), *The Royal Mint*, appendix two, pp. 700–12; and see below, pp. 96–7, 100–1.
30 Mayhew, 'From regional to central minting', p. 102; see below, pp. 69, 146, 168.
31 Craig, *The Mint*, pp. 22–6, 69–70; Mayhew, 'From regional to central minting', pp. 109–10; for buying in precious metal at the mint, see below, pp. 57-8, 65, 69, 142–5, 152, 155–8, 241.
32 Mayhew 'From regional to central minting', pp. 159–63, for mint buildings and equipment in the later Middle Ages; Brand, *The English Coinage*, pp. 18–21. The process of striking coins is described by Craig, *The Mint*, pp. 14–16, 41–43; I. Stewart, 'The English and Norman mints, c. 600 to 1158', in Challis (ed.), *The Royal Mint*, pp. 76–81; Mayhew, 'From regional to central minting', pp. 111–12, 127–30; C.E. Challis, *The Tudor Coinage* (Manchester: Manchester University Press, 1978), pp. 1–29; Sargent and Velde, *The Big Problem of Small Change*, pp. 48–50.
33 See below, pp. 59, 62–4.
34 Brand *The English Coinage*, p. 1; and see below, Chapters 4 and 5, pp. 00–00 for full discussion of these issues.
35 This information was kindly supplied by Dr M.R. Allen from his forthcoming (2012) book on the medieval English coinage.
36 This speculative paragraph is based on discussions with Dr M.R. Allen of The Fitzwilliam Museum, Cambridge; for the role of armies in thirteenth-century monetisation, see below, pp. 191, 212.
37 Brand, *English Coinage*, p. 22; Bolton, 'The English economy in the early thirteenth

century', p. 32 ; Mayhew 'The monetary background to the Yorkist recoinage', 66; see above, p. 12, and below, pp. 69, 143, 158, 159-61.
38 P. Grierson, 'The volume of Anglo-Saxon coinage', *EcHR*, 2nd series, 20 (1967), 153-4 which is a critique of D.M. Metcalf, 'How large was the Anglo-Saxon currency?' *EcHR*, 2nd series, 18 (1965), 475-82; K. Jonnson, 'The pre-reform coinage of Edgar: the legacy of the Anglo-Saxon kingdoms', in B. Cook and G. Williams (eds.), *Coinage and History in the North Sea World c.500-1250: Essays in Honour of Marion Archibald* (Leiden: Brill, 2005), p. 333.
39 M. Allen, 'The volume of the English currency, *c.*973-1159', in Cook and Williams (eds), *Coinage and History in the North Sea World*, appendix two, pp. 503-13 for a list of coin hoards and their size, 973-1158; Grierson, 'The volume of Anglo-Saxon coinage', 155-7.
40 See below, p. 95 and Table 4.1.
41 Grierson 'The volume of Anglo-Saxon coinage', 155-7.
42 J.D. Brand, *Periodic Change of Type in the Anglo-Saxon and Norman Period* (Rochester: private publication, 1984), p. 23.
43 Dolley and Metcalf, 'The reform of the English coinage under Eadgar', pp. 137-41.
44 Dolley, 'An introduction to the coinage of Aethelred II', pp. 115, 118; Allen, 'The volume of the English currency, *c.*973-1159', pp. 496-8 usefully summarises the unresolved debate on this issue; and see below, pp. 64, 91-3.
45 Blackburn, 'Coinage and currency under Henry I', pp. 52-3, 63: W.J. Conte and M.M. Archibald, 'Five round halfpennies of Henry I: a further case for reappraisal of the chronology of types', *Spink's Numismatic Circular*, 98, 1990, pp. 232-6.
46 Grierson, 'The volume of Anglo-Saxon coinage', 153-60; Metcalf 'How large was the Anglo-Saxon currency', 475-82; Allen, 'The volume of the English currency, *c.*973-1159', table ten, p. 501, provides the latest range of estimates of mint output and the volume of the currency.
47 M. Allen, 'Medieval English die output', *BNJ*, 74 (2004), 49.
48 Blackburn, 'Coinage and currency under Henry I', pp. 54-5, discusses the nature of single-find evidence.
49 S.E. Rigold, 'Small change in the light of medieval site finds', in N.J. Mayhew (ed.), *Edwardian Monetary Affairs, 1279-1344* (Oxford: British Archaeological Reports, 36, 1977), pp. 59-80; M. Allen, 'The interpretation of single-finds of English coins, 1279-1554', *BNJ*, 75 (2005), 50-62; D.P. Newton, 'Found coins as indicators of coins in circulation: testing some assumptions, *European Journal of Archaeology*, 9 (2006), 211-27.
50 Britnell, *Commercialisation*, p. 181; and see below, pp. 239-40, 250.
51 Spufford, *Money and its Use*, p. 128: and see below, pp. 92-3, 98-9, 101, 103.
52 See above, p. 59.
53 M.K. Lawson, 'The collection of Danegeld and heregeld in the reigns of Æthelræd II and Cnut', *EHR*, 99 (1984), 726-7; R.C. Stacey 'Jewish lending and the medieval English economy', in Britnell and Campbell (eds), *A Commercialising Economy*, p. 84; Challis, *Tudor Coinage*, p. 210; and see above, Chapter 1, pp. 10-11 and below, Chapter 4, pp. 98-9.
54 Hodges, *Dark Age Economics*, p. 182; P.H. Sawyer, 'The wealth of England in the

eleventh century', *Transactions of the Royal Historical Society*, 5th series, 15 (1965), 158-60; Dolley and Metcalf, 'The reform of the English coinage under Eadgar', 154; Dolley, 'An introduction to the coinage of Aethelred II', 115; D.M. Metcalf, 'Continuity and change in English monetary history, c. 973-1086: part two', *BNJ*, 15 (1981), 63; Jones, 'Devaluation and the balance of payments', 595; I. Blanchard, 'Lothian and beyond: the "English Empire" of David I', in Britnell and Hatcher (eds), *Progress and Problems*, pp. 23-45; in his *Mining, Metallurgy and Minting in the Middle Ages, vol. ii, Afro-European Supremacy 1125-1225* (Stuttgart: Franz Steiner Verlag, 2001), Blanchard repeats his arguments about silver production in Cumbria, but they have been effectively demolished by M. Allen in his review of this book in *EHR*, 118 (2002), 1037-8 and recently (2010) in a forthcoming article in *EcHR*, 'Silver production and the money supply in England and Wales, 1086-c.1500', which also considers production from the Devon mines in the late thirteenth and early fourteenth centuries, concluding that most of the silver for the English coinage had to come from abroad. Spufford, *Money and its Use*, pp. 125, 127-8; R.S. Lopez, *The Commercial Revolution of the Middle Ages 950-1350* (Cambridge: Cambridge University Press, 1971), p. 101; R.W. Kaueper, *Bankers to the Crown: the Riccardi of Lucca and Edward I* (Princeton, NJ: Princeton University Press, 1973), pp. 60-1; C. Cipolla, 'Currency depreciation in medieval Europe', *EcHR*, 2nd series, 15 (1963), 420; Mayhew, 'From regional to central minting', pp. 131-2; for the wool trade and the bullion supply see below, pp. 93, 98, 142, 151-2, 160-3.

55 The phrase was first used by John Day, in his article 'The great bullion famine of the fifteenth century', *P&P*, 79 (1978), 3-54; Spufford, *Money and its Use*, p. 362; these issues are discussed fully below, pp. 232-6.

56 Munro's various and important publications are cited in the bibliography; see also below, pp. 161, 163, 245-7.

57 See below, pp. 240, 248-9.

58 The extension of royal control over mints and exchanges is discussed fully above, pp. 55-8 and below, pp. 88-91, 94-7, 152-3.

59 Mayhew 'From regional to central minting', pp. 109, 132 and n. 164; J.H.A. Munro, 'Mint policies, ratios and outputs in England and the Low Countries, 1335-1420', *NC*, 141 (1981), 95; Rolnick et al., 'The debasement puzzle', 792; Lane and Mueller, *Money and Banking in Medieval and Renaissance Venice*, appendix a and fn 1, pp. 493-94.

60 M. Mate, 'Monetary Policies in England, 1272-1307', *BNJ*, 41 (1972), 50-1; Prestwich, *Edward I*, pp. 246-7, 531.

61 See above, pp. 48, 51, 68 and below, pp. 168-9. The growing obsession about preventing the export of bullion from England can be seen in the list of acts and orders against it given by J.H.A. Munro, 'Bullionism and the bill of exchange in England 1272-1663', in *The Dawn of Modern Banking* (New Haven and London: Yale University Press, 1978), appendices a-e, pp. 216-36.

62 M. Mate, 'The role of gold coinage in the English economy, 1338-1400', *NC*, 18 (1978), 127-32; Spufford, *Money and its Use*, pp. 183-6; Mayhew, 'From regional to central minting', pp. 163-6, argues that excessive seignorage caused the failure, however.

63 T.H. Lloyd, *The English Wool Trade in the Middle Ages* (Cambridge: Cambridge University Press, 1977), pp. 258–62; Mayhew, 'From regional to central minting', pp. 149–52.
64 Mayhew, 'Monetary background', 63; Lane and Mueller, *Money and Banking in Medieval and Renaissance Venice*, pp. 37–41, 62; Munro, 'Mint policies, ratios, and outputs', pp. 71, 76–78, 93–6; Munro, 'Bullion flows and monetary contraction', pp. 110–13, 123–7; Miskimin, 'Money and money movements in England and France', pp. 79, 81–6; and see below, pp. 00–00.
65 See below, Chapter 8, pp. 264–8 and Table 8.1, p. 244.
66 See below, pp. 197, 199, 202–5, 283–4.
67 S. Homer and R. Sylla, *A History of Interest Rates* (New York: Wiley, 4th edn, 2005), pp. 132–41; R.C. Stacey, 'The English Jews under Henry III', in P. Skinner (ed.), *Jews in Medieval Britain* (Woodbridge: Boydell, 2003), pp. 48–9.
68 The general arguments for the use of credit to offset lack of coin are given in Bolton, *Medieval English Economy*, pp. 302–3; see also M. Kowaleski, *Local Markets and regional Trade in Medieval Exeter* (Cambridge: Cambridge University Press, 1995), p. 202, for the importance of credit and financial partnerships in promoting the flow of trade. The best introduction to the monetarist case is P. Nightingale, 'Monetary contraction and mercantile credit in later medieval England', *EcHR*, 2nd series, 43 (1990), 560–75; see also Mayhew, 'Modelling medieval monetisation', p. 67, fn. 44. These complex issues are further discussed below, pp. 263–84.
69 See below, pp. 263, 275–80.
70 Definition of a bill as a written instrument – see OED.
71 A.H. Thomas (ed.), *Calendar of Plea and Memoranda Rolls of the City of London, 1413–37* (Cambridge, 1943), pp. 250, 260–1.
72 M.M. Postan, 'Private financial instruments in medieval England', in Postan, *Medieval Trade and Finance* (Cambridge: Cambridge University Press, 1973), pp. 29–51.
73 Postan, 'Private financial instruments', p. 51.
74 Mayhew, 'Modelling medieval monetisation', pp. 67–8.
75 See below, pp. 280–4, for a fuller discussion of this debate.
76 Rigby, *English Society*, pp. 141–3, argues convincingly against the proposition that there can ever be one main causative factor.
77 Ecclesiastes 10: 19.

PART II

The coinage and the economy 973–1489

A: A MONETISED ECONOMY

4

The coinage from the late tenth century to 1158

The coinage 973–1066

The reform of 973

In 973 Edgar, king of Mercia and of the West Saxons, had himself crowned king of England at Bath. It was a second, symbolic, coronation, intended to show that he was ruler of a united kingdom. To emphasise this, he issued a fourth law code which specifically included north-east Mercia and Northumbria and, at some time between 973 and his death in 975, he ordered a major recoinage. There is no record of this in the *Anglo-Saxon Chronicle* which is frustratingly silent on monetary matters, apart from the weight of the geld, the taxation raised to buy off the Danes. Our information comes from a much later source, the *Flores Historiarum* compiled by the early thirteenth-century monk of St Albans, Roger of Wendover. Under the year 975, he writes 'Then he [Edgar] ordered there to be through the whole of England a new money, because the old had become so corrupt through clipping that the penny had scarcely the weight of a halfpenny in the scales.' This recoinage is said to have marked the beginning of a new and coherent phase in the monetary history of England, 'the beginning of a chapter ... that was to continue uninterrupted by the Norman Conquest until the reign of Stephen', the *renovatio monetae*, with frequent recoinages struck at large numbers of mints.[1]

It was the silver penny that was being recoined, to a new design, and it is upon the silver coinage that this chapter will concentrate. There was some gold in circulation in Anglo-Saxon and Norman England. It was used in the main by the wealthy, by the crown, by lay and ecclesiastical noblemen and by merchants to make payments, either by weight (using the standards of the mancus or the gold mark) or, by the later twelfth century, by coin, the bezant, a Byzantine gold coin. But even when a gold coin or a weight in gold is specified in a transaction, there can be no certainty that payment was actually made in that metal. Equivalent silver values were soon established so that by the thirteenth century the bezant was worth two shillings in silver, the mancus of gold, a weight standard again based on a Byzantine coin, thirty English silver pennies in the tenth century, the ounce of gold 15s and the mark of gold £6 in the late twelfth century.[2] Until the mid-fourteenth century, despite Henry III's experiments with a gold coinage, it was silver that was in mass circulation.

The 'Reform' coinage itself seems to have been introduced over a two- or three-year period. It continued in use in the reign of Edgar's successors, Edward the Martyr (975–8) and Æthelræd II (978–1016) until c.979. As well as bearing Edgar's portrait, the coins carried the name of the place where they were struck and the moneyer there. They were also of exceptionally pure silver. The dies used were consistently of one style, and produced centrally, initially perhaps at Winchester, and then at York. But this centralisation of die supply did not last long. By Edward the Martyr's reign dies were being supplied from three centres, and regional die cutting and distribution seem to have predominated until, perhaps, the latter part of Cnut's reign (1016–35).[3] The coins were struck at a large number of mints. Before the Reform issue, coin hoards suggest that there were some 23 mints in operation. In 973 the number rose sharply to 40 and then, by the end of the century, to about 70. They were also widely distributed geographically, with marked increases in their numbers in the west and north-east of the country and in East Anglia. Dolley and Metcalf have argued that they occurred so regularly throughout the country that their establishment cannot have been anything other than systematic, part of 'the plan of reform of 973'.

This all suggests that Edgar and his advisers embarked upon some grand design, and at least implies some clearly thought-out 'policy' on their part but there can be no certainty of this.[4] As has been seen, no contemporary source mentions the recoinage, while Wendover was only using the example of Edgar's recoinage to stress the need for one in his own time. Edgar's earlier pennies were of a somewhat debased alloy, but probably not so much so that their value had fallen by half.[5] His predecessor, Athelstan (924–39), had decreed in his Grately laws that there be only one coinage for the realm, but the reality was that in his reign regional particularism still prevailed. The weight of his coinage was fairly uniform, but it remained regional in style. Athelstan's power base lay in Wessex and southern and central Mercia, and it was here that mints proliferated. East Anglia and York still lay partly or largely beyond his control, and after his death the Viking kingdom of York reasserted itself, the kings issuing the last Anglo-Norse coinages in 939–44 and 949–54. But, after the death of Eric Bloodaxe in 954, the north-east was brought under the control of the kings of Wessex, and in 973 Edgar proclaimed himself king of England. His great recoinage was an affirmation of that claim. There was now to be one coinage for the whole realm, bearing the king's image, and it is fair to say that that remained the case for the rest of the Middle Ages, even allowing for the upheavals in the reigns of Harold I and Harthacnut (1035–42) and in the 'Anarchy' of Stephen's reign in the twelfth century.[6]

One coinage throughout the realm was to be matched by one standard of weights and measures. That was the language of the law codes which also attempted to control trade by confining it to 'ports', that is, regular markets held in towns. Athelstan's Grately Laws ordered that all transactions involving sums above 20 pence must take place at a 'port', although, in practice this was unenforceable. Later codes concentrated on trying to ensure that goods offered for sale had not been stolen. Law-worthy witnesses were required for all transactions, and late tenth- and early eleventh-century codes prescribed punishment for those who bought goods without due attention.[7] The success of these measures must be doubted, but it is both interesting and important to note that in the late Anglo-Saxon law codes the coinage, weights and measures and the regulation of trade went hand in hand.[8]

Renovatio monetae: the theory

For a king trying to assert his power over all England, tighter control over the coinage made good sense, and perhaps the idea of 'reform' should simply be seen in this light. However, it has been argued that 973 marked the beginning of a radical period in the history of the coinage. There followed nearly two centuries of frequent recoinages, each involving the recall of all or part of the old coinage, and the issue of new pennies of a different design. Between 973 and 1158 there were more than 50 substantive issues, that is, of coins that passed into general circulation. Design changes were often accompanied by changes in the weight of the penny. Each issue now takes it name from the design on the reverse, since the pennies always bore the portrait of the king on the obverse. So in Æthelræd II's reign, the substantive issues are known as First Hand; Second Hand; and Benediction Hand (all showing the hand of God stretching down from Heaven); Crux (a cross); Long Cross; Helmet; and Last Small Cross, while for William I the issues are known as Profile/Cross Fleury; Bonnet; Canopy; Two Sceptres; Two Stars; Sword; Profile/Cross and Trefoils; and

Paxs. It is a quite bewildering series of changes, accompanied until c.1080 by equally bewildering fluctuations in the weight of the penny. If Æthelræd II's First Hand pennies weighed an average of 1.51 grams (23 grains) each, then the Second hand fell to 1.31 grams (20 grains), while the modal weight of the Crux issue was 1.65 grams (25 grains), although that conceals fluctuations between 1.25 and 1.8 grams (19 to 28 grains). Even more bewildering is the wide variation between the weight of coins issued by different mints in different parts of the country, and the fact that there were wide weight variations *within* issues. The same mint could issue 'heavy' coins at the beginning of a new issue and then 'lighter' coins towards its end.[9]

One of the skills of the numismatist is to impose order on chaos, and never more so than in the case of the late Anglo-Saxon and the Norman coinage. In the 1960s, 1970s and 1980s, Michael Dolley and Michael Metcalf argued, with great conviction, that a clear pattern could be adduced from this baffling series of changes. For them, the essence of the reform of 973 was the introduction of a system by which the English coinage was regularly recalled and reissued. They argued that up to 1035, and the death of Cnut, this took place every sixth year (sexennial). The pattern then changed, and between 1035 and 1135 the average duration of each substantive issue, some 42 in all, was two or three years (biennial or triennial).[10] As well as changes of type, there were also changes in weight until late in the reign of William I, when with the Paxs issue of c.1083–c.1086 a new heavier weight standard of 1.38 grams (21.3 grains) was adopted.[11] At the same time, and, again, as has been seen, the number of mints rose substantially, to a maximum of about 70, declining briefly to 12 or 13 in Henry I's reign (1100–35), only to rise again under Stephen (1135–54).[12] For Nightingale, as for Dolley and Metcalf, the Anglo-Saxon monetary system introduced by Edgar and ending with Æthlelræd II stands out as the most sophisticated in northern Europe in that period, equalled only by that of the Byzantine Empire. The production of coin was closely regulated. Moneyers were appointed by the crown and were dependent for their dies on strictly controlled die-cutting agencies, with each man's name being stamped on his work. Finally, the king could exercise a considerable degree of control over the use of the coinage by insisting that all transactions except the most trifling had to be conducted within a 'port' in the presence of official witnesses.[13]

This theory of sexennial and then biennial or triennial recoinages – the *renovatio monetae*, or renewal of the coinage, as it is known – has a powerful symmetry. It adds to the argument that a strong and centralised monarchy was able to survive, in administrative terms at least, both the renewed Danish attacks and the Norman Conquest. These regular recoinages brought the Anglo-Saxon and Norman kings valuable revenues which came at first from payments from the moneyers. It was they who profited both from the successive recoinages, by taking a discount on changing old money into new, and from changing foreign coin into English pennies.[14] Kings taxed these profits in two ways. The moneyers had to pay a fee for each set of dies they used, and another at each recoinage. Effectively, they were paying for licences to operate, although precisely when this system began is not at all clear. The Anglo-Saxon evidence is almost non-existent, and much has to be read back from *Domesday Book* (1085–86). This records that when the coinage was changed, the Worcester moneyers each paid 20s for the new dies, and those at Hereford 18s each. Moneyers at Shaftesbury and other Dorset towns paid an annual fee of one mark of silver to the king, and then 20s when the money was changed. Whether such payments were made throughout the period 973–1086 is simply not known. Domesday probably reflects practices in the time of Edward the Confessor, which may or may not have been of long standing. In his reign the coinage was changed roughly every two years, and at times there were up to 70 mints at work, and many more moneyers engaged in striking the coins, so that he would have obtained an annual income of between £200 and £250 from the coinage. Characteristically, William I demanded much more. The taxes seem to have been shifted from the moneyers to those boroughs where the mints were located, and much larger sums were involved. London had to pay £75, Thetford (Norfolk) £40, Gloucester £20, Malmesbury (Wilts.) £5, and Pevensey (Sussex) £1. By 1086 the crown was drawing an annual income of between £750 and £1,000 from taxing the production of coin, a not inconsiderable part of its revenues.[15]

The geld and the coinage

Tight control over the coinage, and especially the ability to alter the weight of each issue, was essential if kings wished, or were forced, to levy heavy gelds. In general terms it was important to protect royal revenues by ensuring that coin tendered for taxes or for other payments would be worth roughly its face value in terms of its silver content. Frequent recoinages prevented coin becoming too worn, and this also encouraged the general confidence in the coinage essential for all forms of trade.[16] But, between 991 and 1015, taxation was levied on the kingdom at unprecedented rates. Heavy gelds raised the money needed to buy off the Danish armies, and then, between 1012 and 1051, an additional tax, the heregeld, was imposed, to pay for a mercenary fleet. If the figures given in the *Anglo-Saxon Chronicle* are to be believed, in itself a contentious issue, Scandinavian raiders took £127,000

A: A MONETISED ECONOMY

in tribute between 991 and 1012, in coins or ingots. A further £21,000 was paid to Thorkell the Tall and his men in 1014, and then, at the beginning of his reign, in 1018, Cnut demanded the largest single payment of all, no less than £82,500, of which £10,500 came from the Londoners alone. Heregeld is estimated to have cost c. £5,000 a year, and in 1041 Harthacnut raised a total of £32,147, to pay his fleet. The demands of the crown after the Conquest were equally severe. William I's 'stark geld' of 1084 was levied at a rate of 6s a hide (the unit of assessment), while the 4s on the hide taken by William Rufus in 1096 led to the melting down of church plate.[17] The geld remained an important source of income for Henry I. He levied it as an annual tax, and in 1129–30 it brought him about £2,400, or 10 per cent of his total income of £23,000.[18]

These were huge sums, especially when seen in relation to the estimated total volume of coinage in circulation, which was possibly somewhere between £25,000 and £30,000, according to Allen's latest estimates.[19] The ability to pay the geld at these rates is often taken as a measure of the wealth of Anglo-Saxon England, and the strength of its money economy, which is why this question has attracted so much attention. It has been argued that it was essential for the kings to be able, deliberately, and as part of a considered policy, to manipulate the weight of the penny, in order that the taxes could be paid. There were two reasons for this. A lighter weight meant that more coins could be struck from each pound of silver. Secondly, in order to obtain the silver necessary both to maintain the quality and quantity of the coinage in general circulation and to strike the vast numbers of pennies needed to pay off the Scandinavians, the balance of trade had to be altered in England's favour. There was, apparently, plenty of silver available in Europe. At some time between 961 and 968 rich veins were discovered at Rammelsberg, near Goslar, in the Harz mountains in Germany. The mines there came on-stream in the 990s, and the flow of silver from them reached its peak c.1025, but then declined rapidly after 1040.[20] This silver could only be won for England by way of foreign trade. 'Within no more than the duration of two sexennial types [i.e., by 991]', wrote Dolley and Metcalf in 1961, 'the government of Anglo-Saxon England ... [had] not only grasped but implemented the idea that the weight of the coinage could be manipulated as a matter of monetary policy.' Since coin changed hands at face value within England, and as long as kings were prepared to accept light coins at their face value when the type was changed, then it mattered little to the ordinary man if the penny in one year weighed only three-quarters of what it had before. But for the merchant trading to the continent, where the value of money was related to its weight or fineness, a lighter coinage meant that he would have to pay more for goods he bought for import, while he would have been able to sell his exports more advantageously. That should have discouraged imports and encouraged exports, so improving the balance of trade, and drawing silver to England. In Flanders English wool found a ready export market. Sawyer believed that there were more sheep in England in the eleventh century than in the thirteenth and early fourteenth centuries and, although the evidence is slight, argued that the wool export trade to Flanders, with its burgeoning urban cloth industry, was the best explanation for England's growing wealth of silver at this time. That was in 1965. In 1991 the theory received a definitive restatement. For S.R.H. Jones there was no question that England obtained most of the silver it required by running a balance of payments surplus with north-western Europe. That surplus was largely achieved by a policy of devaluation that stimulated exports, cut imports, and encouraged the growth of import substitution.[21]

Careful manipulation of the coinage to attract Goslar silver to England through the medium of the wool-export trade is seen as the key to understanding how such taxation could be paid. When the burden of heavy gelds was finally lifted, after the abolition of the heregeld in 1051, the weight of the penny which had stood at no more than 1.02/1.12 grams (15.74 to 17.28 grains) could be increased to 1.67 grams (25.77 grains).[22] This is seen as almost certain evidence that the varying weight of the coinage was inextricably linked to the payment of heavy gelds. It would seem that between 991 and 1051, and perhaps beyond, the coinage was being managed in a sophisticated and quite exceptional way. Kings and their advisers had apparently and precociously grasped one element of the theory known as the monetary approach to the balance of payments, and put it into operation to secure the bullion they needed.[23] They could order recoinages at regular intervals, vary the weight of the penny, and draw a sizeable income from taxing moneyers and mints. More than that, the sheer size of the gelds is held to demonstrate the wealth of England, and is indicative of the extent to which the use of money had penetrated all levels of society. For historians who hold these views, *Renovatio monetae* symbolises a society in which a 'money economy' had emerged.

Renovatio monetae: the debate

This proposition must be challenged, first in relation to the coinage itself and then, critically, in the context of the question, 'Did a money economy exist in Anglo-Saxon and Anglo-Norman England?', to which the answer offered here will be a resounding 'No'. As far as the coinage is concerned, doubts about the reliability of both coin-hoard and stray-find evidence have already been expressed.[24] The main problem is whether the coins can be dated precisely, so as to establish a sequence for substantive issues that would prove the theory of regular recoinages at fairly precise intervals of at first six years and then two to three years. Dolley was quite emphatic that this was the case, but in 1984 another numismatist, J.D. Brand challenged his theory in detail.[25] He found it difficult to see any triennial pattern under the first two Norman kings, and argued that, while changes of type were frequent in the early years of Henry I's reign, they were less frequent in his last years. Blackburn's work on Henry I's coinage partially confirms that view, since he suggests that there were fourteen different types in the first twenty-five years of that reign, and then only one for the last ten.[26] But at the heart of Dolley's case lay the theory of recoinages at fixed intervals in the late Anglo-Saxon period, accompanied by a deliberate manipulation of weight standards. Brand charged Dolley with making the facts fit the theory. He put forward different chronologies for the main coin types, and concluded that there was no evidence to support Dolley's claim for decennial changes of coin under Æthelræd II and Cnut. Similar doubts were expressed by other numismatists and, eventually, even by Metcalf, Dolley's original collaborator. He, and others, now argue that Æthelræd II's first three issues (First, Second Hand and Benediction Hand) were a single substantive type, and cannot be made to fit a six-year pattern. Doubts have been expressed about the periodicity of other issues, and there now seems to be a consensus that Dolley's rigid theory cannot stand.[27]

Nevertheless, the argument that the Anglo-Saxon and Norman kings were able to recall and demonetise an existing coinage and then strike new coins at varying weight standards through a controlled operation at a large number of mints remains entrenched among historians.[28] Given the current numismatic evidence, such claims cannot be allowed to stand. Up to 1036 the old coinage was completely reminted when the type changed but after that date the evidence is less certain. While the current type had to be used for 'official' payments such as taxes, rents or fines, older issues apparently continued to circulate and could perhaps be used, possibly by weight, for other transactions.[29] This may mean that the volume of coin in circulation could at times have been greater than has been estimated by modern historians, but by how much it is impossible to say. Another central part of the 973 reforms was that coins should be struck at and issued by moneyers working at a large number of mints. In this way, no one would be more than 15 miles from a mint where old coin could be exchanged for new.[30] That there were large numbers of mints cannot be denied, but coins were struck only intermittently and often, apparently, in small quantities at most of them, particularly at those in the West Country, in order to meet specific fiscal needs, notably payment of the geld. What the coin hoards and single finds seem to show is that two-thirds of the coinage was actually produced at only ten mints.

Table 4.1 The ranking of Anglo-Saxon mints by output, 1066

1	London
2	Lincoln
3	York
4	Stamford
5	Thetford
6	Winchester
7	Canterbury
8	Chester
9	Norwich
10	Wallingford

Source: D.M. Metcalf, *An Atlas of Anglo-Saxon and Norman Coin Finds, 973–1086* (Oxford: Royal Numismatic Society, Ashmolean Museum, 1998), p. 18.

In the rankings developed by Metcalf from single-find evidence, London came top, with about 23 per cent of production, followed in descending order by Lincoln, York, Stamford, Thetford, Winchester, Canterbury, Norwich, Chester and Wallingford. The six east-coast ports and trading towns of London, Lincoln, York, Stamford, Norwich and Thetford produced more than half the national coinage in the period 973–1086.[31] This does not necessarily mean that the control exercised by the crown over the issue of dies and licensing of moneyers was any the less rigorous. Indeed, it could be argued that fewer mints producing more coins made for easier administration. But the idea of between forty and seventy mints being kept in continuous production, which somehow seems to have passed into general acceptance, in spite of the reservations of most numismatists, must be discarded. The reality was that ten mints produced most of the coinage, and that has important implications for the regional distribution and use of money, something to be kept in mind when discussing the degree of monetisation in the eleventh- and twelfth-century economy generally.[32]

Weight standards

The major problem with the theory of a centrally controlled coinage with fluctuating weight standards lies in the very complex problem of those weight standards themselves, however. Given relatively crude production techniques, some variation in the weight of the penny within fairly narrow limits was only to be expected. In theory, the king and his advisers declared a specific weight for a new issue which would then be struck within ± a grain or so of that weight. In practice, the variations both within the time span of each issue and regionally, by mints, are so wide as to be baffling. From 973 to 1087 the observable but not necessarily explicable phenomena are these:[33]

(1) There were broad regional variations in the weight of the penny, across the country from west to east. Petersson, in his 1969 study of the coinage from Edgar to the Conqueror, produced histograms of each coin type as a whole, on the basis of a total sample of 44,550 coins. The evidence is strongest for the reigns of Æthelred and Cnut, but patchy after 1035, since fewer specimens have survived. The pattern is unmistakable, however. Mints in the west of the country continually produced heavier coins, while lower weight standards are characteristic of the east of the country, including the Danelaw. As yet there is no satisfactory explanation of this phenomenon. It is possible that the eastern half of the country was more heavily commercialised, and so needed more coin. Perhaps the geld lay heavier on the eastern counties and so, again, there would be a need for more coin to pay the king's taxes. It would therefore make sense for a greater number of lighter coins to be struck from each pound of silver. But these are only suggestions. All that can be said, at this time, is that there was not a national weight standard for each issue.

(2) There were, in fact, declining weight standards over the course of each issue. Heavier coins were struck at the beginning of each new type. The weight usually declined thereafter, with a return to a higher standard at the beginning of the next issue. This was not universally true. The Winchester mint, for example, maintained the initial heavy weight standard throughout each issue, when other mints moved to lower standards. Nevertheless, at most mints, this practice seems to have been adopted. One explanation might be that heavier coins could be struck initially as the old coinage was called in to provide the silver. Thereafter, silver supplies may have declined, and lighter coins would have to be struck. This supposes that bullion shortages

could not be made good through imports but, again, these are pure speculations.

(3) 'National' averages are deceptive, however. Some mints also appear to have operated on different weight standards concurrently, striking 'heavy' and 'light coins' at the same time. The Chichester mint, for instance, struck coins for Edward the Confessor's Facing Bust issue (*c*.1062–*c*.1065) to a tight pattern, with a range of only 0.1 grams around the modal value of 1.12 grams (17.28 grains) yet at York, for the same issue, the weight range was between 0.7 grams and 1.4 grams (10.80 to 21.60 grains), with two peaks at 1.02 grams and 1.17 grams (15.74 to 18.06 grains). Metcalf argues that the York moneyers were not hopelessly clumsy or careless in comparison with their southern counterparts. Rather, they were deliberately striking and issuing heavy and light coins at the same time. Quite why this was so is not explained.

(4) It therefore begins to look as if weight standards were decided not nationally, but regionally, and perhaps on a county basis. This was Petersson's conclusion, based on an analysis of his own data, and his argument has recently (2005) been supported by Jonnson in his study of Edgar's pre-Reform coinage. He concludes that before 973 there was no national policy on the coinage. Decisions were taken at a local level by the ealdorman and local coinage was dominant in each region.[34] It is likely that some of these practices continued after 973, although a national coinage did then emerge. Anglo-Saxon government was, after all, devolved government, through the shires, and minting appears to have been no exception to this. In most counties there was only one mint: where there was more than one, they acted in concert. Nevertheless, the argument for weight variation by county apparently faces a serious problem. If the penny circulated at face value throughout the realm, then it would have been profitable to take old coin for reminting to a mint that offered more, lighter, coins in return. In practice, this would have involved quite long journeys from west to east, and consequently hardly seems likely. Payment by weight may have been encouraged by the existence of heavier and lighter coins in circulation at the same time, while heavier coins could have been culled to use for payments abroad, where weight and fineness, and not face value, counted. These are all imponderables. What does now seem reasonably clear is that actual weight standards, fluctuating around a nominal national level, were decided locally, at the county mints.

The geld, the bullion supply, and the coinage

Given this evidence, it becomes very difficult to argue that there was a conscious policy of carefully controlled variations in weight standards to achieve favourable trade balances. That, in turn, raises serious questions about the weight of the geld and the silver supply, and, indirectly, about the wealth of England and the extent of a money economy in the late Anglo-Saxon period. The weight of the geld and the credibility of the stories in the *Anglo-Saxon Chronicle* became a matter of fierce and, it has to be said, unresolved debate about two decades ago. The heaviest taxation of all was levied at the beginning of Cnut's reign, in 1018. ' In that year', says the *Chronicle*, 'the tribute was paid over all England, nearly 72,000 pounds in all, apart from what the citizens of London paid, namely ten and a half thousand pounds in all.' Given that the circulating medium seems to have been at most £30,000, sums of this magnitude could only have been paid by striking more, lighter, coins, perhaps as many as £40,000 worth, with the balance possibly being made up by payment in ingots. This would have required a great deal of 'new' silver. Some of it was found by melting down plate and jewellery but most of the bullion, it has been argued, came from the profits of the wool-export trade to Flanders. In turn, the Flemish cloth towns were able to pay for the fine English wool they needed because of plentiful supplies of silver from the mines at Goslar in the Harz mountains, which reached their peak around 1025 but diminished rapidly after 1040.[35]

Some silver must have been won for England in this way, but not necessarily in the quantities that would have been needed to double or treble the size of the coinage. It is extremely unlikely that large, favourable trade balances were achieved by deliberate manipulation of weight standards. Nonetheless, an active wool-export trade could still have brought a great deal of silver to England. Yet that, too, seems doubtful. In the late tenth and early eleventh centuries the Flemish cloth industry was still largely rural in character, and producing mainly for a regional market. It relied mainly on local supplies of wool, and not until the late eleventh and twelfth centuries *at the earliest* did it begin to draw heavily on fine-quality English wools. There are no records of English overseas trade in this period, but it is very difficult to believe that it could have earned the quantities of silver needed to make the payment of these huge gelds possible. Could they have been acquired in other ways? Not all the new coins minted in Æthelræd's reign to help pay more modest levels of geld need necessarily have drained abroad to Scandinavia. Some of them must have stayed in England, so increasing the stock of pennies available for reminting at the next recoinage. The amount of bullion made available by melting down plate and jewellery may have been greater than supposed, while some of the payments made to the Danes could have been in kind, rather than in coin or by weight of silver. Land and stock to a certain value may have been taken from those unwilling or unable to pay their taxes, and given to invaders who wished to stay in England. No coins need have been involved in such payments, since money would have been used as a standard of value rather than as a medium of exchange. In these ways, the amount of 'new' silver for recoinages would have been further reduced. This may all be very speculative, but so are many of the arguments about the weight of the geld and the wealth of England in the eleventh century. Nevertheless, it is possible to think in terms of an extra £10,000 or so of coin being struck, to allow heavy gelds of somewhere around £20,000 to be levied, without denuding the country of coin.

The coinage 973-1066: conclusions

Can these wide differences over dating and weight standards be resolved? Probably not, until a great many more coins have been found, and a great deal more research has been undertaken, particularly on the history of individual mints. If one of the most distinguished numismatists of the Anglo-Saxon period declares that 'the governmental purposes behind this remarkable system have defied convincing explanation', then it would be unwise to presuppose that it was the result of conscious and continuous royal policy. Certainly, Dolley's arguments for recoinages first on a sexennial and then on a triennial or biennial basis, accompanied by controlled changes in weight standards, should be treated with some caution. 'We should not', argues Metcalf, 'read back into the eleventh century our own profuse ideas about the management of a national economy through monetary policies. The king and his advisers are likely to have had, by modern standards, only a rudimentary idea of the likely economic effects of their monetary policies – and little or no statistical feedback to show them whether the policies were working.'[36] If payments were made by weight rather than by the face value of the coins, the regional weight variations would not have mattered. Lower weight standards and lighter coins in the east of the country may have stimulated exports and discouraged imports, but there is little or no evidence to support such an argument. That England 'did contain wealth in precious metal necessary to support [geld] payments of the size recorded' now also seems doubtful.[37] The figures given by the *Anglo-Saxon Chronicle* are quite possibly exaggeration for effect and should not be used to make projections of the wealth of England in the eleventh century. England was probably seen as an easy target by the Danish invaders partly because of its relative wealth, but also because the king could raise the money needed to buy them off quickly, through a national taxation system. It was much easier negotiating for large payments from a central source than it was travelling around looting individual monasteries, or being bought off piecemeal by local leaders. As with the Norman Conquest, the great strength of the late Anglo-Saxon monarchy was also its greatest weakness: England was not awash with coin, but with abundant government.[38] But whatever conclusions are drawn, the degree of control exercised by the late Anglo-Saxon kings remains impressive. Edgar's reform did ensure one money for the whole realm, something almost unknown in the rest of Europe, where local noblemen and towns struck their own coins.

The coinage 1066-1158

The new weight standard

The strength of royal control over the coinage was never better demonstrated than in the year 1066. Harold II succeeded Edward the Confessor on 6 January. He was killed at Hastings on 14 October. Within that short period of just over nine months a start had been made on recalling the old coinage and striking a new issue. Evidence that the new coinage had begun to pass into circulation comes from the presence of small numbers of these Pax coins in hoards concealed in that troubled year.[39] William I almost immediately ordered the striking of new coins, but there was no change in his reign (1066-87), or in that of his successor William II (1087-1100), in the general way in which English coinage was struck and issued. The same system of periodic type changes, at intervals of about two years, was maintained. The coins were struck at a large number of mint places, and the ranking of mints, in terms of production, remained the same. Different mints continued to work to different weight standards, until the Two Sceptres issue of *c.*1072-*c.*1074. Then the beginnings of a significant standardisation in the weight of the penny finally appeared. The Winchester mint, which had always issued heavier coins, began to work to a consistent weight of 1.36 grams (20.99 grains). The York mint continued to strike pennies with lower weight values, however, but by the next issue, Two Stars (*c.*1074-*c.*1077), Lincoln had also moved to a heavier weight standard of 1.37 grams (21.14 grains). Other mints continued to strike coins of varying weights for the Sword issue (*c.*1077-*c.*1080) and for Profile/Cross Trefoils (*c.*1080-1083), but then with the Paxs issue of *c.*1083-*c.*1086, all mints worked to one weight standard.[40] The evidence, of course, is limited, but there does seem to be wide agreement among numismatists about this change.

This was a radical reform. The new national weight standard of *c*.1.38 grams (21.3 grains) was maintained until late in Henry I's reign, when it was raised slightly, and then fixed at 1.46 grams (22.5 grains) from the Tealby coinage of 1158 to the recoinage of 1279. With hindsight, it is possible to see that William I had committed the crown to a new and heavier weight standard after 107 years of bewildering fluctuations. Why such a significant change should have been made at a time when trade with Frisia, one of England's main markets, had all but collapsed, and output of silver from the Goslar mines was falling rapidly, is not at all clear.[41] Nightingale sees it as an attempt to solve the problem created by William's wars to defend his duchy. In Normandy coins were exchanged by weight. Since William needed the resources of his new kingdom to finance his continental campaigns, he did not want to pay for them in coins of low weight. The solution was to introduce an English penny of fixed weight and fineness.[42] Given that for the next 138 years England was to be the paymaster for continuous war in defence of the Norman and Angevin territories, this makes sense. It may well explain why his successors maintained the weight of the penny at 1.38 grams (21.3 grains), allowing for some fluctuations, at a time when silver was in short supply. Paying mercenaries and allies was probably more important here than the adoption across north-western Europe of weight measurement standards based on those used in England.[43]

The move to a standard weight for the penny was accompanied by new taxes on minting At what point in the reign they were introduced cannot be firmly established. Domesday shows that in the time of King Edward, before 1066, the crown profited from its rights of coinage by taking fees from the moneyers. At some point William replaced the annual fee and that paid on change of type with a new tax, *de moneta*, levied on each borough with a mint. It produced three or four times more revenue than the previous charges, and there also seems to have been a completely new tax, *monetagium commune*, collected through the boroughs and counties. This may have been, as in Normandy and elsewhere in northern Europe, a periodic general tax, paid by subjects in return for an agreement by the ruler not to make changes in the currency. It may be that the two changes, weight standardisation and the introduction of this tax, should be taken together. But, again, the existence of *monetagium commune* has to be read back from Henry I's later coronation charter, which abolished it. Obviously, its removal in 1100 was a sop to someone, but to whom, and how onerous the tax may have been, are simply not known.[44]

The Norman coinage

The essential problem in trying to construct a history of the coinage between 1066 and 1158, is a lack of evidence which is even more acute than that for the late Anglo-Saxon period. The few coin finds that there have been, either in hoards or singly, mean that only a very basic outline of what happened can be established. There were eight substantive issues in the Conqueror's reign followed by five in that of William Rufus (1087–1100) again at two or three yearly intervals, although it is difficult to date them precisely. Henry I's reign is even more obscure. Altogether, there were fifteen issues, although simply arranging the types in order of issue has proved contentious, let alone dating them. During the reign there were frequent complaints about the state of the coinage. They started immediately, in 1100, with the order to the sheriffs to enforce laws against false coining. In 1108 a reform of the coinage was proposed, and then, in 1124–25, came the savage punishment of the moneyers, discussed further below.[45] The surviving coins suggest that Henry I's coinage was poor in design and badly struck and that there were, until the last decade of the reign, considerable fluctuations in weight standards, although not in fineness. Then, from 1125 onward, there was a return to the heavier penny of 1.38 grams.[46]

The civil war and 'Anarchy' of Stephen's reign (1135–54) is often held to have seen the collapse of centrally controlled minting, and the abandonment of *renovatio monetae*, regular recoinages. Yet this actually seems to have begun in 1125, with the last of Henry I's issues, which was to run for a full ten years, in contrast to the two-yearly intervals proposed by Blackburn for the other issues.[47] Stephen's first issue ran for six years, from *c.*1135 to 1141, the second probably for longer. It is doubtful whether types three to six were substantive issues at all, coming as they apparently did during the Anarchy, but the final type, seven, of 1153, was taken over by Henry II in 1154, and continued in circulation until 1158, a run of some five years. During Stephen's reign, for the first time since 973, coins were issued by his rivals, the Empress Matilda and then her son, Henry of Anjou, the future Henry II, by Henry of Blois, bishop of Winchester, by the northern barons, Eustace Fitzjohn and Robert de Stutteville, and by William of Gloucester in the south-west. This all sounds chaotic, but the coins themselves suggest something different. Stephen's first issue was struck at a large number of mints, of which forty-two have been identified, using dies provided centrally, and to a good weight standard. The last issue was struck at thirty-six mints, and again, to a good weight standard. But between 1141 and 1153 there was civil war and, apparently, monetary chaos. In this case, however, appearances are deceptive. Local mints appear to have operated autonomously but, in some ways, that was little different from practice in late Anglo-Saxon England. Coin circulating in the Midlands in the 1140s is alleged to have been of poor quality, yet there is little or no numismatic evidence on which to base any judgment on that point.[48] Private baronial issues were mostly limited to the North where, at the same time, the mint at York continued to strike good-quality coins in Stephen's name. Coins issued by Matilda and Henry of Anjou circulated only in the south-west, and it is doubtful whether Henry of Anjou issued any coins at all between 1147 and 1153. Stephen, by contrast, controlled London, the south-east and eastern England, the most populated and monetarised areas, and it seems to have been relatively easy to restore a national coinage in 1153. The only significant development in this respect was the striking of coins in the far north-east, at Carlisle by David I of Scotland, and his son, Earl Henry, at Corbridge and Bamburgh. This was to lead eventually to an independent coinage for Scotland, replacing the English coins that had previously circulated there. This apart, until there is much more numismatic evidence for Stephen's reign, it is difficult to reach firm conclusions about the state of the coinage, and the extent to which royal control over its issue did actually collapse.[49]

The bullion supply

If the lack of evidence makes it easier to ask general questions about the Norman coinage than to answer them, this does not mean the questions should not be asked. The first must, again, concern the problem of the silver supply. Output from the Rammelsberg/Goslar mines fell rapidly after the 1040s, and the general European shortage of silver was made worse by outflows to pay for the First Crusade (1096–1100) and then the defence of the new crusading states. Silver also flowed from England across the Channel, either in the form of pennies or ingots, to finance campaigns in Normandy and the diplomacy that went with them. Because there are no royal financial records before the Exchequer pipe roll of 1129–30, it is not possible to give precise figures for such expenditure, nor is it certain where all the money was spent. The heavy geld of 1084, bitterly complained of in the *Anglo-Saxon Chronicle*, was levied to meet the threat of a new Danish invasion, supported by the Count of Flanders, and most of the proceeds probably stayed in England. But when William I went to Normandy in 1086, the *Anglo-Saxon Chronicle* records that he obtained a very great amount of money from his men, and then immediately left for the duchy, implying that he left the men behind and took the money with him. When Robert of Normandy pawned the duchy to William Rufus, he did so for 10,000 marks of silver (£6,666 13s 4d) and there were, again, bitter complaints about the geld of 4s per hide levied to meet the pledge. Henry I was said to have paid out 10,000 marks for his daughter Matilda's marriage to the Emperor Henry V in 1110. The money fief he granted to the Count of Flanders in 1101 cost him £500, and in the same year he promised his brother Robert an annuity of £3,000. Green argues that the geld was levied every year in Henry I's reign, although at a reduced rate of 1s to 2s per hide, and in 1129–30 it accounted for about 10 per cent of his total revenue of £23,000. Henry's financial exactions were harsh, and when he died in 1135 he left 'vast sums of treasure' at Winchester in England and, significantly, at Falaise in Normandy.[50]

It is unlikely that this European shortage of 'new' silver, compounded by outflows to the Near East and from England to Normandy, could have been made good from within the British Isles, discounting Blanchard's repeated claims of exceptionally productive silver strikes near Carlisle in the early twelfth century in the light of Allen's recent work on British silver output.[51] The growing shortage of silver may well have been responsible for the problems with the coinage in Henry I's reign. On the Continent, in an attempt to stabilise prices and attract silver to mints, the weight and fineness of many coinages were reduced, but it is hard to establish convincingly exactly what happened in England.[52] Sifting the reality from indirect evidence and the exaggerations of chroniclers is difficult, yet there does seem to have been some substance to the complaints. In 1100, the already harsh punishment for false coining was increased. Before the Conquest it had been loss of a hand: to this was now added castration. Moneyers were not to exchange money outside their own counties, and no one but a moneyer was to exchange old coin for new. The measures seem to have had little or no effect. By 1108 the chronicler Eadmer recorded in his *Historia Novorum* that the coinage had been so debased and forged that the king decided to reform it with rigour. The penalty for forgery was increased even further to loss of eyes and lower limbs. A favourite trick of forgers was to put a thin coat of silver over coins made of base metal. Pennies were now to be snicked, or marked with a cut before they left the mint, to show that they were of pure metal the whole way through. Interestingly, some of the coin of types seven to twelve, issued between 1107 and 1121, have been found with such cuts, indicating that forgery was a problem. Then, in 1124, came the ruthless punishment of the moneyers. The *Anglo-Saxon Chronicle* records how they were summoned to Winchester and one by one deprived of their right hands and castrated 'because they had ruined all the country with their great false dealing'. Some of the moneyers escaped this horrific purge by paying a fine, but the majority were punished with great severity. This savage attack was followed by an increase in the weight of the penny for the last issue of the reign (type fifteen, c.1125–35), and that issue itself marked a break with the previous pattern of biennial recoinages. Blackburn and others argue that it was also accompanied by a planned restructuring of the mint organisation in which twenty-eight of the fifty-one mints that had previously been operating were closed, mostly the smaller ones, leaving fourteen counties without a mint at all.[53]

The punishment of the moneyers was, however, a consequence of a deeper problem, and only one part of the attempt to solve it. Fluctuations in the weight of the coinage in Henry I's reign were in some way a response to increasing shortages of silver. To attract bullion to English mints, in order to strike the coins needed to pay for the Norman campaigns, it may have been necessary to reduce the silver content of the penny, so that more of them could be struck from each pound of metal, or to lower mint charges. The cost of this would have been borne by the people generally, since they had to change old money for the new lighter coins at each recoinage. The year 1124 was a bad one: a very poor harvest was accompanied by heavy taxation to pay for the suppression of a rebellion in Normandy. The king was probably looking for ways of diverting attention from his own manipulation of the coinage, and the moneyers were an easy target.[54] Blackburn also offers another explanation for the events of 1124/25. He argues that the English penny had long been over-valued in terms of its silver content – that is, its face value was far in excess of its intrinsic value. That made foreign payments for trade and war difficult, and William I had sought to remedy this by introducing the heavier penny. Now, in 1125, by abandoning periodic recoinages, Henry I and his advisers sought the same end. These recoinages seem to have discouraged people from changing any more of their savings into newer, lighter coins than they needed for immediate use. Older coin and bullion continued to circulate unofficially, rather than being taken to the mints for recoinage. The amount of coin of the current issue was thus further reduced, as new silver was in short supply. The king would lose revenue by abandoning periodic recoinages. What he would gain would be a stable, heavier coinage – better, from his point of view, for both making and receiving payments. Whether it would have been any better for his subjects is another matter. Heavy coins containing more silver were worth more. Making small purchases with them would have been difficult, and perhaps one of the reasons why the round halfpenny was issued around 1108 was to provide the small change necessary for day-to-day transactions.[55]

A: A MONETISED ECONOMY

The end of renovatio monetae

Much of this story is conjectural. About the only certainty is that there were increasing shortages of 'new' silver in the early twelfth century. In these circumstances, it is difficult to understand why William I introduced the heavier penny, in complete contrast to what was happening elsewhere in north-western Europe, unless it was for making payments abroad to finance campaigns. Similarly, no contemporary sought to explain why Henry I introduced the round halfpenny, and it is more likely that the king, and not the moneyers, was responsible for the poor state of the coinage. For whatever reason, however, biennial or triennial recoinages did come to an end after 1125, although there was only a limited contraction in the number of mints striking new coins. This did not mean a loosening of royal control over minting. After the Conquest privileged ecclesiastical mints emerged at Bury St Edmund's and Durham, where the abbot and bishop respectively shared the profits of minting with the king, as the archbishops at Canterbury (along with the abbot of St Augustine's) and York had done from time immemorial. At Chester, the fees had been divided between the king and the earl in the time of King Edward, and after 1071, when Cheshire became a County palatine, they seem to have gone exclusively to the earl. But, apart from about a decade in Stephen's reign, there was no other erosion of the king's prerogative of minting, or of his enjoyment of the revenues therefrom. This is in stark contrast to practice in France and Germany, where feudal mints operated to the profit of the local magnates, lay or ecclesiastical, who issued coins to their own design and in their own names.[56] Even in the Anarchy, the extent of private coinage in both volume and circulation should not be exaggerated and the issue of a new national coinage in 1153 seems to have presented few problems. That puts theories of a loss of royal control over minting in a proper perspective.[57] The *renovatio* system may have had its day, but royal control over the coinage had not diminished.

Conclusion: the size of the circulating medium

In the 175 years after 973, Edgar's intention, that there be one money for the whole of England, had been accomplished. This was a remarkable achievement, one unique in north-western Europe, and almost unparalleled outside the Byzantine Empire. But the close identification between crown and coinage brought its own problems. The king clearly bore the responsibility for the issue and maintenance in circulation of good money. It was his duty to ensure that the silver penny was of a good weight and fineness. Failure to do so was certain to cause discontent, and the more the economy became monetarised, the greater such discontent was likely to be. The state of the coinage would become an important political issue, as is shown by Henry I's punishment of the moneyers in response to complaints about a worthless coinage. The king's room for manoeuvre had also been limited by the adoption of a new weight standard around 1080. With the advantage of hindsight it is possible to see that William I had committed the crown to the maintenance of the heavy penny, with a high silver content, something that was to cause considerable difficulties in the late Middle Ages as bullion supplies began to fail.

Yet the scale of the administrative and political achievement should not be allowed to obscure one other very important point, that the size of the circulating medium between 973 and 1158 was relatively small. On the eve of the Conquest it stood at somewhere between £20,000 and £50,000, or 4,800,000 to 12,000,000 silver pennies. That sounds impressive until is seen in relation to the size of the population. The ranges are given above, in Table 2.1 but the lowest estimate, given a population of 1.5 millions and the volume of currency as £20,000, is 3.2d per head, and the highest, with a population of 1.5 millions and the volume of currency £50,000, is 8d per head. The real figure must lie somewhere in between these two points, given inequalities in the distribution of wealth and either hoarding or saving in order to meet future taxation; customary payments to a lord; or simply the general costs of living. Here the figures are taken from Allen's recent (2005) estimates of the volume of currency in circulation but using the older calculations of Dolley and Metcalf produces much the same results.[58] Coin-hoard evidence does suggest that that after 1051 there was a steady decline in the amount of coin in circulation as shortages of silver began to bite. Writing in 1981, Metcalf proposed a figure of about £25,000 in circulation, not too far out of line with Allen's lower estimate for the years 1042–66. At first Dolley agreed with him, but then changed his mind and put forward the widely accepted figure of £37,500 for the size of the circulating medium in the Conqueror's reign.

Table 4.2 Coinage per head of population in 1087: Dolley's estimates.

Volume of the Currency £	Population Millions	Coins (silver pennies) per head
37,500	1.5	6d
37,500	2.0	4.5d
37,500	2.25	4d

Source: M. Dolley, *The Norman Conquest and the English Coinage* (London: Spink, 1966), p. 14.

Allen, however, uses single-find evidence to suggest a sharp decline in the amount of coin in circulation, in line with a general contraction in the European money supply as production from the silver mines in the Harz mountains declined. His estimates of between £10,000 and £25,000 do seem extremely low, but shipment of treasure abroad after 1066 to pay for campaigns in Normandy and for the First Crusade may well have severely depleted England's wealth in silver. Nevertheless, and as he admits, his figures fall below the lowest of the estimates suggested by Dolley (£37,500) and Metcalf (£35-40,000). What happened between 1135 and 1158 is not known but a return to the levels between 1042 and 1066 - that is, £20-50,000 - has been extensively suggested.[59]

One thing is clear, however. Whichever set of estimates is used, it shows that the volume of currency in circulation in the 185 years between 973 and 1158 had at first increased but had then fallen back to earlier levels. The same is true for the amount of coin per head of population and although the Conqueror brought with him from Normandy the Jews who could provide new sources of credit, the basic lack of coin in circulation must have had important implications for the English economy in the late Anglo-Saxon and the Anglo-Norman period, as we shall see in the next chapter.

Notes

1. P. Stafford, *Unification and Conquest: A Political and Social History of England in the Tenth and Eleventh Centuries* (London: Edward Arnold, 1989), pp. 54-6; Dolley and Metcalf, 'The reform of the English coinage under Eadgar', p. 136, citing Roger of Wendover.
2. B.J. Cook, 'The bezant in Angevin England', *NC*, 159 (1999), 255, 258; Nightingale, 'The ora, the mark and the mancus', part ii, 237.
3. Dolley 'An introduction to the coinage of Aethelred II', pp. 117-21; D.M. Metcalf, *An Atlas of Anglo-Saxon and Norman Coin Finds, c.973-1086* (Oxford: Royal Numismatic Society, Ashmolean Museum, 1998), pp. 40, 105, 140; V.J. Smart, 'Moneyers of the late Anglo-Saxon coinage: the Danish dynasty 1017-42', *Anglo-Saxon England*, 16 (1987), 237-8.
4. Dolley and Metcalf, 'The reform of the English coinage under Eadgar' pp. 147-52, and especially p. 148.
5. Metcalf, *Atlas*, p. 40.
6. Dolley and Metcalf, 'The reform of the English coinage under Eadgar', p. 147; *EHD*, vol. i, p. 354; Stafford, *Unification and Conquest*, pp. 32-5, 44-56, 213; Grierson and Blackburn, *Medieval European Coinage*, pp. 323-35; Metcalf, *Atlas*, pp. 145, 282; E. King, 'The anarchy of King Stephen's reign', *TRHS*, 5th ser. 34 (1984), 147.
7. See above, pp. 29-30; *EHD*, vol. i, p. 384; *EHD*, vol. ii, p. 399; R.H. Britnell, 'English markets and the royal administration before 1200', *EcHR*, 2nd series, 31

(1978), 187–8; Britnell, *Commercialisation*, p. 25; R. Fleming, 'Rural elites and urban communities in late Saxon England', *P&P*, 141 (1993), 22.

8 See above, pp. 29–30, for further discussion of the effectiveness of this legislation.
9 For the coinage between 973 and 1086 see Metcalf, *Atlas*, *passim*, and Allen, 'The volume of the English currency', pp. 487–500.
10 Dolley and Metcalf 'The reform of the English coinage under Eadgar', pp. 152–56; Dolley, 'An introduction to the coinage of Aethelred II', p. 120; D.M. Metcalf, 'Continuity and change in English monetary history, *c*.973–1086, part i', *BNJ*, 50 (1980), 20–49, part ii, *BNJ*, 51 (1982), 59–90; Stewart, 'English and Norman mints', pp. 54–5.
11 See below, pp. 100–1.
12 See above, pp. 55–7, 95, 106, and below, pp. 142–4.
13 Dolley and Metcalf, 'The reform of the English coinage under Eadgar', p. 155; Nightingale, 'The ora, the mark and the mancus', part ii, 247; and see above, pp. 29–30, 89.
14 See above, pp. 68–9; P. Nightingale, 'Some London moneyers and reflections on the organization of English mints in the eleventh and twelfth centuries', *NC*, 142 (1982), 47.
15 Stewart, 'English and Norman mints', pp. 55–6; D.M. Metcalf, 'The taxation of moneyers under Edward the Confessor and in 1066', in J.C. Holt (ed.), *Domesday Studies* (Woodbridge: Boydell and Brewer, 1987), pp. 279–93.
16 Warren, *The Governance of Norman and Angevin England*, pp. 54–5.
17 M.K. Lawson, 'The collection of danegeld and heregeld in the reigns of Aethelred II and Cnut', *EHR*, 104 (1984), 721–3; and see below for the debate on the geld, pp. 98–9.
18 J.A. Green, 'The last century of danegeld', *EHR*, 96 (1981), 254; Green, *The Government of England under Henry I*, pp. 69–75; J.A. Green, *Henry I: King of England and Duke of Normandy* (Cambridge: Cambridge University Press, 2006), pp. 249, 311; C.W. Hollister and A.C. Frost, *Henry I* (New Haven and London: Yale University Press, 2001), pp. 352–4.
19 See above, Table 2.1, p. 25–6.
20 Spufford, *Money and its Use*, pp. 74–5, 95.
21 Dolley and Metcalf, 'The reform of the English coinage under Eadgar', pp. 154–5; Sawyer, 'The wealth of England in the eleventh century', 160–4; Jones, 'Devaluation and the balance of payments', 603–6.
22 Metcalf, *Atlas*, p. 158 for a review of the evidence on this point.
23 Jones, 'Devaluation and the balance of payments', 601–6.
24 See above, pp. 57–64.
25 Brand, *Periodic Change of Type*, *passim*; Stewart, 'English and Norman mints', pp. 54–5.
26 Brand, *Periodic Change of Type*, pp. 5–6; Blackburn, 'Coinage and currency under Henry I', pp. 69–71.
27 Metcalf, *Atlas*, pp. 108–21, 126, 129, 131.
28 A. Williams, '*Kingship and Government in pre-Conquest England, c.500–1066* (Basingstoke: Macmillan, 1999), p. 96; R. Bartlett, *England under the Norman and Angevin Kings* (Oxford: Oxford University Press, 2002), p. 371.

29 Blackburn, 'Coinage and currency under Henry I', p. 51, citing evidence from the *Dialogue of the Exchequer*; Metcalf, *Atlas*, pp. 5, 52, 275.
30 Dolley and Metcalf, 'The reform of the English coinage under Eadgar', pp. 148-9; Dolley, 'An introduction to the coinage of Aethelred II', p. 118.
31 Metcalf, *Atlas*, pp. 18-22, 54, 72.
32 See below, Chapter 5, *passim*.
33 For what follows, the evidence assembled in Metcalf, *Atlas*, pp. 56-69, is vital. He, in turn, throughout his discussion of these problems acknowledges his debt to H.B.A. Petersson's analysis of weight standards in *Anglo-Saxon Currency: King Edgar's Reform to the Norman Conquest* (Lund: Bibliotheca Historia Lundensis, 22, 1969); Jonsson, 'The pre-reform coinage of Edgar', pp. 340-3, argues that both before and after 973 there was much regional control of the coinage.
34 Jonnson, 'The pre-Reform coinage of Edgar', p. 328.
35 The debate is to be found in Lawson, 'The collection of danegeld and heregeld', 721-38; Lawson, '"Those stories look true": Levels of taxation in the reigns of Aethelred II and Cnut', *EHR*, 104 (1989), 385-406; Lawson, 'Danegeld and heregeld once more', *EHR*, 105 (1990), 951-61; J.B. Gillingham, '"The most precious jewel in the English crown": levels of danegeld and heregeld in the early eleventh century', *EHR*, 104 (1989), 373-84; Gillingham, 'Chronicles and coins as evidence for levels of tribute and taxation in late tenth- and early eleventh-century England', *EHR*, 105 (1990), 939-50; N.A.M. Rodger, 'Cnut's geld and the size of Danish ships', *EHR*, 110 (1995), 392-403; D.M. Metcalf, 'Can we believe the very large figure of £72,000 for the geld levied by Cnut in 1018?', in K. Jonsson (ed.), *Studies in Late Anglo-Saxon Coinage in Memory of Bror Emil Hildebrand* (Svenska Numismatiska Foreningen Numismatiska Meddelanden, 35, Stockholm, 1990), pp. 165-76; R. Abels, 'Paying the danegeld: Anglo-Saxon peacemaking with Vikings', in P. De Souza and J. France (eds), *War and Peace in Ancient and Medieval History* (Cambridge: Cambridge University Press, 2008), pp. 173-92. Estimated levels of geld are given by Metcalf, *Atlas*, p. 27; Lawson, 'The collection of danegeld and heregeld', 721-23; and Gillingham '"The most precious jewel in the English crown"', 373-4. To these should be added a further £21,099 levied by Harthacnut in 1040-42, to pay off his mercenary fleet, along with £11,048 in heregeld for the 32 ships he retained in his service. For the melting down of plate and jewellery, Lawson, 'The collection of danegeld and heregeld', 726-8. The importance of the wool trade is postulated by Sawyer, 'The wealth of England in the eleventh century', 160-4, but largely dismissed by Lloyd, *The English Wool Trade*, pp. 1-6, and Bolton, 'The English economy in the early thirteenth century', pp. 35-6. In *The English Economy from Bede to the Reformation* (Woodbridge: Boydell, 1992), p. 125, n. 12, A.R. Bridbury suggests that the money stayed in England, and confiscations are discussed by Lawson in 'The collection of danegeld and heregeld', 723-6 and Gillingham, '"The most precious jewel in the English crown"', 382-3. A. Williams, '"Cockles amongst the wheat": Danes and English in the west Midlands in the first half of the eleventh century', *Midland History*, 11 (1986), 11-16 doubts whether there were land transfers, as does M.K. Lawson, *Cnut: The Danes in England in the Early Eleventh Century* (London: Longman, 1993), pp. 163-74. For Goslar silver, Spufford, *Money and its Use*, pp. 76-97.

36 Metcalf, *Atlas*, pp. 57, 281.
37 Lawson, '"Those stories look true"', 404.
38 As Lawson perhaps recognises, 'The collection of danegeld and heregeld', 734–5, and '"Those stories look true"', 404, where he acknowledges that if the estimates of the size of the coinage are reduced then so must those for the size of the geld payments.
39 The coins are so called because the word 'Pax' appears within a banner on their reverse side.
40 Metcalf, *Atlas*, pp. 177, 184, 185, 188–90; as with the Pax issue the word Paxs appears on the reverse of the coins, this time in the four quarters of a cross.
41 Spufford, *Money and its Use*, pp. 95–7.
42 Nightingale, 'The ora, mark and mancus', part i, 250–7.
43 These arguments of new international weight standards have been developed by Nightingale, and they are summarised in 'The evolution of weight-standards and the creation of new monetary and commercial links in Northern Europe from the tenth century to the twelfth century', *EcHR*, 2nd series, 38 (1985), 192–209, *passim*.
44 See above, pp. 142–5 for fuller details of the new fees paid by boroughs; P. Grierson 'Domesday Book, the *geld de moneta* and *monetagium*: a forgotten monetary reform', *BNJ*, 55 (1985), 84–94; Stewart, 'English and Norman mints', pp. 56–7; Brand, *English Coinage*, pp. 20–1; Blackburn, 'Coinage and currency under Henry I', p. 150.
45 See below, pp. 104–5.
46 Blackburn, 'Coinage and currency under Henry I', *passim*.
47 Blackburn, 'Coinage and currency under Henry I', p. 72.
48 William of Malmesbury, *Historia Novella*, ed. and trs. K.R. Potter (London: Nelson, 1955).
49 R.P. Mack, 'Stephen and the Anarchy', *BNJ*, 35 (1966), 38–112, and Blackburn, 'Coinage and currency' are the standard accounts of the coinage 1135–54. See also King, 'The anarchy of King Stephen's reign', 147–52; G. White, 'The end of Stephen's reign', *History*, 75 (1990), 19; Stewart, 'English and Norman mints', p. 67.
50 For the pipe roll, see below, pp. 120–2; D. Whitelock, D.C. Douglas and S.I. Tucker (eds), *The Anglo-Saxon Chronicle* (London: Eyre and Spottiswoode, 1961), pp. 161–2; Green, *The Government of England under Henry I*, pp. 17, 51–4, 74.
51 Blanchard, 'Lothian and beyond', pp. 27–9; Blanchard, *Mining, Metallurgy and Minting in the Middle Ages, vol. ii*, pp. 583–685; Allen, 'Silver production and the money supply in England Wales, 1086–*c*.1500', *EcHR*, 64 (2011), 110–11, 124 and fn. 2; Spufford, *Money and its Use*, pp. 110–11, 124 and fn. 2, for a more sceptical view and comparisons with the output from the very productive mines at Kutná Hora in the late thirteenth and early fourteenth centuries; and see above, pp. 66–7.
52 Blackburn, 'Coinage and currency under Henry I', p. 73, where examples are given.
53 Green, *The Government of England under Henry I*, p. 89; Blackburn, 'Coinage and currency under Henry I', pp. 62–68; Whitelock *et al.* (eds), *The Anglo-Saxon Chronicle*, p. 191.
54 Blackburn, 'Coinage and currency under Henry I', pp. 73–5.

A: A MONETISED ECONOMY

55 Blackburn, 'Coinage and currency under Henry I', p. 75.
56 Stewart, 'The English and Norman mints', p. 57.
57 See above, pp. 102–3.
58 See above, pp. 25–6.
59 Allen, 'The volume of the English currency', pp. 499–500; Metcalf, 'Continuity and change in English monetary history', part ii, 65; Mayhew, 'Modelling medieval monetisation', p. 62; above, table 2.1, p. 25; Bates, 'Normandy and England after 1066', 866–9.

5

A monetised economy, 973–1158?

Introduction

Economic historians may well be interested in the history of the coinage but their prime concern must always be the way in which money actually worked within the economy. Consequently, the purpose of this chapter, and of Chapters 7 and 9, is in each case to ask and answer two main questions in the light of the monetary history of the period they cover. These questions are deceptively straightforward: did a lack or an abundance of coin hold back or stimulate economic development?; had a money economy emerged in the period, was it in the process of emerging, or was it under threat? Here we cannot rely on numismatic evidence alone. Indeed, the way in which coins were used has to be interpreted in the light of written records showing how and for what payments were made and which provide information on measurement, recording, accounting and on the availability of credit and the legal enforcement of credit agreements. But, as we have seen, written records are sparse for the late Anglo-Saxon and Norman period.[1] Consequently, it is not possible to construct from the surviving material the long-run price or wage series that would help chart inflation and deflation and changes in the purchasing power of money. Domesday Book and the Pipe Roll of the Exchequer for 1129–30 are both invaluable sources, yet they stand alone, and the questions posed earlier remains: why are there not more surviving records from these two centuries? Is this simply a matter of survival or were they not made in the first place? The growing use of money ought to have encouraged numeracy, recording and accounting and the lack of financial records may, therefore, indicate that the use of money was limited, and that only a partial or emerging money economy existed in these years.[2] What evidence there is can quite legitimately be interpreted in different ways, however, so that a strong case can be made both *for* and *against* the existence of a money economy in eleventh- and twelfth-century England and both sides of the argument must be examined before any firm conclusion can be reached.

The case for a money economy

The use of money as a medium of exchange

All the available evidence, numismatic and written, certainly suggests that money payments were being made at all levels in society by the late tenth century. The economy of England at this point was overwhelmingly agrarian in character, as it was throughout the Middle Ages. Not surprisingly, therefore, most of the written evidence for the use of money as a medium of exchange comes from the records of agriculture and estate management. The earliest of these is the *Rectitudines Singularum Personarum*, a systematic survey of rights and obligations of workers and tenants on an English estate, whose first version has been dated to the early tenth century. They all had to make some kind of payment to their lord, or to the Church. The nobleman, the *thegn*, owed military service in person to the king, and had to assist in the repair of fortresses and bridges, probably by mobilising the labour required. He also had to help in the equipping of a guard ship and in defending the coast, which effectively meant making a cash contribution, as would his Church dues and almsgiving. The *geneat*, a freeman and possibly an estate official, 'must pay rent'; the *gebur*, a peasant with a substantial amount of land, the equivalent of the later *villanus* of Domesday Book, paid 10d for *gafol* or rent at Michaelmas (29 September); the *kote setla* or cottager did not make land payment (rent) but still owed a hearth penny to the Church at Ascension Day (forty days after Easter) and his Church dues at Michaelmas.[3] Two estate surveys of a century or so later confirm this pattern of regular money payments by the peasantry: the *ceorls* at Hurstbourne Prior's (Hampshire) had to render 40d at the autumnal equinox, while at Tidenham (Gloucestershire) 12d per annum was due from each yardland (*c.*30 acres of arable) and 4d as alms.[4]

Thereafter, the evidence for payments demanded from the peasantry and recorded in money equivalents increases steadily. Domesday shows us that the 238 *villani* on the enormous manor of Leominster (Herefordshire) were required to plough and sow with their own seed 140 acres of the lord's land but also had to pay him £11 and 52 pence each year. At Lewisham (Kent), rents from the *rusticorum* and from 11 mills came to £8 12s 0d, and small groups of rent-payers, *censarii, censores*, or *gablatores* are also found in various counties, but especially in the north. One *villanus* might render

30d, another 10s, 46 cottagers holding between them one hide (*c.*120 acres) paid 30s a year, while other payments were made either in kind or in money. So, 'Here is wood land for the pannage (grazing) of 40 pigs or 54½d', while a gift of fresh fish was worth 12s 9d. The almost contemporary survey of the lands of the Abbey of Bury St Edmunds (Suffolk), the early twelfth-century survey of the Burton Abbey manors in Staffordshire and other estate surveys, as well as Domesday and the *Rectitudines*, all confirm that payment of money rent was widespread among the peasantry of Anglo-Saxon and Anglo-Norman England.[5]

One step up the social ladder from the peasantry were the lessees of the manorial demesnes, who were also used to paying money rents. Land was inequitably distributed in medieval England. Most of it was controlled by the king, the great lay landlords and the Church. In the last days of Anglo-Saxon England, the great earls, and notably those drawn from the Godwine family, grew in landed power at the expense of other nobles, although there were still many thegns with only one or two manors. After the Conquest, great lay landlords were even more prominent. Some 4,000 to 6,000 thegns were replaced by no more than 180 barons, although they in turn granted out (sub-infeudated) land to their followers, the knights, in return for military service. Within this already tight-knit group there was an even closer 'inner circle': some ten men, closely bound to the king, controlled nearly a quarter of the landed wealth of England. The king himself controlled a fifth directly, the Church a further quarter. Wealth, in terms of the tenure of land, was concentrated in far fewer hands in Norman England than it had been before 1066.[6]

All landlords, great or small, faced the same problem, how best to manage their estates to suit their particular circumstances. For most small lords with only one or two manors, taking most of their 'income' in kind was the best alternative. They used their demesnes (a demesne being that part of the estate directly controlled by the lord and cultivated for him largely by the labour of his peasant tenants) to provide themselves with the food they needed to support their households. However, where lords had no demesnes, and in the north and east of the country this was not uncommon, they had to draw their incomes largely from peasant rents in kind or in money. Great households with fixed centres, such as monasteries, also relied on their manors to provide them with food and organised strict rotas so that week by week supplies were sent to them from their estates. The Anglo-Saxon kings had also organised their royal demesnes in this way. The 'farm' of one night from royal manors (a farm or render being in this sense a fixed rent) was designed to supply the king's household with

A: A MONETISED ECONOMY

the provisions it needed when it was in the vicinity. Parts of the royal estates still functioned in this way in the Confessor's reign. Almost all the royal manors in Wiltshire, Somerset and Dorset, either singly or in groups, had to supply the royal court with cash and provisions for a 24-hour stay, when required. Those in Devon, Shropshire, and perhaps Oxfordshire had once been organised in this way, too, and a similar system in Cambridgeshire, Norfolk and Suffolk supplied the court with cash, honey, grain and malt.[7]

But most large estates had outlying manors too far from the centre to make payments in kind practicable, while great lay landlords were constantly, and unpredictably, on the move. They and their ecclesiastical counterparts needed more and more cash to pay their taxes, to buy increasingly expensive military equipment, and to spend on the conspicuous consumption necessary to support a lifestyle where display to emphasise status was all. They looked for alternative ways of exploiting their estates, and found two. Demesnes could either be given over to production for the market or leased for money incomes. Production for the market involved a degree of devolved management. A manorial official would supervise the farming and the local sale of produce. But quite close supervision from the centre was needed if this system was to work. As a result, it was administratively easier and more cost effective to adopt the second method, leasing demesnes for cash rents, or for a mix of cash and produce. How the lessee found the money to pay his rent was his concern. He might sublet parts of the demesne or become involved in production for the market. The evidence suggests that both methods of estate exploitation were found in Anglo-Saxon and Anglo-Norman England, although leasing the demesnes seems to have been the preferred option, particularly after the Conquest.[8]

All this meant that money was in regular use in the countryside. Peasants had to pay some cash rents to their lords, and lords drew incomes in both cash and kind from their estates. When such incomes can be measured, as they can in Domesday Book, they could be astonishingly large. The total recorded value of the king's lands and boroughs in 1086 was about £14,000, although by 1129–30 it had fallen to about £10,700. One of the greatest of his tenants-in-chief, Robert, count of Mortain, held 623 manors in Wiltshire, Dorset, Devon and Cornwall and drew an income of about £1,400 from them. William II de Warenne, earl of Surrey, is supposed to have received about £1,000 from his estates, and the archbishop of Canterbury some £1,200–£1,600 a year between 1086 and 1180. Lower down the scale, the leasable value, in cash, of the estates of St Paul's cathedral in 1086 was £149 3s 4d, with individual leases ranging from £1 per annum at Barling in Essex, to £30 13s 4d for the very large manor of Adulfesness, comprising the Naze promontory and its hinterland in the same county. Comparisons with peasant incomes in this period are difficult because of the limited evidence available to us, but a foot soldier in the royal army was paid a penny a day in Henry II's reign (1154–89) and an agricultural labourer a halfpenny.[9]

Commercialisation, taxation, and lordship

Given these arrangements, a fair degree of commercialisation, specialisation and production geared to markets must have existed, so as to allow cash payments to be made. This is something of a circular argument: without commercialisation money cannot circulate, without money commercialisation is not possible, but the argument is nonetheless valid. Account also needs to be taken of the growing demand created by a steadily rising population, although Langdon and Masschaele argue that commercialisation itself was the main cause of population growth. This growing demand was partly met by the market place and partly by informal trade, between peasants and by merchants from towns buying directly from producers in the fields.[10] Such trade cannot be measured, and not all of it involved the use of money. Exchange between peasants probably relied heavily on barter, but for money to have circulated as freely as it apparently did, a basic, formal marketing structure was essential.

Domesday shows us that it existed after 1086 and thereafter it seems to have grown, so that by 1158 England was covered with a network of daily or weekly markets in towns and villages and, seasonally, at local and regional fairs.[11] Within the countryside, it is difficult to determine the precise number of markets but Britnell has shown the existence of hundredal markets in late Anglo-Saxon England, associated with the basic unit of royal local government. They provided important outlets for local produce and in so doing created small reservoirs of cash so that the king could demand payment of his dues from the hundred in cash and not food renders. After the Conquest, the king and other lay lords began to grant formal charters to markets although at times they were comparatively rare: between 1066 and 1154 only 19 new grants were made by royal charter, and of these 3 were spurious. However, these chartered markets probably represent only a small proportion of the real total. Domesday Book itself lists 112 boroughs, or towns, with populations outside London ranging between 1,000 and 5,000, and a further 59 places with markets. The Domesday evidence is slightly skewed. It seems to suggest that there was more market activity in the west than in the east of the country when, in fact, the reverse was almost certainly true. Nonetheless, it is likely that as much as 10 per cent of the population lived in towns in the eleventh century. After 1086, long-term urban growth, which had been briefly checked by a period of conquest and physical destruction, seems to have resumed. In 1996 King argued forcefully for general economic development in the early twelfth century, which saw an active demand for land, and the development of new ports in eastern and southern England. London, omitted from Domesday, stood head and shoulders above other towns, but its fortunes in the twelfth century are obscure. That it acted as a major centre for the redistribution of imports and collection of exports cannot be doubted, but by the midtwelfth century it faced increasing competition from the growing international fairs at Winchester, Boston, Stamford, St Ives (Huntingdonshire), and Bury St Edmunds.[12]

Money, Britnell argues, flowed from the countryside to the towns as lords spent their incomes on luxury goods or peasants bought pots and pans. There was also a reverse flow, of course, from town to countryside, as merchants bought foodstuffs and raw materials, and invested in rural properties.[13] This encouraged the circulation of money, *but* the main impetus to the use of money, and for its acquisition through exchange, must have come from taxation. The geld may have only raised about £10,000 when it was levied in late Anglo-Saxon England, but this still represented between 20 and 50 per cent of the circulating medium.[14] The Norman kings also levied heavy taxes, and all the evidence suggests that it was the peasantry who bore the brunt of their taxation. The combined burden of rents and taxes probably forced the sale of surpluses by the peasantry in order to raise the money they needed to pay them and the exemptions and preferential treatment granted to the higher nobility and the Church by the Norman kings shifted the tax burden even further towards the small lord and the peasants.[15] It was not only a matter of the geld. By 1130 this had been supplemented by other taxes, 'aids' of counties, cities and boroughs, and from knights, 'aids' being a polite name for compulsory gifts. Feudal military service was being commuted for money payment (scutage) by at least 1100, and the feudal tenure of land by tenants-in-chief and sub-tenants alike was made the vehicle for a whole range of other payments, most notably relief (inheritance duty), wardship (the right to enjoys the profits of an estate when the heir was a minor) and control over the marriage of widows and daughters of tenants, which could be bought for a price. Nor did the Church escape. Archbishops, bishops and abbots also owed military service to the king, and by regalian right he took the revenues of sees and abbacies when there was a vacancy.[16] Kings, by and large, wanted cash, as did their tenants-in-chief, who could demand similar payments from their sub-tenants. Ultimately, again, it was the peasants who through their rents and other dues provided the coin needed to make such payments and the only way for them to find this money was by engaging in the market.

Reckoning, recording and accounting

Taxation thus demonstrated the convenience of money as a medium of exchange and was probably as important in the monetisation of the economy as the growth of demand resulting from steadily rising population levels. Taxation also made the processes of recording and reckoning more and more necessary. The geld itself was levied on taxable units of land, the hide or the carucate (ploughland). These were not precise areas, since the quality of the land – that is, its productive value – was clearly taken into account. Sixty acres of good land might well be worth as much as 120 acres of poor soil. Counties had to be assessed; liabilities to tax had to be worked out at local levels; and records of those liabilities had to be kept. One such county assessment from before 1084 has survived, for Nottinghamshire. It gives the hidage assessment for the Nottinghamshire hundreds (the subdivisions of the county), stating for each how many hides had paid the geld, how many were in demesne, and so exempt, how many owed the king food rents, and how many were waste. It is an impressive document and points to a high degree of recording obligations in terms of area and value.[17] Like the king, lords also needed to know about their revenues. So estate surveys began to appear. They too record area, time and quantity. The *ceorls* of Hurstbourne Prior's had to pay 40 pence (*amount*) at the autumnal equinox (23 September), just before Michaelmas (29 September) which was the chief post-harvest settlement date in the countryside (*time*). The area from which these payments, rents in kind (some measured by weight, others by number) and labour services were due was the hide (*area and quantity*).

Although they were much longer and more elaborate, twelfth-century surveys were simply continuations of well-established Anglo-Saxon practice.[18] It is also likely that the sum of the rents paid was recorded, so that lords could know their yearly incomes from their estates. This is certainly suggested by the evidence in Domesday Book, the first great surviving record of central government. The purposes of Domesday are still much discussed,[19] but, whatever its function, it was above all a record of values, as were the 'satellite' surveys from which it was apparently compiled. Those values were probably taken from other, pre-existing assessments, such as lists of tenants and of dues owed by towns, along with the records of royal lands and all the farms (payments) they owed, thus making possible what

A: A MONETISED ECONOMY

would otherwise have been an astonishingly rapid survey of almost the entire country.[20]

The nature of the inquest can best be seen by looking in detail at one entry, that for Witley in Surrey. Earl Godwine had held the estate before 1066, but it was now in the hands of Gilbert, son of Richer de Aigle. There was land for sixteen ploughs, but only fifteen were in use: two on the lord's demesnes and thirteen by 37 villeins and 3 cottars, to till their own lands and to perform their labour services. There were three acres of meadow, and woodland with pannage for 30 pigs. In the time of King Edward (1065) it had been worth £15, but now (1086) it was worth £16. In village after village across the country, as in Witley, money amounts, measurement in area and number and comparisons over time were being put down together in written record.[21]

But Domesday simply lists and records. Some forty years later the first surviving pipe roll of the Exchequer for the year Michaelmas 1129 to Michaelmas 1130 lists, not only lists and records but also *accounts*, a further prerequisite of a money economy.[22] Royal government is here shown dealing with named individuals rather than with counties in general, and the Exchequer audit recorded the specific obligations of its debtors. The sheriff of each county had to account for farm of the shire, 'old and new', the composite sum which he had agreed to pay the king and which came from the rents of royal estates and the profits of justice. From that sum he was then allowed to deduct any payments he had made on the king's behalf, provided he could prove that he had done so in accordance with royal commands. So, at Michaelmas 1130, Miles of Gloucester, sheriff of Gloucestershire, made his account:

> Miles of Gloucester accounts for 80 pounds and 14 pence blanch for the old farm of the shire. He has paid this in the Treasury. And he is quit
> The same sheriff accounts for the new farm of the shire. He has paid 222 pounds and 13 shillings by weight in the Treasury. He has disbursed:
> In fixed tithes 6 pounds by tale.
> In fixed alms 11 pounds, 2 shillings and 11 pence by tale.
> In fixed liveries 4 pounds, 11 shillings and 3 pence by tale.
> In liveries for a knight and serjeants and a door-keeper at the castle of St Briavels 14 pounds, 5 shillings and 7½ pence by tale.
> In the livery of Walter Pavilly, the clerk, 9 pounds, 2 shillings and 6 pence by tale.
> In the livery for Wibert Savage 76 shillings by tale.
> To the earl of Gloucester 20 pounds by tale for his share of the county.
> In land for cultivation which has been taken within the park of

> Alveston, 72 shillings by tale: and for the tithe of the same land 8 shillings by tale.
> For the transport of wine by the king's writ to Worcester and Bridgnorth 12 shillings and 20 pence by tale to Gilbert of Argentan.
> And he owes 16 pounds and 9 shillings and 10 pence by blanch.

The actual payments had to be made in coin, specified as by weight, blanch or tale, at the Treasury in the Lower Exchequer, the Upper Exchequer being the court of audit. Some of the money had probably been handed over earlier in the year, at Easter, and for this the sheriff would have been given a tally as a receipt. That now had to be produced, as part of the total payment. At the end of his account for the farm of the county a balance was drawn up. The sheriff was either 'quit' or, if he still had money to hand over, he 'owed' the Exchequer.

There then followed a long list of other debts to the crown which he was supposed to collect, such as fines or feudal dues. The record was then divided into two sections: payments outstanding from past years and which had either been partially collected or on which the debtor had defaulted, and liabilities for the current year, 1129–30. So:

> The same sheriff [Miles of Gloucester] accounts for 420 pounds of the old debts of his father in respect of his land and his office. He has paid 50 pounds in the Treasury. And he owes 370 pounds.
> Elias Giffard accounts for 100 marks of silver in respect of the relief of the land which his father held of the earl of Gloucester. He has paid 36 pounds, 13 shillings and 5 pence in the Treasury. And he owes 30 pounds.
> The burgesses of Gloucester owe 30 marks of silver if they can recover through the justice of the king the money which was taken from them in Ireland.
> The same sheriff accounts for 6 pounds, 6 shillings and 8 pence in respect of one murdrum fine in the hundred of 'Botelawia'.

Finally the sheriff had to account for the proceeds of taxation.

> The same sheriff accounts for 42 pounds and 10 shillings in respect of the last Danegeld. He has paid 75 shillings in the Treasury. By writ of the king he has pardoned the following payments. [There then follows a list of those who had been excused payment by royal writ.]

This record has to be treated with some caution. Not all these sums were 'real' debts, since the king often found it politically expedient to respite them in part or whole, or to keep the threat of enforcing repayment as a threat hanging over the head of anyone whose loyalty was suspect.[23]

A: A MONETISED ECONOMY

The Pipe Roll of 1129–30 shows us royal revenues being gathered up at the Exchequer in one centrally audited account. This was new and a major step forward in accounting procedures, one that would be copied by other great lay and ecclesiastical landlords in the management of their estates The abacus, which made it possible, seems to have come to England with the Conqueror, as did feudal tenures, which presented kings with even more opportunities to exploit the resources of their leading subjects.[24] What is important for our purposes is that the pipe roll reveals for the first time the extent to which the demands of the crown forced the majority of the population to use money. Taxes had long been paid in cash. Kings were not interested in payments in kind when the Danes had to be bought off, or wars to defend the Norman frontier financed. After 1066, feudal tenants in chief and their sub-tenants were bound in a new relationship to their overlord. Land and the tenure of land may have lain at its heart, but money payments were demanded by the king from the tenant-in-chief and by the tenant-in-chief from his sub-tenants. They thus had to raise cash incomes from their lands, and ultimately, as with taxation, the money had to come from the peasantry who were forced to enter the market by selling their produce in order to obtain the silver pennies they needed.

Credit

By the first half of the twelfth century most of the building blocks for a money economy seem to be in place: related units of account, measurement of area and weight, reckoning and recording of payments, deferred payments (debts), auditing of accounts, the growth of markets, and increasing demands for money by the state. One last element must now be considered, the growing availability of credit. Credit, it will be remembered, is important because it extends the money supply, allowing a far greater volume of business of all kinds than would be possible if all payments had to be made immediately, in cash.[25] Little, if anything, is known about the availability of credit in late Anglo-Saxon England, but it is highly probable that before, as after, 1066 moneyers acted as major sources of credit. Nightingale suggests that the profits of moneying were not great, and that moneyers drew most of their income from other sources, notably from exchanging coin and, importantly, from moneylending. There were strong links between the London moneyers and the Archbishop of Canterbury, the abbot of Ramsey and the Dean and Chapter of St Paul's, and some of the moneyers of late Anglo-Saxon England were also urban and rural property owners.[26] Property was frequently offered as security for loans. If the borrower defaulted, then the lender acquired the land or the tenements. This is reading back into Anglo-Saxon England what is known about credit after the Conquest, but it would be surprising if moneyers were not major sources of loans.

What is certain is that in 1066 the Jews came to England, almost literally with the Conqueror. There had been a Jewish community at Rouen since the early eleventh century, with connections to the more important and much wealthier Jewish communities in the Rhineland and Champagne. The Jews at Rouen were long-distance traders in luxury goods, dealers in gold and silver plate, and moneylenders. Anglo-Saxon England apparently had no need of them. Its trading links with Flanders and other areas of north-western Europe were already well-established, and there were more distant connections with Italy which brought gold, silk and spices from Venice through Pavia. English merchants controlled overseas trade while English moneyers dealt in gold and silver plate and acted as sources of credit. In Normandy, however, it was the Jews who supplied the duchy with luxuries acquired through long-distance trade, and with Goslar silver. Stacey speculates as to whether the Rouen community financed part of the invasion costs in 1066, thus ensuring them a place within the new regime. William might have hoped to profit from the protection he could offer in England to these new 'outsiders'. If they could challenge the supremacy of the native traders, and especially the merchants of London as dealers in luxury goods and of the moneyers in the changing of plate and coin, then they would be able to provide him with the cash he needed to pay his troops. Such hopes were not immediately realised. English merchants, London merchants, were far too well established in overseas trade for the new Jewish community to pose any threat to them. But by 1130 it is clear that the Jews of London had become a very wealthy community, capable of paying 850 pounds of silver in a single year to the king. The pipe roll records the imposition of a fine of £2,000 on them, for a sick man they were alleged to have killed, of which £600 was paid immediately. The roll also suggests that they were lending money to the crown by 1129/30. Rubigscotsce (Rabbi Josce) was repaid 180 silver marks, and Manasser 85 marks. They were certainly lending money to the lay nobility: Rubigscotsce and his partners offered the king 10 gold marks for his favour in a claim against Ranulf, earl of Chester, and Rubigscotsce, Jacob and Manasser six gold marks for help in their claim against Richard fitz Gilbert. The king here was offering his protection to the Jews by assisting in the collection of their debts, but at a price. Churchmen also borrowed from the Jews: Robert de Chesney, bishop of Lincoln 1148–66, pledged the ornaments of his cathedral to them, against a loan, while Nigel, bishop of Ely 1133–69 and

William de Walterville, abbot of Peterborough (1155–75) used the most precious relics of their churches. During Stephen's reign the community seems to have spread out from London so that by 1158 there were Jewish settlements in York, Lincoln, Norwich, Winchester, Cambridge, Oxford, Gloucester, Worcester, Northampton, Thetford and Bungay. Jewish credit became widely available throughout the realm, although its total volume at this point remains unknown and there is little evidence of who availed themselves of it, beyond the great men of the realm. Later, takers ranged from merchants and knights to wealthy peasants, but whether this was the case before 1158 is just not known. But the Jews were quite clearly a major new source of credit, with repayment of their loans enforced, at a price, by the king. This was to lead to the recording of their debts in the form of bonds or written agreements between the lender and the borrower, copies of which were kept in *archae*, or chests, in specific towns, and to the establishment in the 1190s of a separate Exchequer of the Jews, where they could take legal action to enforce payment of their debts. These methods for the recording of debts and efficient legal redress for creditors were eventually extended to Christian moneylenders in the late thirteenth century and are therefore of considerable importance in the development of the credit market in England.[27]

The case against a money economy

The GDP and the velocity of circulation

The argument for a money economy in eleventh- and early twelfth-century England looks impressive: coin was being used for making payments; regular markets in towns and in the countryside provided outlets for surpluses. There had been some standardisation in weights and measures and, after 1066, there was a substantial increase in the amount of credit available with the pipe roll for 1129–30 demonstrating considerable advances in reckoning, recording and accounting. The only element lacking seems to be the general legal enforcement of debts. The Jews were a special case: actions for recovery through the courts do not yet seem to have existed for Christians. Most of the essential components of a money economy were apparently in place by 1158, if not by 1086.

First appearances can be deceptive, however. A harder look at the evidence suggests that this was in fact an economy where money was in short supply, and being made to work very hard as a result. It is here that the model developed by Mayhew to demonstrate the velocity of circulation (**V**) becomes an important investigative tool. The method for calculating

V in 1086 and 1300 by estimating **GDP** and then dividing it by a figure for the size of the circulating medium has already been discussed above in Chapter 1. Mayhew argues that the high Domesday V score produced by his calculations indicates a society geared to money payments but obliged to extend a money supply basically inadequate for its needs by a variety of non-money expedients, such as deferred payment credits, barter, and rents paid in kind, by labour, or by military service.[28] The calculation of V does provide the best guide to the degree of monetisation in the economy in 1086, but it cannot be made unless reliable estimates of the size of the circulating medium and, most importantly, of the **GDP** can first be established.

Unfortunately, there is now some disagreement among numismatists as to the size of the circulating medium in 1086. The most widely accepted figure is £37,500, taken from Dolley's estimates, but Allen has recently argued that it could have been as little as £10,000–25,000.[29] Mayhew used the higher figure in his calculation of **GDP** in 1086 but the lower figure can easily be substituted to produce an even higher V score and so reinforce his arguments. But estimates of the **GDP** can only be made by using the evidence of the manorial *valets* in Domesday Book, and here there are equally profound disagreements between historians about what the term means. In 1086 the *valet* (literally 'it is worth ...') of the manor of Witley in Surrey was £16. Was this, in some way, a valuation of the surplus from the manor in the form of rents and sales? If so, then by adding together all the *valets* in Domesday and making some allowances for obvious omissions, a notional figure for the **GDP** would emerge. G.D. Snooks firmly believes that this is the right approach. He argues that the manorial system in England at the end of the eleventh century had two essential components, the demesne economy and the subsistence economy. The demesne economy provided the manorial lord and the free peasant with a surplus, to be spent, among other things, on providing a feudal army to fight wars of conquest, or on conspicuous consumption. That surplus was recorded as the *valet* in Domesday Book. The second element was the subsistence economy of the unfree peasantry. According to Snooks, they did not produce a taxable surplus. Rather, theirs was a closed economy in which an unfree workforce provided the labour needed to cultivate the manorial demesnes, and in turn met its subsistence needs from the land granted to it by the lord. Its product, in money terms, can only be estimated, and Snooks and McDonald have provided a complex formula for doing that. The third element was the product of the urban sector. Domesday lists some towns and markets, but it provides us with very little information about them. So, again, estimates have to be made, along with some allowances for the four northernmost counties not covered by the survey. Using the information from Domesday Book, Snooks arrives at an urban income of £10,708 and adds a notional figure for the northern counties, to produce the following estimate of national income, or **GDP**, in 1086.

Manorial Income	£
Recorded Counties:	
demesne economy (aggregate of all Domesday *valets*)	71,573
subsistence economy (estimated)	51,306
omitted counties	3,034
Urban incomes (7.8 per cent of total)	10,708
Total	136,621

He rejects estimates for a population of around 2 millions and instead suggests his own figure of 1.53 million, so that per capita **GDP** was 21.43 pennies or 1.785 shillings. Taking a circulating medium of £37,500, the figure for **V** would then be

$$\frac{136,621}{37,500}$$

or 3.4, a low **V** score which suggests that there was more than enough money in circulation to meet the economy's needs.[30]

There are two major objections to this model: first, it attaches a particular and disputed meaning to the term *valet* and secondly it almost certainly underestimates the nature and size of the peasant economy. For Snooks, Domesday is a tax book pure and simple. Domesday valuations therefore represent the entire value of a lord's holding. Against this Mayhew, following Harvey, Holt and Lennard, argues that the *valet* was actually a valuation of what an estate might be worth if it was let. The Domesday *valets* for 33 counties add up to £72,000 and to this must be added the estimated revenues from the four northern counties not included in the survey and the much under-recorded urban revenues. Certain types of rent-paying tenants, sub-tenants and the landless were also omitted from the survey and the total manorial valuations plus an allowance for omissions can, in any case, only represent a portion of **GDP**, since those paying rent and other dues still had to support themselves and their families, while the better-off may have generated surpluses for sale. Mayhew therefore suggests 'a true figure of at least £100,000 for the *valet* of England as a whole'.

Secondly, Snooks assumes that a tightly structured 'manorial' system, with neatly divided demesne and subsistence economies, obtained all over the country and that unfree peasants, the bulk of the population, did not engage in the market economy at all. This assumption must be challenged, both in general and in its detail. There were wide areas of England where only loose manorial structures obtained, and where there were very substantial numbers of free peasants who still had to pay some rents to a lord. Manorial *valets* in these areas probably do not reflect this extra source of demesne income and should, accordingly, be adjusted upward. Most historians also accept Mayhew's argument that the numbers of rent-paying peasants, together with sub-tenants and the landless, are underestimated in Domesday, and the size of the subsistence economy was certainly greater than Snooks allows. Taking both points together, this would mean a higher figure for the **GDP** than that given by his estimates.

More specifically, Snooks's argument that the unfree peasantry did not engage in the market economy is implausible. It is unlikely that they were forced to hand over 50 per cent of their produce to their immediate lord in the form of rents and dues, barely surviving on what was left to them. Later evidence suggests – and only suggests, since it is based on calculations of compulsory outgoings in the late thirteenth century – that unfree peasants paid between 25 per cent and 40 per cent of their incomes to their lords.[31] It is also quite clear that the unfree had to enter the market, if only to obtain the cash they need to pay taxes to the king and the money rents increasingly demanded by their lords. Mayhew therefore argues that his figure of £100,000 for the *valet* of all England represents about one-third of total peasant income, leaving the peasantry who formed well over 90 per cent of the population in 1100 with the other two-thirds. That gives a total national income £300,000 or perhaps slightly higher if allowances are made for urban households. A **GDP** of £300,000 provides a **V** score of 8, a **GDP** of £400,000 a **V** score of 10.6, compared to the **V** score of 3.4 derived from Snooks's model.[32] A high **V** score means increased velocity of circulation, with each unit of currency having to work harder to offset the relatively low level of coin in circulation.

To these two models providing estimates for the **GDP** and thus for **V** in 1086, a third must be added, that developed by A.R. Bridbury. He believes that the Domesday survey was concerned with the lord's income only, to the exclusion of everyone else's, and that its valuations were based on cash renders (payments) only. If this was the case, any estimates of seigneurial incomes based solely on the *valets* would be serious underestimates. Consequently, the **GDP** was far greater than the £300–400,000 suggested by Mayhew, perhaps by a factor of two or three. Bridbury's purpose is to argue that the Domesday economy was buoyant and the thirteenth-century economy stagnant and a high **GDP** in 1086 is central to his case.

But it is difficult to see how it could have reached £600,000 or more with a circulating medium of only £37,500 or less and consequently a high **V** score of 16.[33]

Given the considerable problems with the estimates of **GDP** provided by Snooks and Bridbury, guarded acceptance of Mayhew's calculations seems legitimate, even allowing for Dyer's cautious footnote to the debate. Consequently the figure of £300,000 for a **GDP** of £300,000 in the late eleventh century will be adopted here. This results in a **V** score of 8, which points, importantly, to a shortage of money in the last decades of the eleventh century.[34] The figures for coinage per head of population already given above in Chapter 4 fully support this conclusion.[35] Estimating population totals causes as much debate and disagreement as trying to calculate the size of the circulating medium before the mid-thirteenth century, but for once that does not matter since the order of change is obvious. Assuming a population of between and 2 and 2.5 million in 1086 and 4.5 to 5.5 million in 1290, the amount of coin per head was somewhere between 3.6d and 6d in the late eleventh century, between 46.6d and 69.3d per head in the late thirteenth, making it far easier to use coin for day-to-day transactions.[36] This would not have been possible in 1086, when there was not enough coin in circulation to allow it and when the regular use of money for making small purchases was inhibited by the high purchasing power of the silver penny. At this time, a whole sheep could have been had for between 2d and 2½d so that with his daily wages of 1d a household servant could have bought half a sheep's carcase but not the half pound of best end of neck to make a stew. There was an acute need for small change in Anglo-Saxon and Anglo-Norman England, in striking contrast with the late thirteenth century when large quantities of halfpennies and farthings were being struck. Cutting silver pennies into halves and quarters was one solution to the problem and some round halfpennies were minted in Henry I's reign, but it seems unlikely that there were enough fractional coins in circulation to meet the demand for them. The money supply was further reduced at times by heavy outflows to Scandinavia and to Normandy. That would certainly have affected the velocity of circulation and the general availability of coin, but how severely cannot be known in either case.[37]

Payments in kind

Taken together, the amount of coin per head and the equally high value of the silver penny in terms of its purchasing power suggest that England between 973 and 1158 had a monetised economy, where money was used as much as a standard of valuation in exchange as a medium of exchange in itself. Between them, the ceorls of Hurstbourne Prior's might well have been able to find the payment of 40d per hide (*c.*120 acres) demanded of them, perhaps collectively, or Aluric the 2s for his two bovates (*c.*30 acres) at Burton (Staffs.) in the early twelfth century. It would not have been so easy for Frawin to find the 16d he had to pay for one dwelling with no land attached to it at Burton, or Ernwill the Gardener 12d for a dwelling and a croft (a small piece of land) unless both had alternative, and unknown, sources of income. Perhaps these bald statements of money rents actually conceal a mix of cash and payment in kind? Such payments certainly persisted at all levels, from feudal military service to food rents paid to the Abbey of Bury St Edmunds from its Suffolk manors in the late eleventh century.[38] But we do not really know how most transactions within the countryside were carried out. Britnell argues that barter must have remained a normal way of obtaining household supplies, in small quantities, and that the English villager's use of cash was probably limited to a minority of the transactions needed for daily life. There was a high degree of self-sufficiency. In Domesday 41 per cent of the recorded country dwellers were villeins, who must have produced most of their own requirements for basic foodstuffs. A further 10 per cent were slaves who were mainly responsible for working the ploughs on the lords' demesnes in return for food and shelter, probably to fairly minimum standards. Over half of the recorded rural population did not rely on the market either exclusively or extensively for its subsistence, and paid much of the rent for its land in labour.[39] Why labour rents should have persisted remains something of a mystery. Hatcher argues that a shortage of manpower forced lords in the eleventh and early twelfth centuries to use their coercive powers to bind unfree tenants to the soil, to ensure the cultivation of their own demesne lands. Britnell finds this an inadequate explanation. Since the population was growing slowly in the first half of the twelfth century, there was increasing demand or competition for land. It was better for a peasant to stay where he was rather than facing the uncertainty and economic insecurity inherent in a move to another estate, even if this meant accepting harsh terms for his current holding. Yet both seem to overlook the fact that there simply may not have been sufficient money in circulation to allow rents to be paid in cash on a large scale, something which would also help explain the persistence of payments in kind. The large numbers of cottagers in Domesday probably worked as hired labourers, and it is highly likely that they would have received their wages in grain or other produce, rather than in coin.[40]

A: A MONETISED ECONOMY

The flow of money to the countryside

Nevertheless, this was not a self-sufficient agrarian society with no need at all for money. Taxes and some rents still had to be paid in money and archaeological excavations show that peasants used pottery and metalwork not made on their own holdings or in their villages and which they presumably had to buy. Their housing often required substantial amounts of timber for framing and was put together in a relatively sophisticated way, probably by craftsmen such as carpenters and joiners who may have been paid at least partly in cash.[41] Towns supplied basic manufactured goods and, at the top end of the scale, luxuries; in return they received back raw materials and foodstuffs. This should have generated bilateral flows, putting money into the pockets of townsmen and country dwellers alike. The problem is judging how strong such flows actually were and, in particular, how much money was transferred from town to countryside. England was covered by an urban and rural market network, but most towns were small, and often largely self-sufficient since they were surrounded by their own fields, which supplied much of their food. For the rest, they drew on the produce of the countryside within a radius of only a few miles from their boundaries. If peasants did spend money raised from sales of surpluses on consumer goods, then much of it probably stayed within the towns, to be used by townsmen for exchange with other townsmen.[42] That would have reduced the amount of money circulating within the countryside even further, unless the chief recipients of rents and taxes, the king and lords both great and small, spent lavishly and regularly there. Lavish spending there may have been, but much of it was irregular. Fixed households, such as monastic communities, needed constant supplies of foodstuffs, but drew much of it in kind from their estates. Great lay households were constantly on the move, either working their way around their estates, or buying supplies as and when they needed them. From 1066, the most opulent of all households, that of the king, with its considerable purchasing power, was often abroad, sometimes for long periods.[43] In recent years, archaeology has shown us that king, lords and especially the Church built impressively in late Anglo-Saxon England. The Normans then tore down most of these buildings, erecting new cathedrals, monasteries, and of course, castles, on an even grander scale. The great cathedral at Durham could not have been built between 1093 and 1133 without a substantial flow of money from the local economy, but this was balanced by substantial flows back into it, to support the construction work there. Roger, bishop of Salisbury, Henry I's Justiciar (his chief royal servant and deputy when he was abroad) spent heavily on manor houses on his estates, as well on a new cathedral at what is now Old Sarum. But this was erratic spending. Its effects were temporary, and often disruptive, since lords would put extra pressure on their tenants to raise the cash for their building works. Britnell argues that, on balance, seigneurial cash outlays of this nature had little effect upon the normal flow of money into the countryside.[44]

Regional variations in the use of money

These are, however, broad generalisations. The reality was that that there were, almost certainly, wide regional variations in the use of money. It has already been seen that there was a hierarchy of mints, with most coin being produced in the east of the country and London standing head and shoulders above the rest. Stray finds can provide useful information about the circulation of coins, always allowing for the smallness of the sample.[45] Frequent recoinages meant that most coins in circulation were no more than four or five years old. It is possible to trace their movement from the towns where they were struck and coins from other mints moving into other towns or regions. London coins moved far and wide, which was only to be expected, given that the city was a great port and a major centre of consumption. Conversely, half the stray finds in London were from mint towns elsewhere. These outward and inward flows are also to be found at Lincoln, York, Worcester and virtually all other towns for which there is evidence. The proportion of local and incoming coins also tends to be roughly the same as in London, and the pattern is uniform throughout the eleventh century.

There were, clearly, substantial inter-regional transfers of money, although they could have resulted as much from the raising and paying of taxes as from internal trade. But the stray-find evidence suggests something else, namely that the focal points for money circulation within England between 973 and 1086 were the half-dozen major trading centres in the eastern counties of England, looking towards the North Sea: London above all, then York, Lincoln, Stamford, Norwich and Thetford. To the west, monetary circulation thinned out, while Yorkshire seems to have been largely self-contained. The currency north of the Humber was to a considerable extent local in origin, with most coins found having been struck at York. It was also significantly different from the currency of southern England, in the sense that York coins do not seem to have circulated widely in the south. There is little evidence for the active and regular use of money in Lancashire, modern Cumbria, or in Northumberland and Durham, although that may be a result of fewer finds in those areas. Regional patterns of minting and of coin circulation strongly suggest that the predominant use of coin was for commercial purposes and involved trade between the east-coast ports and their hinterland. They also suggest that over large areas of northern and western England coin was either not widely available, or not much used, or both.[46]

Conclusion: a monetised economy

Drawing firm conclusions from this uncertain account of the use of money in eleventh- and twelfth-century England is difficult, even perhaps dangerous. But it does seem reasonable, given the present state of the evidence, to make the following points:

First, there was a limited amount of money in circulation, with considerable variations from region to region.

Second, what money there was made to work very hard. The velocity of circulation was high which was characteristic of an economy where the money supply was inadequate for its needs.

Third and consequently, payment in kind was widespread, at all levels in society, from knights performing feudal military service to peasants performing labour services and paying food rents.

Fourth, barter remained common, either because of a shortage of coin or, more likely, because in what was still largely a subsistence economy, it was the most rational way of exchange. That is particularly likely to have been the case during periods of political upheaval and physical destruction. The harrying of the North after the rebellion in 1067 is probably the best known example of such destruction, but there was also a major rebellion during Edward the Confessor's reign (the revolt of the Godwines) and civil wars during Stephen's, while laying waste the countryside was a political weapon much used by the Anglo-Saxon kings.[47] Destruction was certainly limited geographically, and there is much debate about how extensive it was, but barter flourishes both during and in the aftermath of war.

Fifth, the amount of coin in circulation was likely to have been reduced at times by:
    (i) heavy taxation and
    (ii) the flow of money abroad, either as tribute or to pay for continental wars

Sixth, the urban/manufacturing sector of the economy was small, even in terms of a medieval agrarian economy. The evidence here is, again, limited and to some extent contradictory. Towns were sufficiently wealthy to pay substantial sums to their lords as farms, but most were small, and often largely self-sufficient in food.[48] The flow of money to and from towns was probably restricted, and their role as a driving force behind the use of money probably less than is often supposed.

Seventh, in terms of reckoning and recording, the introduction of the abacus and its use by the Exchequer is often seen as a great step forward. Yet, as Murray has said, while it helped arithmetic, at the same time it put limits upon it, and especially on its sophistication and speed. Nor is there any real evidence that literacy and numeracy, both essential components of a money economy, were widespread, something to be discussed further in Chapter 7 below.[49]

Eighth and finally, by 1158 royal control over the coinage was virtually complete. There was to be one further stage in the process, the reduction in the number of mints, and the removal of the moneyers and their replacement by exchangers, and that was to begin later in Henry II's reign. From about 1083 the weight and fineness of the penny were set at a high level. Unquestionably, the English coinage was one of the best, if not the best, in western Europe, but in the long run this was to prove as much a disadvantage as an advantage, especially in the later Middle Ages. In the immediate circumstances of the eleventh and early twelfth centuries, it might have been better for the economy if more coins, of less intrinsic value and with lower purchasing power, had been struck from the limited amount of silver available, so allowing small transactions to be made. The maintenance of 'sound money' at all costs is not always in the best interests of a country's economy.

Given these considerations, it is hard to argue that a full money economy existed in eleventh- and early twelfth-century England. According to earlier definitions, this would have required:

First, enough coin in circulation to allow its use to be normal rather than occasional.

Second, the growth of literacy and numeracy so that recording and accounting could spread from the centre into both urban and rural society.

Third, standard systems of weights and measures to make the exchange of goods and lands equitable throughout the kingdom.

Fourth, the widespread use of credit, with debt recovery enforceable by law.

The late Anglo-Saxon and the Anglo-Norman economy would certainly have failed all these tests. The money supply was pitifully small and despite attempts to establish uniform systems of weights and measures across England, local variations persisted. Exchange within areas using

A: A MONETISED ECONOMY

the same local customs would not be inhibited but exchange between areas with different customs would be. Domesday Book and the pipe roll of 1129–30 are impressive evidence of recording and, in the case of the pipe roll, of reckoning. Yet beyond them, the argument for widespread ability to add, subtract, relate money to weight and area and record the calculations, is largely from silence. Anglo-Saxon historians are adamant that records providing the necessary evidence must once have existed but the reply must be that if the Anglo-Saxons generally were so literate and numerate, then why have more records not survived to show this? In any case, Domesday, the Pipe Roll, geld rolls, estate surveys were produced by central government, by great lords and by royal officials in the countryside. Nothing suggests that below this level there was widespread literacy or numeracy in Anglo-Saxon and Anglo-Norman England and without both a money economy is not possible.[50] Finally, the availability of credit, which could extend the money supply, was limited, and the enforcement of obligations haphazard and mostly dependent on buying the king's favour.

The conclusion must surely be that this was a 'monetised' rather than a 'money economy'. The amount of coin in circulation was limited, there were probably increasing problems with the bullion supply from the late eleventh century onward, credit was restricted, reckoning and recording in their infancy. Coin had to be used to pay taxes and some if not all rents and to make certain types of purchase, but most of the population was still engaged in a subsistence economy where barter was at least as important as cash transactions. If it was, then money may well have acted more as a standard of value than as a medium of exchange. One other possible conclusion might be that the economy in these years was stagnant, and that the money supply was adequate for its needs. There is some truth in this. A subsistence economy with weak urban and manufacturing sectors needs money only for special purposes rather than for day-to-day transactions. However, it is quite possible to turn this argument around, and put a case for expansion being held back by a shortage of coin, partly due to general European shortages of bullion from the late eleventh century onward, and by a weak infrastructure in terms of reckoning, recording and the availability and enforceability of credit. From 1100 onward there seems to have been slow but steady population growth and, as King has argued, some economic development in the first half of the twelfth century, shown by the active demand for land, the foundation of new towns, and increasing local, regional and international trade. Landon and Masschaele contend that this commercialisation of itself stimulated population growth but it is highly likely that economic development was being held back by a simple lack of coin in circulation.[51] There was only one remedy for that, a dramatic rise in European silver output that would allow literally millions upon millions of new coins to be struck in Germany, Flanders, France and, eventually, in England. How and when that happened is the subject of the next chapter.

Notes

1 See above, p. 33.
2 Clanchy, *Memory to Written Record*, p. 21; and see above, pp. 28–30, 33 and below, pp. 133–4, 186, 199–200.
3 P.D.A. Harvey, 'Rectitudines Singularum Personarum and Gerefa', *EHR*, 108 (1993), 21–2; *EHD, vol. ii*, pp. 816–17.
4 *EHD, vol. ii*, pp. 816–17. The Hurstbourne survey is dated c.1050, Tidenham c.1060.
5 F.W. Maitland, *Domesday Book and Beyond: Three Essays in the Early History of England* (Cambridge: Cambridge University Press, 1897), pp. 57–8; *EHD, vol. ii*, pp. 820–1, 825–6; see also pp. 829–33 for other examples from the Peterborough and Ramsey Abbey estates.
6 Loyn, *Anglo-Saxon England and the Norman Conquest*, p. 320.
7 Stafford, *Unification and Conquest*, pp. 492–5; R. Lennard, *Rural England 1086 to 1135: A Study of Social and Agrarian Conditions* (Oxford: Clarendon Press, 1959), p. 130; Britnell, *Commercialisation*, p. 33.
8 The classic work on the leasing of estates 1086–1135 is Lennard, *Rural England*, chapters five to seven, pp. 105–212; the organisation of farming and estate management is also discussed by S. Harvey, 'Domesday England', in H.E. Hallam et al. (eds), *The Agrarian History of England and Wales, vol. ii, 1042–1350* (Cambridge: Cambridge University Press, 1988), pp. 45–136, *passim*; Stafford, *Unification and Conquest*, pp. 205–7; Faith, *The English Peasantry and the Growth of Lordship*, pp. 178–83.
9 Britnell, *Commercialisation*, pp. 39–40; R. Faith, 'Demesne resources and labour rent on the manors of St Paul's cathedral, 1066–1222', *EcHR*, 47 (1994), 660, table 1; *EHD, vol. ii*, pp. 827, 831 for leases of manors in Staffordshire and Huntingdonshire in the early twelfth century; C. Dyer, *Making a Living in the Middle Ages: The People of Britain, 850–1520* ((New Haven and London: Yale University Press, 2002), p. 120.
10 The phrase was coined by Dyer in his study of the West Midlands in the later Middle Ages: C. Dyer, 'The hidden trade of the Middle Ages: evidence from the west Midlands of England', *JHG*, 18 (1992), 141–57.
11 The growth of the market before 1066, and the adverse effects upon it of the Norman Conquest, are considered by Miller and Hatcher. *Medieval England: Towns, Commerce and Crafts*, pp. 18–25, 38–43; the general growth of the market is discussed above, pp. 32–3.
12 Britnell, 'English markets and royal administration before 1200', 183–92; Britnell, *Commercialisation*, pp. 5–10; Miller and Hatcher, *Medieval England: Towns,*

Commerce and Crafts, pp. 18, 40, 42, 43; E. King, 'Economic development in the early twelfth century', in Britnell and Hatcher (eds), *Progress and Problems*, pp. 1–16; R. Holt, 'Society and population 600–1300', in D.M. Palliser (ed.), *The Cambridge Urban History of Britain, vol. i, 600–1540* (Cambridge: Cambridge University Press, 2000), pp. 82–4, 94–5; D. Keene, 'London from the post-Roman period to 1300', in Palliser (ed.), *Cambridge Urban History*, pp. 191–2; P. Nightingale, *A Medieval Mercantile Community: The Grocers' Company and the Politics and Trade of London 1000–1485* (New Haven and London: Yale University Press, 1995), pp. 34–5; E.W. Moore, *The Fairs of Medieval England* (Toronto: Pontifical Institute, 1985), pp. 12–23.

13 Britnell, *Commercialisation*, discusses the flow of money, the growth of the market, and specialisation in trade and industry in Chapter 2, pp. 29–52.
14 See above, Table 2.1, p. 25.
15 Stafford, *Unification and Conquest*, pp. 211, 216; the debate on the regressive nature of taxation in the period is discussed by A. Wareham and X. Wei, 'Taxation and the economy in late eleventh-century England: reviving the Domesday regression debate', in *Anglo-Norman Studies*, 29 (2007), 214–27.
16 Green, *Government of England under Henry I*, pp. 75–81; Green, *Henry I*, pp, 361–6; Hollister and Frost, *Henry I*, pp, 379–90.
17 J. Campbell (ed.), *TheAnglo-Saxons* (Harmondsworth: Penguin, 1991), p. 243.
18 See above, pp. 31–2, and *EHD, vol. ii*, pp. 816–35.
19 The various interpretations of Domesday Book are usefully summarised in N.J. Higham, 'The Domesday survey: context and purpose', *History*, 78 (1993), 8–21 and by N.J. Mayhew, 'Coinage and money in England, 1086–*c*.1500', in D. Wood (ed.), *Medieval Money Matters* (Oxford: Oxbow Books, 2004), pp. 74–9; for Domesday as a 'law book' to settle disputes over land see R. Fleming, *Domesday Book and the Law* (Cambridge: Cambridge University Press, 2004), pp. 1–86.
20 Loyn, *Anglo-Saxon England and the Norman Conquest*, p. 335; S. Harvey, 'Domesday Book and its predecessors', *EHR*, 86 (1971), 753–77; Stafford, *Unification and Conquest*, p. 148.
21 *Domesday Re-bound* (London: Public Record Office, 1954), figures 1 and 2, p. 12; see above, pp. 28–31.
22 For a full discussion of the pipe rolls and why they were kept in roll and not book form, see Warren, *Governance of Norman and Angevin England*, pp. 73–5 and Clanchy, *Memory to Written Record*, pp. 135–44; see also above, pp. 28–31.
23 The extracts are taken from *The Pipe Roll of 31 Henry I* (London: H.M.S.O., 1929), pp. 76–80, translated in *EHD, vol. ii*, pp. 569–75. Tithes were payments made to the Church of a tenth part of the corn crop, vegetables and poultry, and every tenth young animal, or their equivalents in money. Liveries were payments for services, usually on an annual basis. The murdrum fine was levied after the Conquest on the English inhabitants of any hundred in which a Norman had been murdered, a hundred being the administrative sub-division of the shire. For payments by weight, blanch and tale, see above, pp. 46, 99.
24 Murray, *Reason and Society*, p. 165.
25 See above, pp. 8, 30, 72.
26 P. Nightingale, 'Some London moneyers and reflections on the organisation

of English mints in the eleventh and twelfth centuries', *NC*, 142 (1982), 47–48; Fleming, 'Rural elites and urban communities', 36.

27 Stacey, 'Jewish lending and the medieval English economy', pp. 78–89; J. Hillaby, 'The London Jewry: William I to John', *JHS*, 33 (1995), 9–15; Hillaby, 'Jewish colonisation in the twelfth century', in P. Skinner (ed.), *Jews in Medieval Britain* (Woodbridge: Boydell, 2003), pp. 15–29; P. Brand, 'The Jewish community of England in the records of English royal government', in Skinner (ed.), *Jews in Medieval Britain*, pp. 73–9; R.R. Mundill, 'Christian and Jewish lending patterns and financial dealings during the twelfth and thirteenth centuries', in P.R. Schofield and N.J. Mayhew (eds), *Credit and Debt in Medieval England c.1180–c.1350* (Oxford: Oxbow Books, 2002), pp. 42–5.

28 Mayhew, in his important article 'Modelling medieval monetisation', pp. 55–71, argues that in the Fisher Identity **P × T** (prices times the total volume of monetary transactions) represents the total value of goods and services produced in an economy over a one-year period, or **GDP**. So, by manipulating the equation, **V = PT/M**. If values can be calculated for **PT**, or **GDP**, and are known for **M**, then it is possible to calculate **V**, to find out how hard money was being made to work in the economy. The higher the co-efficient for **V**, the harder the money worked. See above, pp. 11, 15, for a definition of **GDP**.

29 See above, p. 107.

30 G.D. Snooks, 'The dynamic role of the market in the Anglo-Norman economy and beyond, 1086–1300', in Britnell and Campbell, *A Commercialising Economy*, p. 33; J. McDonald and G.D. Snooks, *Domesday Economy: A New Approach to Anglo-Norman History* (Oxford: Clarendon Press, 1986), Chapter 7, pp. 117–24, summarises their methodology; J.S. Moore, '"Quot homines?" The population of Domesday England', *Anglo-Norman Studies*, 19 (1997), 307–34; see above, pp. 6–7, 13–15, for the relevance of low and high **V** scores.

31 Rigby, *English Society*, pp. 30–3; Dyer, *Standards of Living*, pp. 109–18.

32 Snooks, 'Dynamic role of the market', pp. 27–41, for a full discussion of his estimates; Mayhew, 'Modelling medieval monetisation', pp. 60–3, 195–6, for a critical appraisal thereof; and see above, pp. 00–00. Snooks also has to argue that a high proportion of the **GDP** went for export, perhaps as much as 20–24 per cent. This is because it could not have been consumed by the unfree peasantry who in his model did not enter the market. This is a higher proportion of the **GDP** in exports than was ever achieved in the nineteenth century when Britain was the workshop of the world. It is based on the assumption of a booming wool-export trade to Flanders, something already challenged, and seems highly improbable; see above, p. 126 and pp. 67, 93, 98–9, 151–2, 160, 164.

33 A.R. Bridbury, 'The Domesday valuation of manorial income', in his *The English Economy from Bede to the Reformation* (Woodbridge: Boydell, 1992), pp. 92–132; the calculation of the **V** score is mine.

34 C. Dyer, 'A note on the calculation of **GDP** for 1086 and *c.*1300', in Britnell and Campbell, *A Commercialising Economy*, pp. 196–7; Mayhew, 'Modelling medieval monetisation', pp. 61–2, 195–6.

35 See above, Tables 2.1 and 2.2, pp. 25–7.

36 See above, Table 2.2, p. 26–7.

A: A MONETISED ECONOMY

37 Harvey, 'Domesday England', p. 57, table 2.1; Britnell, *Commercialisation*, p. 30, who makes the point concerning best end of neck; see above, pp. 25-6, Table 2.1; Mayhew, 'Modelling medieval monetisation', p. 72, Tables 4.5 and 4.6; see below, pp. 189-90, 202, 213-14, for the thirteenth-century evidence and a discussion of the standard of living.
38 *EHD*, vol. ii, pp. 816, 819, 825-6; see also Faith, 'Demesne resources and labour rent on the manors of St Paul's cathedral', 658-9.
39 The figures for categories of rural population in Domesday are taken from Bartlett, *England under the Norman and Angevin Kings*, pp. 317-18, Table 4.
40 J. Hatcher. 'English serfdom and villeinage: towards a reassessment', *P&P*, 90 (1981), 26-32; Britnell, *Commercialisation*, pp. 30-1, 74-5.
41 Dyer, 'A note on the calculation of GDP', p. 197.
42 Miller and Hatcher, *Medieval England: Towns, Commerce and Crafts*, pp. 18-38; Britnell, *Commercialisation*, Chapter 1, pp. 5-52 and Table 1, p. 9, showing the numbers of Domesday boroughs in relation to recorded total population, by region; R. H. Britnell, 'The economy of British towns 600-1300', in Palliser (ed.), *Cambridge Urban History*, pp. 105-26.
43 D. Crouch, *The Image of Aristocracy in Britain, 1000-1300* (London: Routledge, 1992), pp. 247-51; D.C. Douglas, *William the Conqueror* (London: Methuen, 1969), appendix E, pp. 401-7; Green, *Government of England under Henry I*, p. 5; Green, *Henry I*, pp. 298-300; Hollister and Frost, *Henry I*, pp. 360-1.
44 Britnell, *Commercialisation*, pp. 47-8.
45 See above, pp. 64-5.
46 Metcalf, *Atlas*, pp. 191-248, 275-80.
47 Harvey, 'Domesday England', pp. 134-5, argues that it tipped the economic balance in favour of eastern and southern England.
48 See above, pp. 22-3, 117-18, 130.
49 Murray, *Reason and Society*, p. 167; and see below, pp. 199-202.
50 Clanchy, *Memory to Written Record*, chapter seven, 'Literate and illiterate', pp. 224-52; N. Orme, 'Lay literacy in England 1100-1300', in A. Haverkamp and H. Vollrath (eds), *England and Germany in the High Middle Ages* (Oxford: Oxford University Press, 1996), pp. 35-56; J. Barrow, 'Churches, education and literacy in towns 600-1300', in Palliser, *Cambridge Urban History*, p. 149.
51 King, 'Economic development in the early twelfth century', pp. 1-22 *passim*; Langdon and Masschaele, 'Commercial activity and population growth', 42-54.

B: THE EMERGENCE OF
A MONEY ECONOMY, 1158-1351

6

The coinage 1158–1351

Introduction

In 973 Edgar's 'reform' of the coinage brought, for the first time, a silver penny of standard design for the whole of England, one produced in the following two centuries at as many as 70 mints. The situation by 1351 was very different. Now there were no fewer than five struck silver coins in circulation, the penny, halfpenny, farthing, groat (4d) and half groat (2d), and three gold, the noble, worth 6s 8d, with its half and quarter, and there were only two active mints in England, at London and Canterbury, with another just established at the newly won English town of Calais. A loose and essentially local organisation at the mints had been replaced by tight, centralised royal control and the amount of coin in circulation had increased nearly elevenfold between 1100 and 1300. In this period of some 200 years, not only was the coinage transformed but a money economy also finally emerged.

The flood of silver

The first stage in this transformation has to be set against the background of a massive increase in the European silver supply. Until, and unless, that happened there could be no increase in the amount of coin in circulation in England. Bullion could be and apparently was effectively recycled at each recoinage, and losses through wear and tear were made good by limited silver imports. But there had been no appreciable increase in the circulating medium between 973 and 1158. The most recent estimates for the period immediately before 1158, by Allen, suggest that it may have been somewhere between £30,000 and £80,000, allowing for different estimates of die output. Given that European mining output was at a low ebb in the first half of the twelfth century, it probably stood somewhere in the lower half of that range, with only a modest increase since 1086, and possibly none at all.[1] Then, between 1160 and 1230 new sources of silver were discovered in Europe, at Freiberg near Meissen in Saxony, at Montieri in Tuscany, and at Freisach in the Tyrol. However, the productive life of silver mines was relatively short. Limited technology meant that it was only possible to use the ore deposits which lay on or just under the surface. To maintain supplies new deposits had to be found and brought into production, and that is what happened in thirteenth-century Europe. As output fell from Freiberg, Montieri and Freisach, perhaps as early as 1205-14, new silver began to flow from Jihlava (Iglau), on the borders of Bohemia and Moravia; from Schemnitz in Hungary (now Banská Stiavnica in Slovakia); from Golncibánya (Gelnica, Slovak Republic) and Rodna (Transylvania); from Iglesias in Sardinia; and then, right at the end of the century, from Kutná Hora and Pribram in Bohemia (both now in the Czech Republic). Blanchard argues that there were silver shortages at times as production fell at one centre and before the next came online, most notably between 1214 and 1250, 1259-61 and 1275-92. Be that as it may, for much of the 'long' thirteenth century and until the early 1330s, silver flowed into the European economy, north and south. From Central Europe it reached England via the Rhineland and Cologne and the Low Countries, where the expanding cloth industry in the Flemish towns began to draw heavily on supplies of English wool. So, from the late twelfth century onward, thanks largely to favourable trade balances, European silver began to flow to English mints.[2]

Mints and exchanges

This marks the first major difference between Anglo-Saxon and Anglo-Norman and Angevin England. All the major recoinages between 1180 and 1299-1300 took place when European silver supplies were abundant and they also took place at far fewer mints. The reduction in their numbers is quite striking. As many as 70 had operated at times of recoinages in Anglo-Saxon England, and there were still 51 in Henry I's reign. Under Stephen that dropped to between 40 and 46, and then to 29 for Henry II's cross/crosslets Tealby coinage of 1158. The short-cross issue of 1180 was initially struck at 10 mints only, the partial recoinage of 1205 at 16, and the Long-cross coinage of 1247 at 21. The increase in the number of mints in 1247 was necessary because a coinage that had been in circulation since 1180 was being completely and fairly quickly replaced. New mints had to be opened and moneyers attracted, with some difficulty, to work at them. Once the recoinage had been accomplished, then the number of mints in operation fell to five: London, Canterbury and the ecclesiastical privilege mints at Durham, Bury St Edmunds and York. Edward I used only 12 mints during his reign, with production being concentrated more and more at London and Canterbury, the former a major port and by then the capital of England, the latter conveniently near Channel ports and a natural centre for the recoinage of foreign silver.[3]

This reduction in the number of mints was part of a series of significant changes between 1158 and 1262. First, the moneyers were deprived of their right to strike new issues and to exchange old and foreign coins for new and current English money. Even before 1158 some mints were under direct royal control. At others the moneyers still worked for themselves, on the payment of the appropriate fees to the crown, while some boroughs farmed the rights to the mints within their walls. Mint and exchange were usually held together, and it was from the exchange that the real profits flowed, profits that allowed some moneyers, especially in London, to act as moneylenders. The crown was determined, in the long run, to secure these profits for itself, and to subordinate the mints to royally controlled exchanges. The attack on the moneyers began in earnest in 1158, at the time of the Tealby recoinage. They were removed from office en masse, and over the next two decades their successors were made to pay both regular taxation and arbitrary fines for supposed misdemeanours. Then, in 1180, at the time of the major short-cross recoinage, Henry II launched an all-out assault on them, to ensure that the profits from the coinage and the exchange which had previously flowed to the moneyers now came to the crown. The moneyers were replaced by salaried officials, at a considerably reduced number of mints. At the same time, new exchanges were built, at royal expense, and again staffed by salaried officials.

Finally, the practice of frequent recoinages was abandoned once and for all. After 1180, the next and only partial recoinage was in 1205-7, followed by complete recoinages in 1247-9 and 1279-81, another partial recoinage of foreign imitation sterlings, the infamous pollards and crockards, in 1299-1300, and then a comprehensive recoinage of silver and the introduction of a gold coinage between 1343 and 1351. Without the frequent recoinages, the local mints which had more or less recycled the domestic coinage rather than striking foreign silver, were not viable. Henceforth production was to be concentrated on the exchanges and mints to which both domestic and foreign silver were brought, and in the long run that meant London and Canterbury, with the three ecclesiastical-privilege mints at Durham, Bury St Edmunds and York still working but at reduced levels or only intermittently. It is sometimes argued that this centralisation deprived the crown of the regular income from the fees paid by the moneyers, and that

B: THE EMERGENCE OF A MONEY ECONOMY, 1158–1351

it lost money as a result, but this seems unlikely. Henry II was not a king to sacrifice royal rights or royal revenues. The trend towards centralisation of production at certain mints was already under way, even in the Anglo-Saxon period, and at those mints, and particularly at London, the moneyers had become more or less royal officials, rewarded with land, while the king took the profits of mint and exchange. That being the case, then financially the king had little to lose by reducing the number of mints.

In any case, the real profits came from the exchange, and this would explain why Henry II was prepared to lay out large sums for the building of new exchanges, and on the salaries of the officials who ran them. In 1180–81 the Pipe Rolls record payments of between 8d and 16d a day to the exchangers, for the rent of houses for the exchanges in various towns, and for compensation paid to those whose properties had been demolished to make way for a new exchange. All this was quite new, and the sum involved, some £500, was large by twelfth-century standards. Henry II was obviously prepared to speculate in order to accumulate, and he must have thought the risks worthwhile. Whether he did increase his revenues from mint and exchange substantially cannot be known. The profits seem to have been paid directly into the royal coffers, rather than to the Exchequer, where they would have been recorded on the Pipe Rolls. But it is worth repeating that Henry II gave nothing away.

Royal control over mint and exchange was not complete by the end of Henry II's reign, however. Indeed, it was probably not achieved until 1262. Mayhew has described the reforms of that year as 'one of the major landmarks in the administration of the Mint', since they finally claimed such profits as the moneyers still made for the crown. The moneyers became salaried officials of the Exchange, the central office which had been responsible for most of the thirteenth century for the purity and weight of coins issued. Another explanation has been offered for the reduction in the number of mints, however. It is seen as a response to the massive increase in the amount of silver available from c.1180 onward. The widespread granting of minting rights in earlier centuries has been explained as an attempt to make it easier for those who wanted to obtain new coin to take their bullion, be it in the form of old coin or foreign silver, to a mint no further than a day's walking distance, both there and back. Yet the actual location of mints in the Anglo-Saxon and Anglo-Norman periods does not support this argument since there were heavy concentrations in Wessex and Kent and none at all in other areas of the country. In any case, many of the mints worked only sporadically, at times of general recoinages, and the bulk of the coinage in the tenth, eleventh and early twelfth centuries was struck at London, Winchester, Canterbury, and a handful of other mints, mainly in the east of the country. More silver, more coins struck from it, better marketing and distribution systems to push those coins around the country, certainly made it easier to put the coinage into circulation from a limited number of mints, with others working only when required and for short periods at times of major recoinages. But the main impetus for centralised minting, with the Exchange and Mint in London, which from the reign of Edward I onward was situated at the Tower, came from the crown's desire to take the major share of the profits to be made from the coinage for itself. Henry II's attack on the moneyers began a process which was only completed in the second half of the thirteenth century.[4]

The coinage 1158-1290

The Tealby coinage (cross/crosslets) 1158

Between the late twelfth and the fourteenth century the English coinage was transformed and a money economy finally emerged. Progress towards this major economic, social and political change was neither smooth nor planned and was caused as much by exogenous as endogenous factors. It did not simply result from the substantial increase in the amount of money in circulation, but from the interplay of this with the financial and political demands of the crown, with legal and educational change, and, of course, with sustained population growth until at least the early fourteenth century. The result was the commercialisation of society, the emergence of a market economy. Since markets function best when money is used as the main medium of exchange, any discussion of the emergence of a money economy must be based on a proper understanding of how and when the amount of coin in circulation reached the critical mass required to make that possible. This took far longer than is sometimes assumed, and began slowly with the 'Tealby' or cross/crosslets (from the design on the reverse of the coin) issue of 1158. In the last year of his reign (1153) Stephen had ordered a recoinage, which was struck at 46 mints, and apparently to a good weight standard. On his accession, Henry II made no immediate change, but the collection of the geld in 1156 showed that there was still a great deal of poor coin in circulation. Anxious, on the eve of a major campaign in Toulouse, that he should have good money with which to pay his troops and allies, and that the profits of mint and exchange should be his, Henry ordered a major recoinage.

Hindsight has shown us that this was the beginning of a major reform in the coinage, but the immediate pressures behind it were entirely fiscal and

B: THE EMERGENCE OF A MONEY ECONOMY, 1158–1351

political. The new coins were struck at 31 mints and to a new and higher weight standard of 1.46 grams (22.53 grains), to bring the English money system into line with the Troy weight system used in Henry's French possessions. Nightingale argues that the introduction of the Troy pound would also have allowed a fixed mintage and seignorage charge of 1s in the £. The English Tower pound was created by 240 of the new pennies, and their weight was apparently calculated so that twelve pennies would weigh 17.5 grams (270 grains). This equalled the weight difference between the Tower pound of 350 grams and the Troy pound of 367.5 grams (5,401.32 and 5,671.38 grains respectively). By using the Troy pound the mints would be able to strike the 240 pennies of sterling fineness required from the Tower pound *and* a further 12 pennies of the same weight and fineness, which the king would keep for himself. There is no direct evidence to support this argument, but it makes sense, and fits in with changes being made in this period in Flanders and Cologne, two of England's main trading partners. New mint and seignorage charges meant extra expense for those changing money, however, and frequent recoinages would not have been popular. That may have been one of the spurs to the final abandonment of *renovatio monetae*, although, in practice, the intervals between recoinages had already become longer and longer in Henry I's reign.[5]

There is also much uncertainty about the volume of coin in circulation before the mid-1230s. In 1158 the existing coinage was effectively recycled. Using Metcalf's estimate of the number of dies needed to produce the Tealby coinage, and revised calculations of die output, Allen estimates that coins to the face value of somewhere between £30,000 and £80,000 were struck, while Latimer, using the same evidence, suggests much lower figures of between £20,000 and £50,000. The actual figure should lie somewhere in between these low/high estimates, but given that silver was still in short supply a steady growth from £25,000 in 1086 to about £40,000–£45,000 in 1158 seems possible, although that is no more than an educated guess. Initial output is not total output, given that there were topping-up issues between 1158 and 1180. Metcalf estimates total output at between £80,000 and £110,000, Mayhew more, at £125,000 although he also gives low/high estimates of £70,000 and £190,000 and thinks it unlikely that the silver currency exceeded £200,000 in 1180. That means it could still have been within the limits proposed by Metcalf and Mayhew and, given high wastage rates, a circulating medium of around £100,000 on the eve of the short-cross recoinage in 1180 looks possible. From about 1170 onward new European silver was beginning to flow to the English mints, so helping to increase amount of coin in circulation to four times the level it had been in 1086.[6]

The short-cross recoinage of 1180 and the partial recoinage of 1205

As we have seen, the complete recoinage of 1180 was undertaken both to replace a coinage of varying quality and because Henry seems to have been determined to press ahead and finish what had been begun in 1158 – that is, the extension of royal control over mints and exchanges. What he certainly could not have foreseen was that the short-cross coinage was to remain in circulation until 1247, with only a partial recoinage in 1205. Curiously, that meant coins in circulation bearing the name and bust of a King Henry through his reign and those of his successors Richard I (1189–99), John (1199–1216) and Henry III (1216–72), but that did not make them any the less acceptable. All of them were silver pennies, except for very small quantities of round halfpennies and farthings struck during Henry III's reign. The initial recoinage was undertaken at eleven mints, and the coins were of a good weight (1.46 grams), but by the early thirteenth century there were complaints about the number of lightweight pennies in circulation. The Jews were blamed for wholesale clipping, but this was to become the almost standard justification for a recoinage in the thirteenth century, the excuse needed to justify the costs involved, which were in the end borne by the population at large. The original writ and the subsequent assize of January 1205 ordering the recoinage do suggest that lightweight coins were causing problems. Old money, which did not lack more than 2s 6d in the pound, was to remain current, an unusually tolerant limit, suggesting real rather than imagined difficulties. Country-dwellers were to be allowed to have a hole bored through clipped coins, which were then returned to them, for use until they could be exchanged for new coin at the provincial mints reopened across the country for the recoinage.

The new pennies were to be of full weight and standard fineness (92.5 per cent), and were to have an outer circle round the reverse design to prevent clipping. As Mayhew points out, this was entirely impractical. All short-cross pennies since 1180, and the Tealby coins before them, were supposed to have had this outer circle, but when thousands upon thousands of hand-struck coins were made in a hurry, the dies often slipped and the circle was lacking. However, this does seem to have been a genuine attempt to improve the quality of the coinage, although the fact that John, much in need of cash, would have made a profit from the recoinage should not be ignored. By 1207 it seems to have been complete. A special review of the way it had been carried out was held in that year, to which all moneyers, assayers and keepers of the dies, and all masters of the mint were summoned to give advice on the making of coin. The outcome is not known, but this also suggests a genuine desire to maintain the quality

B: THE EMERGENCE OF A MONEY ECONOMY, 1158–1351

of the coinage. After 1207 production was concentrated at London and Canterbury, something that becomes abundantly clear the mid-1230s when written records that allow calculation of mint production begin. From then to the eve of the Long-cross recoinage in 1247 they were striking some 10 million pennies a year on average, which, in spite of the special pleading in 1247, seem to have been at the rate of 240 or at most 242 to the pound, and of standard fineness.[7]

The quality of this coinage is not in doubt: its quantity is. The key questions that should be asked about the short-cross coinage are:

1. how much was produced?
2. did production increase over time, so that more coin was produced after 1220 than before?
3. did the drain of money abroad for war or diplomacy, or hoarding by king, at times reduce dramatically the amount of coin available for making payments of all kinds?

There are no certain answers to any of these questions, but they have to be discussed, because rapid monetary inflation caused by a substantial increase in the money supply is offered as one of the major causes of economic change in the late twelfth and early thirteenth centuries.[8] Let us take first the difficult problems of production and the time scale of the increase in the volume of coin in circulation. On the eve of the short-cross recoinage in 1180 it stood at about £100,000, although estimates vary from £20,000 to £110,000. That was recycled between 1180 and 1182 and new silver was bought to produce somewhere between £9,250- and £18,500-worth of short-cross pennies annually between 1182 and c.1190. In sharp contrast, after the Tealby recoinage of 1138 the annual value of new issues was somewhere between £1,500 and £3,000 in the twenty years from 1160 to 1180, an indication of how rapidly the size of the circulating medium was increasing in the late twelfth century. Between 1180 and 1205 the mints probably produced coin worth in all £500,000. Natural wastage through loss and wear and tear and the heavy drain of coin abroad between 1189 and 1204 to pay for campaigns in defence of the Angevin territories in France would have left about £250,000 in circulation in 1205. The recoinage of 1205–7 may have produced anywhere between £200,000 and £500,000, all in pennies, and a figure of somewhere between £200,000 and £300,000 in circulation from about 1209 to the 1220s seems reasonable. From the mid-1230s, when written mint records become available, estimates take on a greater degree of certainty. Although they can only tell us about mint output, as opposed to the volume of coin in circulation, their evidence suggests a startling period of growth in the money supply in the late 1230s and early 1240s. They also indicate that the total output from English mints during the Long-cross recoinage of 1247–50 was about £585,000. If £150,000 is subtracted from that figure to allow for normal output not connected with the recoinage, that leaves between £425,000 and £450,000 in English coins available for striking into the new Long-cross issue on the eve of the recoinage of 1247.[9]

In short, there had been at least a fourfold increase in the money supply between 1180 and 1247. Silver had poured into England as a result of favourable trade balances, making it possible to strike millions upon millions of new coins. But the pattern of growth was not even. Latimer's estimates for the size of the circulating medium show two possible models. The first is based on a constant growth in the coinage, and shows a smooth upward curve in the money supply. The second shows a more uneven growth, since it takes into account variable yearly mint output, and extraordinary exports of coin. Both figures show that the main increase in the money supply came *after* and not *before* 1220, and particularly from the mid-1230s onward, but it is the second that is the more convincing and which now needs further consideration.[10]

The outflow of coin 1154–1244

From 1154 England became part of a wider 'Angevin Empire', a collection of duchies and counties stretching from south-western France to the English Channel. Henry II and Richard I defended them against all comers but by 1204 John had lost all but Aquitaine. He and his son Henry III, who succeeded his father in 1216, then made a series of abortive attempts to recover them. Successive kings used England as a source of treasure and large sums, in the form of coin, were sent abroad to pay for their wars and their alliances. Figure 6.1 shows Latimer's figures for such outflows, in absolute terms, but they must also be seen in relation to the total volume of coin in circulation since the deflationary consequences of a loss of £50,000 from a coinage of c.£250,000 in 1213–14 would have been more severe than those resulting from the loss of £70,000 from a coinage of c.£450,000 in 1241–43. Even allowing for a steady growth in the population, there would still have been more coin per head of population for use in the expanding economy of the early 1240s. Given this, it can be seen that there were exceptional and probably damaging outflows in the 1190s and early 1200s, to pay for wars with France, the Third Crusade, Richard I's ransom and John's disastrous attempts to recover Normandy in 1213–14. In the 1220s and early 1230s outflows were less on an annual basis, but sometimes quite high when taken over a period of years. Subsidies to the

Figure 6.1 The outflow of coin 1180–1250

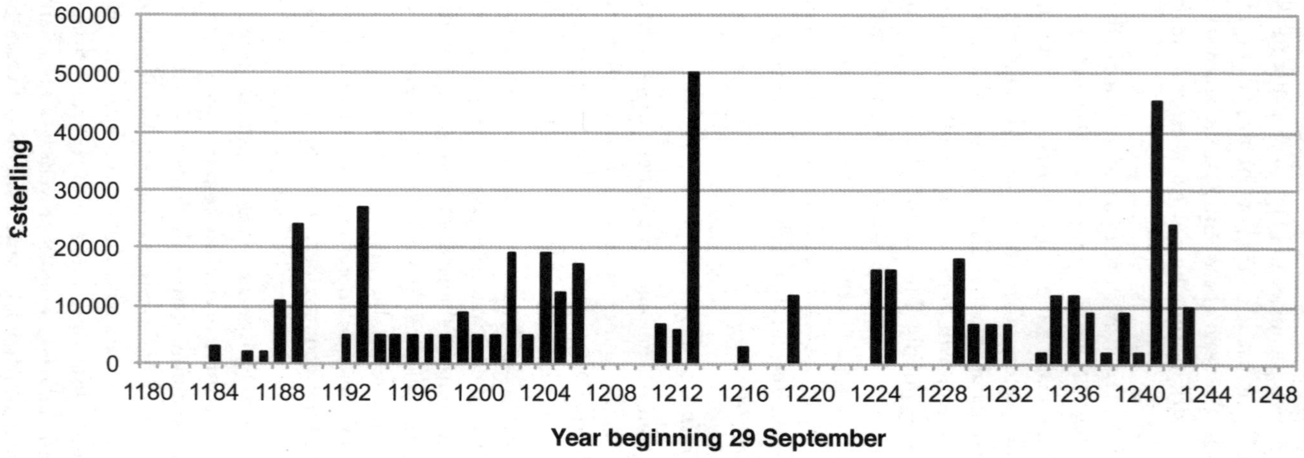

Source: P. Latimer, 'The quantity of money in England 1180–1247: a model', *JEEH*, 32, 2004, Table 5, 651.

duke of Brittany and payments made in Poitou and Gascony cost £7,000 a year between 1230 and 1234, and £12,000 a year was spent on the dowry of Henry III's sister and on Poitevin and Gascon fees from 1235 to 1237. Futile expeditions to Gascony in the early 1240s brought overseas expenditure back to the levels of the early thirteenth century, but possibly with less damaging consequences for the economy because, by then, the money supply was much larger. Not all the money would have flowed abroad, of course, unless it was specifically earmarked for the payment of papal taxes, subsidies to allies, a king's ransom or a sister's dowry. Foreign expeditions meant substantial expenditure within England on shipping, equipment, fodder for horses and foodstuffs for men, while some of the money paid in fees, wages and expenses for service abroad would have been brought or sent home. Nevertheless, losses from silver shipped abroad were at times very substantial.[11]

Silver imports 1154-1247

On the credit side of the balance sheet were imports of silver, without which the increasing volume of new coins could not have been struck. The main way in which bullion was acquired was through favourable trade balances, largely the result of wool exports to Flanders, but the flow of silver to the mints was subject to constant interruptions. The politics and warfare of the late twelfth and the first half of the thirteenth century meant that trade with Flanders was often brought to a standstill. Between the late 1170s and 1193 it flowed freely, but then the war between Richard I and Philip Augustus led to such a severe slump that Baldwin IX, count of Flanders, was forced to abandon his French alliance in favour of one with England, in order to secure wool supplies for the Flemish towns. Freedom of trade did not long survive the renewed outbreak of war between John and Philip Augustus, and between 1205 and 1213-14 the position of Flemish merchants in England was precarious. These were years when Flemish merchants dominated the wool-export trade, and if they could not move freely within the realm, without fear of reprisal, then silver would not flow to the mints. From 1218 to 1223 normal trading relations seem to have been resumed, but there were continuing difficulties with Flanders and France in the late 1220s. Lloyd argues that the major expansion in the wool trade came only after 1236, with only a brief interruption in its growth at the time of Henry III's Gascon expedition of 1241-42.[12]

The consequences of losses of coin abroad and fluctuations in the supply of silver for both mint output and for the volume of coin in circulation have been estimated by Latimer. He shows that there was a sharp rise in the circulating medium in the 1180s, albeit from a fairly low base, followed by a period of contraction in the 1190s and early 1200s due to a combination of coin exports and shortages of silver at the mints, a recovery in the second decade of the century, especially as the wool trade picked up between 1218 and 1223, then a sharp fall back in the late 1220s and early 1230s until new supplies of silver brought a very rapid rise in the circulating medium from about 1235–36 onward. The amount of coin in circulation may also have been severely affected between 1207 and 1213–14 by royal hoarding, a subject to be discussed further below when late twelfth- and early thirteenth-century inflation is considered. The lesson to be learned from Figure 6.1 is clear, however, and would certainly remain the same whatever figures were used for the size of the circulating medium, namely that although there was a significant rise in the money supply in the late twelfth century, we should look to the late 1210s and early 1220s and then to the decade after about 1235–36 for the most substantial increases. The implications for the expansion of the economy are of considerable importance.[13]

The long-cross coinage 1247–79

By 1247 the short-cross coinage had been in circulation for 67 years. One might perhaps suppose that the coinage must have been old and worn, but it should be remembered that the coinage was constantly being renewed, to replace losses of up to £250,000 a decade through wear and tear. A new coinage was ordered in 1247, but with the curious proviso that 'all great and good pennies and halfpennies of the old money not clipped should be current with the new'. So, old short-cross and new long-cross coins ran side by side for a brief transitional period. Then, four months after the introduction of the long-cross pennies, a commission was convened at Westminster to compare the old and the new money. The old short-cross and the new long-cross pennies were assayed and, while the new coins were found to be no more than 6d less than pure, the old ones were declared 10d less than pure 'wherefore it was clear to all that it [the old coinage] was not good or lawful'. This was used as justification for a complete recoinage, and the valuation of the old coinage, at 10d in the pound light, was applied to all the old short-cross pennies brought to the exchanges. It was not a favourable exchange rate. In addition to the king's seignorage of 6d, bullion holders suffered a further deduction of 10d in each pound, 6d for the traditional mintage costs and a further 4d because of the better quality of the new coin. That meant a deduction of 16d in the pound, but on top of that there were further charges to allow for the light weight of the old coin. The chronicler Matthew Paris, who speaks of a deduction of only 13d in the pound, nonetheless says that the people suffered great hardship as a result: 'twenty shillings could scarcely be obtained from the money changers for thirty, without the trouble and expense of several days duration and tedious expectation'. Modern metal analysis has found that there was in fact little or no difference between the purity or fineness of the short-cross and long-cross coins, and the problem appears to have been mainly one of light weight. This does raise the question of the need for a recoinage, and of who needed it. There is some evidence that worn coin was causing price increases in the years immediately before 1247, but it is worth speculating that a king deprived of regular taxation was looking rather desperately for an additional source of revenue, while his brother, Richard of Cornwall, who financed the initial costs of the recoinage, stood to make a handsome profit.[14]

The new coinage was struck principally at London, Canterbury and Bury St Edmunds. Additional provincial mints were opened, first at Norwich, Northampton, Exeter, Winchester and Lincoln, and then at Wallingford, Bristol, Ilchester, Hereford, Newcastle-on-Tyne, Nottingham, Carlisle, Shrewsbury and Wilton. All, except perhaps Nottingham, were in operation early in 1249 but were closed again by 1250. The accounts for London and Canterbury show that coins to the value of £287,470 were struck between November 1247 and July 1250. Hoard evidence suggests that about the same amount was struck at the provincial mints in the same period, and so the whole recoinage produced in about three years £550,000–575,000 or some 138,000,000 pennies, of controlled weight and fineness, at a daily rate of about 150,000 coins. Of this, between £425,000 and £450,000 came from recycling the old coins, and the rest from foreign silver, which means that the foreign silver coming to the mints in 1247–50 equalled in face value the circulating medium in 1180. As Mayhew says, the administrative achievement was considerable, and the level of technical competence and speed with which the recoinage was accomplished impressive.[15]

The actual amount of coin in circulation was always less than the total amount of coin produced by the mints. Losses through wear and tear came to about £250,000 per decade, and to make them good, and to add to the currency, the London and Canterbury mints remained in constant production after the main recoinage was over. They were particularly active in the 1250s, striking pennies to the value of £5,000–6,000 per annum, but there was a sharp fall in output in the 1260s, at the time of the mint reorganisation of 1262, with some recovery thereafter until the 1270s when it fell to below £2,000 a year. Archibald estimates that between 1247 and 1278

B: THE EMERGENCE OF A MONEY ECONOMY, 1158–1351

£1,700,000-worth of pennies were produced, and that total losses were £1,033,016, leaving some £666,984 in circulation in 1278, on the eve of the next recoinage. Allen opts for a broader range of between £500,000 and £600,000 in circulation while Latimer estimates it at between £500,000 and £700,000. This would suggest steady growth in the size of the circulating medium during the period of the long-cross coinage, after the sharp rise in the 1230s and 1240s. Perhaps the political upheavals and civil wars between 1258 and 1267, and then the accession of a new and distrusted king in 1272 held back expansion. Whatever the reasons might have been, it is clear that the next, and massive expansion in the money supply was to come in the decade after the recoinage of 1279.[16]

A failed experiment: gold in 1257

Before the end of his reign, Henry III tried and failed to introduce a gold coinage. Some foreign gold coins were already in circulation in twelfth- and early thirteenth-century England, and were used both to make payments and for ceremonial alms-giving. Thanks to the work of Carpenter and Cook, it is now clear that the main gold coin in use was the bezant from the Byzantine Empire, which was 20½ fine (that is, 93 per cent pure gold), weighed up to 4.4 grams (67.90 grains) and when it was used in England for making payments its value was two shillings. Payments were also being made by the ounce of gold, equal to 15s in silver, and the mark of gold, at £6. These were not just moneys of account nor payments that had once been made in gold and were now being made in the equivalent amount of silver. Carpenter and Cook both insist that gold bezants were actually used, and Carpenter has shown how between 1243 and 1253, and then between 1253 and 1258, Henry III set about building up two gold 'treasures', or hoards. The first he was forced to spend to finance a campaign in Gascony in 1253–54, since he could not persuade the barons to grant him taxation to meet his costs; the second was sold in London and Paris in 1259–60 and in London in 1261. Henry acquired his gold in the form of dust, leaf and in coins: bezants, a few of the Emperor Frederick II's magnificent augustales, and dinars and double dinars of the Almohad dynasty – the Moors or Arabs who ruled large parts of Spain and North Africa between 1130 and 1269. The king demanded payment in gold in return for grants of privileges such as the right to keep a warren, or to hold markets and fairs, and also for the fines levied for not taking up the dignity of knighthood. The Jews were also made to pay fines in gold, but the expansion of Henry's treasure after 1249–50 was certainly the result of a deliberate policy of using silver to buy gold.[17]

Between 1243 and 1258, and by various means and in various forms, Henry had amassed a gold treasure worth, in silver equivalent, some 28,390 marks or about £19,000. Why he acquired this gold is not at all clear. It may have been to finance his proposed crusade to the Holy Land, since by the mid-thirteenth century gold was the preferred method in the Mediterranean world for making large payments, for both war and trade. If this was the reason, then his plans were frustrated by the need to pay for the Gascon campaign in 1253–54. On his return from that failed enterprise, Henry set about acquiring another treasure, and this time its purpose was to pay for an army in Italy to establish his son Edmund on the throne of Sicily. But, in the summer of 1257 a new problem loomed, the need for a new campaign against the Welsh and no money to pay for it. If Henry had simply sold his gold on the open market, then the price per ounce would have fallen sharply, as was indeed to happen in 1259–61. Instead he decided to mint his own gold coins, fix their value and insist that they be accepted. If they were, then he stood to make a handsome profit from seignorage, as merchants brought gold to the exchanges for reminting. The new gold pennies were issued in the summer of 1257. Each was worth 20 silver pennies, at a gold:silver ratio of 1:10, since the new coin was of pure gold and weighed two silver pennies. In all, some 52,480 gold pennies with a silver value of £4,373 6s 8d were struck, but the experiment ended in compete failure. By the November of 1257 the mayor and citizens of London, when asked whether the gold coinage was of use for the common benefit of the kingdom or not, replied emphatically that it would do great harm to the realm and especially to the poor people whose chattels were not worth one gold coin. These may have been crocodile tears since, given the small amount of gold in circulation and the high value of each coin, the peasantry would never have seen let alone used gold pennies. The real reasons for the failure are not hard to see. Henry's vigorous purchases of gold had pushed up its price, but then he suddenly released a substantial quantity of the metal in the form of the new pennies, and the price of gold fell sharply. This hit the pockets of those merchants who held gold and it meant that one gold penny was simply not worth twenty silver pennies, so the coins were rejected. In any case, there was at this point neither enough gold in England nor coming to England to sustain a new and substantial coinage. When compared to a silver coinage of about £550,000 in 1257, or 132,000,000 pennies, the amount of gold put into circulation, some £4,400, was tiny. A new gold coinage was not needed in mid-thirteenth-century England. Silver still reigned supreme.[18]

B: THE EMERGENCE OF A MONEY ECONOMY, 1158-1351

The recoinage of 1279-90

Edward I's reasons for ordering a complete recoinage in 1279 are not at all clear, perhaps because they were not entirely honest. There is some evidence to suggest that, after 30 years in circulation, the long-cross coinage was becoming old and worn. The trend of prices for both grain and livestock was steadily upward in the 1270s, with some sharp increases immediately before the recoinage. The escheator in Cornwall went as far as to complain that the coinage was in such a poor state that the collection of taxes was proving almost impossible.[19] Against this monetary background, in 1277 the king embarked upon his conquest of Wales. The campaign was brief and relatively inexpensive, since the accounts show it cost about £23,000. There were still castles to be built, however, to control the newly conquered lands and it was clear that another campaign would be needed to complete the conquest. A subsidy, or tax on moveable property, of a fifteenth had been granted in 1275, but it was still being collected in 1279. The king's Italian bankers, the Riccardi of Lucca, had advanced him £22,476 for the first Welsh war, and in 1277-78 they lent him a further £18,233. They, and other Italian bankers, had to be repaid, from the proceeds of the fifteenth of 1275 – and from the tempting profits of a major and thorough recoinage.[20]

The recoinage of 1279 was precisely that. Edward I did not give his subjects a choice. In August 1280 he forbade any further use of long-cross coins and so successful was this demonetisation that they have not been found in coin hoards deposited after 1279-80.[21] High seignorage and mintage charges were set, at 9d and 10d in the pound respectively, something that was only possible when there was a compulsory recoinage. Seignorage was raised to 12d in the pound in 1280 but then fell back to 9d in 1281. Those who held long-cross coins had no option but to take them to be exchanged for the new coins, although the high charges do seem to have deterred merchants from bringing foreign silver to the mints. Nevertheless, the king's profits were substantial. Mate suggests that between 1279 and 1281 the London mint alone yielded the crown £18,219, and that in all the king received about £25,000 from the recoinage. That was a valuable addition to royal finances, at a time when the king needed to repay loans made to cover the costs of his Welsh campaign.[22]

A compulsory recoinage, ordered as much to raise revenues as to improve the coinage, had to be justified. Edward sought to do so in a distasteful and for him profitable way. At the start of his reign he had launched an all-out attack on coin clipping and particularly on alleged coin-clipping by the Jews. This culminated in 1279 with what amounted to a show trial.

Commissioners of inquiry were sent into the various counties of England, charged with the task of discovering and arresting those who were clipping coins, and officials who were conniving at coin clipping for their personal profit. As a result, 480 Jews and 1,110 Christians were arrested and then brought to trial at the Guildhall in London, 269 Jews were then convicted and hanged, but only 29 Christians. The Jews suffered out of all proportion to their involvement in coin-clipping and related offences, since much less evidence seems to have been required to convict a Jew than a Christian. It is hard to avoid the conclusion that the king was as much interested in the profits of justice as in justice itself, since the fines and sale of forfeited goods brought him no less than £10,815 14s 4d. The show trial also helped to undermine the confidence in the old coinage, as did the trial and execution of two mint officials, Philip de Cambio and William de Harlewyn, for adding more than the permitted amount of copper to the silver from which coins were being struck. Attacks on the Jews were always popular and what better way to justify a complete recoinage than to provide 'proof' that the long-cross coins had suffered from extensive clipping, especially when it could be done at a considerable profit?[23]

This was the background to what was to prove one of the most important re-coinages in medieval England. The new pennies were of the same fineness as, and only 0.41 per cent lighter than, the previous issue. Initial output was not high. Allen estimates that the face value of the silver available for recoining was between £500,000 and £600,000, but because the old coins were of light weight, this provided bullion for a lesser amount of new money. Significantly, given the needs of an increasingly commercialised economy for small change, round farthings were minted for the first time in 1279 and, when they proved popular, round halfpennies were struck from August 1280.[24] Lastly, and much influenced by the growing practice abroad, Edward issued a new, heavier, silver coin, the groat, worth four pennies. It was a failure. As with Henry III's gold penny twenty-two years earlier, there was no need as yet for such a high-value coin.[25]

By 1281 the initial recoinage was complete. It had been struck mainly at London and Canterbury, but there were also eight other mints in operation, the ecclesiastical-privilege mints at Durham, York and Bury St Edmunds, and five others opened or reopened for the purpose at Bristol, York, Newcastle on Tyne, Lincoln, and Winchester. The ecclesiastical mints continued working after 1281, when the provincial mints closed. At the same time Edward I ordered a major recoinage in Ireland which began in May 1280, and in Scotland Alexander III followed the English king's example, as he had already done in 1250, by issuing new pennies, halfpennies and farthings, the single-cross coinage which lasted from 1280 to 1351. Substantial quantities of both Irish and Scottish coins then passed into circulation in England.[26]

There then followed a quite extraordinary expansion in the volume of coin in circulation. Allen estimates that by 1282 there were pennies to the value of between £760,000 and £800,000 in circulation, plus £20,000–50,000 in groats, and *c.*£40,000 in halfpennies and farthings, making a total of somewhere between £800,000 and £900,000, compared with £425,000–450,000 on the eve of the long-cross recoinage in 1247. By 1290 that had risen to between £900,000 and £1,100,000 in pennies, £40,000 in halfpennies and farthings, and between £90,000 and £170,000 of foreign sterling imitations, the notorious pollards and crockards, making a total of between £1,000,000 and £1,300,000, although these estimates have been criticised by Mayhew as being too high.[27] The money supply seems to have roughly doubled in ten years, an astonishing rate of growth quite outstripping anything that had happened in the previous century. The explanation for this is quite simple: a massive influx of foreign silver. The high seignorage and mintage charges had at first discouraged merchants from bringing new silver (as opposed to old coins) to the exchanges. At the height of the recoinage, between October 1280 and March 1281, the Canterbury mint received only £813 of foreign silver, and it had to rely almost entirely on recycling old coins for the bullion it needed. Then, in February, Edward I reduced his seignorage charges from 12d to 9d, so that from each pound of old English money he received only 16d instead of 19d and from each pound of foreign silver only 14½ d. The effect was almost immediate. The mint price offered was now very attractive, compared with that at other mints in north-western Europe, and the English mints were almost swamped by a tidal wave of silver. Between March and 3 May 1281, the amount of foreign silver brought to Canterbury more than doubled, between May and September 1281, it reached £15,936, and in the following year £23,000, compared to old English coins worth only £1,688. The figures for London are even more startling. Between September 1281 and April 1290 the London mint received and recycled English coins worth £89,645. During the same period £218,708 of new or foreign silver was brought to the mint.[28] Not all the new coins struck from it stayed in the country. The foreign merchants who brought the silver to England took the new money they received out of the country, and so, to stop the drain of coin abroad, in 1283 Edward I forbade the export of English money. This did not lead to the desired or expected result. Foreign princes began to strike imitation sterlings of slightly lesser weight and fineness, but accepted in England as true silver pennies. So there began a long and unsuccessful battle to prevent them passing into circulation. Extra searches were ordered at the ports and in 1284 a detailed schedule of the different kinds of false coins was circulated, but it is doubtful whether foreign imitations were a real problem before 1290, or even in the 1290s. England at this time seems to have had a voracious appetite for coin, and foreign imitations were an important supplement to the circulating medium.[29]

The circulating medium in 1290

In 1180 somewhere in the region of £100,000-worth of coin was in circulation. By 1290 that figure stood at between £1,000,000 and £1,300,000, including foreign imitations which accounted for about £140,000 to £170,000, and halfpennies and farthings (but no groats) worth between £50,000 and £60,000. The significant increases had come not between 1180 and 1220, as has traditionally been claimed, but in the 1230s and 1240s, and then in the 1280s when, in less than one decade, the circulating medium doubled. Coinage per head of population had reached new levels by 1290 and that is of significant importance in any discussion of when a money economy finally emerged in medieval England. But from 1290 onward the country entered a period of political crisis and of monetary instability caused first by too many and then by not enough silver coins in circulation and then, with the introduction of a gold coinage in 1343–44, by the problems inherent in bimetallic currencies and by an acute shortage of silver.

Monetary instability 1290–1343: the crisis of silver

1290–1300: pollards and crockards

The 1290s were a decade of war with France and Scotland, of rebellion in Wales, of heavy taxation of the laity and clergy, of new export duties upon wool, and of acute political crisis. In three years alone, between 1294 and 1297, no less than £750,000 was raised in taxation of all kinds and, of that, £550,000 was shipped abroad, mostly to pay for an elaborate system of alliances to contain France. At the same time there was a sudden and almost complete collapse in the quantity of silver coming to the exchanges. English coins were in such short supply that they were not being brought for reminting, and foreign silver was simply not to be had. Given the heavy drain of coin abroad, and the normal processes of wear and tear, this meant that the coinage was not being replaced. Mint activity almost ceased, and that at Canterbury had to close between 1296 and 1299 because of a shortage

B: THE EMERGENCE OF A MONEY ECONOMY, 1158–1351

of silver. There was little coin to be had in an England where society had become accustomed to using money for making payments of all kinds. As a result, the yield of taxation declined between 1295 and 1297 and grain prices fell sharply as a result of monetary deflation. If there were no English coins available then substitutes had to be found, in the form of foreign imitations of English sterlings, the infamous pollards and crockards.[30]

War, or rather the costs of war, cannot alone explain this crisis in the currency. The underlying problem was the collapse in silver imports. In part this was due to difficulties in the wool trade, which had earned so much bullion in the 1280s. Wool exports initially continued at high levels, reaching a peak in the early 1290s. When war broke out they fell sharply, but they recovered quickly after 1297. The underlying reasons for the silver shortage were thus more complex. There was a temporary shortage of silver in Europe, a foretaste of things to come. The older mines were gradually becoming worked out and new supplies from Kutná Hora did not come on stream until about 1300. International competition for bullion became intense. Edward I's adversary, Philip IV of France, faced the same costs of war but lacked his rival's ability to tax his subjects effectively. He turned instead to a cynical manipulation of the coinage for his own gain. The devaluation and revaluation of the currency brought howls of protest within France, but diverted bullion that might have come to England to the French mints. There was further competition for silver from mints in the Low Countries where, ironically, imitation sterlings were being struck. Minting these imitations had begun in Brabant in 1283, when Duke Jean I issued coins of like weight and fineness as the new English pennies. They had the same design on the reverse but a lion and shield on the obverse, instead of the king's head. These coins were then imitated by his neighbours, and began to pass into circulation in England. Then, starting about 1290, Guy of Dampierre, as count of Namur, issued a new type of coin, identical to the English penny except that the king's head on the obverse was bare instead of crowned. Later, the duke of Brabant thought of putting a garland of roses around the king's head, and other princes followed his example. These imitations came to be known as pollards and crockards and the mints issuing them offered attractive prices for silver. Merchants would receive more imitations for each pound of silver they took to these mints than they would English pennies at London or Canterbury, and pollards and crockards were being widely accepted in England. The attractions were obvious and silver flowed to mints in the Low Countries and France and not to the English mints.[31]

All attempts to keep them out of the country failed and by 1299 there were perhaps between £300,000 and £350,000 of them by face value in circulation.[32] They have received a 'bad press'. They have been blamed for causing high prices, since it took more coins of poor quality to buy any given article, and there were familiar murmurings about bad money. Yet such complaints should be treated with caution. Some of the coins were of poor quality, but many were scarcely distinguishable from pennies in weight and fineness, and this is confirmed by the exchange rate of 22s of pollards and crockards to 20s sterling which actually brought them within the legitimate weight range for English sterlings. Heavy pennies were often culled, or picked out, for their silver content, leaving the lighter and sometimes clipped coins in circulation, barely distinguishable from imitations which fitted well into the English monetary system. Given the shortage of silver at the English mints and the drain of coin abroad, pollards and crockards may have been needed in an economy increasingly starved of coin.[33]

The recoinage of 1300-2

For the English crown the influx of foreign imitations was more serious. If silver was not flowing to English mints, then the king was being deprived of valuable revenue from seignorage. The government believed that the imitations only began to arrive in substantial quantities with the return of the English army from Flanders in 1298, and there may be some truth in this. It was at about this time that men began to insist on debts being paid in good and lawful sterlings, always a bad sign for the currency. Edward I faced a choice. He could either debase, and so attract foreign silver back to the mint, or he could order a partial recoinage in the hope of eliminating the pollards and crockards. He chose the latter course, but his first step, by the Statute of Stepney of May 1299, was to prohibit the export of English coins and silver in plate, and to order more rigorous searches to prevent the import of false coins. Only sterlings or hall-marked plate of standard fineness could be used for commercial transactions within England, except when they were made by written book transfers involving eventual payment in cash. The effectiveness of this legislation was almost completely undermined by the privileges given to the king's Italian bankers, however, and in any case it did not deal with the large quantities of crockards and pollards already in general circulation. So, in December 1299 it was proclaimed that pollards and crockards were to be current for only half their face value (a halfpenny rather than a penny) and that from Easter 1300 they were to be demonetised. This had some curious consequences. It was now more profitable to take the pollards and crockards to the exchanges, where, because of their good silver content they were worth more than their face value of a halfpenny. At the same time, many refused to take the imitations in payment for goods, or accept them in repayment for debts, demanding good sterlings instead. But the partial recoinage of 1300-2 was, in the end, a considerable success. Its purpose was quite specific, the elimination of pollards and crockards, which had to be taken to be taken to the mints for striking into substantial quantities of new English money. The mint accounts show that over £262,000 was recoined between 1300 and 1302, and although pollards and crockards were never completely eliminated, nevertheless the great bulk of the coinage was now English pennies, along with substantial quantities of halfpennies and farthings.[34]

Early fourteenth-century problems: monetary fluctuations

The consequences of the second recoinage in Edward's reign were much the same as those of the first. Silver in quite staggering quantities suddenly flowed to the English mints. Much of it came from the profits of a boom in the wool trade, as native merchants in particular brought back foreign silver for recycling. It has also been argued that the English mint price for silver was more attractive than that being offered at continental mints, so that silver that in the past had been taken to mints in the Low Countries and France now came to England. Lloyd has shown that between 1303 and 1309 were coined 634,381 lbs. of silver, with an aggregate face value of £642,362 and that 99 per cent of this silver was foreign. Between 1311 and 1321 (there is a gap of two years in the records after 1309) mint activity was at a lower level, with output falling significantly after 1313, but, even so, 259,705 lbs. of silver were coined, with a face value of £268,009 and, again, 98 per cent of this silver was foreign. Much of the coin seems to have stayed in England, thanks to the enforcement of the laws against the export of coin, and the result was a very substantial increase in the money supply. Allen argues for much higher figures than have previously been advanced, with possible totals of between £1,500,000 and £2,000,000 in 1310 and between £1,900,000 and £2,300,000 in 1319, all in silver coins although, as we have seen, Mayhew has considerable reservations about the methodology used to arrive at these estimates and suggests that they should be substantially lower. In some ways the actual figures are not of importance, however. What can be said, with certainty, is that in terms of volume, this was the high point of the medieval English currency. Never again was there to be as much coin in circulation, and particularly silver coin, pennies, halfpennies and farthings, the money used by the poor, of whom there were many.[35]

Boom was inexorably followed by bust. In 1309 foreign silver worth

£93,336 had been brought to the London mint but by 1317–18 this figure had fallen to just over £12,663 and by 1321–22 to £1,118. After 1324 the mint at Canterbury closed, because no silver was available, and scarcely any new money was made at London. It is also quite possible that after 1324 and perhaps as early as 1319 more money was being taken out of the country than was being minted, so reducing the volume of coin in circulation, as continental rulers began to offer more attractive mint prices for silver. There was no recovery in silver supplies in the 1330s, and by 1335 the only course of action left to safeguard the silver coinage seemed to be debasement. Between 1335 and 1344 only halfpennies and farthings were struck at ten ounces fine as against the standard sterling fineness of 11 ounces 2 pennyweights, so reducing the silver fineness and weight by 13.1 per cent. This had the effect of attracting some silver to the mints, but it also undermined confidence in the coinage, both at home and abroad. The halfpennies and farthings were intended for use in England, but their debasement cast doubt on the coinage as a whole. There was little point in bringing silver to English mints only to receive back new coins of suspect fineness, while within England itself the men of Devon refused to use the new halfpennies and farthings in 1339. It is quite clear that the volume of silver coin in circulation was falling fast. Allen's figures for 1331 suggest that it stood at only three-quarters of what it had been in 1319, and Mayhew believes the fall to have been even greater, from about £1,100,000 in 1311 to only about £500,000 by the early 1340s. Complaints about the lack of coin grew at the same time as prices fell, certainly as a result of monetary deflation. The chronicler Knighton saw the shortage of money as the main cause of low prices in 1336 and the remembrancers of the parliament held at Westminster in 1339 also complained about the general scarcity of coin. The crown sought to remedy the situation by banning the export of both coin and plate. Ordinances in 1331 and 1335 forbade the export of English coin and ordered that all foreign coins brought to England must be taken to the mints for reminting. The searchers at the various ports were offered rewards if they discovered money being smuggled out of the realm, and in 1340 the Statute of Westminster required every merchant to bring back to England two ounces of silver for each sack of wool exported. None of this seems to have been of any avail. When 'black' money called 'turneys' containing little or no silver was made in Ireland, the king immediately banned its circulation but then had to allow it 'on account of the scarcity of sterling money'.[36]

By the 1340s the volume of silver coin in circulation had probably fallen back to the level it had been in 1247, to no more than about £500,000. The

B: THE EMERGENCE OF A MONEY ECONOMY, 1158-1351

immediate causes for this sharp decline are fairly straightforward. Between 1323 and 1329 the balance of trade deteriorated rapidly. A bitter civil war in Flanders had serious consequences for wool exports and although they recovered between 1329 and 1336, no new silver flowed to the English mints as a result. At the same time, coin began to flow abroad to pay for wars. Considerable sums were paid to the Scots in protection money in Edward II's reign. Durham paid over £2,000 in 1313 and the people of the Western March were blackmailed into handing over £1,466 in 1313-14, a sum they could ill afford. All this went straight into the coffers of Robert the Bruce, and it may help explain the large quantities of English silver to be found circulating in Scotland in the early fourteenth century.[37] The costs of defending the English possessions in Gascony during the War of St Sardos (1324-25) were a further drain and then, from 1337, came the opening stages of the Hundred Years War. Between 1338 and 1340 Edward spent about £400,000 in the Low Countries. Most of it was raised abroad, by loans from Italian banking houses such as the Bardi and Peruzzi and by calling on money that would otherwise have come back to England. The greater part of all wool exported between August 1336 and the summer of 1343 was despatched in the king's name, and the income from its sale expended in the Low Countries. The profits from the sale of such wool as was exported privately by native and alien merchants, outside this scheme, were handed over to the king in Flanders as loans which were to be repaid in England, in sterling, from tax revenues. Consequently, very little silver came to the mints from the profits of the wool trade and the results were obvious.[38]

In a sense these were immediate problems, peculiar to the 1320s, 1330s and 1340s. Of much more long-term significance was the growing general shortage of silver in western Europe as mining output began to fall. First the Villa di Chiesa mines at Iglesias went into sharp decline in the 1330s and 1340s and then those at Kutná Hora a little later. But what made matters worse was the continuing flow of silver from western Europe to the near East to pay for the increasing volume of imported luxury goods. Two handbooks compiled by member of great Italian trading companies, the Venetian *Zibaldone da Canal* of about 1311 and what is usually known as Pegalotti's list but more properly his *Practica della mercatura*, drawn up for the Bardi of Florence in the 1340s, show how silver from Germany and central Europe went to pay for imports of primary products and for silk from China, spices from the East Indies, precious stones and spices from India, and pearls from the Persian Gulf. Such silver losses were sustainable when mining output was high, but once it fell, then they began to cause problems, first for the Mediterranean world and then for western Europe, because the general pool of silver was being depleted.[39]

The silver losses resulting from trade deficits were compounded by what are known as 'bi-metallic flows', the exchange of silver for gold, and gold for silver. The theory behind such flows may be briefly stated thus. If gold is plentiful in one area while silver is in short supply and much in demand, then silver will be more highly valued than gold, and a relatively small amount of silver can be exchanged for a much greater weight of gold. If, conversely, silver is plentiful in another area, and gold is not, but again in high demand, then a small quantity of gold can be exchanged for a much greater amount of silver. It follows that silver will flow to the area where it is in demand, to be exchanged for gold, and vice versa. This, roughly speaking, was the situation that obtained between southern Europe and northern Africa. Gold had always been used in the Mediterranean world and, has been seen, Frederick II's augustales, Byzantine bezants and Almoravid and Almohad dinars circulated widely, even reaching England.[40] Then, in 1252 and almost simultaneously, Genoa and Florence started striking their own gold coins, the ducat and the florin respectively. Sufficient gold was now available from northern Africa via trade routes across the Sahara to the Western Sudan, its source, to allow this. They needed such coins for their trade in the Mediterranean, and particularly for the transit trade between the Maghreb and the Levant. Venice was not as heavily involved in this trade and stocks of gold were slow to accumulate there, but by 1284 it too was striking gold ducats, of similar fineness to the florin.

Gold was now established as the preferred currency for international trade and for financing wars and its use spread, slowly, northward. Attempts first by Henry III of England and then by St Louis (Louis IX) of France to introduce gold coinages were failures. There was neither as yet sufficient gold available in the north to launch successful coinages nor at that point any real need for gold coins in either England or France. But by 1296 when Philip IV of France attempted to introduce a gold coinage for the second time, he met with more success. The bullion his mints needed came from Italy along the trade routes across the Alps and up the Rhône valley, but then, from about 1320 onward, large quantities of gold began to flow from the Hungarian mines at Kremnica. Gold was highly valued in France, and silver flowed out of the country to pay for it, so much so that between October 1329 and September 1330 and then from March 1334 to February 1336 all the French mints were closed for want of silver. When they did resume production, attractive mint prices were set, which drew

B: THE EMERGENCE OF A MONEY ECONOMY, 1158–1351

silver from England. By 1337 there was enough gold in France for Philip VI to strike an enormous issue of écus, and the opening stages of the Hundred Years War were paid for in gold by both England and France. As a result gold coins, high in value and low in bulk compared to silver ingots, became the preferred way of making large payments in north-western Europe for both war and trade. Mints in Brabant, Hainault, Cambrai and Guelders all began to mint gold for the first time in 1336–37 and silver began to flow southward to Italy and south-eastward to Hungary in increasing quantities to pay for it. Thence, via Venice and Genoa, it flowed to the Near East, where it was highly valued, and from Spain to North Africa, where a lucrative export trade in forged silver dihrams developed.[41]

For England the spread of gold posed a peculiar and particular problem. Edward III may have tried to prohibit the use of gold coins in England, but the fact of the matter was that they were in circulation and in substantial quantities. Wool exports were being paid for in gold, and it is often argued that it was the difficulties caused by the fixed exchange rate between the gold florin and sterling that finally decided Edward to mint his own gold coins. The wholesale trade in wool in the Netherlands was conducted in gold florins, which were priced at 3s sterling, far more than they were worth on the open market. The merchants alleged in parliament that because of this fixed exchange rate they were losing 'one third on all merchandise imported thence'. Prestwich has shown that this was unlikely since exchange rates in the early fourteenth century fluctuated widely. This caused problems for the Italians who dealt in bills of exchange, where profits came from differences in exchange rates between country and country. Edward III had forced his bankers, the Bardi and Peruzzi, to accept an artificial fixed rate of exchange of 3s to the florin, although this did not apply to the English wool exporters. Rather, debasement of the French silver coinage and the heavy output of gold from Flemish and French mints meant that the gold florins English merchants brought home with them were probably worth less in 1343 than they had been in previous years, but this had nothing to do with Edward's agreement with the Bardi and Peruzzi.[42]

By 1343 there was a general crisis in the English currency. Gold had come to command a higher price in England than on the continent, something that persisted for the rest of the Middle Ages. As a result, silver was leaving the country at an alarming rate, and even the partial recovery of the wool-export trade did not bring enough silver to the mints to alleviate a desperate shortage of coin in the winter of 1342–43. The debased halfpennies and farthings were being refused, and the wool exporters could not sell the gold they earned abroad to the mint, at a profit, simply because there was as yet no English gold coinage. Complaints in parliament about the state of the coinage were growing and the export of all bullion had been forbidden. A general debasement seems to have been considered, and rejected, but it was quite clear that a general silver recoinage was now necessary, and that some action had to be taken over gold. What cannot have been so obvious to contemporaries was that much of the problem was caused by events beyond their control, namely growing shortages of silver as a result of falling mining output, adverse international trade balances and bi-metallic flows.

The revaluation of silver and the introduction of gold, 1343-51

On 3 December 1343 an important decision was made, to lower the weight of the silver coinage and simultaneously to introduce a gold coinage. It was ordered that new pennies should be struck, the first since 1335, of like weight and standard (fineness) as the old, which was taken to mean 266 pennies (22s 2d) from a pound of silver. The contract of 9 July 1344 with Percival de Porche of Lucca as mint-worker confirmed this, but on 23 June 1345 the rate was raised to 266 pennies (22s 4d) from the pound, to give an extra 2d to merchants bringing silver to the mint. From 28 July 1346 there were to be struck 270 pennies from the pound (22s 6d) with halfpennies at 555 to the pound and farthings at 1,109. More of the lesser denominations were struck from the pound of silver to allow more profit for the mint master, to cover the extra costs involved in striking these smaller coins. To meet popular demand, it was also ordered that only halfpennies and farthings were to be struck for the next five years. Finally, from 1 July 1351, and fixing the weight and fineness of the silver coinage until 1411–12, there were to be 300 pennies (25s) to the pound, and new coins – the groat worth four pennies and the half groat of two pennies – were to be struck. They were needed as wage rates had shot up in response to labour shortages after the Black Death had reached England in 1348 and coins of higher value were now acceptable in general circulation, which had not been the case in 1279. The penny was still 92.5 per cent fine, but its weight was now only 1.166 grams (18 grains), compared to 1.44 grams (22.22 grains) in 1279. The groat weighed exactly four times as much, at 4.66 grams (71.91 grains) and the half groat 2.33 grams (35.95 grains). This was not debasement since the fineness of the coins was maintained, although their weight was reduced to take account of the rising price of silver on the international market, as shortages began to bite. Had this reduction not been made, the intrinsic value of each coin – and thus its purchasing power – would have increased, making buying and selling in small quantities difficult. All future changes in the silver coinage in the later Middle Ages were to take the form of weight reductions, rather than alterations in fineness. Moreover, the weight of the silver coins now had to be taken in relation to the value of the new gold coins. There had to be an acceptable relationship between gold and silver based on the value of both metals on the international market, so that one unit of gold was worth so many units of silver, as expressed now in ratios such as 1:10, 1:12 or 1:14.

Side by side with the progressive reduction in the weight of the silver coins came the introduction of a gold coinage. It was thought that gold would be used in international trade and for making large payments abroad which would solve the problems faced by the wool exporters and release silver for use on the domestic market, but the crown seems to have underestimated the difficulties involved in introducing a bi-metallic currency. Unless an acceptable gold:silver ratio was established, the new gold coins would not pass readily into circulation. It took nearly eight years before that was accomplished, and there was a bewildering sequence of coins issued and then withdrawn, and of alterations in weight and fineness. First, on 3 December 1343 the minting of three new gold coins was ordered, the double leopard, to be worth two little florins of Florence or 6s according to the fixed exchange rate of 3s to the florin, the leopard of 3s and the half leopard of 1s 6d (18d). They were to be of fine gold, 23 carats, 3½ grains pure (24 carats being pure gold), and £15 by value was to be struck from the Tower pound. The gold:silver ratio was effectively 1:12.4 and this was far too high. Seignorage was also set at an unacceptably high rate, so that not enough gold came to the mints to make a major issue of these coins possible. By June 1344 the king was forced to order a proclamation that they need only be accepted by those willing to take them, more or less acknowledging that they had failed, and then on 20 August 1344 they were withdrawn from circulation. A new contract for striking the gold coinage was drawn up, at a more attractive rate of seignorage, and the new coins were to be nobles, worth 6s 8d, with their halves and quarters, at 3s 4d and 1s 8d – that is, the equivalents of 80, 40 and 20 silver pennies. The gold:silver ratio was 1:11 which was probably too low, but this time the coins did pass into circulation, and further adjustments were made to their weight in June 1345 and July 1346 to bring it to a more realistic 1:11.5. Finally, in 1351, the last weight adjustment for half a century was made: from the Tower pound were to be struck 45 nobles, each of a weight of 7.78 grams or 120 grains. Seignorage and mintage were lowered significantly to attract bullion to the mint and a gold coinage was finally and successfully launched.[43]

Conclusion

The readjustment of the gold and silver coinages in 1351 marks another important stage in the history of the English coinage in the Middle Ages. In 973 there had been one struck silver coin, the penny. Now there were eight, and of two different metals. Frequent recoinages had been abandoned after 1158–80, and the numbers of mints had fallen from 70 or more effectively to three, at London, Canterbury and Calais, although its major role in producing coin lay in the future.[44] The major readjustments to silver and the introduction of gold brought as many problems as they solved, however. The gold:silver ratio was still higher than on the continent where it had fallen from the high point of 1:14.2 at Venice in 1305, a level maintained across Europe until *c.*1330, when it dropped precipitously to 1:10 by 1350 and in Florence to as low as 1:9.4.[45] Gold was still fetching a higher price in England than elsewhere in north-western Europe, and it was profitable to ship silver to mints in France and the Low Countries, in return for gold. So far from being simply the currency of international trade, so releasing silver for the domestic market, English gold coins had to be used internally. Silver stocks may have risen from the low levels of the late 1330s and early 1340s, but the long-term trend was inexorably downward. Just as important was the composition of the silver coinage. Small change was badly needed, but after 1351 the preferential rates to compensate for the extra work involved in striking the smaller coins were abandoned. The mint staff favoured the striking of larger coins, because of the lower labour costs, and the result was growing shortages of pennies, halfpennies and farthings. Almost inevitably, foreign substitutes came into circulation, the 'lushbournes', an inferior imitation penny in the late 1340s, and Venetian galley halfpennies later in the fourteenth century.[46] A clever balancing act was now required to maintain gold:silver ratios which accurately reflected the price of both metals on the international market. As silver shortages grew, significant and regular reductions in the weight of the penny might have been expected. But the upheavals of the late 1330s and early 1340s made it more and not less difficult for the crown to interfere with the coinage without stirring up parliamentary opposition. The debate on bullionism had now begun in earnest, and the crown's room for manoeuvre from 1351 was now far less than it had been in the thirteenth century when Europe had been awash with silver.

Notes

1 Spufford, *Money and its Use*, pp. 95-7; Allen, 'The volume of the English currency, 973-1158', 499-502; for die output calculations, see above, pp. 59-64; see above, Table 2.1, p. 26.
2 Spufford, *Money and its Use*, pp. 109-31; Bolton, 'Inflation, economics and politics', 3-4; Harvey, 'English inflation', 1-30; I. Blanchard, *Mining, Metallurgy and Minting in the Middle Ages, vol. iii, Continuing Afro-European Supremacy, 1250-1450* (Stuttgart: Franz Steiner Verlag, 2005), pp. 926-34.
3 Brand, *The English Coinage*, pp. 18-57; Mayhew, 'From regional to central minting', pp. 83-4, 96-7; R. Eaglen, 'The evolution of coinage in thirteenth-century England', in Coss and Lloyd (eds), *Thirteenth Century England V* (Woodbridge: Boydell and Brewer, 1992), pp. 20-2; M. Allen, 'Henry II and the English coinage', in C. Harper-Bill and N. Vincent (eds), *Henry II: New Interpretations* (Woodbridge: Boydell, 2007), pp. 261-6, 271.
4 Mayhew, 'From regional to central minting', pp. 87-117; Eaglen, 'The evolution of coinage in thirteenth-century England', 19-22; Brand, *The English Coinage*, pp. 18-48; see above, pp. 55-7, 90.
5 Warren, *Henry II*, pp. 264-5; Nightingale 'The evolution of weight standards', 204-6; Mayhew, 'From regional to central minting', pp. 89-90; Allen, 'Henry II and the English coinage', pp. 260-7; see above, pp. 90, 94, 102.
6 D.M. Metcalf, ' A survey of numismatic research into the pennies of the first three Edwards', in N.J. Mayhew (ed.), *Edwardian Monetary Affairs (1279-1344)* (Oxford: British Archaeological Reports, 36, 1977), pp. 6-7, 26-31; Allen, 'The volume of the English currency, 1158-1470', 598-9, 607; P. Latimer, 'The quantity of money in England 1180-1257: a model', *JEEH*, 32 (2003), 642-8.
7 Mayhew, 'From regional to central minting', pp. 83, 92-107; Brand, *The English coinage*, pp. 1-4, 25-27, 36, 43-47, 49-57, 61; Bolton 'The English economy in the early thirteenth century', pp. 31-2, and see above, Chapter 2, Table 2.1.
8 See below, pp. 176-82.
9 N.J. Mayhew, 'Frappes de monnaies et hausse des prix en Angleterre de 1180 à 1220' in J. Day (ed.), *Études de histoire monétaire, XIIe-XIXe siècles* (Lille: Université de Paris VII, 1984), pp. 163-5; N.J. Mayhew, 'Money and prices in England from Henry II to Edward II', *AgHR*, 35 (1987), 125; Brand *The English Coinage*, pp. 43-6; Allen, 'The volume of the English currency, 1158-1470', 599-601, 607; Latimer, 'The quantity of money in England 1180-1257', 642-52.
10 Latimer, 'The quantity of money in England 1180-1257', 646, 648, 652.
11 Latimer, 'The quantity of money in England 1180-1257', 651, 655-9.
12 Lloyd, *The English Wool Trade*, pp. 15-20, 22; Bolton 'The English economy in the early thirteenth century', 36-7, 40; Latimer, 'The quantity of money in England 1180-1247', 647-59.
13 Latimer, 'The quantity of money in England 1180-1247', 652 and Figure 3; and see below, pp. 176-82.
14 Mayhew, 'From regional to central minting', pp. 107-9, citing Matthew Paris, *Chronica Majora, vol. v*, ed. H.R. Luard, Rolls Series (London: Public Record

Office, 1880), pp. 18–19. Mayhew describes the justification for the recoinage as 'breath-taking effrontery'.

15 Mayhew, 'From regional to central minting', p. 113; Allen, 'The volume of the English currency, 1158–1470', 600–01; Latimer, 'The quantity of money in England 1180–1257', 644–59.

16 M. Archibald, 'Wastage from currency: long cross and the recoinage of 1279' in Mayhew (ed.), *Edwardian Monetary Affairs,* p. 174; Allen, 'The volume of the English currency, 1158–1470', 601–2; Latimer, 'The quantity of money in England 1180–1257', table 1, 642.

17 D.A. Carpenter, 'The gold treasure of King Henry III', in P. Coss and S.D. Lloyd (eds.), *Thirteenth Century England I* (Woodbridge: Boydell and Brewer, 1986), pp. 64–9; D.A. Carpenter, 'Gold and gold coins in England in the mid-thirteenth century', *NC*, 154 (1987), 106–13; Spufford, *Money and its Use*, p. 183; Cook, 'The bezant in Angevin England', 255, 258–63, 267–71.

18 Carpenter, 'The gold treasure of King Henry III', 74, 77–81; Spufford, *Money and its Use*, pp. 183–5; Cook, 'The bezant in Angevin England', 273–4.

19 D.L. Farmer, 'Some livestock price movements in thirteenth-century England', *EcHR*, 2nd series, 22 (1969–70), 12–14; M. Mate, 'Monetary policies in England' 41; Prestwich, *Edward I*, p. 247.

20 Mate, 'Monetary policies in England', 43; Prestwich, *Edward I*, pp. 182, 239–40, 247; M. Jurkowski, C.L. Smith and D. Crook, *Lay Taxes in England and Wales 1188–1688* (Surrey: Kew, 1998), p. 20.

21 N.J. Mayhew, 'Numismatic evidence and falling prices', 4.

22 Mate, 'Monetary policies in England', 50–1, 54, 76, 79; Prestwich, *Edward I*, p. 247.

23 Z.E. Rokeah, 'Money and the hangman in late-thirteenth-century England: Jews, Christians and currency offences alleged and real', part I, *JHS*, 31 (1988–90), 34–109, part ii, *JHS*, 32 (1993 for 1990–92), 159–218, *passim*; W. Johnson, 'Textual sources for the study of Jewish currency crimes in thirteenth-century England', *BNJ*, 66 (1966), 21–32 *passim*, but especially 30–31 and fn. 45; D.C. Skemer, 'King Edward I's articles of inquest on the Jews and coin-clipping', *HR*, 72 (1999), 1–26; R.R. Mundill, *England's Jewish Solution, 1262–90: Experiment and Expulsion* (Cambridge: Cambridge University Press, 1995), pp. 26, 104–7. Mate, 'Monetary policies in England', 37–44, takes a more charitable view of Edward's actions than that given here.

24 Mate, 'Monetary policies in England', 45; Munro, 'Bullionism and the bill of exchange', p. 188; Allen, 'The volume of the currency in England, 1158–1470', 601–2. Halfpennies and farthings formed 7.4 per cent of the output at London between 1 January 1280 and 20 September 1281. The coins were also struck at four other mints, but not at Canterbury: M. Allen, 'The volume and composition of the English silver currency, 1279–1351', *BNJ*, 70 (2000), 41, fn. 15.

25 Spufford, *Money and its Use*, pp. 234–6; Allen, 'The volume and composition of the English silver currency, 1279–1351', 41.

26 Mate, 'Monetary policies in England', 44–54; I. Stewart, 'The volume of early Scottish coinage', in D.M. Metcalf (ed.), *Coins in Medieval Scotland* (Oxford: British Archaeological Reports, 45, 1977), pp. 69–70.

27 Allen, 'The volume of the currency in England, 1158–1470', 601–3 and Table 1, 603; N.J. Mayhew, 'Coinage and money in England, 1086–c.1500', in D. Wood (ed.), *Medieval Money Matters* (Oxford: Oxbow Books, 2004), pp. 81, 86 fn. 41.

28 Mate, 'Monetary policies in England', 71, Table 1.

29 M. Prestwich, 'Edward I's monetary policies and their consequences', *EcHR*, 2nd series, 12 (1969), 408–9; Mate, 'Monetary policies in England', 56–7; Archibald 'Wastage from currency', p. 176; see below, pp. 161–2.

30 Prestwich, 'Edward I's monetary policies', 408, 411; Mate, 'Monetary policies in England', 62, Fig. 2; Mayhew, 'Numismatic evidence and falling prices', 11–12; M. Prestwich, 'The crown and the currency: the circulation of money in late thirteenth- and early fourteenth-century England, *NC*, 142 (1982), 52–4; Prestwich, *Edward I*, pp. 408–9; Mayhew, 'From regional to central minting', p. 135.

31 Mate, 'Monetary policies in England', 57; N.J. Mayhew and D.R. Walker, 'Crockards and pollards: imitation and the problem of fineness in a silver coinage', in Mayhew (ed.), *Edwardian Monetary Affairs*, pp. 126–7; J.R. Strayer, *The Reign of Philip the Fair* (Princeton: Princeton University Press, 1980), pp. 394–7.

32 Mate, 'Monetary policies in England', 58–9; Munro, 'Bullionism and the bill of exchange in England', pp. 187–90.

33 Mayhew and Walker, 'Crockards and pollards', pp. 125–30, 132; Mate 'Monetary policies in England', 63–72.

34 Prestwich 'Edward I's monetary policies', 411–12; Mate, 'Monetary policies in England', 63–72; Mayhew and Walker, 'Crockards and pollards', 129–37; Mayhew, 'From regional to central minting', pp. 139–40; Allen, 'The volume and composition of the English silver currency, 1279–1351', 42–4.

35 M. Mate, 'High prices in early fourteenth-century England: causes and consequences', *EcHR*, 2nd series, 28 (1975), 1–5; Lloyd, *English Wool Trade*, pp. 98–9; Allen, 'The volume of the English currency, 1158–1470', 602–3; Mayhew, 'Coinage and money in England, 1086–c.1500', pp. 81, 86 fn. 41; see below, pp. 174–5, 211–14.

36 *R.P.*, ii, pp. 62, 105; Mayhew, 'Numismatic evidence and falling prices', 12; Mate, 'High prices in early fourteenth-century England', 9, 12; M. Prestwich, 'Currency and the economy in early fourteenth-century England', in Mayhew (ed.), *Edwardian Monetary Affairs*, p. 48; Munro, 'Bullionism and the bill of exchange in England', pp. 190–1, 216–18, 222–3.

37 Prestwich, 'Currency and the economy in early fourteenth-century England', 46; Lloyd, *The English Wool Trade*, pp. 123–43; E.M. Carus-Wilson and O. Coleman, *England's Export Trade, 1275–1547* (Oxford: Oxford University Press, 1963), p. 122; C. McNamee, 'Buying off Robert Bruce: an account of monies paid to the Scots by Cumberland communities in 1313–14', *Transactions of the Cumberland and Westmoreland Antiquarian and Archaeological Society*, 92 (1992), 77–84; D.M. Metcalf, 'The evidence of Scottish coin hoards for monetary history, 1100–1600', in D.M. Metcalf (ed.), *Coinage in Medieval Scotland (1100–1600)* (Oxford: British Archaeological Reports, 45, 1977), pp. 1–15.

38 Prestwich 'Currency and the economy in early fourteenth-century England', p. 46; Lloyd, *English Wool Trade*, pp. 108–9.

39 Mayhew, 'Numismatic evidence and falling prices', 2, 12; H.A. Miskimin, *The Economy of Early Renaissance Europe, 1300–1460* (Cambridge: Cambridge

University Press, 1975), pp. 112-15. Spufford, *Money and its Use*, pp. 152-6, 240; Blanchard, *Mining, Metallurgy and Minting, vol. iii*, pp. 927-70.

40 See above, p. 154.

41 A.M. Watson, 'Back to gold - and silver', *EcHR*, 2nd series, 20 (1967), 1-34 and Blanchard, *Mining, Metallurgy and Minting, vol. iii*, pp. 927-70 are the best guides to the complex problem of bi-metallic flows; Spufford, *Money and its Use*, pp. 176-8, 271-6.

42 Craig, *The Mint*, p. 63; M. Prestwich, 'Early fourteenth-century exchange rates', *EcHR*, 2nd series, 32 (1979), 470-82; for bills of exchange, see below, pp. 285-7.

43 Oman, *The Coinage of England*, pp. 169-79; Craig, *The Mint*, pp. 59-75; Reddaway, 'The king's mint and exchange', 1-5; Lloyd, *The English Wool Trade*, pp. 109-12; Prestwich, 'Early fourteenth-century exchange rates', 479-82; Mayhew, 'From regional to central minting', pp. 144-8, 163-8 and Appendix 2, pp. 700-8; Blanchard, *Mining, Metallurgy and Minting, vol. iii*, pp. 962-9.

44 Some coins were still struck at the ecclesiastical privilege mints of Bury St Edmunds, Durham and York. For output at Durham see M. Allen, *The Durham Mint* (London: Spink for the British Numismatic Society, 2003), pp. 52-60.

45 J.H.A. Munro, 'Medieval monetary problems: bimetallism and bullionism', *JEH*, 43 (1983), 294.

46 'Lushbourne' was a corruption of Luxembourg, where the coins were minted: Craig, *The Mint*, p. 68; Mayhew, 'From regional to central minting', p. 149.

7

The making of a money economy
1158–1351

Introduction

Between 1086 and 1300 the English population more than doubled, from 2–2.5 million to 5–6 million people. In that same time the money supply rose at least twenty-seven and perhaps as many as forty times, from between £25,000 and £37,500 in 1086 to £1,00,000 in 1300, with most of the increase coming after 1220. More significantly, the average amount of silver coin per head of population rose from between 4d and 6d to between 46.6d and 69.3d in 1290, an elevenfold increase. After 1279 it was also easier to spend that money, because large quantities of fractional coins, halfpennies and farthings were put into circulation.[1] Virtually all medieval economic historians agree that during the 'long' thirteenth century, between about 1180 and the early 1300s, total output expanded. More land was taken into cultivation than at any time before the world wars of the twentieth century, agricultural production rose as more land was taken into cultivation and lords and peasants alike engaged directly in the market, a market served by a growing number of towns, village markets and fairs, while the wool-export trade boomed. There was a darker side to this picture, however. By the late thirteenth century there are signs of increasing and sometimes acute rural poverty, and in the early fourteenth century there was a severe economic crisis. The Great Famines of 1315–17, followed by sheep murrains and cattle plagues and then more bad harvests in the early 1320s, coupled with monetary and price instability brought the expansion to an abrupt end. From 1337 onward, with the opening stages of the Hundred Years War, the combined weight of all taxes, lay and clerical subsidies, papal taxes, and duties on and in wool again reached the levels of the 1290s. Edward I levied about £529,143 in direct lay and clerical taxes between 1290 and 1297 and his grandson, Edward III, well in excess of

£500,000 between 1337 and 1342. The tax burden bore heavily upon the country and it has even been argued that increasing poverty led to demographic decline before the Black Death arrived in 1348, although there is no general agreement on this point.[2]

The difficulty is not so much in describing what happened as in explaining why it happened. Many historians have seen population growth as the driving force behind expansion, as there were more mouths to be fed, more people to be clothed and housed and supplied with consumer goods. This interpretation has been challenged by Britnell who has focused on the increasing commercialisation of society, the growth and expansion of the market, which went hand in hand with improved agricultural productivity and innovative economic development. Society came to rely increasingly on the market and market forces to regulate its affairs in town and countryside alike, on exchange and the use of money as a medium of exchange, and on organised markets in towns and at fairs, governed by strict rules and regulations.[3]

Some, but not all, monetary historians would take the argument even further, however, and have pressed the case for change in the money supply, M, as the crucial factor in economic expansion or contraction. For them the 'long' thirteenth century began with rapid price and wage inflation between 1180 and 1220, followed by an upward price trend which reached its peak in the early 1300s before falling rapidly as the money supply contracted in the late 1330s and early 1340s. In particular, a justly famous article written in 1973 by Paul Harvey, has influenced the monetary case more than any other and has framed much of the subsequent debate. He argued that it was the inflation of 1180–1220 which triggered economic change. Rising demand caused by a population just beginning to push against the limits of its subsistence, coupled with an influx of new silver from the profits of the wool-export trade, led to sudden and rapid price and wage inflation. Great landlords faced both rising costs and falling revenues since their manors had been let out on long leases at fixed rents which depreciated in value as inflation soared. The answer to their problems seemed to be to take control of their demesne lands back into their own hands and to manage their estates in order to maximise their incomes by producing grain and wool to sell at higher prices on expanding markets. To secure the labour they needed to cultivate their estates, they imposed or re-imposed labour services on a peasantry which therefore became increasingly unfree. The rapidly rising volume of coin in circulation, combined with the need to market surpluses and the equally pressing need of the peasantry to participate in the market to raise the cash to pay other dues to their lords and taxes to the king, accelerated the commercialisation of society. Old towns expanded, new ones were founded, markets and fairs proliferated across the countryside. The expansion of the thirteenth century was under way, launched on a flood of silver.[4]

Two different but not necessarily mutually exclusive explanations of how the very substantial increase in the money supply affected the economy have thus been offered. One focuses on price and wage inflation and their consequences. The other is more subtle, and involves looking at how money helped change the way in which the economy worked, from top to bottom. If in 1180 English society was not commercialised, by the early fourteenth century it certainly was. Access to and participation in the market was now essential for peasant, townsman and lord alike. One of the driving forces behind this commercialisation was the growing use of money in exchange and the emergence, for the first time, of what can properly be called a money economy. That, as has already been suggested, was not simply the result of an increased money supply. There had to be, at the same time and certainly stimulated in part by more money and more markets, general advances in literacy and numeracy, in recording and accounting, and in the availability of credit and the legal enforceability of credit agreements. This approach shifts the argument away from inflation as the main cause of economic change towards an understanding of how and why a money economy developed in the second half of the thirteenth century and why, at a time when the population was at its medieval peak and rural poverty was increasing, it was important for the survival of at least some of the peasantry that it had finally emerged.[5]

Inflation in England, 1199-1247

The case for economic expansion as a long-term consequence of the monetary inflation of 1180–1220 remains strong, however, and it is now necessary to re-assess its importance, in the light of the monetary and price-wage history of the thirteenth century as a whole. Here Latimer's work, which looks again at the evidence for the prices of wheat, oxen, sheep, wool, wax and textiles, is of considerable importance. He broadly confirms the pattern of inflation established by Farmer in *The Agrarian History of England and Wales*, published some fifteen years after Harvey's seminal article. Latimer argues that the beginnings of inflation can first be seen in the late 1170s and 1180s, but it was checked abruptly in the 1190s when prices fell back to the levels of the 1160s. Then, between 1199 and 1204-5 there was a sudden and quite unexpected surge in prices. After this shock, prices fell back, albeit to newer and higher levels than those in the 1180s and 1190s, and then remained remarkably stable well into the 1230s and 1240s and beyond, taking into account the temporary effects of fluctuating harvest yields and outbreaks of livestock disease. This is a different pattern from the four decades of continuing inflation from 1180 to 1220 proposed by Harvey. It suggests that there were only five years of severe inflation and at other times either deflation or higher but stable prices, and it needs explaining.[6]

According to Latimer, what caused the severe deflation from about 1187 to 1199 was the outflow of money to pay for the Third Crusade, Richard I's ransom and then the costs of defending Normandy against the French king, Philip Augustus, which together led to a significant fall in the English money supply.[7] But why there was then this sudden and completely unexpected surge in prices over a brief six-year period from 1199 to 1205 remains something of a mystery. The chronicler Ralph of Coggeshall gives graphic accounts of bad weather in the summer of 1201 and in April 1203, and then of a winter so cold in 1205 that the Thames froze over and the land could not be ploughed between 1 January and 25 March. The harvest failed and the price of a summ or measure of wheat which could have been had for 12d in Henry II's reign rose to 13s 4d. This might explain some of the price rises but the major harvest failure was in 1205, and the sharp rise actually began in 1199. Coggeshall also comments on money so corrupt through clipping that a recoinage was necessary, and Latimer sees the serious deterioration of the coinage in the years immediately before 1205 as the prime explanation for the rapid price inflation. In such circumstances people hoarded what they believed to be good coin and spent, if they could, what they thought to be bad. He argues that much of the money stock in the last decade of the twelfth century was being held in hoards, but when a recoinage seemed likely, then confidence in the old money collapsed and there was a sudden change from accumulation to spending. The release of the hoarded stock and *not* the sudden influx of silver sent prices shooting upward, as **M** was dramatically increased. The recoinage of 1205 stabilised prices, in much the same way as those in 1247 and 1279 were to do, but they did not fall back to their pre-1199 levels, remaining on a higher plateau until the mid-1240s.[8]

Latimer offers the most convincing explanation so far for sudden price rise of 1199–1205. What he is not able to explain quite as convincingly is why prices did not continue to rise sharply after 1206, and then, beyond John's reign, in the 1220s and above all in the 1230s and 1240s when there was another substantial increase in **M**. This period needs more considera-

B: THE EMERGENCE OF A MONEY ECONOMY, 1158-1351

tion than it has so far been given. First, what probably held prices back after 1206 and until 1214 was the weight of King John's exactions and his hoarding of the money raised by them. Royal revenues passing through the Exchequer rose from a relatively modest £22,000-23,000 per annum in the opening years of the reign, to £30,000 in 1205-6, then to £52,000 by 1210, and to £83,000 in 1211. That was the peak year: by 1212 they had fallen back to £56,000, although this was still more than twice what they had been in 1200. Nor do these figures represent all John's income. Money was extorted from religious houses, and particularly from the Cistercians, and from the Jews through heavy tallages or arbitrary taxes. These were not part of the traditional revenues of the crown and did not pass through the Exchequer. When they are included in the totals, then John's income in 1211 was somewhere in the region of £145,000. Moreover, perhaps up to 75 per cent of that was paid in cash, and most of that cash came not from the exceptional payments by the Church and the Jews but from the ordinary revenues collected from the country at large. Between 1210 and 1212 those revenues contributed £118,115 of a total of £157,051. It was, as Barratt says, the greatest level of [fiscal] extortion seen in England since the Conquest.[9]

Some of this money was spent abroad, on the expedition to Poitou in 1206 and on subsidies to allies between 1206-7 and 1212-13; some was spent in England, on the expenses of the household, on building; and some on the army for the Welsh campaign in 1213. A great deal of it actually stayed in the country, however, and was not spent at all. From at least 1207 John was intent on building up large reserves of money, in coin, and storing them in castle treasuries across England. He was determined that they should be ready, on call, for his great and ultimately abortive expedition to recover Normandy, which had been lost to Philip Augustus in 1204. The sums involved were very substantial. In July 1207 an amount of 20,000 marks (£13,333 6s 8d) was taken from the central 'treasure' at Winchester and sent to the castle treasuries at Devizes and Marlborough, and a further £7,333 6s 8d was sent to Nottingham. The decentralisation of the king's treasure continued throughout 1207-8, until there was on deposit across the country somewhere in the region of £44,333 6s 8d or about 18 per cent of the coinage in circulation in 1205-7. John then began to build up his war chest in earnest. Joliffe has suggested that by 1213 the regional treasuries could have provided him with something like £133,333, the equivalent of about half the circulating medium in 1205-9.[10]

Even allowing for regular expenditure on the household, on necessary political largesse and on campaigns within Britain, such as that against Scotland in 1209 and the Welsh expedition of 1213, John was still withdrawing very large sums from circulation for long periods. It is also highly unlikely that shortages of coin could be made good by striking more money from silver brought into the country as profits from the wool-export trade. There is no numismatic evidence to suggest that this was done and anyway the wool trade was in the doldrums at this point, a victim of the wars between John and Philip Augustus. The king's hoards were far greater than any private hoards, from which money would have had to be released to pay taxes, fines and proffers. Considerable quantities of coin were being kept out of circulation, causing monetary deflation which would have pulled prices back after the sharp rise between 1199 and 1205-6.[11]

This will not explain why prices remained relatively stable, albeit at new, higher levels, thereafter. After all, John's hoarding was a temporary phenomenon: much of his treasure was spent in the three years after 1213-14, although most of it seems to have gone abroad, and stayed there, with deflationary consequences which held back prices in the first years of Henry III's reign (1216-72). There were further outflows of coin in the 1220s, 1230s and early 1240s, again probably with deflationary consequences, but the real puzzle is why, given a doubling of the money supply between 1205 and 1247, with most of the rise coming from the mid-1230s onward, prices did not respond as they should have done. Any sustained increase in **M** should lead to similar increases in **P**, according to the workings of the Fisher Equation. Movements in wage rates are also difficult to interpret. It is well known that John had to pay two shillings a day to hire a mercenary for whom Henry II would have paid eight pence, but the higher wages paid to knights and men-at-arms when John was at war with France may well reflect the going rate on the international market for a limited supply of trained men and not rampant inflation. Widespread evidence for other wage rates, for skilled agricultural and building workers on piece work, is much harder to come by and such as there is comes from the account rolls of one or two great estates or from the royal records. Estate records have a regional bias and what was true on the bishop of Winchester's estates in Hampshire may not have been true in the West Midlands, East Anglia or the North. The crown often used impressment, especially for its building projects, and workers may not have been paid the going market rate. Yet even this limited evidence shows a similar pattern to price movements, with a sharp rise in the first decade of the thirteenth century and then remarkable stability up to about 1250.[12] Why the rise in **M** in the first half of the thirteenth century from £250,000 in 1205 to £450,000 on the eve of the recoinage of 1247 did not lead to the sustained inflation predicted by the terms of the Fisher Equation remains puzzling.

B: THE EMERGENCE OF A MONEY ECONOMY, 1158–1351

Matters are further complicated by an alternative and contentious explanation for price rises, one which focuses on the functions of **V** rather than upon changes in **M**. Goldstone and Miskimin argue that where a large market network already exists, a small amount of coin can be made to work very hard, to meet the monetary needs of a rising population so that **V**, velocity of circulation, would probably rise at a much faster rate than **T**, the total volume of transactions, thus pushing up **P**. They developed this argument to explain the price revolution of the sixteenth and early seventeenth centuries, to challenge the primary role traditionally given to the huge influx of silver from the Americas. It could also be applied to the early thirteenth century, however, since coin was still in limited supply. The amount per head had barely risen between 1205 and 1247, possibly because the increase in the money supply was matched by an increase in the population. In these circumstances, and given that there was a growing market network, an increased velocity of circulation (**V**) could have helped keep prices at their new, higher levels after the initial surge in inflation between 1199 and 1205.[13]

Goldstone and Miskimin's theory has been vigorously challenged both by early-modern historians and by medievalists. Mayhew, for instance, entirely rejects it on the grounds that there was enough coin in circulation to allow for a fall in **V**. This, he argues, was not a cash-starved economy where money had to change hands rapidly and shortages of coin were such that there were queues of creditors waiting for payment. A high velocity of circulation actually made buying and selling more difficult, and all the evidence points to greater urbanisation and monetisation in the first half of the thirteenth century. Increased supplies of money meant a falling velocity of circulation, so freeing one transaction from dependence on another. It would no longer be necessary to sell before buying, and reserves could be accumulated to allow greater flexibility in purchasing and payment. There is much to agree with here, yet for **V** to fall **M** must rise substantially and **T** would rise at the same time, as more trade was carried out and more payments were made in coin. If the rise in **T** cancels out the fall in **V**, it still means that any significant rise in **M** should have caused a sustained price rise in England between 1199 and the early 1240s, and even up to the mid-1270s. Yet this does not seem to have happened.[14]

Can these conflicting theories be resolved? Not easily, not entirely convincingly and not, as yet, by developing an alternative model that will encompass all the variables. However, a possible explanation for price movements in the later twelfth and the first half of the thirteenth century can be attempted. In the late 1170s and early 1180s an influx of silver was pushing up prices, and possibly wages. These rises were checked, and then reversed, as massive outflows of coin and hoarding caused monetary deflation between 1187 and 1199. Then, between 1199 and 1205–6 there was a sudden and quite unexpected price rise, perhaps as a result of bad harvests and of release of coins from hoards in anticipation of the partial recoinage that came in 1205. Thereafter, prices fell back but to the new and higher levels at which they broadly remained until the mid-1240s and then, after the recoinage of 1247, until the mid-1270s. An inexorably increasing money supply did not push prices relentlessly upward, as is sometimes supposed. On the contrary, the quantity of money in circulation was temporarily reduced by hoarding, as in John's reign, and then by the outflow of coin during the 1220s, 1230s and 1240s. That should have had deflationary consequences, but here Goldstone and Miskimin's argument may apply, although not quite in the way that they themselves intended. A shortage of coin meant that money had to work harder within the economy. The velocity of circulation therefore rose, cancelling out the effects of any temporary fall in **M** and producing a degree of price stability.

From the 1230s onward prices should have risen, as favourable trade balances brought more silver to England and an increasing population stimulated demand. What held them back can only be a matter of speculation. It is possible that production was increased to meet demand, although the balance of evidence suggests that this is unlikely.[15] A better explanation is perhaps provided by looking at the way in which money worked within the market economy itself. On the one hand, the increase in **M** allowed for a fall in transaction costs, so improving the marketing and distribution of goods, and that helped keep prices down. But there was still not, as yet, sufficient money in circulation to make the market work as effectively as it might have done. Coin per head rose very little between 1205 and 1247, or indeed 1279.[16] The velocity of circulation may well have been much greater in mid-century, given continuing population increase, and that would have helped keep prices higher than they might otherwise have been. This is speculative, but it does emphasise the need for more consideration to be given to the functions of **V** in the Fisher Equation, since **M** cannot be taken in isolation, as an abstract or absolute figure. It has to be seen in relation to the population, to the amount of coin per head and to how hard each silver penny had to work. By mid-century and perhaps even by the 1270s the coinage had still not reached that critical mass essential for a money economy in which fluctuations in **M** could produce sharp price movements. As for wages, after an initial and sharp rise, they too remained relatively stable over a long period.[17] This can best be explained in terms of supply exceeding demand. Most early thirteenth-century landlords, great and small, relied on a combination of *famuli*, staff permanently employed to work on the demesne, labour services provided by the increasingly unfree villani or villeins and day-wage labour, to cultivate their estates. As the century wore on, the attraction of day-wage labour as a cheaper alternative to labour services that could be commuted (converted) into money rents became even greater, given the growing pool of surplus labour in the economy. A growing population was the controlling factor in stable wage-rates, rather than the money supply.[18]

Inflation in England, 1247-1351

If further confirmation is needed that increases in the money supply did not necessarily lead to rampant inflation, then it comes from the period before 1290. Prices fell back after the recoinage of 1247 and thereafter remained reasonably stable until the early 1270s. Then they began to rise again, quite sharply. Again, there is no evidence that this was the result of an influx of silver. The volume of coin in circulation rose steadily but not spectacularly between 1247 and 1279, and mint output was actually falling in the 1270s.[19] It has been argued that these higher prices were a consequence of a deteriorating and clipped coinage, and that may be partly true, but it is also worth considering an alternative argument. By the 1270s England's medieval population was fast approaching its peak. The marketing network, in terms of size if not efficiency, was also at its peak, with few successful towns or new markets being founded after the middle of the century.[20] If there was not yet sufficient coin in circulation to meet the monetary needs of this expanded economy, then the Goldstone-Miskimin theory as to the effects of an increased velocity of circulation would apply. Each penny was being made to work harder, and so prices rose.

It is almost impossible to determine what the effects of the recoinage of 1279-81 may have been because in the 1280s the English mints were almost awash with silver. By 1290 coinage per head had risen from between 22.7d and 32.0d, the level in 1247, to between 46.6d and 69.3d, with much of that rise coming after 1281. Grain prices should have responded rapidly to the very substantial increase in **M**, but they did not do so. Rather, and irrespective of whether harvests were good or bad, they remained at the new, higher levels to which they had risen immediately before 1279.[21] Why they were held back is, again, a matter for speculation, but the 1280s seem to mark the point at which the money supply finally matched the needs of an economy driven forward by the last stages of population expansion. With sufficient

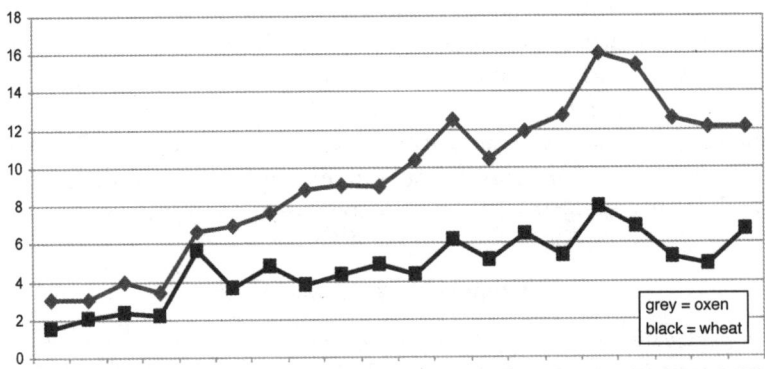

Figure 7.1 Wheat and oxen sale prices by decades 1160–9 to 1350–6, in shillings per quarter for wheat and shillings per one oxen.

Source: D. Farmer, 'Prices and wages', in H.E. Hallam (ed.), *The Agrarian History of England and Wales, vol. ii* (Cambridge: Cambridge University Press, 1988), table 7.1, p. 734 and table 7.4, p. 748.

coin in circulation for it to change hands easily, the market would work more effectively, and at the same time the velocity of circulation would fall. Both together helped hold down and stabilise prices. But the critical factor here was probably improved market efficiency which worked against the inflationary consequences of a sharp rise in **M**. At the same time, and interestingly, wages show only a slow upward trend, as the spare labour capacity in the economy caused by population growth continued to rise.[22]

If this argument holds good, then the decade 1279–89 certainly marks an important stage in the emergence of a money economy in England. Society at all levels was now accustomed and more importantly able to use coin for the majority of payments, because there had been such a dramatic increase in the money supply. Not surprisingly, then, between 1291 and 1351 prices in a thoroughly monetised economy responded almost entirely in the ways predicted by the Fisher Equation. It must be remembered that there had not been a thorough-going debasement. Until the 1340s, there was no significant change in the silver content of the coinage. Nor did silver shortages begin to bite hard until the 1330s, so pushing up the intrinsic value of the coins in spite of weight reductions. In these circumstances, the erratic nature of price movements is readily intelligible in terms of changes in the money supply, according to the strict workings of the Fisher Equation and accepting Mayhew's argument that **V** will fall when coin is plentiful. In the 1290s serious shortages of coin helped hold back prices, although they rose immediately before the recoinage of 1299–1300, in spite of good harvests in 1297 and 1298. Then, from 1303, well before the disastrous harvests and cattle plagues of 1315-25 and the destruction in the North caused by Scottish raids, prices rose to unprecedented levels. From this point they almost always responded to changes in the money supply, with severe inflation up to the 1330s, when European-wide shortages of silver coupled with crippling war taxation began to bite. Interestingly, agricultural wages also rose sharply in the opening decades of the fourteenth century, but then fell back in the 1330s and 1340s, until the catastrophic depopulation caused by the Black Death eventually led to an acute shortage of labour.[23]

Inflation 1180-1300: conclusion

An explanation of price and wage movements from 1180 to *c.*1300 which relies solely upon changes in the money supply will not stand. It is now quite clear that the pattern of inflation was uneven. A very sudden price rise between 1199 and 1205 was followed by nearly seventy years of relative stability. Prices rose to new levels in the late 1270s at which they remained until the extraordinary influx of silver in the first two decades of the fourteenth century. These periods of stability were the complex product of a series of interacting and sometimes countervailing tendencies. Monetary deflation caused by the temporary outflow of coin to pay troops and allies could be cancelled out by the inflationary tendencies of a rising velocity of circulation. An increase in the money supply that should have led to higher prices also meant more coin available per head of population. Buying and selling became easier, transaction costs were lowered, the already extensive market network worked more effectively and that held back price rises. Between 1180 and 1300 the population at least doubled, without there being any general improvements in agricultural productivity. Yields per acre were static and intensified methods of agriculture were the exception rather than the rule. As a result, more and more land had to be taken into cultivation to meet the demand for wheat, barley, oats and rye, but even as early as 1270 the physical limits of expansion had been reached in many places.[24] At the same time the money supply rose tenfold, and the combination of extra demand and extra coin should have pushed prices sky high, yet they rose by a factor of only three or four. For long periods both prices and wages remained stable, apart from the short-term fluctuations resulting from the flow of coin abroad or harvest failures. It is wrong to characterise the thirteenth century and particularly the seventy-odd years between 1205 and 1279 as an age of continuous price rises caused either by monetary inflation or by population growth.

Inflation, the direct management of great estates and 'the crisis of the knights'

If we accept that prices and wages were stable in the thirteenth century, then two major historical interpretations based largely or at least partly upon the premise of continuous inflation need careful reconsideration, namely that great landlords returned to the direct management of their demesnes to produce for the market, and the so-called 'crisis' of the knightly class. 'The coincidence between the period when estate owners were turning to demesne farming [direct management] and the period of rapidly rising prices is very striking', wrote Harvey in 1973. He went on to argue that estates were taking exactly the right steps to meet the new inflationary situation. Even if rents could have been raised to new levels, there would always have been a time lag in which lessees would have benefited unduly from the increased prices that their landlords and others would have had to pay for the produce they sold, and direct management was the only way to avoid this. There was an inextricable link between monetary inflation and the adoption of direct management, and in a second important article Harvey proposed a chronology of change. Using evidence from the pipe rolls between 1155 and 1216, he found that in the 1170s demesnes were still leased: by 1210–14 it was to be found on the two-thirds of all estates surrendered to the king.[25] No direct connection was made with inflation but since the second article appeared within a year of the first, the inference could clearly be drawn. Monetary inflation was a root cause of the change to direct management.

As we have seen, inflation could not have offered incentive to change until at least 1199, however, and the extraordinary price rise that followed was short-lived. After 1205 prices remained relatively stable and, as Bridbury has argued, once the shock of change had worn off, experience offered no clear guidance as to how they should proceed to those who managed the big estates. He also pointed out that management decisions varied constantly. One year a group of manors might be leased out, another taken directly in hand, as the perceived needs of the particular institution and families changed. So, in 1186–7 the archbishop of York managed most of his demesnes directly, but in 1212–15 nearly half of them were again on lease. Flexibility seems to have been the key throughout the thirteenth century. Estates had to be managed to provide food for the household and a cash income for spending, rather than investment.[26] More imported consumer goods were available, while new architectural styles made building or rebuilding on the grand scale very tempting. Towards

B: THE EMERGENCE OF A MONEY ECONOMY, 1158-1351

the end of the century the demands of both king and pope became heavier and heavier, and money had to be raised quickly from almost any source to meet them. If that meant switching to cash rents for demesne lands and substituting money payments for customary labour services, then so be it.

It does now seem unlikely that monetary inflation between 1180 and 1220 *of itself* forced great landlords to reconsider the ways in which their estates were managed. Other causes should therefore be sought, and most notably the consequences of changes in the laws of property and possession. Henry II's legal reforms gave free tenants far greater protection against landlords. Possession was now nine points of the law, and leases granted for long terms of years could harden into perpetuity. As a result, landlords stood to lose estates granted out in this way and were forced, where possible, to take them back into their own hands and begin managing them directly.[27] Management required managers, however, while marketing the surpluses from estate production would need an effective exchange system involving a far greater use of coin in transactions. The spread of literacy, numeracy and administrative training provided the one, the increase in the money supply the other. Together these two factors were of more importance for the management of great estates than a relatively brief period of rapid price inflation.[28]

Inflation has also been accused of forcing social change, most notably in what has become known as 'the crisis of the knights', where the knightly class is broadly defined as all those beneath the ranks of the baronage who held by military tenure and were manorial landlords, whether they took the title or not. Coss argued that this group was overtaken by financial problems and material collapse stemming from the rapid inflation of 1180-1220, which continued at a slower pace until 1260, since its members did not possess sufficient land to allow them to produce for the market. To maintain their social pretensions they borrowed heavily, notably from the Jews. Eventually they were forced to sell up to meet their debts, finding willing buyers especially from ecclesiastical houses and other lords eager to expand their demesnes or their rent rolls.[29]

This thesis has considerable implications for the politics and local administration of thirteenth-century England, and not least for the involvement of the knightly class in the barons' wars of the mid-century. It has not withstood the test of time, however. The most convincing attacks upon it have come from Carpenter and Faulkner. Carpenter, basing his arguments on evidence from Oxfordshire, pointed to a knightly class for the most part successfully holding on to its prosperity. Faulkner sees not so much the collapse of a class as its stratification. Knighthood was becoming less a profession of arms and more a ceremonial rank, whose trappings were expensive to maintain. Those who did not wish to do so simply dropped out or, perhaps better, failed to opt in. They did not lose their lands but simply abandoned the dignity of knighthood. In any age and in any society there are those who prosper and those who fail. Society is always fluid and in the thirteenth century there were new men on the make, judges, lawyers, administrators, merchants, soldiers, willing and able to move into what might be called 'the middling ranks'. Without the credit facilities offered by the Jews and by others, the land market would have been more static and far less able to respond to the ambitions of these acquisitive newcomers. Most importantly, the underlying assumption that inflation lay at the root of all ills must be challenged. Before the early 1300s, and except for two brief periods from 1199-1205 and 1270-79, inflationary pressures were relatively mild. Whether to spend extravagantly on the greater variety of consumer and luxury goods that became available or to live within one's means was essentially a matter of personal choice. Borrowing to allow one to live ostentatiously was also a matter of choice which had little to do with inflation and the crisis of a whole class should not be adduced simply from the failure of some individual families.[30]

The emergence of a money economy

It is now time to consider the general proposition that by 1300 there was a money economy in England. As we have seen, this was not the case in 973, in 1180 or even in 1247. Two important points need to be re-stated and re-emphasised here, before taking the argument further. First, the growth of a market economy cannot be attributed simply to a vast increase in the money supply. Demand was created in the main by population increase, resulting from an earlier age of marriage due to the greater availability of land to support the family, from more surviving children of the marriage and from more opportunities for those children and their successors to earn a living in an increasingly commercialised society.[31] Supplying that demand, however, meant that exchange had to move beyond the primitive processes of barter or the use of money simply as a standard of value. Secondly, there had to be a sufficiency of coin in circulation to allow money to become the main medium of exchange. Goods were still supplied in return for service, but what manorial court records show is that such transactions were increasingly being given nominal money values. By the late thirteenth century, society at all levels was thinking in monetary terms and, as will be seen, using coin as the main way of making payments.[32]

B: THE EMERGENCE OF A MONEY ECONOMY, 1158-1351

So, had a money economy emerged in England by 1300? The first and most obvious question to be asked is 'What were the practical consequences of the elevenfold increase in the money supply between 1180 and 1300?' The second, and more complex, is 'What was required in terms of advances in reckoning, recording and accounting, in the development of credit mechanisms and the enforcement of debts and contracts if money was to work more effectively in the market economy?' There is much more involved here than the increasing availability and use of coin, including most importantly literacy and numeracy and legally enforceable debts and contracts. Taxes, which were paid mainly in money, had to be granted by a political assembly, which began to voice its own opinions on the state of the coinage and the bullion supply. In each case the growing use of money acted as one of the stimuli to educational, legal, and political developments, but only one. There were many others, and the arguments here need to be set alongside those of Clanchy on the rise of literacy; Brand and Palmer on changes in the law; Prestwich, Harriss, Ormrod and others on the politics and financing of war; and Britnell, Campbell and Masschaele on the growth of commercialisation. Without developments in these spheres a money economy could not have emerged. In turn, however, these changes could not have occurred without a vast increase in the money supply. Money, as Francis Bacon nearly said, is like manure: it helps things grow.[33]

The coinage and the rural economy

The answer to the first of the two substantive questions asked above, concerning the practical consequences of the elevenfold increase in the money supply between 1180 and 1300, is relatively straightforward. More and more payments were made in coin, although it is not possible to measure the scale of the increase. At no point can we know the total size of the market, and it has to be emphasised that this was still in some ways a subsistence economy. On the estates of the bishop of Winchester and Westminster Abbey more grain was consumed by the household than was sent to the market. It has been estimated that only about 10 per cent of all peasant land was used to produce crops for sale, rather than for consumption. London and other towns were drawing on wider areas for their supplies of foodstuffs, fuel and raw materials, thus increasing the flow of money from town to countryside, but the size of the urban population in 1290 is a matter of debate. Dyer has adopted a broad approach and has estimated that urban dwellers comprised 20 per cent of the English population as a whole while Campbell estimates it as just under 10 per cent of the population of England and Wales in 1290. In truth, there is no certain figure but the 'pull' of urban markets should not be exaggerated. Even London's was limited to an area of only about twenty miles around the city. Most country dwellers ate the crops they grew themselves, and by the end of the thirteenth century many of them lived precariously on the margins of subsistence.[34]

Nevertheless, in rural areas the impact of money is all too obvious. Coin was substituted for payments previously made in labour or in kind. In the late twelfth and early thirteenth centuries labour services were imposed or re-imposed on the peasantry in many areas. There may have been an increased need for demesne labour by lords involved in the direct management of their estates or, as has been argued, as lords sought to redefine status in order to exact more seigneurial dues from an unfree and dependent peasantry. By the late thirteenth century, however, the relationship between lords and peasants was based firmly on cash payments, as Kosminsky and others have demonstrated. The unfreedom of the peasantry could also be exploited through a whole range of other seigneurial dues which were paid in cash. An heir could be made to pay an inheritance duty or entry fine to gain possession or seisin of the family holding. There was also a death duty, a heriot, to be paid, either in kind, the beast or the best possession, or in money. A payment known as merchet was demanded when daughters were married, a fine was levied in cases of female immorality (lerywite or legerwite) and for permission to live off the manor (chevage). Breaches of manorial discipline were punished in the manor courts by money fines, while lords, great and small, had often acquired new lands for the money rents they produced. The level of these payments may well have been fixed by custom, but they still had to be made, and mainly in cash.[35]

Peasants had other lords, both spiritual and temporal. The Church took its dues in both kind and cash, mainly from tithes and mortuary payments, and then, in the 1290s, the burden of direct royal taxation and of purveyance became nigh intolerable.[36] Taxation had to be paid, physically, in coin. Purveyance or prise was the seizure of goods theoretically for the provisioning of the royal household, but actually for supplying royal armies. Payment was made, but often at arbitrarily low rates and after some time. If in the meantime the peasant household went short, then food would have to be bought on the market, or borrowed against future repayment from another member of the family or, more usually, from a richer peasant.[37]

The most recent attempt to model the peasant budget in late thirteenth-century England has estimated that a customary (unfree) tenant had to pay over about a third (34 per cent) of his cash revenues to meet his seigneurial

B: THE EMERGENCE OF A MONEY ECONOMY, 1158-1351

dues. A further 22 per cent was spent on 'consumption' goods, that is on house maintenance, and the purchase of utensils and furnishings, candles, clothes, shoes and salt and pepper. Money also had to be spent on the upkeep of horses and other draught animals and the repair of ploughs and carts. Kitsikopoulos calculates that the income of a peasant farming about eighteen acres of arable and with access to about two acres of meadow came to 57s 7d a year in the late thirteenth century. After all payments had been made, the family might be left with a surplus of about 7s 7d to set aside for a rainy day or to buy barley for malting. His conclusion is that the margins of subsistence were perilously narrow, a point to which we must return. Such estimates of the peasant budget have been made before, notably by Titow and Dyer, and in some ways this new work merely confirms their earlier findings, although Kitsikopoulos would argue that the minimum holding needed for subsistence was nearer eighteen than the ten acres they thought necessary. His calculations are as much open to challenge as all the others. The typical peasant did not exist. In many areas survival was possible because of other sources of income, from rural industries or enhanced opportunities for wage labour. Some soils were more productive than others, and in some regions farming more intensive, cash incomes higher.[38] The important point to note here is that the family had to raise a substantial amount of cash each year from the sale of produce, wage labour and renting-out its carts to meet its bills. The income of 57s 7d is purely notional. It is, however, of an order that could not have been reached in 1200 or even in 1240, because there would not have been sufficient coin in circulation to allow it. Only when the money supply had reached a figure of around £1,000,000 would it have been possible for cash receipts and payments to have reached this level.

Dyer's recent work on the use of coins by peasants adds considerable weight to this argument. His initial survey of coin finds on thirty-three excavated village sites in England and Wales yielded unpromising results. On sixteen no coins were found at all, and the remaining seventeen produced only sixty, with some jettons or counters sometimes used as coin-substitutes. That might point to little use of coin, but he would argue strongly against this. Rents and dues had to be paid, and consumer goods bought, and coins were so precious to peasants that they simply did not lose them in their houses. Accidental losses in the fields were another matter, and here Dyer's analysis of single coin finds from Warwickshire, together with Rigold's samples from excavations on all types of medieval site and Mayhew's figures for coin finds notified to the Ashmolean museum in Oxford produce some fascinating results. 'Losses of coins reflecting the population of coins in circulation were especially numerous in the case of coins minted between 1279 and 1351. The finds of coins minted after 1351 reduced to the same level as those in the twelfth and early thirteenth centuries.' Dyer again stresses that much exchange was conducted without the use of coin, but his findings are significant since more coins lost meant more coins in use, as his evidence is drawn from stray finds and not from hoards. His conclusion is that the use of money had developed to a high level in the last decades of the thirteenth century, that peasants owned and used coins, were embedded in a market economy and were money conscious. The striking point, however, is the correlation between high levels of stray finds and the huge increase in the money supply from 1279 onward.[39]

Credit and the market economy

If peasants had become accustomed to the use of money and were embedded in the market economy, so were all the ranks above them: artisans, craftsmen, merchants, minor and major landlords. By the end of the thirteenth century it was the market economy, along with taxation and the payment and movement of armies, that helped turn the coinage into a truly national currency.[40] That much is clear, but the growth of credit in the economy is a much more complex subject. At a low level much of it was informal, and evidence of borrowing and lending in all their various forms only appears in recorded court actions, when something had gone wrong. Little or nothing is known about credit transactions that worked smoothly and it is therefore impossible to calculate the total amount of credit in the medieval economy at any time. In modern economic thinking credit is held to add to the money supply in all but its narrowest definition, M_0 which refers only to the physical amount of money in circulation. Broader definitions of money add to M_0 savings deposits and any other funds that are easily accessible for spending which, in the Middle Ages, would have included gold and silver plate, and that is M_1 while M_2 includes savings deposits and money created through loans or credit operations.[41] Some modern economic historians have chosen to use the narrowest definition of money, M_0 and to argue that the amount of credit available was directly linked to the size of the money supply. In the Middle Ages what was borrowed in coin had to be repaid in coin. If money was 'tight' – that is, in short supply for any reason – then credit dried up. Creditors could not lend, borrowers could not repay. Mercantile credit was also very much tied to trade cycles. When English wool was sold abroad, this released funds

B: THE EMERGENCE OF A MONEY ECONOMY, 1158–1351

that could then be lent to those who wished to buy goods in the Netherlands to sell in England. If markets were interrupted, then there were no profits to be made, no money to be lent. Even during 'normal' years money would be 'tight' or expensive to borrow at certain times. When the wool or cloth fleets were loading for export, merchants scrambled for credit, and when they returned with imports for sale, money was easier. There were almost certainly similar cycles in the countryside, related to the wool clip and the grain harvests, although these are much more difficult to measure, because of lack of evidence.[42]

This argument concentrates too much on international trade, however. There were different credit cycles and different credit needs within the economy. A peasant might have to borrow to avoid starvation, a bishop to pay his papal taxes, a knight to support his lifestyle, a merchant to pay for his wares, a king to finance his wars. There were also different forms of credit. Often it was not a matter of taking a direct loan, but of accepting or offering deferred payment for goods, or of borrowing by way of partnerships. In each case, however, one of the parties involved had to have either liquid capital to advance or sufficient resources to allow him or her to wait for repayment, or both.

At first sight, the connection between the amount of coin in circulation and the availability of credit seems an obvious one. More coin should have meant greater liquidity, and a greater ability to accumulate cash balances to lend, provided there was not excessive taxation or a drain of money abroad. There were always those in medieval society who, for a variety of reasons, had more liquid wealth than others and so were able to lend both on the grand scale and at very low levels. A 'money market' had emerged, but it was far less flexible and far less accessible than that which exists today where it is still relatively easy to borrow, even given credit squeezes. It was not quite that straightforward in the thirteenth century, and, almost inevitably, any analysis of the credit market is skewed by the evidence. It tells us much about lending and borrowing in the upper and middling ranks of society but little about peasant access to credit. At times of bad harvests and heavy taxation the poorest sections in rural society, the smallholders with few assets, needed to borrow to survive. They often found it necessary to do so and were forced to sub-let or sell portions of their land to raise the cash needed to buy food. In line with the evidence available, what follows is also badly skewed, leaving discussion of the vital rural credit market until last, when it should be first.[43]

Loans and partnerships

Before discussing who did lend money, it is best to consider the various ways by which credit was advanced and commercial partnerships were financed. Some form of security against a loan is always essential and in an agrarian society what better security could there be than land? During the course of the twelfth and thirteenth centuries the mortgage emerged, although not quite in the form we know it today. The author of the late twelfth-century legal treatise known as *Glanvill* discusses two different ways of 'gaging' moveable property, lands, tenements or rents: the vifgage and the mortgage. In both, the creditor (lender) took possession of the property. Under the vifgage any income he received went towards paying off the debt whereas under the mortgage the creditor took the income, but as profit. It did not go towards paying off the debt, which had to be repaid, in full, at the end of the specified term of years. *Glanvill* regarded this as usurious, and so it was, since taking the profits from the land was a form of interest. There were dangers for the creditor, especially from the second half of the twelfth century onward. His tenure of the land was less secure because he could be summarily dispossessed by the use of one of Henry II's new possessory assizes and so lose both profit and security for repayment.[44] In the thirteenth century this type of mortgage was replaced by one more favourable to the creditor. He now had a 'gage' of the land for a limited period only. If he was not repaid by the due date, then the land passed to him in perpetuity. He became the freeholder, and could sell the land to recover his debt, if he so wished, or add it to his estates. The Jews, who were the principal source of credit in the early thirteenth century, had their right to hold land, fees and gages confirmed to them by King John in 1201. From 1234 onward it was gradually taken away from them until, in 1271, it was completely removed. This was not the prime cause of their decreasing importance as providers of credit, however, because they had usually sold on estates acquired from defaulting debtors to willing Christian buyers in what was a land-hungry society.[45]

These were credit transactions to raise cash against the security of land. Other material objects could also be offered as collateral: plate, jewellery, armour, clothes, almost anything of value. If the debt was not repaid, then the creditor could sell the articles pledged. Other credit transactions were slightly more complicated. There was an unmeasurable degree of what might be called credit in kind, the loan of goods or equipment, or a promise to perform certain services. This all looks very much like barter, but clear cash values were given to such transactions. Failure to perform the services or use the equipment to perform a specified job resulted in a penalty, and these must be regarded as forms of credit. More common (or more measurable because of the weight of the evidence) were the various forms of sales credits. The simplest was the promise to buy an article at far more than its market price in return for a cash loan. No interest was charged on the loan itself. It was taken instead, heavily disguised, through the eventual purchase of a hat worth, say, 5s for 25s in return for a loan of 100s.[46]

Much more common, indeed almost standard, was the forward sale or purchase contract where the buyer or seller provided deferred credit terms. At its simplest this might involve a peasant lending a bushel of wheat to another peasant. It might be returned in kind, but more likely in a money equivalent. An abbey, or by the early fourteenth century, a knight who wished to borrow could use as security the current or, more dangerously because of the risk of sheep disease, the future wool clip. In the late thirteenth and early fourteenth centuries demand for English wool was at its height and exports ran at record levels. So the wool clip from the estate for several years in advance along with as much more wool as the debtor (the borrower) could put together from other sources, and notably from peasant flocks, would be offered as security for a loan. In this case the buyer, effectively the Flemish, English, or Italian exporter, was advancing the credit. This type of transaction could be turned around so that the manufacturer, often the clothier or cloth producer, accepted deferred payments, that is, over time, to his customers. There is a tendency to concentrate on evidence drawn from the activities of major wool exporters and, later, cloth manufacturers and their clients, but it is likely that these forms of sale credits were, along with the gage of land, the most common types of credit throughout society, remembering again that most credit transactions are unknown to us, either because they were successfully completed or have left no written evidence. It must also be stressed that they were credit transactions in the full sense. Creditors had to have the liquid capital to advance and the liquid resources available to them so that they could wait for deferred payments.[47]

Finally, there were commercial partnerships, which were themselves forms of credit arrangement. In a classic article Postan identified three types: 'service', where one person provided the capital or stock, the other the trading or manufacturing skills; 'finance', where the merchant hired the capital – that is, borrowed money or stock to finance his operations; and 'complete', where all parties contributed capital or goods and services. It goes without saying that these distinctions were often blurred in practice, but credit and deferred payments were clearly involved in all three. Whether partnerships were also made to disguise loans at interest is nigh impossible to discover. In addition, there were other forms of commercial credit agreements. A merchant living in one town or one country might consign his goods to a merchant or to a factor or servant living in another, to sell on his behalf, on a commission basis. He was essentially advancing credit to his agent through the capital tied up in his goods, until they were sold, and he realised his profits and the agent received his commission.[48]

Credit, then, can take various forms, but there are certain elements common to all of them. Creditors must have or have access to capital or capital assets, which could take the form of cash, but could also be stocks of food, materials, manufactured goods or equipment that they could advance to the debtor. Such advances were always made over time and the longer the time and the more complex the transaction, then the more need there was for a written record, a bond or recognizance, stating the terms of the loan and its repayment.[49] Then there was, or rather is, the matter of interest and the rates at which it was charged, or whether it was charged at all. From the mid-twelfth century the Church's attitude towards the taking of interest hardened, and notably so after the Fourth Lateran Council of 1215 and the Council of Lyon in 1234.[50] Up to the middle of the thirteenth century the Priory of Christ Church, Canterbury, borrowed extensively from both Jews and Italians and the rates of interest it had to pay were recorded in its accounts. For a loan of 420 marks (£280) from Roman and Sienese merchants in 1220 they had to pay 117½ marks (£78 6s 8d) interest while in 1240 a loan of £20 from Master Jacob, Jew, cost the house 4 marks (£2 13s 4d) in usury over a year. Then, apparently, there was a significant change in attitude and the outright recording of rates of interest charged disappeared. This could be interpreted as marking the disappearance of usury itself, in the face of the Church's growing disapproval of the practice, but that seems highly unlikely. What appears to have happened is that interest was disguised or taken, as it always had been, in a variety of different ways. If prompt repayment of a loan was not made, then 'damages' could legitimately be charged. More wool might be delivered than was paid for when forward contracts were made or, effectively, a lower price was set for the wool initially.[51]

Interest, therefore, could be, long had been and long was to be paid in kind. The king in particular had a great deal of patronage at his disposal. Advantageous marriages could be arranged, the administration of a minor's lands (wardship) or an office of profit granted, preferential customs duties levied on exports, embargoes on trade waived, convenient terms for the lease of land arranged, all in return for loans. In spite of the Church's teachings, the crown regularly paid interest on loans from its Italian bankers in the late thirteenth and early fourteenth centuries. The Frescobaldi were

B: THE EMERGENCE OF A MONEY ECONOMY, 1158-1351

owed £21,635 in 1310, of which interest and 'compensation' amounted to £12,000, while in 1348 Edward III owed the Bardi £63,000 plus a further £40,000 in 'charges'. The Italians also paid interest on some of the money deposited with them by great men, while in the diocese of Canterbury in the 1290s the Church courts found it nearly impossible to enforce the usury laws. It was difficult to do so when it was said in open court of one defendant that he took less for his loans than the archbishop himself charged his debtors. Most judges did not make the attempt and it probably has to be accepted that in disguised form and in various ways interest was charged on most if not all loans. Lastly, most lending, formal or informal, depended on the creditworthiness of the lender, the debtor, as it still does. If that was good, then the repayment might well be extended beyond the due date, at an extra cost, which was licit or legal interest on the original sum, or more funds would be advanced to ensure that a venture was successful, and that all monies or goods were recovered. But, ultimately, there had to be a degree of enforceability so that debts in any or all forms could be recovered through legal action. Without that protection, an active credit market could not have developed and we will return to this subject later in this chapter.[52]

The Jews and the Italians

It is quite usual to focus on the Jews and the Italians as the chief sources of credit in the thirteenth and early fourteenth centuries, because they had access to large reserves of liquid capital and enjoyed privileges that allowed them to secure the speedy repayment of debts owed to them. By the late twelfth century the Jews were certainly able to lend on a large scale to religious houses and to the nobility, as well as paying heavy tallages to the crown. William Fossard, a tenant-in-chief of the crown with extensive estates in Yorkshire, used them as security for loans amounting to £1,200 from Aaron of Lincoln c.1180 and nine Cistercian abbeys owed Aaron over £4,000. Some idea of their liquid wealth can be had from the £72,333 they paid in royal tallages between 1241 and 1256. Recent work has suggested that by the mid-thirteenth century at least their lending had moved a long way down the social scale so that by the early 1260s their clients included the gentry, wealthy peasants and artisans and craftsmen. They were providing credit to a rural society, on a wide scale, before the statute of Jewry of 1275 prohibited them from making loans at interest against the security of land or moveable goods. The statute of 1275 attempted to turn Jews from moneylenders into merchants and it has been argued that they became in effect commodity brokers, dealing in forward contracts in wool and grain. Most historians still believe that such contracts were simply a disguise for loans at interest, for which there was still a real need. A draft statute of c.1284-86 proposed that Jewish moneylending at interest should again be authorised, at a fixed annual rate of either 8s 8d in the £ or at a lower rate of 6s 8d. Nothing came of this, but it does suggest that the Jews were still of some importance as a source of credit for 'small' men in town and countryside alike. By 1290 they may have been nearly bankrupt, however, as a result of crippling royal taxes, and were increasingly seen as a community apart, religiously unacceptable and no longer of utility to the realm. Their expulsion in 1290 left a gap in the credit market that had, somehow, to be filled.[53]

The Jews had played an important role in the expanding economy of the thirteenth century but it was not just a matter of access to reserves of liquid capital that made it possible for them to lend in the way they did. What is often overlooked is that for nearly a century this literate and numerate community received special protection from the crown for the recovery of its debts. In 1194 a network of chirograph chests (*archae*) was established where the written records of all Jewish moneylending against the security of debtors's lands and of all repayments due on such debts were deposited. At first such chests were kept in six or seven towns only, but the practice soon spread and what it gave the Jews was an effective method for the written registration of debts due to them. Just as important, and again in 1194 or shortly after, the crown offered direct executive assistance in the collection of their debts. No prolonged legal procedure was necessary to establish the debtor's liability to pay. Debts to the Jews had to be paid when they were due, unless some compromise was reached between creditor and debtor. Within a few years the Exchequer of the Jews had emerged, which had jurisdiction over all debt litigation between Christians and Jews.[54] So it was not simply a matter of their having large reserves of cash to lend at interest that made the Jews the pre-eminent moneylender of the late twelfth and early thirteenth centuries. The system for the written registration of debts, and the effective legal means for their enforcement, gave them advantages not available to Christian lenders until the later thirteenth century. Not that they were always ruthless in making their creditors pay up. Time and again they would reach settlements with them, and accept lesser sums in ready cash than those that were due to them. Fiscal realism would often triumph over legal obligation. But, during the thirteenth century, perhaps from as early as 1234, Jewish privileges were gradually whittled away, and then finally removed by the statute of Jewry in 1275, fifteen years before their expulsion. Until then, and for almost a century, they alone had had clear legal protection for the recovery of their debts.[55]

Who was to replace them? Neither the Flemings who controlled the wool-export trade for much of the thirteenth century nor the Cahorsins, the wealthy merchants from southern France, engaged in the general credit market in England. Nor did the much better known or perhaps more widely studied Italians. They came to England in the first half of the thirteenth century both as merchants and as papal tax collectors. The money they gathered for the pope meant that they did have large reserves of money to lend, but Lloyd believes that their own trading operations in England provided them with the capital they needed. By the late thirteenth and early fourteenth centuries they had become the major royal financiers, providing through their loans the cash flow the crown needed, particularly for war. Their price was protection and privilege, so that by the late thirteenth and in the early fourteenth century they were able to dominate the wool-export trade, then at its medieval peak. They acted as deposit bankers for great noblemen and they controlled the exchange market, the transfer of funds by written instruments to and from the Continent, making their profits and sometimes losses from the fluctuating exchange rates. The Pulci-Rimbertini, Riccardi, Acciaiuoli, Frescobaldi, Bardi and Peruzzi seem to have dominated the upper end of the English credit market from the mid-thirteenth to the mid-fourteenth century. They had all the advantages the Jews had once had, access to large reserves of liquid capital, literacy, numeracy and privileged protection, since there is evidence that Edward I and probably his successors allowed them to use the Exchequer court to recover their debts.[56]

Nevertheless, the Italians did not fill the gap in the money market left by the impoverishment and then the expulsion of the Jews. There is no evidence to suggest that the Flemings, Cahorsins and Italians lent widely outside the privileged circle of crown, lay and ecclesiastical magnates, religious houses, wealthy royal officials and wealthy merchants.[57] The tempting assumption is that in general the Jews were replaced by Englishmen, who lent money at interest to their own countrymen. It has also been assumed that the amount of credit available automatically expanded in line with the increases in the money supply, the implication being that this was in the long run to the advantage of English lenders. The evidence for this substantial shift from the Jews and the aliens to the English seems at first sight to confirm both assumptions. More and more cases of debt, detinue (unlawful retention of goods) and account (failure to account properly for financial dealings where, say, a merchant had employed an agent to sell on his behalf) were being brought in courts at all levels, from the manor to the common bench. Recognizances, formal and binding acknowledgements of debt were being recorded on the close rolls and on the exchequer memoranda rolls in increasing numbers, and by towns in their own courts.[58] Then, in 1283 and 1285 came the statutes of Acton Burnell and Merchants. They provided for the formal registration of debts (although not of the interest due on them) on special rolls kept at certain specified towns, rather in the manner of the Jewish *archae*, and that, of course, produces more evidence of a widening credit market.[59] Nevertheless. there are dangers in such an interpretation. More evidence can be the result of the greater survival of records, and so there may be nothing new in all this. What did happen, however, was the gradual development of a legal framework for the recovery of debts, so that by the last quarter of the thirteenth century what had previously been the privilege of the Jews and the Italians was now widely available to the English.

Literacy and numeracy

There was no one cause for these important legal changes. Rather, they were the result of a whole series of interacting developments within English society in the thirteenth century. The first of these, as we have already seen, was the growth in literacy which in the late twelfth century was the accomplishment of the few but by 1300 had spread to the upper ranks of the peasantry.[60] Unquestionably the driving force here was the developing central administrative and legal bureaucracy. A growing body of trained administrators served that bureaucracy and their skills spread downward. The late twelfth-century *Treatise on the Laws and Customs of England*, commonly known as *Glanvill* after its supposed author Ranulf de Glanville, justiciar of England, shows a system of royal justice in which most actions at law were initiated by the *writ* which, as its name suggests, was a small written instrument ordering someone to do something. Royal courts also began to show a preference for written over oral evidence. It had long been recognised that a sealed charter (the seal being the mark of authenticity throughout the Middle Ages) gave added protection to property rights. As the pre-amble to an Anglo-Saxon charter succinctly put it:

> Whatever is transacted by men of this world, to endure for ever, ought to be fortified with ranks of letters [i.e., put in writing], because the frail memory of men in dying forgets what the writing of letters preserves and retains.[61]

B: THE EMERGENCE OF A MONEY ECONOMY, 1158-1351

Henry II's legal reforms made it much easier to challenge both the title to and possession of land. A written record whose authority could be proved by the witnesses to it and their seals now carried greater weight in courts than oral testimony and by 1300 this was as true for the peasant as for the knight.[62] There was also a growing and parallel need to record and to account. Literacy and numeracy need to be taken together. Land transfers had to be recorded both in terms of future ownership and possession, and in terms of extent, how many acres of arable, meadow and pasture, and of worth, how much was to be paid for the land, what it should yield in rent or other payments. Manorial lords interested in maximising the income from their estates required records of financial obligations, of customary payments due to them, rents, entry fines and heriots, as well as fines levied in the manorial courts for breaches of manorial discipline. Debts and contracts needed writing down since what was owed, in numerical terms, was after all a vital part of such instruments, along with the day or days on which payment was due, in part or whole.[63] The increasing use of money made more and more demands on literacy, and the downward spread of numeracy was as important as the general growth of literacy.

Unfortunately, numbers are not as attractive to the historian as the written word. There is no comprehensive study of numeracy to compare with Clanchy's study of literacy, partly because of the nature of the evidence available to us. A great deal is known about the development of the Exchequer and its practices. There has also been a considerable amount of work on how such practices were taken up on the estates of great lords to help in the administration of their estates. The localities had to account to the centre and used methods based on the Exchequer charge/discharge model. Expenditure was set against income and all liabilities recorded, so that a fixed balance of what owed from the manor could be struck. The accounting official then had either to pay over that balance, or acknowledge his future liability to pay. Such systems seem to have been developed earliest on the estates of the bishops of Winchester, and Vincent has shown in detail how and why that was.[64] In the first part of the thirteenth century the bishop's officials came from the localities to the centre to make their accounts, much as the sheriffs came to the Exchequer. The important change came mid-century when there were enough trained personnel to allow the accounts to be drawn up and written down locally, by local officials. This marked another important stage in the downward spread of skills. There were by then in the local communities sufficient clerks (men in minor holy orders) and, perhaps, laymen, who could read, write and number.[65]

Interestingly, the mid-thirteenth century also saw the beginnings of a parallel development, the keeping of written records of the proceedings of manorial courts, the court rolls. Razi and Smith noted this phenomenon and followed Harvey in rejecting the idea that recording payments such as the fines and amercements received by the bailiff or the reeve provided the impetus for these new records, something which could have been done just as effectively by making lists of such payments, as the bishops of Winchester's officials did on their central manorial accounts from the first decades of the thirteenth century onward. For them, the mid-century saw a struggle between the royal and local courts for business. New procedures and new actions were making the royal courts more attractive. To win back some of that business and therefore local influence, landlords began offering similar procedures in their own courts, and written record of proceedings to serve as proof in the future, if decisions were challenged. It is a persuasive case and Razi and Smith also see a correlation between the gathering momentum of manorial account-keeping and the appearance of the written court roll from the 1270s onward. This also happens to be the period of the greatest increase in the money supply and in the physical use of money at all levels. Keeping notes of payments due on the side of central accounts would no longer do. Local accounting was surely necessary and local officials had to undertake it.[66]

By the mid-thirteenth century there were manuals to instruct them in the task of estate management: Robert of Grosseteste, bishop of Lincoln, set down his *Rules*, Walter of Henley his *Husbondrie*; and then about 1265 there came a practical manual on how to keep – that is, administer – a manorial court. Seigneurial administration and elementary legal procedures were taught informally at Oxford, outside the university, and specimen formulae showing how courts should be kept and accounts drawn up began to circulate.[67] Kosminsky argued that at the time of the Hundred Roll inquests the lords of small estates had no need for keeping accounts. He may well have been right, but change was on its way. By the early fourteenth century Sir Lionel de Bradenham, a minor landlord in north Essex, and several of his contemporaries were keeping their own estate accounts. In towns, these too were the years when record-keeping emerged. Rules and regulations were written down and urban courts increasingly became the forums where commercial disputes were settled.[68] What are lacking are merchant and peasant accounts, to show how numeracy had spread with literacy, but it is possible to construct a convincing argument from the records that have survived. From top to bottom society was being called to account for money owed, for royal taxes and prises, for rents, for customary payments and for debts. Men and some women had to respond to financial demands made in writing. They had to be aware of what was required of them, of what their liabilities were and of their ability to pay them. As we have already seen, Kitsikopoulos estimates the annual income of a peasant farming 18 acres of land in the late thirteenth- and early fourteenth century to be 57s 7d. This is the equivalent of 691 silver pennies or, more likely, a mix of pennies, halfpennies and farthings which had to be collected from and paid to a variety of officials and individuals, customers, friends, relatives, employers and employees. An elementary knowledge of addition and subtraction was required, along surely with an awareness of what written figures meant. There is, as yet, no way of proving that wealthy peasants at least kept some sort of written accounts or reckonings, in however elementary a form, but it would be surprising if they did not.[69]

The recovery of debts and the enforcement of contracts

The payment of debts and performance of contracts had to be enforceable at law, however. It has already been argued that it was only with the statutes of Acton Burnell (1283) and Merchants (1285) that the English achieved the procedures for the enrolment and recovery of debts that had been available to the Jews since 1194. This being the case, the terms of both statutes are worth looking at in detail. Acton Burnell was made in response to the increasing problems experienced by English and alien merchants, particularly the Flemings, in the recovery of debts. It was proving very difficult to enforce judgments, even where it was all too apparent that the debtor had the resources to meet his obligations. The statute provided for the registration of debts before the mayors of London, Bristol and York. The terms of repayment were specified and if they were not met, then the mayor had the power to seize and sell the debtor's moveable goods and burgage tenements up to the value of the debt.[70] If the debtor had nothing that could be seized within the mayor's jurisdiction, then the sheriff within whose jurisdiction he did have possessions was to levy the debt instead. If that did not work, then the debtor could be imprisoned until arrangements for repayment had been made. Within two years this whole system had to be revised and by the terms of the statute of Merchants the number of towns where the debts could be registered was increased from three to fifteen, and since sheriffs had proved unwilling to implement the new procedures for distraint (seizure) of goods if a debt was not paid promptly, debtors were to be imprisoned immediately. They were then given three months to raise the necessary money. Failure to do so meant that the creditor would receive all the debtors' lands and goods until the debt was fully paid off from the proceeds.[71]

Together, Acton Burnell and Merchants introduced rigorous procedures for the recovery of debt and, as they became established and accepted, for the enforcement of other contracts. The use of such procedures was certainly limited to the relatively wealthy, to merchants and substantial landholders, and they were open to abuse. A corrupt moneylender, such as Walter Langton, Edward I's infamous treasurer, could exploit them quite ruthlessly to collect far more than had ever been lent. Consequently, in 1311 their use was restricted to merchants and the number of towns where debts could be registered was reduced to twelve. These amendments were subsequently repealed, in 1322, and on balance the statutes did provide merchants and especially alien merchants with effective ways of recovering debts. More importantly, they were symbolic of the growing use of courts at all levels to recover debts, and of debts being recorded formally to provide the written proof needed in such actions.

There is a growing volume of evidence of registration and recovery of debt from the second half of the thirteenth century onward. It comes from the records of manor, borough and fair courts, from the eyre rolls of the royal justices on their progresses through the counties, from the central courts of Common Pleas and King's Bench which respectively heard cases between private individuals and those involving the crown, and from the Chancery close rolls and the Exchequer memoranda rolls. Because the evidence survives, it is tempting to assume that the measures for the recovery of debt were growing generally from about 1250 onward. Lack of evidence makes comparison with earlier periods nigh impossible, however, and growing literacy may have produced more written evidence of what was already existing practice. Yet there is a real sense here of a growing and ascending series of courts where debts could be registered and recovery at least attempted. Lesser lay courts, hundredal and seignorial, continued to hear debt litigation throughout the thirteenth century and beyond. Neither they, nor manorial courts, were actually stopped from hearing cases involving sums over 40s by the statute of Westminster I of 1275. There was no attempt to impose such a limit before the last decade of the thirteenth century, and then more by accident than design. By the early 1290s it was being argued that a royal writ was necessary to initiate cases for recovery of debts above 40s, and since there were no such writs for initiating actions in lesser courts, they were effectively removed to the king's courts.[72]

It is sometimes argued that procedures in these courts were inflexible and cumbersome and actually hindered recovery of debt. The Law

B: THE EMERGENCE OF A MONEY ECONOMY, 1158–1351

Merchant, or rather the law of merchants, used in borough and fair or pie powder courts, is often seen as being much quicker. Almost instant judgments were delivered locally, by men with greater understanding of matters of debt and contract than the justices in the common law courts. Yet recent research has shown this idea to be something of a myth. Town and fair courts were important but they ran in parallel with rather than counter to the common law courts. They were being held in places where a great deal of trade took place, but they heard a multitude of cases, concerning everything from prostitution to dung heaps and blocking roads and not just matters of debt. They did offer swift judgments, and certainly at Yarmouth, London and in the Cinque ports registers were kept where debts could be enrolled, long before Acton Burnell and Merchants offered a similar service. At the same time, however, the crown allowed debts to be enrolled on the close and memoranda rolls, two of the most important records of the workings of central government, and royal courts were quite happy to hear cases according to the rules and procedures of the law merchant. This is important. Developments in one set of courts tended to influence practice and procedures in others. New actions, particularly of account and detinue, which developed in the royal courts, were copied eventually in manorial courts. The registration of debts was probably practised first in borough courts: it passed up to the royal courts, while after Acton Burnell and Merchants many borough courts copied the procedures they established.[73]

It is easy to be far too optimistic about the effectiveness of debt recovery. A court's jurisdiction was often limited to the specific area of a manor, hundred, borough or county. This meant it was difficult to enforce payments outside those jurisdictions, and Acton Burnell and Merchants offered solutions for the few rather than the many. Nevertheless, the growth of formal recorded proceedings was important. They provided written records of obligations, and courts were increasingly favouring written over oral evidence. It had been and remained possible to prove one's case by swearing an oath that the evidence given was true and then bringing oath-helpers to swear to the same effect. By the end of the thirteenth century, however, much more credence was being given to written evidence, to charters in land disputes, to written agreements, bonds and recognizances, in cases of debt or contract. An entry in a court roll could act as a formal recognizance of debt. It could also provide a preliminary negotiating point for an out-of-court settlement. Arbitration, formal and informal, was used throughout the Middle Ages as a way of settling disputes. If an action of debt, detinue or account was entered, then both sides might find that an

THE MAKING OF A MONEY ECONOMY, 1158-1351

out-of-court settlement, possibly for a lesser sum, saved time and trouble. Much debt still went unrecorded, however, and many disputes probably did not reach the courts at all, making it all the more difficult to reach even general conclusions about the level or amount of indebtedness and thus, indirectly, about the demand for credit. Yet it does seem to have been rising in the late thirteenth century. Monetary historians tend to see this as a result of the greater liquidity created by a vastly increased money supply. In so doing, they ignore the importance of the basic shift in the legal balance in favour of all creditors. Written credit agreements could at last be generally enforced in many courts and at a very local level. What had previously been the privilege of the Jew and the Italian was now available to the English.[74]

Credit provision by the English: lay and ecclesiastical moneylenders

The obvious answer to the question posed earlier, 'Who replaced the Jews?' should be, the English. It must again be stressed that the total amount of credit advanced by Englishmen cannot be quantified, making direct comparisons between the scale of their activities and those of the Jews and the Italians difficult, except perhaps in the narrow area of royal finances. What can be done is to identify those now willing, or able, to lend, and to draw some tentative conclusions. Moneylending by Christians was not new. In the late twelfth century, and before the quasi-monopoly of the Jews, William Cade of St Omer and William Trentegeruns of Rouen were major royal financiers and lent extensively to a variety of wealthy English clients. The list of Cade's debts, as acknowledged in the Pipe Rolls after his death in 1166, amounted to some £5,600. It shows that he lent to earls, barons, bishops and archbishops, to religious houses and most notably to those of the new Cistercian order. Postan also suggested that Cade was making forward contracts for wool, a practice usually associated with the Italians in the late thirteenth century. Henry II's quite arbitrary seizure of Cade's debts after his death seems to have discouraged other Christians from lending even to these 'blue chip' clients, however. Although there is some evidence of lending by prominent Londoners, such as Gervase of Cornhill, in association with the famous Jew, Aaron of Lincoln, by and large the credit market seems to have passed to the Jews. They too lent extensively to the Cistercians and other religious houses, as well as to the laity.[75]

Other moneylenders gradually emerged. As has been seen, Christ Church Priory, Canterbury, was using Italians to transfer funds to Rome and regularly borrowing from them in order to pay their papal taxes by the

B: THE EMERGENCE OF A MONEY ECONOMY, 1158-1351

early thirteenth century. At the same time the house was also borrowing from the Jews and from its lay and ecclesiastical neighbours. Prominent Kentishmen were often willing to lend substantial sums to the priory, apparently without expecting interest to be paid on them, which was only to be expected in the light of the Church's condemnation of usury at the Second (1139), the Third (1179) and the Fourth (1215) Lateran councils. Often these loans were repaid in instalments, and Mate argues that in effect the house was acting as a deposit banker. Mate also speculates that other lay and ecclesiastical lords were willing to lend to their fellows without expectation of profit from usury but of interest taken in the form of spiritual services, the employment of relatives or the need for a safe deposit for their cash. Christ Church may have acted altruistically but Thomas de Multon, the abbot of St Mary's, York, in the early fourteenth century certainly did not. He was a notorious moneylender and his corrupt activities were recounted two hundred years later in the *Little Gest of Robin Hood*.

Two of his contemporaries, Archbishop William de Melton of York (1317-40), and Edmund Fitzalan, earl of Arundel (1306-26), acted in much the same way. Melton used the profits of his archiepiscopal see and from his various offices to make no fewer than 700 loans and gifts to private persons resident in the northern province as a whole and even further afield. He lent to Yorkshire knights and barons, to Yorkshire abbeys and priories, to secular clergy, and to citizens of York, Beverley, Hull and Ripon. The loans were spread over the whole of his pontificate, but mostly came in the 1330s, when by 388 bonds, recognizances and pledges of plate he lent no less than £23,551 18s 1¼d. One of Melton's debtors was the wool merchant Simon Swanland, originally of Hull and later mayor of London, his kinsman and banker, and through him and his brothers Nicholas and Thomas Swanland he was connected to the Bardi and Peruzzi. Similarly, when the earl of Arundel was arrested and executed for treason in 1326 his records and accounts were seized and among them was a list of sums due to him by writings obligatory, or bonds. They amounted to £6,025 in all. John Lestrange, lord of Knocton and his wife Matilda owed him £2,000 'by a certain Statute Merchant made at Shrewsbury', Sir John de St John another £2,000 by a letter obligatory. John le Walsh, merchant of Shrewsbury owed Fitzalan £484 while more than sixty Shropshire men, members of the gentry, merchants and a humble parson, sums ranging between 400 marks (£266 13s 4d) and 40 marks (£26 13s 4d). Arundel maintained substantial reserves in cash, often acquired by less than legal means, and he seems to have been only too willing to lend it to others. Again, it should not be assumed that he took usurious interest since most of his loans were made to buy local support, and the wealth of the Fitzalans was quite extraordinary by late medieval standards. Nevertheless, he, Thomas de Multon, William de Melton and Christ Church, Canterbury, are good examples of the part played by great landlords in holding deposits for and advancing credit to friends and neighbours. There was perhaps nothing new in this, yet one cannot but be struck by the amount of liquid capital at the disposal of these two religious houses and of great nobles at the end of the thirteenth and in the early fourteenth century, and by Fitzalan's use of statute merchant bonds and letters obligatory.[76]

What does seem to have been new in the period was the growing provision of credit by royal and seigneurial officials and lawyers, who were often one and the same person or persons. The growth of the royal administration in the thirteenth century, in the Chancery, the Wardrobe and the courts of justice, saw an increase in the number and importance of the king's clerks.[77] According to Bowers, they were men of ambition, often in minor clerical orders, seeking advancement in the Church through their careers but with every legal device at their fingertips. They were among the first to use the enrolled recognizance as a means of guaranteeing repayment of debts, including money advanced by them in usurious loans. Using the lucrative profits from their offices, income from benefices, attorneys' fees, investments in land and the rights to marriages and wardships, some of them lent on the grand scale. Robert Burnell, bishop of Bath and Wells and Chancellor from 1274 to 1292, Adam de Stratton, chamberlain of the Exchequer, William Hamilton, chancery clerk and Chancellor 1305-7, and Walter de Langton, bishop of Lichfield and Coventry and Treasurer in the reigns of Edward I and Edward II were among the most notorious. Their resources were vast. Adam de Stratton alone had £12,500 in cash in his coffers when he fell victim to the purge of the judges in 1289, Langton probably much more than that. But the evil reputation of these men has overshadowed the much more important activities of these royal clerks, and of judges and lawyers like Sir John Stonor in the early fourteenth century and even the Masters of the Royal Mint. Most of them lent much more modest sums, most repayments were met, and most of their clients seemed satisfied.[78]

Credit provision by the English: the merchants

By the second half of the thirteenth century and within what might be called the upper ranks of landed society there existed webs of credit outside and alongside those established by the Jews and then the Italians. They were

B: THE EMERGENCE OF A MONEY ECONOMY, 1158-1351

based on the wealthy and the not so wealthy lending to clients, servants, those whose favour or influence they wished to secure, and to friends and relatives. The earl of Arundel could lend to the lord of Knocton, and the Archbishop of York to religious houses and to the merchants of the most important northern towns. Rural clergymen had money to lend from the sale of tithes and from offerings and oblations, while wealthy tenants on the royal manor of Havering, Essex, could borrow from others to finance the purchase of more land.[79] To this growing band of English creditors must be added the merchants great and small. The growing participation of English merchants in the wool-export trade and their ability to advance large sums on forward contracts is well known. The Basings and Cornhills from London, the Ludlow brothers of Shropshire and then, later, merchants from York, Beverley, Hull, Louth and Lincoln began to replace the Flemings and the Italians as the principal wool exporters, and as major suppliers of credit against the future wool clip. They also began to lend to the crown on a grand scale, especially in the opening stages of the Hundred Years War. After, and even before the collapse of the Italian companies, John Pyle and Adam Frauneys of London, and the de la Poles from Hull were becoming as important to Edward III as the Bardi and Peruzzi, as the Frescobaldi had been to Edward II and the Riccardi to Edward I. They lent from their own resources, and organised syndicates to raise even larger sums for the crown, much as the Italians had done. Acton Burnell and Merchants were passed to help men such as these and they made full use of the courts for enrolling recognizances of debt and taking actions of account where their factors or servants at home or abroad had defaulted on their obligations. The legal framework for recording and recovery of debts now allowed them to exploit their growing reserves of liquid capital to their own best advantage.[80]

There is also a growing body evidence for the use and extension of credit at a lower level. By the late thirteenth century the leading London pepperers already had extensive debts to their suppliers from Southern France and Lombardy. Then, in the early fourteenth century the expansion in the money supply meant even more imports bought on credit, with the average debt falling to about £14 per head. The records of the mayor's court in London also show credit, but at a much more modest level: refusal to pay the balance due on the sale of handbills; for failing to pay for six oxen; for failing to honour an agreement for the forward purchase of coal; for ale sold on 'tick'; for firewood sold and not paid for; and for hay.[81] More interestingly, outside London, pleas of debt and broken contract were being heard at Colchester in the early fourteenth century while the certificates sent to the Exchequer in 1287–89 by William fitz Robert of Goldington show recognizances made in Appleby in Westmorland. They relate to unpaid debts, many of them for wool owed to him by local growers, at values ranging between £1 16s 0d and £70. But there is also a list of goods he had sold on credit to local men in Cumberland and Westmorland, for sums ranging between 10s and £20 and mostly for short periods of between six and twelve months. Here, in a remote part of England, the legal processes for the recording and recovery of debt were known and used in the late thirteenth century.[82]

Credit provision by the English: village moneylenders

Lastly, least known but perhaps most vital were those who provided credit to villagers. Here we have to look beyond London and the other major urban centres and the credit flowing from town to countryside and back again. Feeding the capital, supplying it with firewood and other raw materials may well have had a major effect on the credit market at the manorial level in the Home Counties and the south-east generally. Rural money, or rather rural credit lines, flowed back into the towns for the purchase of manufactured and imported goods. Britnell has shown, however, that markets in late thirteenth- and early fourteenth-century England were by no means as well integrated as is often supposed.[83] Much trade was at the very local village level, be it in grain, livestock and animal products, pottery or firewood and building materials. Most of it was between the villagers themselves and we know very little indeed – currently – about how it was financed. Local butchers and corn dealers probably extended credit to villagers, but often through bargains made in the fields and by oral agreements. As the thirteenth century wore on, there was also an increasing need for peasants to borrow to pay taxes and other dues, to buy food in the famine years of 1315–16, or to participate in the active peasant land market that does seem to have existed, to a greater or lesser extent, almost everywhere in England.[84] The difficulty here is that, at present, we know little about how and from whom money could be borrowed in villages, small country towns and at the network of small fairs held at regular intervals across the countryside. Nevertheless, as long ago as 1970 Hyams suggested that in the earlier part of the century the Jews played some role in moneylending at the village level, and there is now growing evidence to support his argument. The German merchant Terricus of Cologne, for example, was acquiring property and land in Stamford and the surrounding countryside in the first half of the thirteenth century, often from vendors who

B: THE EMERGENCE OF A MONEY ECONOMY, 1158-1351

needed cash to pay debts to the Jews. Mundill has shown how in the 1260s the Jews were lending extensively to artisans, craftsmen and wealthier villagers in Herefordshire, Lincolnshire and Kent, and possibly in other counties.[85]

This was credit from outside sources being extended to the wealthier members of these rural communities. Who lent to the less well-off? Hyams pointed to the activities of Henry Wade, an established moneylender on the manor of Wakefield (Yorks.) in the early fourteenth century. He was also one of the most important dealers in land in the village, and this connection between landed wealth and the extension of credit was also firmly made by Smith and Campbell in the 1980s. They mainly focused on evidence from the 'crisis' decades of 1290-1320, to show that in years of poor or disastrous harvests that led to severe famine there was often an active trade in peasant land. For the most part it passed from smallholders to wealthier peasants seeking to enlarge their own holdings. Smallholders may have thought or hoped they would be able to buy back their land when the crisis years were over but that seldom seems to have happened. Schofield went further than this in 1997 in his study of dearth, debt and the local land market in the Suffolk village of Hinderclay. He developed Maddicott's argument that the combined weight of heavy taxation and purveyance led to the general impoverishment of the peasantry between 1294 and 1341. What Schofield found at Hinderclay was that the heavy taxation of the 1290s led creditors to withdraw their loans and to invest instead in land, so removing credit at a time when it was most needed, causing further distress to an already struggling class of smallholders.

More recent research has confirmed that village credit in the late thirteenth and early fourteenth centuries ran along vertical rather than horizontal lines, between the rich and the poor, with little evidence of lending within family or kin groups. Briggs has also investigated the workings of rival manorial courts to demonstrate that some were more efficient than others in hearing cases and bringing them to a conclusion, so drawing business to themselves. The group of seven Cambridgeshire manors he has studied bear more resemblance to those in the open-field villages of midland and southern England than to those in the small-holding and intensively-farmed settlements of Norfolk and Suffolk, making his evidence more widely applicable. In truth, however, the two regions differed little in terms of credit structures, with vertical lines of obligation predominating in both.

More significantly, Briggs has shifted the argument about village credit away from the crisis years of late thirteenth- and early fourteenth-century rural England, to a wider chronological framework, while adding useful comparisons with credit arrangements in rural western Europe. Outside the crisis years it is possible to see, from an admittedly limited amount of evidence, that there were fully functioning lines of credit within villages in eastern England with the emphasis being not on the straight cash loan, as in western Europe, but on the future performance of contracts, the loan of foodstuffs to be repaid when the next harvest came in or of services to be performed in return for the use of equipment such as ploughs or carts. This was mainly internal credit, within the village, although wealthier peasants producing for the market were also debtors to merchants in small towns.[86] There were others in most villages who might also be willing to lend, reeves and other manorial officials with cash balances waiting to be paid in and local clergymen with spare cash from the sale of tithes. The poor had to rely on the wealthy who inevitably looked after their own interests when times were hard. Finally, two important points must be borne in mind, both here and in later chapters. First, money was always involved in credit transactions, either as a standard of value or in penalties imposed for the non-performance of contracts. Secondly, as with the cases originating from the legislation enacted by Acton Burnell and Merchants, pleas in manorial courts record failed agreements. The total amount of credit extended was always far greater than that calculated from such evidence, because most debts were paid on time or settlements reached out of court. Ultimately, however, there had to be legal means for the enforcement of credit agreements and by the later thirteenth century they were available in courts high and low, from common pleas to the manor.

The money market

None of this is to argue that there was a highly organised 'money market' in the modern sense of the term in late thirteenth- or early fourteenth-century England. Some of its characteristics did exist. Money could be 'tight' or 'easy' according to trade cycles, harvest fluctuations, heavy taxation and short- or long-term changes in the money supply. Creditworthiness was important and judged in much the same way as it is today, according to potential assets or income and personal reputation. There were some opportunities for outsiders to invest in commercial partnerships, and rich men could put money on deposit with the Italians or with religious houses. What did not exist, however, was a general banking system operating on the fractional reserve principle, that is accepting deposits from a wide range of clients but maintaining on demand only a percentage of their capital, with the rest being lent out at specified and variable rates of interest. The Jews and the Italians perhaps came nearest this model in their credit dealings, but only for the Jews was moneylending their main business. Others lent money as and when it suited them and from the profits of their other main occupation or office. William de Melton, archbishop of York, and Henry Wade of Wakefield, the one a great officer of Church and state, the other a wealthy peasant, had that much in common. Ironically, and perhaps in a quasi-modern way, credit was all too often called in when it was most needed, in times of subsistence crisis or heavy taxes or both combined, while its availability does seem to have depended heavily in the upper ranks of society on personal and interfamilial relationships. Lords lent to their clients, and vice versa, and mercantile loans and partnerships often reveal connections by birth or marriage. As we have seen, the reverse seems to have been true among the peasantry, insofar as the evidence will allow us to see credit and debit across the whole of rural England rather than simply in the eastern counties.

This was scarcely an independent money market in the modern sense, nor was there borrowing for capital investment. That did not happen. Money was borrowed for many purposes, to pay taxes, finance buildings, to buy foodstuffs or land, for the income and status it would bring. On some great estates profits were calculated in crude ways, but mainly to determine which type of farming practices would bring the best income, but income to spend. The idea of investment for capital formation seems to have been foreign to thirteenth- and early fourteenth-century England.[87] The only transition that does seem to have taken place was the growth of the money contract between lord and client to replace the bond previously based on land and the tenure of land. Feudalism, it seems, was replaced by 'bastard' feudalism. Exactly when and why that happened is the subject of a vigorous debate, but one in which the question of the money supply seems to have been largely ignored. Yet it deserves consideration. John rewarded his household knights with lands, wardships and marriages. By Edward I's reign the money retainer was much more common, and not just for knights, but for judges and household servants, while the large armies raised for the Welsh, Scottish, and French wars mostly fought for wages. Between the two reigns there had been at least a fourfold increase in the amount of coin in circulation.[88]

With no organized money market and little sign of the much-discussed transition from feudalism to capitalism, it might seem that the massive increase in the money supply had had little structural effect on the economy by the end of the thirteenth century. This would be quite wrong.

The growth of literacy and numeracy, in recording and accounting, and in the legal enforceability of debts and contracts created a framework within which money could work far more effectively than it had done a century earlier. This had serious implications for the development of the market and of commercialisation. There is considerable disagreement about both the size and the function of the market c.1300. Some see it as being highly integrated, ironing out inequalities in supply, and very much geared to serving the needs of the largest fifty or so English towns. Others believe that it was for the most part uneven in quality, with the majority of medieval producers operating only or mainly in localised small markets which were likely to be volatile and subject to disruption. Doubts have also been cast about the extent to which specialisation and craft industries could provide alternative employment and income for the very large numbers of smallholders at times of harvest failures and subsistence crises. It was precisely at those times that the demand for craft products was likely to collapse, so depriving the peasant smallholder of the income the family needed to survive in those desperate years.[89]

Yet much of the argument revolves around the nature, scope and effectiveness of the market and it is worth thinking, or speculating, as Bailey has in his study of rural poverty in the late thirteenth century, about the relationship between markets and money. However limited, however imperfect the market, it did help sustain a population that had doubled or trebled in size between 1086 and 1300. The market could not provide the panacea for all ills. There were years of real crisis, of harvest failure and crippling taxation between c.1290 and the early 1320s and then again in the 1340s, and it is worth noting that these coincided with periods of great volatility in the money supply. But, by the early fourteenth century, England could not have sustained the level of population that it did, however precariously, had there not been both a money economy and a market economy, and the one was absolutely vital for the other. The extent to which this was now a money economy can be seen precisely by the response of prices to fluctuations in the money supply and in the velocity of circulation. It can also be seen in the way in which some, many, peasants were forced to sell what little they had to raise money to buy food. This is perhaps one of the most telling pieces of evidence for the widespread use of money by the early fourteenth century and of how deeply engrained buying and selling had become in the economy, from the top to the bottom of society. Cash and credit went together, and the size and effectiveness of the market was much greater not simply because there was more coin in circulation, but because literacy, numeracy, accountability and enforceability cut transaction costs

B: THE EMERGENCE OF A MONEY ECONOMY, 1158-1351

and allowed money to work more effectively. All that was perhaps lacking was negotiability of written instruments, so that they could act as fiduciary or paper money and so supplement the money supply. This is an issue to be discussed later, and at much greater length in the following chapters. For the moment it is worth, again, speculating, that when England was awash with silver there was little need for any new forms of money. It was only when there was a shortage of bullion and of coin that the need grew for new forms of money in the shape of negotiable written instruments. What can and should be argued here is that without the massive increase in the money supply in the second half of the thirteenth century and the parallel development of a framework within which it could work effectively, the consequences of the early fourteenth century crises might have been much greater than they all too obviously were.

Notes

1 See above, pp. 25-6, and Table 2.1, 54, 157, 162.
2 I. Kershaw, 'The great famines and the agrarian crisis in England 1315-22', *P&P*, 59 (1973), 3-50; J.R. Maddicott, *The English Peasantry and the Demands of the Crown, 1294-1341*, *P&P* supplement no. 1 (Oxford: Oxford University Press for the *P&P Society*, 1975), pp. 1-75; A.R. Bridbury, 'Before the Black Death', *EcHR*, 2nd series, 30 (1977), 393-410; M. Prestwich, *War, Politics and Finance under Edward I* (London: Faber and Faber, 1972), pp. 92-113, 117-203; Prestwich, *Edward I*, pp. 398-400, 568-71, ; B. Harvey ' Introduction: the crisis of the early fourteenth century' in B.M.S. Campbell (ed.), *Before the Black Death: Studies in the Crisis of the Early Fourteenth Century* (Manchester: Manchester University Press, 1992), pp. 1-24; W.M. Ormrod, 'The crown and the English economy, 1290-1348' in Campbell (ed.), *Before the Black Death*, p. 182; W.C. Jordan, *The Great Famines: Northern Europe in the Early Fourteenth Century* (Princeton, NJ; Princeton University Press, 1996); M. Bailey, 'Peasant welfare in England, 1290-1348', *EcHR*, 2nd. series, 51 (1998), 223-51; Dyer, *An Age of Transition?*, pp. 29-33; B.M.S. Campbell, 'The agrarian problem in the early fourteenth century', *P&P*, 188 (2005), 3-70.
3 Britnell, *Commercialisation*, pp. 79-151, 228-31; see above, pp. 89, 117-119, 130.
4 Harvey, 'English inflation', 3-30; P.D.A. Harvey, 'The pipe rolls and the adoption of demesne farming in England', *EcHR*, 2nd series, 27 (1974), 345-59; A.R. Bridbury, 'Thirteenth-century prices and the money supply', *AgHR*, 33 (1985), 1-21; N.J. Mayhew, 'Money and prices in England from Henry II to Edward III', *AgHR*, 33 (1985), 121-32; Bolton, 'The English economy in the early thirteenth century', 27; Latimer, 'The English inflation of 1180-1220 reconsidered', 3.
5 See below, pp. 211-14.
6 P. Latimer, 'Early thirteenth-century prices', in Church (ed.), *The Reign of King John*, pp. 41-73; see above, pp. 149-51.
7 See above, Figure 6.1, p. 150.

8 J. Stevenson (ed.), *Radulphi de Coggeshall Chronicon Anglicanum*, Rolls Series (London, 1875), pp. 129, 142, 151: D.L. Farmer, 'Prices and wages', in Hallam et al. (eds), *The Agrarian History of England and Wales, vol.ii, 1042–1350*, pp. 715–78; Latimer 'Early thirteenth-century prices', pp. 41–73; Latimer, 'The English Inflation of 1180–1220 reconsidered', 3–29.

9 N. Barratt, 'The revenue of King John', *EHR*, 111 (1996), 841–3; Bolton, 'The English economy in the early thirteenth century', p. 34.

10 J.E.A. Joliffe, 'The chamber and castle treasuries under King John', in R.W. Hunt, W.A. Pantin and R.W. Southern (eds), *Studies in Medieval History Presented to F.M. Powicke* (Oxford: Oxford University Press (1948), pp. 133–5, 140–1; Bolton, 'The English economy in the early thirteenth century', p. 34.

11 Lloyd, *The English Wool Trade*, pp. 7–8, 11–14; Bolton, 'The English economy in the early thirteenth century', pp. 34–6.

12 W.L. Warren, *King John* (Harmondsworth: Penguin Books, 1966), p. 163; Farmer, 'Prices and wages', p. 767 and Fig. 7.9, p. 770 and Fig 9.10; Bolton, 'Inflation, economics and politics', p. 4; Latimer, 'Early thirteenth-century prices', p. 70; P. Latimer, ' Estate management and inflation: the honor of Gloucester, 1183–1263', *Albion*, 34 (2002), 201–2; see above, pp. 25–6, and Table 2.2.

13 Britnell, *Commercialisation*, pp. 79–127 discusses fully the growth of the market; Masschaele, *Peasants, Merchants, and Markets*, pp. 57–72; see below, pp. 00–00.

14 H.A. Miskimin, 'Population growth and the price revolution in England', *JEEH*, 4 (1975), 179–86; Miskimin, 'The impact of credit on sixteenth-century English industry' in F. Chiapelli (ed.), *The Dawn of Modern Banking* (New Haven and London: Yale University Press, 1979), pp. 275–89; J.A. Goldstone, 'Urbanization and inflation: lessons from the English price revolution of the sixteenth and seventeenth centuries', *American Journal of Sociology*, 89 (1984), 1122–60; Mayhew, 'Modelling medieval monetisation', p. 70; Britnell, *Commercialisation*, 73–127; N.J. Mayhew, 'Population, money supply and the velocity of circulation in England, 1300–1700', *EcHR*, 2nd series, 48 (1995), 238–57; S.H. Rigby, 'Introduction', in R. Horrox and W.M. Ormrod (eds), *A Social History of England, 1200–1500* (Cambridge: Cambridge University Press, 2006), pp. 22–7. R.C. Palmer has further argued in 'The economic and cultural impact of the origins of property: 1180–1220', *LHR*, 3 (1985), 381–9, that reforms in the common law in the late twelfth and early thirteenth centuries strengthened proprietary rights, encouraged a lively land market and so caused a build-up of inflationary pressures by increasing the velocity of monetary circulation. It seems unlikely that the land market could develop so suddenly and on a sufficient scale to have had a marked effect on prices.

15 J.Z. Titow, *Winchester Yields: A Study in Medieval Agricultural Productivity* (Cambridge: Cambridge University Press, 1972), pp. 9–33; D. Postles, 'Cleaning the medieval arable', *AgHR*, 37 (1989), 130–43; E.I. Newman and P.D.A. Harvey, 'Did soil fertility decline in medieval English farms? Evidence from Cuxham, Oxfordshire, 1320–1340', *AgHR*, 45 (1997), 119–36; B.M.S. Campbell, 'Economic rent and the intensification of English agriculture 1086–1350' in G.G. Astill and J. Langdon (eds), *Medieval Farming and Technology: The Impact of Agricultural*

Change in Northwest Europe (Leiden: Brill, 1997), pp. 233–5; B.M.S. Campbell, *English Seigniorial Agriculture 1250–1450* (Cambridge: Cambridge University Press, 2000), pp. 306–75; Campbell, 'The agrarian problem in the early fourteenth century', 65–8.
16 See above, p. 26, Table 2.2.
17 Farmer, 'Prices and wages', p. 767, Fig. 7.9.
18 J. Hatcher, 'English serfdom and villeinage: towards a reassessment', *P&P*, 90 (1981), 3–24; J. Kanzaka, 'Villein rents in thirteenth-century England: an analysis of the Hundred Rolls of 1279', *EcHR*, 2nd series, 55 (2002), 594–617; Campbell, 'The agrarian problem', 4–10, 24–44; Dyer, *Making a Living in the Middle Ages*, p. 133; C. Dyer, 'The ineffectiveness of lordship in England, 1200–1400' in C. Dyer (ed.), *Rodney Hilton's Middle Ages*, *P&P*, 195 (2007), supplement no. 2, 69–70, 85; Z. Razi, 'Serfdom and freedom in medieval England: a response to revisionists' in Dyer (ed.), *Rodney Hilton's Middle Ages*, 182–7.
19 See above, pp. 153–4, 156.
20 Britnell, *Commercialisation*, pp. 81–2; G. G. Astill, 'General survey', in Palliser (ed.), *Cambridge Urban History*, Vol. i, pp. 46–9.
21 Farmer, 'Prices and wages' pp. 737–9; Prestwich, *Edward I*, p. 248.
22 Farmer, 'Prices and wages', p. 719, Fig. 7.1.
23 See above, Table 2.2, pp. 26–7, and pp. 163–4 for full details of changes in the money supply in the early fourteenth century; Farmer 'Prices and wages', p. 767, fig. 9; Ormrod, 'The crown and the English economy', pp. 182–3.
24 S.H. Rigby, 'Introduction: social structure and economic change in late medieval England', in Horrox and Ormrod (eds), *A Social History of England, 1200–1500*, pp. 23–9.
25 Harvey, 'English inflation', 5; Harvey, 'The pipe rolls and the inception of demesne farming in England', 353–4; Bolton, 'The English economy in the early thirteenth century', p. 27.
26 Bridbury, 'Thirteenth-century prices', 4; Rigby, *English Society*, pp. 127–43; Dyer, *Making a Living*, pp. 127–8; H. Kitsikopoulos, 'Technological change in medieval England: a critique of the neo-Malthusian argument', *Proceedings of the American Philosophical Society*, 144 (2000), 397–449; Campbell, *English Seigniorial Agriculture*, pp. 18–22.
27 S.L. Waugh, 'Tenure to contract: lordship and clientage in thirteenth-century England', *EHR*, 101 (1986), 812–3; R.C. Stacey, *Politics, Policy and Finance under Henry III, 1216–1245* (Oxford: Clarendon Press, 1987), pp. 66–73; N. Vincent, 'The origins of the Winchester Pipe Rolls', *Archives*, 20 (1994), 35.
28 See below, pp. 199–202, for further discussion of these topics.
29 P.R. Coss, 'Sir Geoffrey de Langley and the crisis of the knightly class in thirteenth-century England', *P&P*, 65 (1975), 3–37; D.A. Carpenter, 'Was there a crisis of the knightly class in the thirteenth century? The Oxfordshire evidence', *EHR*, 722–4; P. Coss, *The Origins of the English Gentry* (Oxford: P&P Publications, 2003), pp. 69–108.
30 Carpenter, 'Was there a crisis of the knights', 738–9; K. Faulkner, 'The transformation of knighthood in early thirteenth-century England', *EHR*, 111 (1996), 21–3; C. Carpenter, 'England: the nobility and the gentry', in S.H. Rigby (ed.),

A Companion to Britain in the Later Middle Ages (Oxford: Blackwell, 2003), pp. 262-4; Coss, *Origins of the English Gentry*, pp. 69-108.
31 Langdon and Masschaele, 'Commercial activity and population growth' 36-42.
32 See above, pp. 189-91.
33 These topics can be pursued further in: Prestwich, *War, Finance and Politics*; G.L. Harriss, *King, Parliament and Public Finance in Medieval England to 1369* (Oxford: Clarendon Press, 1975); R.C. Palmer, *The County Courts of Medieval England, 1150-1350* (Princeton, NJ: Princeton University Press, 1982); Prestwich, *Edward I*; Clanchy, *From Memory to Written Record*; P. Brand, *The Origins of the English Legal Profession* (Oxford: Blackwell, 1992); W.M. Ormrod, *Political Life in Medieval England, 1300-1450* (London: Macmillan, 1995); Britnell, *Commercialisation*; R.H. Britnell, 'Specialization of work in England 1100-1300', *EcHR*, 2nd series, 54 (2001), 1-16; Langdon and Masschaele, 'Commercial activity and population growth', 35-81.
34 Titow, *Winchester Yields*, pp. 1-33; B.M.S. Campbell et al., *A Medieval Capital and its Grain Supply: Agrarian Production and Distribution in the London Regions c.1300* (London: Institute of British Geographers Historical Geography Series, 30, 1993), pp. 172-83; Rigby, *English Society*, p. 65; Bailey, 'Peasant welfare in England, 1290-1348', 237; Campbell, *English Seigniorial Agriculture*, pp. 193-212; H, Kitsikopoulos and H. Fox, 'Review article. Campbell on late-medieval English agriculture: two views', *JEH*, 62 (2002), 213-16; H. Kitsikopoulos, 'Urban demand and agrarian productivity in pre-plague England: reassessing the relevancy of von Thunen's model', *Agricultural History*, 77 (2003), 482-522.
35 E.A. Kosminsky, 'The Hundred Rolls of 1279-80 as sources for English agrarian history', *EcHR*, 1st series (1930-31), 16-44; Kosminsky, *Studies in the Agrarian History of England in the Thirteenth Century* (Oxford: Blackwell, 1956), 152-96; Maddicott, *The English Peasantry and the Demands of the Crown, passim*; Hatcher, 'English serfdom and villeinage', 6-14; Britnell, *Commercialisation*, 111-12; C. Dyer, 'Taxation and communities in late medieval England', in Hatcher and Britnell (eds), *Progress and Problems in Medieval England*, pp. 168-74; C. Reed and A.M. Dross, 'Labour services in the thirteenth century', *JEEH*, 26 (1996), 333-46; Kanzaka, 'Villein rents in thirteenth-century England', 593-618; P. Schofield, *Peasant and Community in Medieval England 1200-1500* (London: Palgrave Macmillan, 2003), pp. 11-33; S. Raban, *A Second Domesday? The Hundred Rolls of 1279-80* (Oxford: Oxford University Press, 2004), pp. 131 ff.; Razi, 'Serfdom and freedom in medieval England', 182-7.
36 J.A.F. Thomson, 'Tithe disputes in later medieval London', *EHR*, 78 (1963), 1-4 for urban tithes paid in cash; Maddicott, *The English Peasantry and the Demands of the Crown*, pp. 11-14; C. Dyer, 'Peasants and coins: the uses of money in the Middle Ages', *BNJ*, 67 (1997), 41.
37 See above, pp. 209-11.
38 J.Z. Titow, *English Rural Society 1200-1350* (London: Allen and Unwin, 1969), pp. 64-96; Dyer, *Standards of Living*, pp. 109-50; Rigby, *English Society*, pp. 30-4; H. Kitsikopoulos, 'Standards of living and capital formation in pre-plague England: a peasant budget model', *EcHR*, 2nd series, 53 (2000), 237-61; P.R. Schofield, 'The social economy of the medieval village in the early fourteenth century', *EcHR*, 2nd

B: THE EMERGENCE OF A MONEY ECONOMY, 1158-1351

series, 61 (2008), 38-63; the best guide to regional variation is the various chapters in Hallam (ed.), *The Agrarian History of England and Wales, vol. i.*

39 Dyer 'Peasants and coins', 30-47 where on 39 he defines 'coins' as silver pennies, and cut and minted halfpennies and farthings.

40 M. Prestwich, 'The crown and the currency', 52.

41 M_0 can be defined as cash in circulation with the public and in the commercial banks' tills and cash balances held by the banks at the Bank of England: Mackintosh et al., *Economics and Changing Economies*, p. 378.

42 Nightingale, 'Monetary contraction and mercantile credit in later medieval England', 561-4; Britnell, *Commercialisation*, p. 122; J. Kermode, *Medieval Merchants: York, Beverley and Hull in the Later Middle Ages* (Cambridge: Cambridge University Press, 1998), pp. 165-7, 245, 306; A.F. Sutton, *The Mercery of London: Trade, Goods and People, 1130-1578* (Aldershot: Ashgate, 2005), pp. 132-8, 236.; credit cycles in the countryside await thorough investigation. For later international trade and credit cycles see: R.C. Mueller, *The Venetian Money Market: Banks, Panics and the Public Debt 1200-1500* (Baltimore and London: Johns Hopkins University Press, 1997), pp. 305-14; F. Guidi Bruscoli and J.L. Bolton, 'The Borromei bank research project', in L. Armstrong et al. (eds), *Money, Markets and Trade in Late Medieval Europe: Essays in Honour of John Munro* (Leiden and Boston: Brill, 2007), pp. 471-81.

43 See above, pp. 209-11.

44 S.C. Milsom, *Historical Foundations of the Common Law* (London: 2nd edn, Butterworth, 1981), pp. 134-43; R.C. Palmer, 'The origins of property in England', *LHR*, 3 (1985), 1-50; Palmer, 'The economic and cultural impact of the origins of property, *LHR*, 3 (1985), 375-96; Warren, *The Governance of Norman and Angevin England*, pp. 113-17.

45 Rigby, *English Society*, pp. 286-8; see above, pp. 185-7.

46 L.H. Butler, 'Archbishop Melton, his neighbours and kinsmen', *Journal of Ecclesiastical History*, 2 (1951), 58-9; H.G. Richardson, *The English Jewry and Angevin Kings* (London: Methuen, 1960), pp. 76-7; R.H. Helmholz, 'Usury and the medieval English church courts', *Speculum*, 61 (1986), 366.

47 Lloyd, *The English Wool Trade*, pp. 288-99; Britnell, *Commercialisation*, p. 99; P. Nightingale, 'Knights and merchants: trade, politics and the gentry in late medieval England', *P&P*, 169 (2000), 36-62; Nightingale, 'The English parochial clergy as investors and creditors in the first half of the fourteenth century', in P.R. Schofield and N.J. Mayhew (eds), *Credit and Debt in Medieval England* (Oxford: Oxbow Books, 2002), pp. 89-105; A. Bell, C. Brookes and P. Dryburgh, *The English Wool Market, c.1230-1327* (Cambridge: Cambridge University Press, 2007), pp. 68-112.

48 M.M. Postan, 'Partnership in English medieval commerce', in his *Medieval Trade and Finance* (Cambridge: Cambridge University Press, 1973), pp. 66-7.

49 Thirteenth-century bonds and recognizances are discussed in J. Biancalana, 'The development of the penal bond with conditional defeasance', *Journal of Legal History*, 26 (2005), 103-17.

50 J. Gilchrist, *The Church and Economic Activity* (London: Macmillan, 1969), pp. 65-9, 112-15; Helmholz, 'Usury and the medieval English church courts', 365-7; Wood, *Medieval Economic Thought*, pp. 161 ff.; Nightingale, 'English parochial

clergy', 89; L. Armstrong, 'Usury', in *The Oxford Encyclopaedia of Economic History* (Oxford: Oxford University Press, 2003).

51 M. Mate, 'The indebtedness of Canterbury Cathedral Priory 1215–1295', *EcHR*, 2nd series, 26 (1973), 183–94.

52 M. Prestwich, 'Italian merchants in late thirteenth-century and early fourteenth-century England' in Chiapelli (ed.), *The Dawn of Modern Banking*, pp. 85, 86–7; E.B. Fryde, 'The deposits of Hugh Despenser the younger with Italian bankers', in his *Studies in Medieval Trade and Finance* (London: Hambledon Press, 1983), pp. 346–59; Helmholz 'Usury', 377; see above, pp. 202–5.

53 J.C. Holt, *The Northerners: A Study in the Reign of King John* (Oxford: Clarendon Press, 1961), pp. 166–7; Richardson, *The English Jewry*, 60; S. Menache, 'Faith, myth and politics: the stereotype of the Jews and their expulsion from England and France', *The Jewish Quarterly Review*, 75 (1985), 351–74; Miller and Hatcher, *Medieval England: Towns, Commerce and Crafts*, pp. 381–9; R.C. Stacey, 'Jewish lending and the medieval English economy', in Britnell and Campbell, *A Commercialising Economy*, p. 93; N. Fryde, *Ein Mittelalterlicher deutscher Grossunternehmer: Terricus Teutonicus de Colonia in England, 1217–1247* (Stuttgart: Franz Steiner Verlag, 1997), pp. 95–103 and cartulary, nos 40 and 42; Mundill, *England's Jewish Solution*, pp. 146–208, 209–48; P. Brand, 'Jews and the law in England, 1275–90', *EHR*, 115 (2000), 1140–58; R.R. Mundill, 'Edward I and the final phase of Anglo-Jewry' in Skinner (ed.), *The Jews in Medieval Britain*, pp. 55–70.

54 Richardson, *The English Jewry*, pp. 135–60; Brand, 'Jews and the law', 1138–40; Brand, 'The Jewish community of England in the records of English royal government', in Skinner (ed.), *Jews in Medieval Britain*, pp. 73–83.

55 Stacey, 'Jewish lending', pp. 91–2; P.R. Hyams, 'The Jews in medieval England, 1066–1290', in A. Haverkampf and A. Vollrath (eds), *England and Germany in the High Middle Ages* (Oxford: Oxford University Press, 1996), pp. 173–92; Mundill, *England's Jewish solution*, pp. 249–85; Brand, 'Jews and the law', 1140–58; see above, pp. 202–5.

56 E.B. Fryde, 'Loans to the English crown, 1328–31', *EHR*, 70 (1955), 205; Kaeuper, *Bankers to the Crown: The Riccardi of Lucca anad Edward I* (Princeton, NJ: Princeton University Press, 1973), pp. 121–4; R.W. Kaeuper, 'The Frescobaldi of Florence and the English crown', *Studies in Medieval and Renaissance History*, 10 (1973), 41–95; Mate, 'Indebtedness of Canterbury Cathedral Priory', 183–94; Fryde, 'The deposits of Hugh Despenser the younger with Italian bankers', pp. 344–59; Harriss, *King, Parliament and Public Finance*, pp. 125, 224, 238, 241–3; Lloyd, *The English Wool Trade*, pp. 82–3, 86; Prestwich, 'Italian merchants', 83–91; T.H. Lloyd, *Aliens in England in the High Middle Ages* (Brighton: Harvester Press, 1982), pp. 166–203; E.S. Hunt, 'A new look at the dealings of the Bardi and Peruzzi with Edward III', *JEH*, 50 (1990), 149–62; E.B. Fryde, 'The bankruptcy of the Scali of Florence in England, 1326–1328', in Britnell and Hatcher, *Progress and Problems*, pp. 107–20; Bell et al., *The English Wool Market, c.1230–1327*, pp. 25–6. 116–17.

57 Mate, 'Indebtedness of Canterbury Cathedral Priory', 183–97; Prestwich, 'Italian merchants in England', pp. 95–7; Lloyd, *Aliens in England*, pp. 94–7 (Cahorsins), 98–116 (Flemings/Brabanters), 166–203 (Italians); Bell et al., *The English Wool Market*, pp. 116–17.

B: THE EMERGENCE OF A MONEY ECONOMY, 1158-1351

58   F.W. Maitland, *Select Pleas in Manorial and other Seignorial Courts, vol.i, Henry III -Edward I* (London: Quaritch for the Selden Society, 1889), pp. xii-xiii, 118, 140, 144, 150-2, 158; Maitland, *The Court Baron* (London: Quaritch for the Selden Society, 1891), p. 47; M. Bateson, *Borough Customs, vol. i* (London: Quaritch for the Selden Society, 1904), pp. 186-8, 202-3, 209-11, 213-14; Bateson, *Borough Customs, vol. ii* (London: Quaritch for the Selden Society, 1906), pp. 183-92; C. Gross, *Select Cases concerning the Law Merchant, vol. i, Local Courts:* AD 1270-1368 (London: Quaritch for the Selden Society, 1908), pp. 1-8, 14, 17, 19-20, 97-100; A.H. Thomas, *Calendar of the Early Mayor's Court Rolls* AD 1298-1307 (Cambridge: Cambridge University Press, 1924), pp. 27, 75-6, 81, 106-7, 112, 115, 119, 122, 129, 139; H. Hall, *Select Cases concerning the Law Merchant, vol. ii, Central Courts:* AD 1239-1633 (London: Quaritch for the Selden Society, 1930), pp. 1-3, 19-21; Butler, 'Archbishop Melton', 59; G.H. Martin, *The Early Court Rolls of the Borough of Ipswich* (Leicester: University College, Leicester, 1954), pp. 17-18; R.H. Britnell, *Growth and Decline in Colchester, 1300-1525* (Cambridge: Cambridge University Press, 1986), pp. 104-5. The close rolls contain copies of writs concerning grants from the crown to particular persons and for particular purposes, not being intended for public inspection but closed and sealed. The memoranda rolls record details of Exchequer business concerning the crown and the proceedings of the Exchequer court.
59   C. McNall, 'The business of the statutory debt registries, 1283-1307' in P.R. Schofield and N.J. Mayhew (eds), *Credit and Debt in Medieval England c 1180-c.1350* (Oxford: Oxbow Books, 2004), pp. 68-9.
60   See above, pp. 33.
61   S. Keynes, 'Royal government and the written word in late Anglo-Saxon England' in R. McKitterick (ed.), *The Uses of Literacy in Early Medieval Europe* (Cambridge: Cambridge University Press, 1990), p. 226.
62   F. Pollock and F.W. Maitland, *History of the English Law before the time of Edward I, vol. ii* (Cambridge: Cambridge University Press, 2nd edn, 1923), pp. 203-4, 219-26; Clanchy, *Memory to Written Record*, pp. 294-327; M. Bailey, *The English Manor c.1200-1500* (Manchester: Manchester University Press, 2002), pp. 173-6, S. Walker, 'Order and law' in Horrox and Ormrod (eds), *Social History of England*, p. 98.
63   See above, pp. 8-9, 28-9, 31, 73-4 and below, pp. 280-4.
64   Vincent, 'The origins of the Winchester pipe rolls', 25-42.
65   P.D.A. Harvey, *Manorial Records of Cuxham, c.1200-1359*, Oxfordshire Record Society, 50 (London: H.M.S.O., 1976), pp. 12-21; Harvey, *Manorial Records* (British Records Association, Archives and their use, 5, 1999), pp. 8-9; Bailey, *The English Manor*, pp. 18-20, 35, 97-100, 167-9.
66   Maitland, *Select Pleas in Manorial and other Seignorial Courts*, pp. xii-xv, 118, 130-7, 140-1, 144, 150-2, 158; Maitland, *The Court Baron*, pp. 110-11, 117; Z. Razi and R. Smith, 'The origins of manorial court rolls as a written record: A Puzzle', in Z. Razi and R.M. Smith (eds), *Medieval Society and the Manor Court* (Oxford: Clarendon Press, 1996), pp. 36-68; L. Poos and L. Bonfield (eds), *Select Cases in Manorial Courts 1250-1550: Property and Family Law* (London: Selden Society, 1998), pp. xv-xxvii, lxx.

67 H.G. Richardson, 'Business training in medieval Oxford', *American Historical Review*, 46 (1941), 259–80; D. Oschinsky, *Walter of Henley and other Treatises on Estate Management and Accounting* (Oxford: Clarendon Press, 1971); P.D.A. Harvey, 'Agricultural treatises and manorial accounting in medieval England', *AgHR*, 20 (1972), 170–82; Clanchy, *Memory to Written Record*, p. 276.

68 R.H. Britnell, 'Production for the market on a small fourteenth-century estate', *EcHR*, 2nd series, 19 (1966), 380; R.H. Britnell, 'The economy of British towns 600–1300' in Palliser (ed.), *The Cambridge Urban History of Britain*, p. 121; J. Campbell, 'Power and authority in British towns 600–1300', in Palliser (ed.), *The Cambridge Urban History*, pp. 70–3.

69 Titow, *English Rural Society 1200–1350*, pp. 64–96; Dyer, *Standards of Living*, pp. 109–118; Kitsikopoulos, 'Standards of living and capital formation', 397–449; see above, p. 33. Tallies or notched sticks may well have been used to record income, expenditure and liabilities.

70 Moveable goods can be defined as personal possessions, livestock, crops and grain surpluses above and beyond those needed for the maintenance of the household. Agricultural implements and other tools of the trade were also exempt: Jurkowski et al., *Lay Taxes in England and Wales*, p. xxx. A burgage tenement was a specific plot of land within a town, held freehold at a fixed and low rent, which was devisable at will, meaning that it could be sold or mortgaged freely. It was also heritable, according to the custom of the town.

71 H. Hall, *Select Cases Concerning the Law Merchant, vol. iii, AD 1251–1779, Supplementary, Central Courts* (London: Quaritch for the Selden Society, 1932), pp. xiv–xxv ; Prestwich, *Edward I*, pp. 278–9; McNall, 'Business of statutory debt registers', pp. 68–9.

72 Gross, *Select Cases Concerning the Law Merchant*, pp. 19–20; Hall, *Select Cases Concerning the Law Merchant, vol .ii*, pp. xix–xxiii; Hall, *Select Cases Concerning the Law Merchant, vol. iii*, pp. xiv–xxix; J.S Beckerman, 'The forty-shilling jurisdictional limit in medieval personal actions', in D. Jenkins (ed.), *Legal History Studies, 1972* (Cardiff: University of Wales Press, 1975), pp. 110–17; R.H. Bowers, 'From rolls to riches: king's clerks and moneylending in thirteenth-century England', *Speculum*, 58 (1983), 62; Prestwich, *Edward I*, pp. 278–9; P.R. Schofield, 'Peasants and the manor court: gossip and litigation in a Suffolk village at the close of the thirteenth century', *P&P*, 159 (1998), 5–9; C.D. Briggs, 'Manor court procedures, debt litigation levels and rural credit provision in England c.1290–c.1380', *LHR*, 24 (2006), 519–27.

73 Hall, *Select Cases Concerning the Law Merchant, vol. iii*, pp. xiv–xxv, 1–3, 19–21; Butler, 'Archbishop Melton', 56–9; Bowers, 'Rolls to riches', 62–5; J.S. Rogers, *The Early History of Bills and Notes: A Study of Anglo-American Commercial Law* (Cambridge: Cambridge University Press, 1995), pp. 27–8; see below, pp. 283–4, n. 58.

74 Butler, 'Archbishop Melton', 56–9; Bowers, 'Rolls to riches', 61, 65; Nightingale, 'Monetary contraction and mercantile credit', 569–74; P. Nightingale, *A Medieval Mercantile Community: The Grocers' Company and the Politics and Trade of London, 1000–1485* (New Haven and London: Yale University Press, 1995), pp. 87–8; P.R. Schofield, 'Dearth, debt and the local land market in a late thirteenth-

century village community', *AgHR*, 45 (1997), 1–17; Schofield, 'Peasants and the manor court', 5–9, 16–17.

75 H.R. Jenkinson, 'William Cade, a financier of the twelfth century', *EHR*, 28 (1913), 209–20; Richardson, *The English Jewry*, pp. 51–3; M.M. Postan, 'Credit in medieval trade', in his *Medieval Trade and Finance* (Cambridge: Cambridge University Press, 1973), p. 10; E. King, 'William Cade', *Oxford Dictionary of National Biography*; see above, pp. 123–4.

76 Butler, 'Archbishop Melton', 55–9; Mate, 'Indebtedness of Canterbury cathedral priory', 183–97; J.R. Maddicott, 'The birth and setting of the ballads of Robin Hood', *EHR*, 93 (1978), 282–5; C. Given-Wilson, 'Wealth and credit, public and private: the earls of Arundel 1306–1397', *EHR*, 106 (1991), 2–4; ; Kermode, *Medieval Merchants*, p. 236; the origins of bonds obligatory and recognizances are discussed in Biancalana, 'Development of the penal bond with conditional defeasance', 103–17; see below, pp. 281–2.

77 The chancery was literally the writing office while the wardrobe had expanded from being the body responsible for the king's personal household to a central financial department of state. There were substantial profits to be had from holding office in either department.

78 Bowers, 'Rolls to riches', 60–71; P. Jeffries, 'Profitable legal practice and landed investment: the case of Judge Stonor', *Southern History*, 15 (1993), 18–35.

79 M.K. McIntosh, *Autonomy and Community: The Royal Manor of Havering 1200–1500* (Cambridge: Cambridge University Press, 1986), pp. 167–8; Kermode, *Medieval Merchants*, pp. 237–8; Nightingale, 'English parochial clergy', pp. 89–102.

80 A.H. Thomas, *Calendar of Plea and Memoranda Rolls of the City of London, vol. i, 1323–1364* (Cambridge; Cambridge University Press, 1926), p. 217; Lloyd, *The English Wool Trade*, 60–143; Lloyd, *Alien Merchants*, 94–7; E.B. Fryde, 'The wool accounts of William de la Pole', in his *Studies in Medieval Trade and Finance* (London: Hambledon, 1983), pp. 3–31; E.B. Fryde, *William de la Pole: Merchant and King's Banker* (London: Hambledon, 1988), pp. 41–50, 53–86, 87–134; Nightingale, *Medieval Mercantile Community*, pp. 135, 170; Kermode, *Medieval Merchants*, pp. 197–9; Nightingale, 'Knights and merchants', 3–49; Bell et al., *The English Wool Market c.1230–1327*, pp. 1–10.

81 Thomas, *Calendar of Plea and Memoranda Rolls, vol. i*, pp. 104, 113, 173–4, 179, 214, 223; Nightingale, *Medieval Mercantile Community*, pp. 96–7.

82 Lloyd, *The English Wool Trade*, pp. 300–1 and Table 18; Britnell, *Growth and Decline in Colchester*, pp. 98–9, 119–20.

83 Masschaele, *Peasants, Merchants and Markets*, pp. 147–8; R.H. Britnell, 'Urban demand in the English economy 1300–1600', in J. Galloway (ed.), *Trade, Urban Hinterlands and Market Integration c.1300–1600* (London: Institute of Historical Research, 2000), pp. 1–21.

84 P.R. Hyams, 'The origins of a peasant land market in medieval England', *EcHR*, 2nd series, 23 (1970), 18–31; P.D.A. Harvey (ed.), *The Peasant Land Market in Medieval England* (Oxford: Clarendon Press, 1984), 'Introduction', pp. 19–28; J. Williamson, 'Norfolk: thirteenth century', in Harvey (ed.), *Peasant Land Market*, pp. 30–105; B.M.S. Campbell, 'Population pressure, inheritance and the land market in a fourteenth-century peasant community', in R.M. Smith (ed.), *Land,*

Kinship and Life Cycle (Cambridge: Cambridge University Press, 1984), pp. 87-134; R.M. Smith, 'Families and their land in an area of partible inheritance, Redgrave, Suffolk, 1260-1320', in Smith (ed.), *Land, Kinship and Life Cycle*, pp. 135-95; C. Dyer, 'The hidden trade of the Middle Ages: evidence from the west Midlands of England', *JHG*, 18 (1992), 141-57; Schofield, 'The social economy of the medieval village', 38-61 and comprehensive bibliography, 61-3; C.D. Briggs, *Credit and Village Society in Fourteenth-century England* (Oxford: Oxford University Press for the British Academy, 2009), pp. 90, 153, 155, 162, 191-3, 196-7.

85 Gross, *Select Cases Concerning the Law Merchant*, pp. 1-8, 14, 17, 97-100; Hyams, 'Origins of a peasant land market', 20; E. Wedermeyer Moore, *The Fairs of Medieval England* (Toronto: Pontifical Institute, 1985), pp. 85, 110-22; Stacey, 'Jewish lending and the medieval English economy', pp. 92-100; Mundill, *England's Jewish Solution*, pp. 16-44, 108-45, 209-48; Fryde, *Ein mittelalterlicher deutscher Grossunternehmer*, pp. 90-103; R.R. Mundill, 'Christian and Jewish lending patterns and financial dealings during the twelfth and thirteenth centuries', in Schofield and Mayhew, *Credit and Debt*, 43-63.

86 Hyams, 'Origins of a peasant land market', 20; McIntosh, *Autonomy and Community*, pp. 166-7; Bailey, 'Peasant welfare' series, 243-4; Schofield, 'Dearth, debt and the land market', 10-13 and fns. 46, 47; Schofield, 'Social economy of the medieval village', 61-3, for a bibliography of works on credit and debt; Briggs, *Credit and Village Society*, pp. 146-8.

87 Dyer, *Making a Living in the Middle Ages*, pp. 127-32; Campbell, *English Seigniorial Agriculture*, pp. 17-24, 411-30.

88 The debate on feudalism and bastard feudalism is extensive. These are some starting points: J.R. Maddicott, *Law and Lordship; Royal Justices as Retainers in Thirteenth- and Fourteenth-century England*, P&P supplement no. 4 (Oxford: Oxford University Press for the P&P Society, 1978), pp. 10-21; Prestwich, *War, Politics and Finance*, pp. 41-91; P.R. Coss, 'Bastard feudalism revised', *P&P*, 125 (1989), 27-64; D.A. Carpenter and D. Crouch, 'Debate: bastard feudalism revised', *P&P*, 131 (1991), 165-89; P.R. Coss, 'Bastard feudalism revised: reply', *P&P*, 131 (1991), 190-203; Bolton, 'Inflation, economics and politics', pp. 8-9; M.A. Hicks, *Bastard Feudalism* (London: Longman, 1995), pp. 19-21; S.D. Church, *The Household Knights of King John* (Cambridge: Cambridge University Press, 1999), pp. 74-99; D.A. Carpenter, 'The second century of English feudalism', *P&P*, 168 (2000), 30-71.

89 Bailey, 'Peasant welfare', 230-3, 236-8; Britnell, 'Specialization of work in England, 1100-1300', 1-16; Campbell, 'Agrarian problem', 1-70; Schofield, 'Social economy of the medieval village', 38-63.

C: THE MONEY ECONOMY CHALLENGED, 1351-1489

8

The coinage 1351–1489

Introduction: infrequent recoinages

The story of the English coinage in the late Middle Ages is short but extraordinary. Between 1351 and 1489 there were only two major recoinages involving both gold and silver coins and a recoinage of the gold but not the silver coinage. The first recoinage was ordered in 1411, began in 1412 and was complete by 1417. The second began in 1464–5, lasted until 1470 and involved the striking of new coins of different face value to those that had been in circulation since 1351. The gold nobles struck in the recoinage of 1412–17 proved to be of poor quality and their recoinage to a new standard was ordered in 1421–22, as will be seen. Two and a half coinages in 138 years has to be compared to six major recoinages and one partial recoinage in the 193 years between 1158 and 1351 and more than fifty substantive issues, that is, of new coins that passed into general circulation in the 185 years between 973 and 1158. Put more crudely, there was one recoinage every 55.2 years between 1351 and 1489 compared to one every 29.7 years between 1158 and 1351 and one every 3.7 years between 973 and 1158.[1]

It is a startling change but perhaps not a surprising one, given the political and economic turmoil caused throughout Europe and the near and middle East by war, famines, bullion shortages and the return of plague after an absence of nearly 650 years.[2] The four horsemen of the apocalypse seemed to roam the world unhindered, but quite why their depredations should have affected the coinage and, directly and indirectly, the economy of a small set of islands off the coast of mainland Europe may not be immediately obvious.[3] A good starting point for an answer to this question is what two fifteenth-century poets and one seventeenth-century polemicist said in, respectively, *The libelle of Englyshe polycye* (anonymous, c.1436), 'On England's commercial policy' (anonymous, c.1461) and

C: THE MONEY ECONOMY CHALLENGED, 1351-1489

England's Treasure by Forraign Trade, written in the 1620s by Thomas Mun, a London East India merchant, and published posthumously by his son John in 1664.[4] They may have been written at different times and for different purposes but a common theme runs through them, that England's prosperity depended on controlling the country's foreign trade to ensure that the value of exports always exceeded in value that of imports. In that way bullion, gold and silver, would be won for the land. If such a policy was not followed, then, as the *Libelle* put it when complaining bitterly about the commercial practices of Venetian and Florentine merchants in England,

> Also they bere golde oute of thy slonde
> And souke the thryfte away oute of oure honde;
> As the waffore souketh honye fro the bee,
> So mynuceth oure commodite.[5]

In its section on foreign trade, 'On England's commercial policy' closely followed the earlier *Libelle*, leaving Thomas Mun in the seventeenth century to put the case more succinctly than in the fifteenth-century texts:

> The ordinary means therefore to encrease our wealth and treasure is by *FORRAIGN TRADE*, wherein wee must ever observe this rule: to sell more to Strangers yearely than we consume of theirs in value ... because that of oure stock [exports] which is not returned to us in wares [imports] must necessarily be brought home in treasure [bullion].[6]

The message was the same in all three cases: the bullion on which England's wealth depended could only be won through foreign trade. What exactly was meant by 'wealth' is not always clear, however. The anonymous author of 'On England's commercial policy' was the most pragmatic in his approach:

> Ther is noothir pope, emperoure, nor kyng,
> Bysschop, cardynal, or any man levyng,
> Of what condicion, or what maner degree
> Duryng theyre levyng thei must have thynges iij
> Mete, drynk, and cloth, to every mannes sustynaunce,
> They leng alle iij, without varyaunce.[7]

Our immediate interest is in the coinage and the bullion supply, however, for the one depended on the other and both on the profits of foreign trade and the mint price set by the ruler. The difficulty is that none of these factors can be taken in isolation from what was happening in both the 'North Sea' economy, which in fact stretched from the Baltic and Scandinavia down to the south-western coast of France, and in the Mediterranean and near East. In 1300 English overseas trade had largely been concentrated along two main routes. Wool went directly to the great Flemish cloth towns and wine came from Bordeaux and the English lands in Gascony. By 1400 the wool trade to Flanders, now routed through the staple at Calais, was in decline as cloth exports grew. Cloth travelled much further afield, to the Low Countries and the growing international markets at Antwerp and Bergen-op-Zoom, to the Baltic in both Hanseatic and English ships and then on to central Europe, down the river and land routes that led from the mouths of the Rhine to southern Germany and by sea routes to Italy and North Africa. The gold for English nobles came from Hungary and from Africa, via Alexandria in Egypt and the camel routes across the Sahara to north and west African ports and then to Europe via Venice and Genoa. The dwindling silver supplies came from Bohemia and Serbia and, much later in the fifteenth century, from the Rhineland and southern Germany.[8]

Trade and bullion did go hand in hand. It was the merchants, be they English or alien, who brought new gold and silver to the king's exchanges both at times of major recoinages and year-on-year, in order to replenish the existing coin stock. If trade routes were disrupted or markets depressed by falling demand, then the bullion supply could be interrupted or even fail. This is what happened in Europe and the near East between c.1350 and c.1460 and it is the reason why the problems of the English coinage in those years have to be set against the background of war, pestilence, famine and death.

War and its consequences

From the 1290s onward a long period of relative peace came to an end with the simultaneous spread of destructive and almost constant warfare in the eastern, central and western Mediterranean, in the Levant, in Italy, Spain and southern France, in north-western and central Europe, and in the Baltic lands. The Hundred Years War between England and France (1337–1453), into which many other kingdoms and principalities in western Europe were also drawn, is the best known of these conflicts, probably because it has been the most studied. Historians of England tend to overlook wars outside north-western Europe but they are foolish to do so. Munro has argued that constant and disruptive land war led to a major realignment of Europe's international trade routes. Before the 1290s they had mainly been overland, running from the Low Countries and northern France via the fairs of Champagne and one through the Alpine passes to Italy and the Mediterranean world. They were now replaced by direct sea

C: THE MONEY ECONOMY CHALLENGED, 1351-1489

routes from Genoa, Venice, Florence and Barcelona through the Straits of Marrock (Gibraltar) to Flanders (to Bruges and its outports Sluys and Arnemuiden) and to England (London, Southampton and Sandwich). Paradoxically, this change raised rather than lowered transaction costs. The new sea routes were much longer than the old. The overland route from Venice was only about 20 per cent of the distance by sea at a time when the costs of sea transport were rising rapidly. Ships had to be heavily armed and manned in time of war, of increasing corsair raids from northern Africa and of general piracy along all routes, but especially those through the English Channel. Wage bills rose correspondingly as did maritime insurance premiums on both hulls and cargoes. The consequence, according to Munro, was a greater concentration on high-cost luxury goods that would bear the increased costs of transport and to fundamental changes in cloth production in the Low Countries, from the cheaper textiles of the thirteenth century to the fine broadcloths of the fourteenth and fifteenth centuries.[9]

Falling demand from the Flemish textile industry was one of the reasons for the decline in England's wool exports from 30,000-40,000 sacks per annum in the 1350s and 1360s to less than 10,000 sacks per annum in the 1470s and 1480s.[10] That decline was partly offset by rising volume and value of cloth exports, but English merchants had to fight hard to sell their broad and narrow cloths in difficult markets such as the Low Countries and the Baltic. Trade was frequently interrupted by embargoes, piracy and outright warfare and almost inevitably England's bullion supply suffered. It was through the wool trade that much of the silver and gold needed for striking the huge coinages of the first half of the fourteenth century had been acquired. From the last decades of that century both the wool trade and the bullion supply began to suffer even more from the politics of the interminable war between England and France. England's most important allies in the fifteenth century were the Valois dukes of Burgundy. A cadet branch of the French royal family, their main interest lay in keeping France weak while they built up their own territories in the Low Countries, where England's main markets for wool and cloth lay. What complicated matters further was that Burgundy and France paid for their wars with England and with each other from the profits of frequent remintings of their coinages, involving both devaluations and revaluations, at a time when bullion was becoming increasingly scarce throughout Europe. So, alongside the prolonged military campaigns there were also bullion wars, the fiercest of which were probably those between England and Burgundy. These had profound implications for the English coinage, as will be seen.[11]

Plague and depopulation

With war came plague, which followed the paths of armies as well as spreading along trade routes. The story is so well known that there is no need to repeat it at length here. The disease spread by ship from the Crimea, where the plague-ridden Tartar armies were besieging the Genoese trading outpost at Caffa, to southern Italy in 1347 and reached the south coast of England in the summer of 1348. It raged through the British Isles until 1351 and has traditionally been seen as a mixture of both primary bubonic and secondary pneumonic plague, striking in both summer and winter, although this is now a controversial issue. Death rates were appallingly high, with one recent (2004) study suggesting 62.5 per cent for England, the only country in Europe for which there are enough surviving records from which reasonably accurate estimates can be made. These high death rates released a flood of land on to the market, perhaps allowing earlier marriage, higher birth rates and a temporary recovery in population levels after 1351. Then came renewed outbreaks of plague in the 1360s and 1370s, however, and the start of a cycle of demographic decline that lasted well into the mid-fifteenth century and beyond, with the population of England in 1450 having fallen to c.2.5 million, about half its total in 1300 and little more than it had been in the late twelfth century. The causes and consequences of this level of population decline have been much debated in recent years although, as usual, many of the important questions have still not been answered. Some argue that the demographic disaster could not have been caused by bubonic plague and offer alternative causes, such as outbreaks of anthrax or haemorrhagic fever, but contemporary evidence simply does not support such explanations. Postan and his followers have seen this drastic depopulation as the root cause of the economic stagnation which they argue typifies the fifteenth century in England. In sharp contrast, monetarist historians, led by Day and Nightingale, believe that if there was a depression in the fifteenth century, it was caused as much by lack of coin and consequently of credit as by lack of people, but Postan's ideas still command wide support.[12]

Famine and economic downturn

Hunger was common in medieval England, at its worst in the late spring and summer before the new harvest was brought in. If that harvest failed, then distress became more acute in the following year, while a series of harvest failures, such as those that struck England and north-western Europe in the 1430s, brought famine, with the widespread starvation and outbreaks of the enteric disease that accompany it. London eventually had to send to Danzig for emergency supplies of grain, but it was north-east England that suffered the most. There the effects of depopulation and a crisis in the agrarian economy were so severe that the north-eastern economy went into a sharp decline from which it was not to recover for the next two centuries. This had little to do with shortages of money, regionally or generally, since coin had always been in short supply in the pastoral north. Rather, it was the cumulative result of plague and famine, and this must be borne in mind when assessing the consequences of the bullion crises and the shortages of coin and credit for the northern economy in the later Middle Ages.[13]

The bullion crises

Depopulation as a result of plague, the impact of war and the high costs of paying for it, famines and other forms of epidemic disease such as the 'sweating sickness' of 1485 have all been offered as explanations for the economic and social changes that are so evident in the near century and a half after the Black Death. Indeed, population decline has been used as an almost monocausal explanation of such changes. Historians who adopt this approach often pay little attention to the parallel changes in the volume of currency in circulation, to the almost unique preference in England for gold over silver or to so-called 'bullion famine' of the later Middle Ages.[14]

In fact, there were at least two bullion famines, with the first beginning in the last quarter of the fourteenth century and lasting until c.1410–15 and the second running from the 1440s to the 1460s. Their root causes can be briefly summarised thus. First, there was a collapse in mining output. The production of silver from the Bohemian mines fell rapidly after 1350, a decline that was hastened by political and religious uncertainties that culminated in the vicious Hussite wars of the 1420s and 1430s. New silver mines were opened in Serbia but most of their output flowed to the Levant and to the Islamic world, through Venice, leaving Europe desperately short of silver. Transylvanian mines, then under Hungarian control, had supplied some of the gold for the frenzied minting of new coins in the first half of the fourteenth century but, again, production from them fell rapidly after 1387, fading away to nothing by the second half of the fifteenth century. However, most of Europe's gold came from western Sudan, travelling northward either via Alexandria in Egypt or by camel routes across the Sahara to Timbuktu, where it was exchanged for salt. It then crossed the Mediterranean via western Africa or through Tunis and Tripoli in northern Africa to Genoa or Venice. Both routes suffered major interruptions in the late fourteenth and early fifteenth centuries. An acute crisis in the Egyptian monetary system, caused by the disruption of the trans-Sahara camel routes, led to shortages of gold on the Alexandrian market and a collapse in its export to Europe via Venice. The camel routes themselves were controlled from the late thirteenth century by the empire of Mali until it disintegrated into dynastic wars and tribal anarchy in the late fourteenth century. The result was a significant decline in gold supplies to Europe and a consequent sharp rise in its price on the Bruges and Antwerp markets. Bullion prices in Europe only began to fall in the late fifteenth century when first the new method of production by mercury-amalgamation increased gold output from the Rhineland and then new silver came on stream from the south German mines.[15]

Shortfalls in the supply of precious metals were made much worse by two other factors: the drain of specie to the east, to pay for the luxury goods that Europe seemed to crave, and the workings of bi-metallic flows. Paying for imports from the Levant and ultimately from the East Indies and China was a perennial problem for Europe. Ashtor has estimated that in the fourteenth and fifteenth centuries the value of European imports from the Levant exceeded the value of exports by approximately 400,000 Venetian ducats a year, a deficit that could only be settled in coin or specie, gold or silver. Creating a sterling equivalent for this is difficult because of fluctuating exchange rates, but in the mid-1430s the ducat was worth about 43d sterling in London, making 400,000 ducats worth roughly £71,666, at a time when the total value of the gold and silver currency in circulation in England was about £1 million. This suggests that in each decade Europe lost the equivalent in value of nearly three-quarters of the English currency through adverse trade balances with the east.[16]

The theory of bi-metallic flows is, in essence, simple. As we have seen, if gold is valued more in one country or region than silver, while silver is valued more than gold in another, then gold will flow to the first region and silver to the other. Watson has argued that such flows existed between the Islamic world and Europe from at least the year AD 1000 and that by the first half of the fourteenth century silver had become the desired metal in the east and gold in the west. Bi-metallic flows between the two regions continued into the fifteenth century, although perhaps at reduced rates. Even so, much more specie moved between them than was needed simply to cover the adverse balance of trade. If there was a bullion famine in later medieval Europe, the argument continues, it must be seen in terms of silver and not gold, since bi-metallic flows ensured that the Muslim world had

C: THE MONEY ECONOMY CHALLENGED, 1351-1489

the precious metal it wanted, silver, while sufficient gold still flowed northward to help every region in Europe maintain one kind of gold currency until the end of the Middle Ages.[17]

For whatever reason, there do seem to have been severe difficulties with the European bullion supply in the century or more after 1351. Two scholars, Day and Spufford, have isolated what they believe to be periods of acute 'crisis' or contraction in the general European economy caused by the lack of gold and particularly of silver in these years. Using what he calls

> assorted figures concerning foreign trade, bullion prices, mint production and coinage issues, supported by a considerable amount of non-quantitative evidence relating in particular to emergency measures initiated by various states in an effort to counteract the effects of monetary stringency and to prevent mints falling idle

Day has identified 'a major "liquidity crisis"' lasting about a generation (c.1395 to c.1415) that affected to a greater or lesser degree the whole of Europe and the Near East, and was destined to cast its shadow over most of the fifteenth century'. Its causes have already been described, with the emphasis being placed by Day on the imbalances in trade, on falling mining output and, interestingly, on the personal expenses of European pilgrims and others travelling to the near East. The cumulative weight of his evidence points to 1409-10 as marking the height of the crisis, judging from mint output everywhere in Europe, but for the rest of the century bullion shortages prevented sustained economic recovery.[18] Spufford, however, argues that there was a further period of 'crisis' from the late 1430s onward, a crisis that was at its severest between 1457 and 1464. Across western Europe mints were forced to close down altogether, from lack of bullion, not just for months or years but for decades. The mint of the duchy of Brabant at Brussels struck no silver for 29 years from 1437 onward, and in 17 of these years no gold either. The English mint at Calais struck practically nothing from 1439 onward and then closed permanently in 1442. The French royal mint at Tournai was closed for political reasons in 1435 but after it was re-opened in May 1440 it was impossible to find bullion for minting in seven of the next 27 years. The Rhineland mints closed, there was no bullion to be had in Austria and eventually even Venice, the greatest commercial and financial centre in Europe, was affected by the shortages. In 1464 there was no silver at all in the city and in that year, in Florence, there was a series of spectacular bank collapses, triggered by the severe shortage of coin. It was, wrote one Florentine, 'the greatest calamity that had happened in this city since 1339'. From lack of money, Spufford argues, the economy of Europe ground to a halt at every level, 'from the humblest purchases of bundles of leeks, up to the great merchants, whose galleys had to row away with goods unsold'.[19]

These are truly apocalyptic views of the effects of the bullion crises, from which no part of Europe seems to have escaped. Other factors apparently made the situation even worse in north-western Europe. It has long been argued that there was a perpetual imbalance in trade and payments between northern and southern Europe which, in the end, could only be settled by the transfer of bullion. The Italians exported luxury goods to the north, most importantly to Bruges and London, but could find little to buy in return except English wool. As the English cloth industry expanded, so supplies of wool dried up. The Italians found it increasingly difficult to make their returns, that is, to balance their trade and exchange, and credit balances built up in Bruges and London which could not easily be remitted to Italy thanks to ever more stringent regulations prohibiting the export of gold and silver, especially from England. Difficulties were compounded by the regular flow of money to the papacy, to pay first fruits and tenths for bishoprics and other major benefices, for papal bulls of appointment or granting or confirming privileges. Together, the imbalance of trade and payments to the papal curia led in the end to a flow of specie from north to south which contributed to the apparent disequilibrium in the European economy in the fifteenth century.[20]

There was also another imbalance in trade requiring settlements in specie, this time between north-western Europe and the Baltic. English merchants may have failed to break the Hanseatic monopoly there but after 1441 the Dutch certainly did. By 1500 they had taken over much of the region's export trade in low-value naval stores, grain, furs and other primary products, supplying in return manufactured goods from western Europe. The Baltic lands were still under-developed, however, and could not absorb more than certain quantities of relatively expensive cloth, the principal export from the Low Countries. Trade deficits could only be settled by the transfer of bullion, in coin or in silver bars, since credit and credit instruments were little used in the Hanseatic regions. Although this was to become a critical problem in the sixteenth and seventeenth centuries – and much debated by modern historians – it placed yet more strain on the limited supplies of bullion in north-western Europe and thus on the ability of mints to strike the desperately needed coins.[21]

What this meant in practice was fierce competition among rulers for limited supplies of precious metals, rulers here meaning anyone who controlled a mint or mints that issued coins which passed into general circulation. In north-western Europe this effectively meant the kings of England, Scotland and France, with the English king also controlling the Irish mints and the mint at Calais; the dukes of Brittany; the dukes of Burgundy who from 1381 onward gradually brought under their control the mints of Flanders, Holland, Zealand and Brabant, England's main trading partners; and the various towns and principalities in the Lower and Upper Rhineland that minted Rhenish florins. At one time or another all these rulers faced the demands of war and were tempted by the profits to be made from recoinages which might be accompanied by devaluations or revaluations (*renforcements de la monnaie*) in bewildering sequence. Devaluation did not always mean debasement. At times it was necessary to reduce the weight of both silver and gold coins so that their intrinsic value reflected the current price of both metals on the open market. At other times gold coins might be overvalued in terms of silver or vice-versa and a proper ratio between the two metals had to be restored, again according to prices for bullion on the open market. If this was not done, then one or the other metal would drain 'abroad' to another mint where better prices were being offered. Revaluations or *renforcements* could also take place, for these reasons, but the temptation to debase, in order to profit from seignorage, was too great for most European rulers. Between the mid-1350s and the mid-1380s the Flemish gold coinage was altered no fewer than 24 times, leading to an overall debasement of 59 per cent. In 1385 Charles V ended 20 years of monetary stability by debasing both the gold and the silver coinages. There then followed a period of monetary stability in both Flanders and France, only ended once again in the 1410s and 1420s by the demands of war, civil and international, but by the 1430s strong money had returned in both cases.[22] All the time, however, there was a need to replenish the existing coinage, whether it be gold nobles or silver pennies, *écus de la couronne* or *deniers tournois*, *riders* or *groots*.[23] In the decades of bullion shortages this could only mean fierce competition for such precious metals as there were in north-western Europe.

The English coinage 1351-1489

It is against this general background of war, famine, plague and local and international bullion shortages that the two major and one partial English recoinages between 1351 and 1489 must be set. Complete recoinages meant, or should have meant, the recall and demonetisation of all existing coins and the re-striking of new coins from the bullion they provided and from extra supplies from abroad. The latter could only be obtained if the mint prices for gold and silver and the gold: silver ratios were set at acceptable levels. If they were not, then bullion would not flow to the mints and the new coinage would be rejected by the merchants and the populace at large who were only too well aware of the intrinsic value of coins and the relationship of one metal to the other. Among the many matters discussed at the parliament held in May 1421 was the state of the coinage and the recoining of the gold noble was ordered 'to abolish frauds which have long been in existence in the realm among sweaters, clippers and counterfeiters'. It was the only other recoinage between 1411-12 and 1464 and was to be accomplished by November 1422. The immediate consequence, according to the *Great Chronicle of London*, was a rush to buy scales. In the December Parliament of the same year it was further ordered that for the true weighing of the gold noble, the half-noble and the gold farthing (the quarter-noble) weights were to be sent to all cities and substantial towns so that people could have recourse to them to ensure that they were of the correct weight.[24]

In Flanders or at Calais, weighing coins was standard practice. The Celys, wool merchants at the staple in the 1470s and 1480s kept scales and balances at the counter in their warehouse there. Very little sterling (English money, gold and silver) was then in circulation in the town and they had to deal with a mixture of Flemish and other coins. They were weighed to establish their value in terms of their bullion content which could then be given a sterling equivalent. A simple face-value to face-value conversion was not possible. The coins might be 'light' or 'heavy', in terms of the precious metal they contained, and that, in the end, was what mattered to the Celys, as it was to the Borromei Bank in Bruges in 1438. The manager, Paolo da Castagnolo, accepted a payment in cash of £491 10s 3d *flemish* on 7 November consisting of a mixture of Anglo-French gold saluts, Flemish nobles, écus de la couronne of France and Flemish riders, another gold coin. The saluts were exchanged at the current rate of 47 groschen (Flemish pennies) per salut but the other coins were weighed as specie and came to £136 10s 3d *flemish*. This was only to be expected in a region where many currencies of widely varying quality were in use. In England, only English coins were supposed to circulate and yet the same precautions had to be taken, as the legislation cited above makes clear. It does not refer simply to merchants but to the people generally, remembering that the silver equivalent of the quarter noble was twenty pennies, a sum not beyond the reach of the wealthier artisan or peasant. Thomas Hoccleve, a privy seal clerk and a poet who was fond of complaining about how poorly he was paid, wrote bitterly in his *Dialogue with a Friend* that

C: THE MONEY ECONOMY CHALLENGED, 1351–1489

because of the widespread clipping and washing of coins, people insisted on weighing them before accepting them as payment. He then went on to refer to the legislation of 1421 and said: 'Reson axith that it obeyed be'. Distinguishing between 'good' (heavy) or 'bad' (light) became more of a problem in late medieval England, thanks to the bullion shortages and the long intervals between major recoinages.[25]

The opportunity was also taken at the recoinage of 1411–12 to adjust the gold and silver content of the coinage to bring their value in line with international bullion prices. This had already been planned in 1409 when the indenture with Richard Garner, the newly appointed master of the mint, stated that he was to strike new gold nobles weighing 7.28 grams (112½ grains), a sharp reduction from the 7.77 grams (120 grains) of 1351, while the silver penny was to weigh 1.036 grams (16 grains) compared to the 1.166 grams (18 grains) of 1351. These weight reductions were not adopted but they do show how overvalued the English coinage had become in terms of current bullion prices and so, in 1411–12, the recoinage was ordered at a weight of 6.68 grams (105 grains) for the noble of 6s 8d and 0.97 grams (15 grains) for the penny, with proportionate reductions for the lesser gold and silver coins.[26] These were the weights at which the coins remained for the next half-century, through all the supposed vicissitudes of the second bullion crisis, until the second major recoinage of the fifteenth century was more or less forced upon the crown in 1464–65. The first attempt, in 1464, was a failure. The noble of 6.8 grams (105 grains), with its halves and quarters, was now given a face value of 8s 4d and the weight of the penny was reduced to 0.78 grams (12 grains), with the weights of all other silver coins, groats, half groats, halfpennies and farthings being adjusted accordingly. These weights were simply not accepted by the merchants and the populace generally and prompted the London chronicler, William Gregory, to comment, that '… at the be-gynnyge of thys money men grogyd passing sore, for they couthe not rekyn that gold not so qukley as they dyd the olde golde for that it was alloyed. And men myght goo throughe oute a strete or throughe a whole paryshe or that he myght change hit'.[27] The gold coins were seriously overvalued and the crown was forced to abandon this first attempt and to try again in 1465. This time there was to be a completely new gold coin, the rose noble or noble ryal, weighing 7.78 grams (120 grains) and with a face value of 10s, with commensurate halves and quarters at 5s and 2s 6d. The old noble, with a face-value 6s 8d, was resurrected at 5.18 grams (80 grains) in weight, but was now called an angel, with promises of a half angel at 3s 4d and a quarter angel at 1s 8d, although the half angel was only struck after 1471 and the quarter never. The penny remained at

0.78 grams (12 grains), with groats, half groats, halfpennies and farthings at multiples or subdivisions thereof.[28] This time the coinage was accepted and minting continued until 1471.

These were the only major recoinages of the period and of them the second was the most complete since the gold and silver ratio, at 1:12, was in line with that of England's main trading partner, Burgundy, and the Anglo-Burgundian treaty of 1469 enshrined it at that level. Substantial quantities of old and worn coins were brought to the mint and those bringing bullion received in return a greater amount of new coins, even after seignorage and mint expenses had been deducted. At long last England had been provided with a realistic coinage, in the sense that it was acceptable to the merchants, to the country at large and on the international market, in terms of the intrinsic value of the precious metals the coins contained.[29] Between these two recoinages, and against a background of parliamentary complaints about the shortage of coin, there were topping-up issues, the restriking of the gold noble in 1421-22, already discussed, the limited striking of more halfpennies and farthings in 1445 and of more silver generally in the 1450s, but that is all.[30] This should be compared with what was at times frenetic mint activity on the continent between 1351 and 1464-65 and with something unknown in England, the striking of 'white' and 'black' money to ease the acknowledged shortage of small change. 'White' money contained a small amount of precious metal, usually silver, 'black' money or billon none at all, and throughout continental Europe both were in wide circulation and essential for small sales and purchases. Counters or tokens, similar to the tradesmen's tokens of the seventeenth century, were also widely used in Europe but not, apparently, in England, although there is still some debate on this issue.[31]

That there was a dearth of small change in late fourteenth-century and fifteenth-century England cannot be denied. The complaints in parliament and in contemporary literature are too frequent to be ignored. The petition of 1445 asking for the striking of more halfpennies and farthings sums up contemporary feelings:

> To the most worshipful and discreet commons assembled here in this present parliament, may it please your wise and high discretions to consider the great harm which the poor commons of this noble realm of England suffer at this time for lack of half pennies and silver farthings, in so much that men travelling over countries [counties], for part of their expenses must of necessity divide our sovereign lord's coin, that is to wit, a penny in two pieces, or else relinquish the entire penny for payment of a half penny: and also the poor common retailers of victuals

C: THE MONEY ECONOMY CHALLENGED, 1351–1489

and other small necessities, for lack of such coin of half pennies and farthings, often are unable to sell their said victuals and items, and many of our sovereign lord's poor liege people who would buy such victuals and other small necessities cannot buy them for lack of half pennies and farthings on the part of either the buyer or the seller.

The petitioners went on to ask that only a limited number of small coins should be allowed in the payment of large sums and, more radically, that there should be a weight reduction in the smaller coins. The purity was to remain the same, but in future they asked that halfpennies and farthings to the face value of 33s should be struck from each pound of silver, instead of 30s to the pound.[32] This would have produced smaller coins and more of them and there is no reason to doubt that they were needed. Cut half and quarter pennies have been found in coin hoards and in the early fifteenth century Venetian *soldini* or 'galley halfpennies' were in wide circulation in London, in spite of frequent complaints about their worthlessness.[33] Other foreign coins were also circulated, particularly the imitation gold nobles struck in the Low Countries in what Munro has described as 'The War of the Gold Nobles, 1388–1402'. They were so near in weight and fineness to the English coins that they were widely used in England, in spite of frequent prohibitions, forming perhaps between 10 and 20 per cent of the circulating medium at the time. Like the pollards and crockards of the thirteenth century, these coins were much criticised in parliament but were much used publicly.[34]

The mints: the Tower and Calais

For the most part, however, the coin in circulation remained firmly English. It was mainly struck at the Tower in London and at the new mint at Calais. Of the provincial mints, Bury St Edmunds and Reading were permanently closed after 1351, while minting at Canterbury was sporadic and insignificant, in contrast to its earlier output which had sometimes exceeded that of the Tower. The ecclesiastical mints at York and Durham were kept open, to supply coin for the cash-strapped North, but only the mint at Calais could equal London's output. Calais and its environs became English territory in 1347 and the English wool staple was established there in 1363. It was to remain in the town for the next two centuries, with only temporary relocations to Middleburg in Zeeland from 1383 to 1389, to staple towns in England in 1391 and then, briefly, back to Middleburg in 1392.[35] All wool exports from England to the Low Countries had to pass through Calais and, since the wool trade was still England's main source of foreign earnings in the late fourteenth century, it made sense to establish a mint there to convert those earnings, in the form of either coins or bullion ingots, into English coin. Flemish, Brabantine and Dutch merchants were, in any case, given little option. Only English coins were current in Calais so they had to exchange their own money before they could buy English wool.

The Calais mint opened in February 1363 and was active in its first phase until March 1403, during which time it struck coins of almost the same value, weight and denomination as those minted in London. After the issue of the imitation Flemish nobles, gold was attracted to the duke of Burgundy's mints, where a better mint price was being offered, and as a result gold issues at Calais declined sharply and the mint was closed in 1404. But in December 1421 the Commons in Parliament petitioned for the mint to be reopened and it began work again in July 1422. Between then and 1436 prodigious quantities of silver coins were struck, especially between 1428 and 1436, although quite what happened to most of them remains something of a mystery. After the siege of Calais in 1436 the mint was closed for a year and, although production continued until about 1450, it never again reached the heights of the 1360s and 1420s. The fluctuations in its fortunes and the change from minting large quantities of gold to minting similarly large quantities of silver groats, half groats and pennies have to be seen against the background of the bullion famines, the resulting struggles between England and Burgundy for gold and silver and the management of the wool-export trade as both a monetary, diplomatic and military bargaining factor in the Hundred Years War.[36]

If Calais is taken, as it should be, as an outpost of the London mint, then it shows the extent to which minting had become centralised between 973 and 1441. The main exchanges, where foreign currency could be changed for English coin and the bullion then sold to the mint, were also in London, at the Tower and in the city itself, first at Servat's tower, a house in Bucklersbury, Cheapside, in 1344, then moving to Lombard Street in 1378. There were other exchanges at Dover and Great Yarmouth for travellers to and from the Continent, at mints temporarily opened for recoinages and, of course, at York and Durham.[37]

The volume of coin in circulation

There are no records from which the volume of coinage in circulation after the recoinage of 1412-17 can be estimated. Allen suggests that the demonetisation of the old stock was not complete, since pre-1412 issues of gold and silver have been found in post-1412 hoards, even as late as

Figure 8.1 Calais mint output 1363–1450.

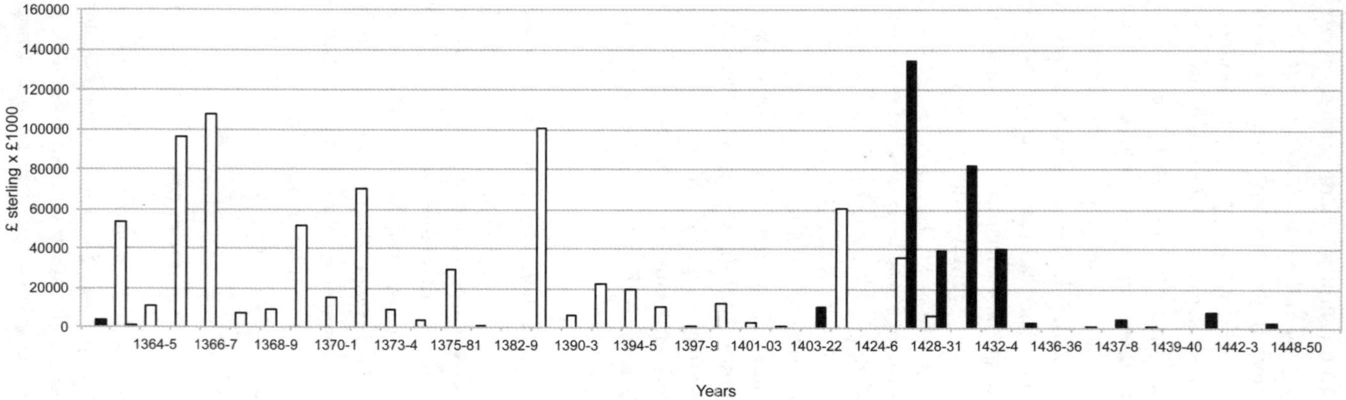

White column = Gold   Black column = Silver

Source: M. Allen, 'The output and profits of the Calais mint, 1349–1450', *BNJ*, 80 (2010), 136–7.

1464, on the eve of the next recoinage. He estimates that in 1421-22, after the re-minting of the worn gold nobles, the circulating medium stood at somewhere between £950,000 and £1,000,000, not much different from what it had been in 1351, except that the balance between silver and gold had been reversed. The recoinage of 1464-65 to 1471 was more complete, according to Mayhew, but he and Allen disagree about the size of the subsequent circulating medium. Allen believes it had shrunk to between £750,000 and £950,000 while Mayhew calculates that it was still about £1,000,000. As Table 8.1 shows, given the sharp decline in population, there was now much more coin per head than in earlier centuries. In 1290, when the coinage was all silver, the figure had stood at 48d per head. By 1351 it had risen to 64d per head, to 83d per head in 1422. Then, according to Allen's lower estimate it fell slightly, to 72d per head after 1464-65, but rose to 95d if Mayhew's estimate is used. There are too many variables here to make these figures any more than a very rough guide but they seem to show that there was indeed more coinage per head available for use in the late fourteenth and fifteenth centuries than there had been at any time before then, even allowing for hoarding, cash balances kept by noblemen, churchmen and merchants, sharp inequalities in the distribution of wealth and the drain of coin abroad, and at a time of bullion famines.[38]

These figures for coinage per head include all coins, however, both gold and silver, and are therefore misleading. Gold was supposedly the coinage used by princes for war and merchants for trade and above all for international trade. The common people, by far the greater part of the rural and urban population, used silver coins for their day-to-day transactions. The small denominations – groats, half groats, pennies, halfpennies and farthings – made it possible to buy and sell goods in small quantities and for wages to be paid to the increasing body of daily-paid craftsmen and labourers. As has already been seen, lack of small change became a constant cause of complaint everywhere in Europe, let alone in England, and the last column in Table 8.1 shows why. From a high point of 56 silver pence per head in 1351, there was a sharp fall to 13 pence per head by 1422, with the first signs of recovery coming by 1470, whichever set of figures is used. Mayhew attributes this revival to the realistic mint prices set by Edward IV's government, but it may also have been the result of new supplies of silver from the Rhineland and south Germany reaching the market.[39] From at least the beginning of the fifteenth century and probably from the 1380s and 1390s until the late 1460s there was an acute shortage of silver coins in late medieval England. In 1422 silver levels per head of population had fallen to those of the late twelfth century and only reached

C: THE MONEY ECONOMY CHALLENGED, 1351-1489

Table 8.1 Coinage and coinage per head of population 1290-1470

Date	Silver (£)	Gold (£)	Total (£)	Population (millions)	Coinage per head (d.)	Silver coinage per head (d.)
1290	1,000,000	Negligible	1,000,000	5	48	48
1351	700,000	100,000	800,000	3	64	56
1411	—	—	—	—	—	—
1422	150,000	800,000	950,000	2.75	83	13
1470 (A)	350,000	400,000	750,000	2.5	72	33.6
1470 (M)	302,250	689,560	991,810	2.5	95	29

Sources: M. Allen, ' The volume of the English currency, 1158-1470', *Economic History Review*, liv (2001) = (**A**); N. Mayhew, 'The monetary background to the Yorkist recoinage of 1464-1471', *British Numismatic Journal*, 44 (1974) = (**M**).

those of the mid-thirteenth century by the 1470s, in an economy which had become thoroughly inured to using money as the main way of making payments and storing wealth.[40]

The Commons in Parliament were well aware of these general shortages. Led by Londoners sitting for the city itself, for neighbouring Middlesex and for other boroughs, a group of merchant MPs who represented ports, major provincial towns and even some county constituencies, complained in the majority of parliaments between 1363 and 1487 about one or another of a series of related 'problems': the poor state of the coinage and the lack of small change; the imbalance in trade and the drain of gold and silver from the land and how both were to be remedied; and the alleged responsibility of all aliens, but especially the Italians, for this dire situation. The answer to their insistent petitions was usually 'Let the statutes in these matters be enforced' or '*Le roi s'avisera*', the king will 'take advice' [on these matters] which meant in practice that no action would be taken. Yet at times, usually when the Commons could take advantage of the crown's temporary political weakness, there were 'clusters' of legislation on these matters. The first came between 1377 and 1381, at a time of political and social upheaval; the next in 1399-1404 during the crisis of the Lancastrian succession; and then in 1407-14, when there was faction in the royal household and struggle for power between the ailing king Henry IV and his sons Henry and Thomas. The recoining of the gold noble produced another batch of complaints in 1420-23, as did the political and economic crisis with Burgundy between 1429 and 1441-42, after the passing of the bullion ordinance of the Staple in 1429 and the reversal of alliances at the Treaty of Arras in 1435. There was another cluster before the major recoinage of 1464-65 and again in

1478 when Edward found himself in serious financial difficulties. These parliamentary petitions were couched in much the same terms, but they do follow the persistent themes outlined above which were repeated in contemporary literature and which now deserve our attention.[41]

Bullionism and the balance of trade

The first and best statement of bullionist ideas about the balance of trade and the drain of 'good money' abroad came in 1379. The Lords and Commons asked the government, which meant in practice John of Gaunt, duke of Lancaster, since Richard II was not yet of age, to summon the officers of the Tower mint before him to explain why they were no longer striking any coins of gold or silver, 'to the great damage of the king and his commonwealth'. Replies to the articles with which they were charged were given by two mint officials, Richard Leycester and one 'Crantren', who remains unidentified, along with John Lincoln, a goldsmith, and Richard Aylesbury and John Hoo, both aldermen of the City of London and members of the Grocers' Company with great experience in foreign trade. Aylesbury was also the largest supplier of bullion to the king's exchange and thus to the Tower mint, after the Master of the Mint, Walter de Barde. The answers these men gave were almost identical, as if learnt by rote. They said that shortages of coin were the result of the money of England, especially the gold noble, being so strong and that across the sea (i.e., in the Low Countries) so weak that nobles drained from both Calais and England. Any bullion brought to England was promptly sold to those who then re-exported it to the Low Countries, thus compounding the loss. Moreover, the money of Scotland was so feeble (quite true) that English silver was much in demand across the border and was replaced by inferior Scottish groats and pennies. Within England, clipping was so bad that £100 at face value would scarce buy £80-worth of goods at market, which is in itself evidence of clear understanding of the difference between the face and intrinsic value of coins. If all this continued unchecked, then the greater part of the gold and silver money of England would be lost and what remained would be so clipped that it would be worthless.

How were these ills to be remedied? The reply to this question was unanimous. The only way of ensuring ample supplies of bullion for the minting of more coin and for the general well-being of the realm was by making certain that the balance of trade was in England's favour. The country was spending far too much on unnecessary imports. If every merchant, and particularly alien and above all Italian merchants, importing

C: THE MONEY ECONOMY CHALLENGED, 1351–1489

goods spent as much if not more on English goods for export, then bullion would flow into the land. There should be employment laws, as they are called, to ensure this, to make all aliens spend the profits from the sale of their imports on English wool, cloth and tin for export. All exports of bullion, whether in coin or ingots, should be banned and the existing regulations rigorously applied. Payments to the papal curia by bills of exchange should also be controlled, as should payments made abroad by pilgrims and clergy and, again, these were familiar targets. The money of Scotland and Flanders should not be current in England and the Master of the Mint should be ordered to strike more halfpennies and farthings to alleviate the shortage of small change. The laws against clipping should be vigorously enforced and there is also the suggestion, made quite explicit in Hoo's answers, that to overcome the present difficulties coins should circulate not by weight but by their face value. Aylesbury went even further. The answer to the lack of coin was a lighter noble, with more of them being struck from the Tower pound of gold which would mean more of them passing into circulation.[42]

What followed in the rest of the fourteenth and in the fifteenth century was a series of variations on these themes, with a crescendo in 1429 in the Bullion Ordinance of the Staple, which demanded payment in full in gold or silver for all wool bought at Calais. This enraged the duke of Burgundy since it deprived his mints of the gold and silver they so desperately needed and was a major cause for his change of alliance from England to France in 1435.[43] Such was the importance of this Ordinance that an exemplification (or copy) of it from the Parliament Roll, although with slightly different wording, is to be found in the archive of the Borromeo-Arese family on Isola Bella, Lake Maggiore, north-west Italy. The Borromei were international bankers and traders with a keen interest in the wool trade at Calais and would have been seriously affected by the Ordinance, hence their interest in its provisions.[44] Whether the bullion won by the English in this way was worth the price of the Burgundian alliance and the subsequent slump in exports from which the wool trade never recovered is another issue.[45] Another high point of protest came in the Parliament of 1439–40, with the grant of the first tax specifically on aliens resident in England in the first session held at Westminster and then the Hosting Statute, in the second session at Reading. The tax itself raised little more than £700 and was more a sop to the Commons and especially the Londoners than anything else, coming as it did after the failure of the peace negotiations with the French held at Gravelines. The hosting legislation was more serious and was aimed at achieving a favourable balance of trade, so that bullion would be brought to and kept in the realm. All alien merchants arriving or already living in England were to be assigned an English merchant host who was to record all their sales of imports and purchases of exports and return the account to the Exchequer. Any profits made from selling imports were to be spent on buying English goods for export, so ensuring a favourable balance of trade and ample supplies of bullion. The statute was supposed to last for seven years, but it was not renewed. Careful examination of such returns as have survived suggests that it was in fact unnecessary: the value of exports and particularly of Italian exports was always far greater than the money earned from the sale of imports. Despite the claims made in parliament, the trade balance was actually in England's favour for much of this period.[46]

In between these high points of protest there were constant demands for other restrictions on aliens to be put in place or simply enforced. Exchanges to the Court of Rome were a favourite target, with the Italians who carried them out being required to buy English goods for export to the same value as the sum exchanged. There were occasional bans on credit sales to aliens because, as the *Libelle* alleged, they (the Italians) transferred their ready money to Flanders and there lent it again by way of exchange to English merchants and so 'wipe our own nose with our own sleeves'.[47] The export of bullion in either coin or plate was, of course, completely forbidden as was the import and circulation of foreign, debased coins. From 1360 to 1463 specific amounts of bullion were supposed to be delivered to the mint for every sack of wool or other goods exported by aliens. This was yet another attempt to ensure that profits from the sale of imports stayed in England, but how often it was actually done is not known. All this protest and occasional legislation ran alongside successive demands for more small coins to be struck, couched in the same terms and addressing the same issues as those raised in 1377 or earlier. Nor were such complaints and the proposed remedies simply an English phenomenon. The Four Members of Flanders, the body representing the great towns of Bruges, Ghent and Ypres and the rural 'Franc' of Bruges, said much the same things to the duke of Burgundy while the Hanseatic Diet, having been constantly warned about the evils of credit sales and purchases, legislated against their use by Hanseatic merchants.

Alongside these protests there ran another constant and slightly contradictory plea to rulers: not to interfere with the coinage and to maintain sound money.[48] Yet gold was out of balance with silver and the obvious remedy in 1379 was to change the money by a recoinage which, by adjusting the weight of the coins, would have brought the gold:silver ratios into line

C: THE MONEY ECONOMY CHALLENGED, 1351–1489

with those elsewhere in north-western Europe. The remedy may have been obvious but Leycester and Aylesbury, who fully understood the problem, still argued that nothing should be done because altering the coinage would be to the universal damage of the lords, the commons and the whole realm. Directly or indirectly, the ideas of Nicholas of Oresme that money is essentially established and devised for the good of the community seem to have taken root in England where, in any case, the Commons in Parliament were arguing that according to the Ordinances of 1311 and the terms of the Statute of Purveyors of 1352, no changes could be made to the coinage without their consent. Aylesbury and Leycester had the right answer in 1379 but the politics of the economy would not allow any changes to be made.[49]

The background against which all this political protest and legislation took place was, of course, the bullion famines themselves. They also formed the background to the bullion 'wars' between England and the duchy of Burgundy that Munro has studied in such detail. In fact these 'wars' were more like games of monetary chess, with an English move such as the Bullion Ordinance of 1429 being countered by the Burgundian embargo on the sale of English cloth in the duke's territories other than Flanders, where its sale had already been banned since 1359. The political nature of these disputes cannot be ignored because trade was constantly used as a political and military weapon in the Hundred Years War. Nevertheless, at their heart lay intense competition for limited supplies of bullion. Curiously, and perhaps inevitably, each side achieved its ends. The dukes of Burgundy were determined to provide their territories with an adequate silver coinage or, perhaps more accurately, their territories were determined that the dukes should provide them with a stable silver currency and that seems to have happened, insofar as it was possible during bullion famines. Conversely, either the English crown or the English merchants in parliament or both, working together, opted for a stable gold currency, and Figure 8.1 and Table 8.1 above show the result. Stability could only be achieved at a price, however, and that price was high. English gold nobles were often over-valued in term of their specie content and so drained abroad, causing shortages at home or the circulation of thin coins that had to be weighed before being accepted. If gold was to be won from Burgundian or other mints, then it had to be paid for in silver and Table 8.1 again shows the consequences quite starkly. Yet, even at the height of the bullion crises, the Tower mint did not stop working, as the mints of so many other European rulers did. It might not have been able to strike many coins and at times hardly any pennies, halfpennies and farthings at all, but it was never completely closed.[50]

Monetary historians argue that the shortages of bullion and thus of coin crippled the European economy in the late Middle Ages: others believe that they have overstated their case. After the instability of the late fourteenth century, there appears to have been no lack of gold or silver in France, according to Bompaire and Sussman. Their case is that the evidence for crisis is at present lacking for Germany and fragmentary for Italy, while for France itself documentary evidence is very sparse. Sussman maintains that it would have been impossible for western Europe as a whole to have run a balance of payments deficit with the East at the same time as it was itself experiencing acute shortages of bullion. Here he is adapting the modern economic theory known as the Monetary Approach to the Balance of Payments (MABP) to prove his point. According to this, current-account or balance of payment movements are driven by changes in the worldwide demand for and supplies of money. Changes in spending patterns are then caused by changes in relative prices that result from capital and reserve flows. A simple model runs thus: if the world is divided into two countries, one with a balance of payments surplus, the other with a balance of payments deficit, then the deficit country has to send bullion – both gold and silver – to the surplus country to pay for its imports from that country, while the surplus country has to absorb the bullion received for its exports. The theory then explains how increases in the money supply in the surplus country will eventually cause inflation and a rise in export prices, while the outflow of bullion from the deficit country will cause deflation, making its goods cheaper, so that eventually the two countries will move towards equilibrium and a current-account balance. In late medieval western Europe's trade with the East that does not seem to have happened. Bullion flowed almost continuously to the east and that would have been impossible had there been serious bullion famines in the west. Sussman further argues that where individuals have an excess supply of money, they will not necessarily use it to purchase commodities. Instead, they may hoard it and when excess demands for money are made by, say, the state, then those demands can be met by dishoarding rather than by a trade surplus.

Consequently, there could not have been bullion famines in late medieval Europe and there were certainly no shortages of silver in France between 1360 and 1415. As Spufford has pointed out, hoarding in itself reduces the amount of coin in circulation and so worsens the effects of bullion shortages, and as Bompaire admits, Day, Munro and Spufford have convincingly shown that there were monetary crises in the Low Countries, northern France and England, although they were not perhaps as severe in England as they were in other parts of north-western Europe.[51]

C: THE MONEY ECONOMY CHALLENGED, 1351-1489

The shortages of silver

Why should this have been the case? Because for much of the fifteenth century England may have been running a balance of payments surplus, even allowing for the costs of war with France, and so may not have been quite as short of bullion as parliamentary petitions would have us believe. To counter that, most numismatists and historians would argue that while gold may have been won through trade, it was the acute shortage of silver coins of small denomination that was the real problem, as has already been seen. That may be so, but a much closer look at the gold coinage is necessary before any judgment, however tenuous and provisional it might be, can be made about the lack of coin. Gold is all too often used as a blanket term for the noble or later the ryal and angel, coins with high face values of 6s 8d and 10s and with a bullion content that made them worth even more. These were far too valuable for everyday use. Not all gold coins had these high face values, however. Half and quarter nobles worth 3s 4d and 1s 8d were also struck until the recoinage of 1464-65, the latter being known as the gold farthing, and half ryals and half angels worth 5s and 3s 4d respectively during that recoinage. The difficulty lies in knowing how many were minted and how widely they circulated. Allen has meticulously examined the evidence from the indentures made with the Master of the Mint for the proportions of denominations to be struck, the trials of the pyx when a sample of all coins produced was tested for weight and fineness, die output and the coins hoards and is still not able to draw any firm conclusions. There does seem to have been more emphasis in the fifteenth century on striking silver pennies and halfpennies rather than groats, perhaps in response to the parliamentary petitions, but the problem of how many of the smaller gold coins were actually struck remains unresolved. The indenture of 1361 specified that from each pound of gold 4 ounces of nobles (16.7 per cent of coins, given their heavier weight), six ounces of half nobles (50 per cent) and two ounces of quarter nobles (33.3 per cent) should be struck. This was the theoretical ratio. In practice, it does not seem to have been followed by any of the mint masters, although it remained in force until *c*.1409. In 1422, the indenture with the new Master of the Mint, Bartholomew Goldbeter, changed the ratio. Eight ounces of nobles (44.4 per cent), three ounces of half nobles (33.3 per cent) and one ounce of quarter nobles (22.2 per cent) were now to be struck from the pound of gold, pointing to a reduction in the amount of small gold struck. However, the evidence from the trials of the pyx in 1414 and then between 1422 and 1432 at London, Calais and York suggests otherwise. That for 1414 at London is exceptionally important as it is the only one of the records that explicitly states the quantities of each denomination actually minted. Quarter nobles were being struck at the rate of two ounces to the pound, but the remaining ten ounces was divided between nobles and half nobles in a ratio of about 2:1 by weight instead of the 2:3 ratio of the indentures. Thereafter there is no written evidence of the proportions but at the trials of the pyx for which records have survived quarter nobles represent between 42 and 57 per cent of all the gold coins presented. Die-output and die studies are of more use for determining the proportions of the silver coinage than the gold, but the smaller gold coins do appear in the hoards, although never in large quantities, with the quarter nobles being more prominent.[52]

Allen's article raises almost as many questions about the composition of the coinage in terms of proportions of gold and silver coins as it provides answers. Was it simply that more quarter nobles were presented for the various trials of the pyx rather than half or full nobles? If not, then why are the quarter nobles not better represented in the hoards than they are, or could that be a function of selection by whoever deposited the hoard? Nothing can be certain, but half and especially quarter nobles do seem to have been more widely in circulation and use than is generally supposed. It would not have taken that long to run up a credit account with a local merchant that could be settled with coin worth 1s 8d and yearly rents could have been paid with a mix of gold and silver coins. On the other hand, it is only fair to say that Dyer found little evidence of the use of gold in his examination of single-coin finds in the later Middle Ages and indeed discovered little evidence of the use of any coin by the peasantry in the mid-fifteenth century. He was not surprised by this because, in his view, all coins from the farthing and halfpenny upward then had a purchasing power too great for them to be lost casually.[53] Yet, in spite of all these caveats, the main thrust of the arguments put forward by the monetarist or bullionist historians that there were shortages of coins and notably of small silver coins still seems to hold good. Whether this had the dire consequences for the economy that are sometimes alleged now remains to be seen.

Notes

1 See above, pp. 89–90, 93–5, 143–4.
2 J.R. Maddiccott, 'Plague in seventh-century England', *P&P*, 156 (1997), 7–54.
3 Revelation 6: 2–8, although St John of Patmos named only one of them: 'Behold, a pale horse, and his name that sat on him was Death.' The well-known print by Albrecht Dürer dramatically conveys the destruction and chaos they were thought to bring with them.

C: THE MONEY ECONOMY CHALLENGED, 1351-1489

4 Sir G. Warner (ed.), *The libelle of Englyshe polycye* (Oxford: Clarendon Press, 1926); 'On England's commercial policy' in T. Wright (ed.), *Political Poems and Songs Relating to English History, vol. ii*, Rolls Series (London: Longman, 1861), pp. 282-7; T. Mun, *England's Treasure by Forraign Trade* (London: 1664, reprinted by Elibron Classics, Chestnut Hill, MA, 2005).
5 *Libelle*, lines 396-9.
6 Mun, *England's Treasure*, pp. 7-8.
7 'On England's commercial policy', p. 283.
8 I. Blanchard, 'Egyptian specie markets and the international gold crisis of the early fifteenth century', in Armstrong et al. (eds), *Money, Markets and Trade*, pp. 383-407.
9 J.H. Munro, 'The symbiosis of towns and textiles: urban institutions and the changing fortunes of cloth manufacturing in the Low Countries and England, 1270-1570', *JEMH*, 3 (1999), 20-66.
10 A 'sack' of wool was the unit on which customs duties were levied. It equalled 364 lb of shorn wool: E.M. Carus-Wilson and O. Coleman, *England's Export Trade, 1275-1547* (Oxford: Oxford University Press, 1963), pp. 13-14.
11 M-R. Thielemans, *Relations politiques et économiques entre les Pay-Bas Bourguignons et l'Angleterre, 1435-1467* (Brussels: Presses universitaires de Bruxelles, 1966); Lloyd, *The English Wool Trade*, pp. 239-48, 257-83; J.H.A. Munro, 'An economic aspect of the collapse of the Anglo-Burgundian alliance, 1428-1442', *EHR*, 85 (1970), 225-44; Munro, *Wool, Cloth, and Gold*, Chapter 2, pp. 44-63, which sees Anglo-Burgundian relations 1384-1415 in terms of the war of the gold nobles; R. Vaughan, *Valois Burgundy* (London: Allen Lane, 1975); W. Prevenier and W. Blockmans, *The Burgundian Netherlands* (Cambridge: Cambridge University Press, 1986); W. Blockmans and W. Prevenier, *The Promised Lands: the Low Countries under Burgundian Rule, 1369-1530* (Philadelphia: University of Pennsylvania Press, 1999). See also R.Vaughan's biographies of the successive Valois dukes: *Philip the Bold* (London: Longman, 1962); *John the Fearless* (London: Longman, 1966); *Philip the Good* (London: Longman, 1970); *Charles the Bold* (London: Longman, 1973). See above, pp. 245-6, 248.
12 For recent debates on the nature and consequences of plague, see G. Twigg, *The Black Death: A Biological Reappraisal* (London: Batsford, 1984); S. Scott, *Biology of Plagues: Evidence from Historical Populations* (Cambridge: Cambridge University Press, 2001); W.G. Naphy and A. Spicer, *The Black Death: A History of Plagues, 1345-1730* (Stroud: Tempus, 2001); S.K. Cohn, *The Black Death Transformed: Disease and Culture in Past Time* (London: Arnold, 2002); O.J. Benedictow, *The Black Death, 1346-53: The Complete History* (Woodbridge: Boydell Press, 2004); W.G. Naphy, *Plague: Black Death and Pestilence in Europe* (Stroud: Tempus, 2004); J. Arbeth, *The Great Mortality of 1348-50: A Brief History with Documents* (Boston and New York: Bedford and St Martin's Press, 2005). Two articles suggest severe population decline in England in the second half of the fifteenth century, J. Hatcher, 'Mortality in the fifteenth century: some new evidence', *EcHR*, 2nd series, 39 (1968), 19-38 and J. Hatcher, A. Piper and D. Stone, 'Monastic mortality: Durham Priory, 1395-1529', *EcHR*, 2nd series, 59 (2006), 667-87. Their argument is supported by B. Harvey, *Living and Dying in England, 1100-1540*

(Oxford, 1993), Chapter 4, pp. 112 ff. and B. Harvey and J. Oeppen, 'Patterns of morbidity in late medieval England: a sample from Westminster Abbey', *EcHR*, 2nd series, 54 (2001), 215-39. J. Hatcher, *Plague, Population and the English Economy, 1348-1530* (London: Macmillan, 1977) remains the best short 'Postonian' account of the late Middle Ages but should now be supplemented by Hatcher, '"The Great Slump" of the mid-fifteenth century', in Britnell and Hatcher (eds), *Progress and Problems in Medieval England*, pp. 237-72 and Hatcher and Bailey, *Modelling the Middle Ages*, in which monetary problems are given short shrift (pp. 186-92). The present author's views on the late medieval English economy were given most recently in '"The world upside down": plague as an agent of economic and social change', in W.M. Ormrod and P.G. Lindley (eds), *The Black Death in England* (Stamford: Paul Watkins, 1996) but as a result of writing this book his opinions on the role of monetary deflation have changed. Economic issues are discussed fully in Chapter 9, below. For population recovery after the first outbreak of plague see J. Hatcher, *Plague, Population and the English Economy, 1348-1530* (London: Macmillan, 1977), pp. 32-3 and Z. Razi, *Life, Marriage and Death in a Medieval Parish: Economy, Society and Demography in Halesowen, 1270-1400* (Cambridge: Cambridge University Press, 1980), pp. 135-7; Dyer, *An Age of Transition*, pp. 156-7, 235 for comparisons between slow population recovery in England compared with France and Italy.

13 W. Langland, *Piers Plowman*, ed. and translated by A.V.C. Schmidt (Oxford: Oxford University Press, 1992), passus vi, p. 73; A.H. Thomas and I.D. Thornley (eds.), *The Great Chronicle of London* (London: Corporation of London, 1938), pp. 173-4; J. Stow, *A Survey of London*, ed. C.L. Kingsford (Oxford: Clarendon Press, 1971, reprint of 1603 edition), p. 179; E. Joachim and W. Hubatsch (eds), *Regesta historico-diplomatica ordinis Sanctae Mariae Theutonicorum, pars ii, Regesta privilegiorum ordinis Sanctae Mariae Theutonicorum* (Göttingen: Vandehoeck and Ruprecht, 1948), nos 2471, 2475; D. Nicholas, *Medieval Flanders* (London: Longman, 1992), pp. 360-3; Dyer, *An Age of Transition*, pp. 29-33; A.J. Pollard, *North-eastern England during the Wars of the Roses: Lay Society, War and Politics, 1450-1500* (Oxford: Clarendon Press, 1990), pp. 50-1; H. Lamb, *Climate, History and the Modern World* (London: Routledge, 1995), pp. 179-80, 186.

14 Day, 'The great bullion famine', 3-54; Spufford, 'The bullion famines of the later Middle Ages', Chapter 15 of *Money and its Use*, pp. 339-62; Munro 'Mint policies, ratios, and outputs', 93; Munro, 'Bullion flows', 97-126 for a general discussion of explanations of the bullion shortages, notably those advanced by Miskimin and Postan. However, in 'Wage-stickiness, monetary changes, and real incomes in late medieval England and the Low Countries, 1300-1500', in A.J. Field, W.A. Sundstrom and G. Clark (eds), *Research in Economic History*, 21 (Amsterdam: Elsevier, 2003), pp. 214-15, Munro argues that additional if not *alternative* [my italics] explanations for periodic shortages of bullion, and thus of coin, should be sought. They are to be found in the behaviour of bullion flows and specifically in two sets of adverse changes in the income velocity of money ... related to the pernicious effects of warfare and plague from the 1370s onward. This seems to be his current position. The theory that bullion shortages in northern Europe were the result of bullion flows to the south to settle adverse trade balances between Italy and the

C: THE MONEY ECONOMY CHALLENGED, 1351-1489

Low Countries has been most cogently advanced by R. de Roover, *The Rise and Decline of the Medici Bank 1397-1494* (New York: Norton, 1966), pp. 123, 317. It has, however, been challenged recently by Bruscoli and Bolton, 'The Borromei Bank Research Project', pp. 468-81.

15 Spufford, *Money and its Use*, pp. 352-3, 368-9; Day, 'The great bullion famine', 37-8; Blanchard, 'Egyptian specie markets and the international gold crisis of the early fifteenth century', figures 1-5, pp. 394-6 and pp. 405-7. He argues that chaotic conditions on the market in Alexandria, again caused by the disruption of the trans-Saharan camel routes, led to a flow of gold from Genoa to Egypt, where it was exchanged for primary products. 'Eclipsing the effects of the mining crisis of 1375-1500, this was the principal cause of the European gold crisis during the years 1400-32' (p. 407). It eased only when gold production was established in the Rhineland using the mercury-amalgamation process. This is explained in his *Mining, Metallurgy and Minting in the Middle Ages, vol. iii*, pp. 1075-6.

16 Spufford, *Money and its Use*, p. 389: E. Ashtor, *Les Métaux précieux et la balance des payements au proche-orient à la basse époque* (Paris: S.E.V.P.E.N., 1971), p. 96; the calculations of sterling equivalents are based on the exchange rates in the ledger of Filippo Borromei & co. of London, 1436-39, Archivio Borromeo dell'Isola Bella, libro mastro no. 7. They should only be used as rough indicators of the monetary size of the problem.

17 Watson, 'Back to gold – and silver', 1-34, and especially 6-7, 31-6; J.H.A. Munro, 'Wage-stickiness, monetary changes and real incomes in late medieval England and the Low Countries, 1300-1500', in A.J. Field et al. (eds), *Research in Economic History*, 21 (Amsterdam: Elsevier, 2003), pp. 214-15.

18 Day, 'The great bullion famine', *passim*, quotations, 3, 25.

19 Spufford, *Money and its Use*, 356-62; de Roover, *Medici Bank*, p. 360.

20 De Roover, *Medici Bank*, pp. 271, 352-3, 373-4. See above, pp. 245-7, for further discussion of de Roover's thesis.

21 Spufford, *Money and its Use*, p. 381; Spufford, *Power and Profit*, p. 348; C. Wilson, 'Trade and trade Balances: the mercantilist problem', *EcHR*, 2nd series, 2 (1949), 153-6; P. Dollinger, *La Hanse (xiie-xviie siècles)* (Paris: Aubier, 1964), 211, 256-9, 281-2, 366-71; G.V. Scammell, *The World Encompassed: The First European Maritime Empires, c.800-1650* (London: Methuen, 1981), pp. 51, 375-9; Postan, 'The trade of medieval Europe: the north', pp. 300-5; J.H.A. Munro, 'Patterns of trade, money and credit', in T. Brady et al. (eds), *Handbook of European History, vol ii, 1400-1660: late Middle Ages, Renaissance and Reformation* ((Leiden: Brill, 1994), p. 160.

22 Spufford, 'The scourge of debasement', Chapter 13 of *Money and its Use*, pp. 289-319, *passim*; Contamine et al., *L'Économie médiévale*, pp. 318-24.

23 Coins in circulation in England, France and Flanders.

24 *RP, iv*, pp. 130a, 155a; A.H. Thomas and I.D. Thornley (eds), *The Great Chronicle of London* (London: Corporation of London, 1938), p. 119; C. Given-Wilson et al. (eds), *The Parliament Rolls of Medieval England, 1275-1504* (Leicester: Scholarly Digital Editions, 2005), introduction to the parliament of May 1421. 'Sweating' silver coins was done by placing a quantity in a bag and shaking it vigorously so that silver dust would be created by the friction. This could later be removed from

the bag, for re-use or re-sale.
25 A. Hanham, *The Celys and their World: An English Merchant Family of the Fifteenth Century* (Cambridge: Cambridge University Press, 1985), p. 171; Archivio Borromeo dell'Isola Bella, libro mastro no. 8, f.143.1 *dare*; see also ff. 147.1 and 374.3 where 43 gold nobles of light weight were sold in Bergen-op-Zoom at a loss of £2 *flemish* to the Bank. The ledger of Filippo Borromei & co. of Bruges is now available on line at www.queenmaryhistoricalresearcg.org; Thomas Hoccleve, *Dialogue with a Friend* (Various editions), lines 99–140; J. Burrows, 'Thomas Hoccleve: some re-datings', *Review of English Studies* (1995), 369.
26 Mayhew, 'From regional to central minting', pp. 172–3; *RP, vol. iii*, p. 658.
27 William Gregory, 'A chronicle of London', in J. Gairdner (ed.), *The Historical Collections of a Citizen of London in the Fifteenth Century* (Westminster: Camden Society, 1876), p. 227.
28 C.E. Challis, *Royal Mint*, appendix 2, mint contracts, 1279–1817, pp. 712–13; N. Mayhew, 'Monetary background, 62–3; Craig, *The Mint*, pp. 92–3.
29 Mayhew, 'Monetary background', 64; Craig, *The Mint*, pp. 92–3.
30 Mayhew, 'From regional to central minting', p. 176; *RP, vol. iv*, pp. 108b, 109a; see above, pp. 237–8, for the re-striking of the gold nobles in 1422; see above, pp. 250–1 for further discussion of parliamentary complaints about the coinage.
31 Spufford, *Money and its Use*, pp. 328–35, 361–2, 371–3; Dyer, 'Peasants and coins' p. 40.
32 *RP, vol. v*, pp. 108b–109a.
33 *RP, vol. iii*, pp. 108b–109a, 498a and b, 600a, 644a; *RP, vol. iv, 69b*; *PROME*, introductions to the parliaments of 1411 and 1415; Spufford, *Money and its Use*, p. 328. Galley halfpennies were prohibited by name in 1399, declared forfeit in 1409, prohibited again in 1411, ordered to be taken to the mint immediately they came into the country in 1414, and prohibited again in 1423, a sure sign that they were in wide circulation: Craig, *The Mint*, pp. 81–2.
34 Munro, *Wool, Cloth and Gold*, pp. 49–63. The first ban on Flemish nobles came in 1389, *Calendar of Close Rolls, 1385–89* (London: H.M.S.O., 1921), p. 647. There was a new parliamentary ban in 1401, *RP, vol. iii*, p. 470, but it was only when the recoinage of 1411–12 reduced the weight of the English noble that the problem, if it was a problem, disappeared. See also J.H.A. Munro, 'A maze of medieval monetary metrology: determining mint weights in Flanders, France and England from the economics of counterfeiting, 1388–1469', *JEEH*, 29 (2000), 185–94.
35 Lloyd, *The English Wool Trade*, pp. 216–33; Sutton, *Mercery of London*, pp. 151–4.
36 M. Allen, 'The output and profits of the Calais mint, 1349–1450', *BNJ*, 80 (2010), 130–8, revises all previous work on the Calais mint.
37 Challis, *Royal Mint*, pp. 95, 157–8; Reddaway, 'The King's mint and exchange in London', 3, 6–9; M. Allen, *The Durham Mint* (London: Spink for the British Numismatic Society, 2003), p. 34.
38 Allen, 'Volume of the English currency', pp. 606–8; Mayhew, 'Monetary background', 62–8. Estimates of population totals are notoriously changeable but if the pre-plague population stood at 5 millions, then it was probably 2.5 millions by the mid-fifteenth century and had shown little signs of recovery before 1489: Hatcher, *Plague, Population and the English Economy*, pp. 13–20, 68–9; Allen, 'Volume of

the English currency', p. 608, n. 92; and see above, p. 16 and n. 10.

39   See above, pp. 229, 233 and Munro, *Wool, Cloth and Gold*, pp. 15-16.

40   See above, pp. 25-7 and Tables 2.1 and 2.2, and pp. 187-8 for the emergence of a money economy.

41   J.L. Bolton, 'Alien Merchants in England in the reign of Henry VI', unpublished Oxford B.Litt. thesis, 1971, pp. 7-15, 235-51, for discussions of the nature of the parliamentary complaints and of the mercantile interest in the commons. This interest is also discussed in the introductions to each parliament between 1351 and 1489 in *PROME*. The appendices to Munro, 'Bullionism and the Bill of Exchange' contain detailed lists of all parliamentary statutes and royal proclamations concerning bullion. M. Allen, 'The proportions of the denominations in English mint outputs, 1351-1485', *BNJ*, 77 (2007), 192-4, has an excellent account of the complaints about the lack of small change.

42   *RP, vol. iii*, pp. 126-7; unfortunately, the full text with translation has not been made available in the digital version, Given-Wilson et al., *PROME*. The enquiry has been redated to 1379 by W.M. Ormrod, 'The Peasants' Revolt and the Government of England', *Journal of British Studies*, 29 (1990), 27; Mayhew, 'From regional to central minting', pp. 170-1; Nightingale, *A Medieval Mercantile Community*, p. 258, n. 2.

43   Munro, 'An economic aspect of the Anglo-Burgundian alliance', 225-44, *passim*: Munro, *Wool, Cloth and Gold*, pp. 84-113, *passim*: *RP, vol. iv*, p. 359. In the November parliament of 1381 the first navigation act, requiring all English overseas trade to be carried in English ships, was also passed: *RP, vol. iii*, p. 120.

44   Archivio Borromeo dell'Isola Bella, box file 669, item 39.

45   See below, pp. 272, 308.

46   *RP, vol. v*, pp. 6, 24-5; the changing definition of who was regarded as an alien is discussed by J.L. Bolton in his introduction to *The Alien Communities of London in the Fifteenth Century* (Stamford: Paul Watkins, 1998), pp. 3-5; the yield of the alien subsidy is given in S. Thrupp, 'The alien population of England in 1440', *Speculum*, 32 (1957), 262-3; the Hosting returns are discussed by Bolton in 'Alien merchants in England in the reign of Henry VI', pp. 212-14; Bolton, *Medieval English Economy*, pp. 305-15. His argument has been reinforced by subsequent work on the Borromei bank in London and for this see Guidi Bruscoli and Bolton, 'The Borromei Bank Research Project', pp. 466-70. London's involvement in lobbying parliament in these years is discussed by C. Barron, 'London and parliament in the Lancastrian era', *Parliamentary History*, 9 (1990), 357.

47   Munro, 'Bullionism and the bill of exchange', pp. 205-8; *Libelle*, lines 390-455.

48   Munro, 'Bullionism and the bill of exchange', appendices a-e (un-numbered pages) for a complete survey of all English material on bullion and credit regulations; the term used, here in French but in various other languages, was 'la bonne monnaie, fort et durable, pour l'or et pour l'argent'; Contamine (ed.), *L'Économie médiévale*, p. 320; Dollinger, *La Hanse*, pp. 252-6.

49   *RP, vol. iii*, pp. 126b-127a for Aylesbury's and Leycester's replies; for Oresme, see above, pp. 35-6 and for the economic implications of the failure to adjust the coinage, see below, pp, 293-5.

50   Munro set out his case in 1972 in *Wool, Cloth and Gold*, and has maintained it ever

since although, as noted earlier, he now places more emphasis on flows of bullion to the east and changing transaction costs than he does on falling mining output. Spufford's views have also been noted above, pp, 233-4, n. 14, 253, nn 14 and 15.

51 L.D. Johnston, 'Balance of payments', in J. Mokyr (ed.), *The Oxford Encyclopedia of Economic History, vol. i* (Oxford: Oxford University Press, 2003); N. Sussman, 'The late medieval bullion famine reconsidered', *JEH*, 58 (1998), 126-7 and *passim*; Sussman, 'Debasements, royal revenues, and inflation in France during the Hundred Years War, 1415-22', *JEH*, 53 (1993), 47-70; Sussman, 'Minting trends in France and the bullion famine hypothesis: regional evidence (1384-1415)', in I. Zili (ed.), *Fra spazio e tempo: studi in onore di Luigi de Rosa* (Naples: Edizioni scientifiche Italiane, 1995), pp. 769-91; M. Bompaire, 'Essor et crise d'une économie monétaire européenne', Chapter viii, Contamine et al. (eds), *L'Économie médiévale*, pp. 314-37. R.A. Goldthwaite, *Wealth and the Demand for Art in Italy 1300-1600* (Baltimore: Johns Hopkins, 1993), pp. 50-1 and *The Economy of Renaissance Florence* (Baltimore: Johns Hopkins, 2009), pp. 57-63, also argues that the bullion famines had little effect in Italy.

52 Allen, 'Proportion of the denominations, *BNJ*, 77 (2007), pp. 194-5, 202-6.

53 Dyer, 'Peasants and coins', pp. 36-40. Nightingale has recently (2010) suggested that the quarter noble may have been for peasant savings, to pay yearly bills, thus releasing more silver coins for everyday use: P. Nightingale, 'Gold, credit and mortality: distinguishing deflationary pressures on the late medieval English economy', *EcHR*, 2nd series, 63 (2010), 1084-5.

9

Testing the money economy, 1351–1489

Introduction: the nature of the evidence

Modern historians face considerable difficulties when they try to explain the consequences of the plagues and bullion famines of the later Middle Ages. This is not so much because of a lack of evidence but rather because of a quite radical change in its nature, especially for the agrarian sector in which about 80 per cent of the population were involved. Faced with falling prices for agrarian products and rising labour costs, great institutional landlords such as cathedrals, monasteries and leading members of the lay aristocracy stopped managing their estates directly and largely became rentiers. Their records became lists of apparently decaying and uncollectable rents and once their demesnes were leased their manorial records no longer provide modern historians with detailed information about agriculture in the open fields.[1]

The lessees of these demesnes and wealthier peasants who took the opportunity to enlarge their own holdings into small farms have left few records of their achievements. This being so, it makes it very difficult to judge whether Humphrey Newton of Cheshire, a man of enterprise who invested in his estates in the late fifteenth century, or some of the enterprising gentry and yeomen whom Dyer has studied, were typical of the whole. Any generalisations as to how far such men were held back by constraints on credit for investment or for trade in the markets where they bought and sold are therefore difficult, if not impossible.[2] There is only one known surviving set of English mercantile accounts for the late Middle Ages, those of Gilbert Maghfeld, a failed London ironmonger in the reign of Richard II. Whether lack of credit due to a contracting money supply led to his insolvency is a moot point, but his accounts have certainly been used to show this.[3] After that, we have to wait for the Paston letters from about

1440 onward and the letters and papers of the Cely family from the 1460s to the 1480s for more evidence about land and trade. The Pastons were a Norfolk family whose letters are one of the main sources for English political history during the Wars of the Roses, but they left no estate accounts as such. There are passing comments in the letters about the shortage of coin and the lack of buyers for their barley, but these are no real substitute for the records that would show the day-to-day or even the year-to-year running of their manors.[4] In sharp contrast, the Celys were wool exporters, based in London and Calais in the 1460s, 1470s and 1480s, when wool played only a minor part in English overseas trade.[5] Their reliance on credit both in buying and selling wool and on the complex exchange and money markets in London, Calais and the Low Countries is obvious, and without their letters and papers our knowledge of the workings of the fifteenth-century wool trade would be severely limited. But as to their typicality, there are no other surviving records of a merchant family in the same period that would allow comparisons to be made. Two recent studies of major London companies, the Grocers and the Mercers, have added significantly to our knowledge of internal and external trade in the period, as has Kermode's work on the merchants of York Beverley and Hull and the publication of local and national customs records for Southampton and London.[6]

Modelling the late medieval economy

The lack of evidence for England's later medieval economy has encouraged the construction of models to explain some of the broadly observable phenomena. It is not an easy task. Few societies in recorded history have had to cope with both severe depopulation and monetary deflation at one and the same time. Much effort has been expended by economists and economic historians on the consequences of over-population and price/wage inflation, but comparatively little on the effects of depopulation and the unlikely combinations of low prices and high wages, rising standards of living and a contracting money supply, a contraction in credit and the increasing use of written instruments both to record and to pay debts. The purpose of this chapter, therefore, is to examine the various models of the late medieval economy constructed by the leading historians of the period, to assess what part the problems of the money supply play in them, and then to look at what we actually know about the working of money, in coin and in credit, within this difficult period. In particular, we must examine why did the crown not take the advice given to it in 1379 and devalue the currency by adjusting the fineness of both gold and silver coins. Had it

C: THE MONEY ECONOMY CHALLENGED, 1351–1489

done so, shortages of silver might have been less severe, as more would have been earned from an expanding export trade. There are disadvantages in devaluation. The pound in your pocket does lose its value, in spite of one British Prime Minister's claims to the contrary, since, as he also admitted, 'prices will rise'.[7] There are also disadvantages to economic modelling, because historians seem to use exactly the same evidence to reach completely different conclusions. Yet the evidence, as it now stands, will allow one firm conclusion to be reached: the money economy was in a more robust state in 1489 than it had been in 1351. In order to justify this rather surprising proposition, it is necessary to look first at the existing models and then at the strong case for innovation through adversity, since necessity is supposedly the mother of invention.[8]

'Stagnation tinged with gloom'

Few short pieces of historical writing have had such an effect on the historical interpretation of the late medieval English economy as 'Revisions in economic history IX: the fifteenth century' by M.M. Postan, published in *The Economic History Review* in 1939. It was, he argued, an era of stagnation tinged with gloom. The collapse in the population and the consequent decline in agrarian prosperity in the later Middle Ages induced a severe contraction in the value of goods which were traded and in the size and fortunes of most towns. The majority of village markets ceased to function in the fifteenth century and town after town sought relief from taxation and other payments by complaining to the crown about depopulation and impoverishment. The growing value of labour, as wages rose and prices fell, and the redistribution of income in favour of the peasantry did stimulate expansion in some areas, principally those serving the growing demand for basic consumer goods which had previously been unaffordable. Demand for woollen textiles was exceptionally buoyant both at home and abroad, particularly for cloth of medium quality, and production flourished in a number of rural areas as the countryside enjoyed the advantage over towns of a less regulated environment and a supply of labour that was both cheap and flexible. Nevertheless, in the long run, falling agricultural prices made manufactured goods relatively more expensive and after a period of expansion in the late fourteenth century manufacturing faltered and then declined. Nor could the domestic demand for woollen textiles offset the loss of overseas markets in the mid-fifteenth century. So, although the volume of trade and non-agricultural production in the late fourteenth and fifteenth centuries may not have fallen as much as population, in an overwhelmingly agrarian economy with a pronounced emphasis on arable farming, it was inevitable that no major sector would escape recession. 'That the total national income of wealth was declining is shown by almost every statistical index available to the historian.'[9]

The authors of *Modelling the Middle Ages* have examined Postan's arguments in their discussion of what they have called the population and resources model of the economy, essentially based on the ideas of Malthus and Ricardo. Yet neither Postan nor his modern followers make any allowance for the consequences of a much reduced and a much changed money supply. Could the increased intrinsic value of both silver and gold coins caused by international shortages of bullion have been largely responsible for the fall in prices? One silver penny might now, in the fifteenth century, buy twice as much as it had in the late thirteenth, so that falling prices reflected the changing value of money and not declining demand. When in 1959 Robinson chose to argue that this was the case, Postan's reply was entirely dismissive, as he had been in his earlier paper on the rise of a money economy. There was, he said, a huge store of bullion within the country, the legacy of the expansion of the thirteenth century, while the population had been halved. There could not possibly be any shortage of coin and falling prices for agricultural products, in common with falling rents for agricultural land, could only be the result of severe population decline.[10]

Other models of the late medieval economy

In essence, Postan set the agenda for all discussions of the late medieval English economy in the last seventy years by placing population decline at the centre of the debate. Some historians have tried to prove him completely wrong, as Bridbury did in a brilliant short survey published in 1962.[11] Others have acknowledged the problem of sustained population decline but have put forward different explanations for the changing structure of economy and society in the fifteenth century, not all of them by any means as gloomy. One approach is based on a discussion of class, power and property relations and the transition from feudalism to capitalism, both as defined by Marx, and better known as the 'Brenner debate', after the publication of the latter's major articles in 1976 and 1982 and the vigorous disagreements his views provoked.[12] Brenner saw class struggle and the role of the state in supporting landlords against peasants as the 'key variable' in the divergent social evolution of England, France and eastern Europe. As Rigby has pointed out, there is rarely ever a 'key variable' among the complex causes of social change and the Brenner debate has largely fizzled out because empirical historians have shown that what actually happened in the English countryside differed greatly from what is largely a theoretical model.[13]

For our purposes, the important point is that there is no place at all in Brenner's theory for the consequences of a change in the money supply. A second approach to the late medieval economy adopted in recent years has been a renewed focus on the workings of the market, on commercial activity and technical progress and the ways in which they interact with population growth and decline and social change. If Postan looked to Malthus and Ricardo, then the proponents of commercialisation owe a great debt to Adam Smith and his theories of free trade and to Johann-Heinrich von Thünen who examined the link between urbanisation, the degree of commercialisation and intensification of agricultural production.[14] This theoretical model has been increasingly applied to the later Middle Ages by Britnell who argues that while population decline almost inevitably led to fewer markets, those that survived were better integrated[15] leading to better distribution of goods and services in a society where general consumer demand was on the rise. This in itself led to more effective market clearing, so that supply could meet demand and thus keep prices low. There is a central role for money in this theory but chiefly as a medium of exchange rather than as a causative factor in change. Much the same can be said of the approach to the role of money in the economy in the most recent and most elegant of the challenges to Postan's thesis by Christopher Dyer which concludes that the later Middle Ages were an 'Age of Transition'. Just as commercial growth in the thirteenth century prepared the way for the structural changes of the fifteenth, so developments before 1500 can be connected with trends in the early modern period. Importantly, he argues that, in spite of the difficulties caused by severe depopulation, there was continuing investment in both the agrarian and industrial sectors and the emergence of a class of wage labourers, not yet 'the proletariat' essential for capitalism, but well on the way to becoming one.[16] His approach to the question of money, the money supply and credit is of great interest because it will be developed further later in this chapter. There were, he says, periods of depression in the early fifteenth century and in the 1450s and 1460s, but recession itself often forces change. The shortages of coin and particularly of silver coins were an obstacle to be overcome and not an overwhelming hindrance to the economy. Peasants and producers on a more substantial scale had to pay rents and taxes in cash and they expected to be able to spend money in the local markets but, where possible, they avoided using coins. They engaged in transactions of all kinds, the buying and selling of goods, hiring labour and paying rents for land sublet to them without handing over any money, or perhaps with no more than a few pence in 'earnest money' to seal the bargain. After the passage of time debtors and creditors would meet and draw up a 'reckoning' or a 'conter' in which various transactions would be put together and might even cancel each other out, leaving the parties on a level footing or able to settle debts with a modest payment. Though faced with practical problems, the market was still able to maintain a high level of activity in the fifteenth century.[17]

'Money answereth all things.'

In marked contrast with Postan, Brenner, Britnell and Dyer who either ignore or minimise the problems raised by shortages of coin, other historians believe that 'money answereth all things'.[18] As has already been seen, it was Day who re-stated and refined earlier arguments for an acute shortage of bullion in Europe between c.1390 and c.1420 and Spufford who drew attention to the second bullion famine from the late 1440s to the late 1460s. Interestingly, Spufford excluded England from the direst consequences of the second famine, but Hatcher argues strongly for a general crisis of the economy from the 1450s to the 1470s, with shortages of coin and thus also of credit contributing substantially to a severe fall in aggregate demand in the third quarter of the fifteenth century.[19] This slump in trade in the agrarian and the urban sectors cannot be ignored, but one crisis does not make a prolonged recession. Moreover, as in the Great Depression of the 1930s, when there were very different regional responses to the general economic trends, so in the fifteenth century there was a sharp contrast between the experience of northern and especially north-eastern England and that of other regions.[20] For Pollard the famine-induced agrarian crisis of 1438-40 marked the beginning of an economic depression in the northeast which lasted well into the seventeenth century, and his opinions have been reinforced by Dodd's recent work about production by peasants on the estates of Durham Priory. Contemporary opinion also saw this as a northern crisis, and the anonymous author of the poem about the battle of Towton in 1461 had the impoverished northerners boasting that, once victorious, they would dwell in the south country and take all that they needed.[21] The tales of woe coming from the northern towns which lacked coin, credit and commercial outlets are also well known and it has to be acknowledged that if there was a recession or slump throughout England in the 1450s and 1460s, then in the north and notably the north-east there was a wholesale depression.[22]

Monetary deflation, prices and wages

We should accept, then, that there was a general recession in the 1450s and 1460s and a depression in the north from the 1440s. Monetarist historians take the argument further, however, and posit that in a money economy a shortage of coin must severely affect both the level of transactions and prices for a whole range of basic products, on a nationwide basis and not just regionally, and that there is a direct link between the money supply and the availability of credit. If **M** falls substantially, as it did in the case of silver, according to the strict workings of the Fisher identity, even though **V** may rise as each unit of currency is made to work harder and **T** fall as sales decrease as a result of population decline, there must be a substantial fall in prices for goods not requiring high labour inputs and thus in **P** generally. This, they argue, is what happened in the 'long' fifteenth century, after a period of price and wage inflation in the decades of economic and social turmoil immediately following the outbreak of plague. Monetary deflation must therefore be seen as one of the prime causes of the low prices characteristic of the period from c.1370 to 1500.

Deflation has many causes. It is characterised by a fall in general price levels, often caused by a reduction in the supply of money or credit. Deflation can also be brought about by direct contraction in government, personal and investment spending, although in the Middle Ages it is likely that the last two were more important than the first. The resulting lower level of demand in the economy usually causes unemployment and lower nominal wages, paid in cash, for daily, weekly and seasonal labour. In the two decades after the Black Death, the severe depopulation caused by the first wave of plague and made worse by the second and third outbreaks in 1360–62 and 1369 had confusing effects on the economy, however. Wages did rise, as a result of labour shortages, but prices remained stubbornly high. The purchasing power of labour actually fell in the twenty-five years between 1350 and 1375, according to Farmer's statistics, although this is disputed by Hatcher in his analysis of the aftermath of the Black Death.[23] Thereafter, wages rose and remained high in both nominal (cash) and real terms. Real wages can best be defined as the physical quantity of goods and services that the artisan, craftsman or labourer can buy with his or her money wages, *plus* all the material fringe benefits that the employee receives in kind as further payment for his or her labour in terms of food, clothing, shelter and other rewards. Today real wages are expressed by a standard formula:

$$\text{Real Wages} = \frac{\text{Nominal (Cash) Wage Index (NWI)}}{\text{Consumer Price Index (CPI)}}$$

Changes in real wages can be expressed in terms of an index where a base year or set of years represents 100 and the movement of real wages, up and down, is plotted in terms of that base. Constructing wage/price indexes for the late Middle Ages involves many difficulties, however. The best evidence for wages come from the records of payments made to builders and other craftsmen working for institutions such as cathedrals, monasteries, Oxford and Cambridge colleges or on the constant payments for repairs to London Bridge, but these may not accurately reflect wages paid to agricultural day labourers or other industrial workers. Much the same criticisms can be made of the evidence for prices which again is mainly institutional. A further problem is that it is very difficult to calculate the value of the 'fringe' benefits discussed above and so most historians simply ignore them. In place of a comprehensive CPI historians construct what is called a 'basket of consumables' based on an estimate of how a household

Figure 9.1 Real wages of building workers in southern England expressed in terms of a composite unit of consumables. 1450–75 = 100.

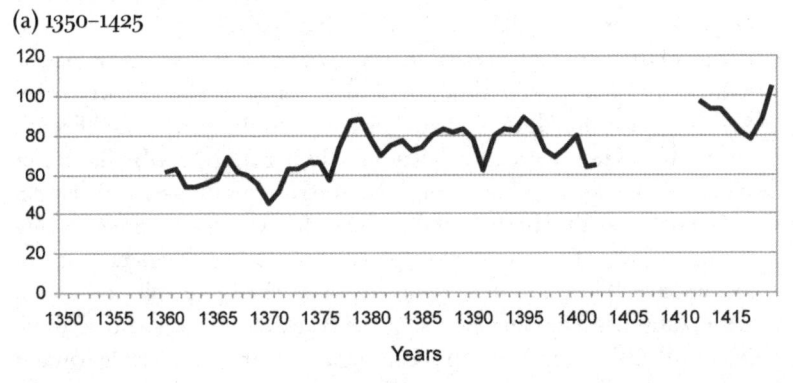

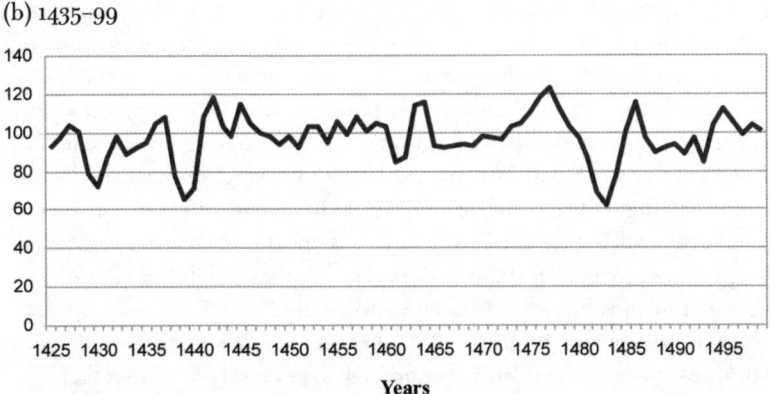

(a) 1350–1425

(b) 1435–99

would spend its earnings – so much on grain for baking and brewing, so much on dairy products and so much on manufactured goods.

The most commonly used wage/price index is that constructed by Phelps Brown and Hopkins, based mainly on institutional builders' wages and the price evidence gathered by the pioneering Victorian historian and M.P., J. Thorold Rogers, whose work has been much criticised but so far never bettered.[24] Prices and wages in the twenty-five years between 1451 and 1475 were used by Phelps Brown and Hopkins as the base of 100, with all previous and subsequent changes in real wages being expressed in terms of that base. Their results for the period from about 1380 onward only confirmed what Thorold Rogers had already stated in 1903: 'the fifteenth century and the first quarter of the sixteenth were the Golden Age of the English labourer, if we are to interpret the wages he earned by the cost of the necessities of life'.[25]

If we separate prices from wages, however, a further difficulty arises. Prices certainly fell after 1380 but wages remained stubbornly high. Most historians now seem to accept one part of the Postan-Abel thesis that falling prices were a function of a sharp decline in aggregate demand due to a halving of the population. What they also accept is that severe monetary deflation, or rather a severe shortage of silver coins, also had a part to play in keeping prices low from the late fourteenth to the end of the fifteenth century. However, if monetary deflation held back prices, why did it not also hold back wages? In both nominal and real terms they remained high. Critics would say that because the evidence for wage rates comes mainly from the records of institutional employers in southern England it is not representative. There are also arguments as to whether employees took a different attitude to employment after the Black Death, choosing to work when it suited them, rather than accepting the yearly contracts demanded by the Statute of Labourers, and spending more leisure time on breaks between jobs or down at the pub. If so, then actual earnings were probably lower than figures calculated from day-wage rates for 250 working days per year (allowing for Sundays and saints' days) would suggest, so that Figure 9.1 may give a false impression of the purchasing power of money. But irregular work-patterns can only have increased shortages of labour, leading to higher wage rates which would have made it easier for workers to take time off. Figure 9.2 shows the almost inexorable rise in a carpenter's wages between 1380 to 1500 and explaining these high levels remains a considerable problem for monetarist historians.[26]

One answer might lie in the phenomenon economists call 'wage stickiness', used to explain why nominal wages rarely fall when there is a

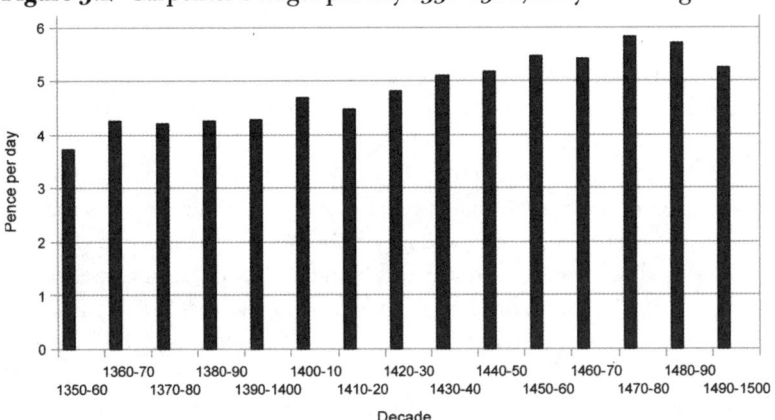

Figure 9.2 Carpenter's wages per day. 1350–1500, ten-year averages.

Source: D.L. Farmer, 'Prices and wages, 1300–1500', in E. Miller (ed.), *The Agrarian History of England and Wales, vol. iii, 1350–1500* (Cambridge: Cambridge University Press, 1991), Table 5.8, p. 471.

recession and unemployment is high. Various theories are offered, differing according to whether the economist writing belongs to the Neoclassical or Keynesian school of thought. Neoclassicists believe that unemployment is entirely voluntary, that workers leave their jobs when pay starts to fall in an economic downturn. This stops wages falling and makes them appear inflexible or 'sticky'. The idea that unemployment in a recession is voluntary would be regarded as fairly absurd today and this version of the theory cannot be applied to England in the fifteenth century, when male labour shortages may have created new employment opportunities for women.[27] However, the Keynesian explanation does not fare much better, although it has slightly more relevance to late medieval conditions. Its disciples argue that wage stickiness can be caused by government intervention in labour markets; by explicit contracts that last for more than a year; by implicit contracts between employer and employee that prevent wage cutting for the sake of the employer's reputation; and by the efficiency wage theory that if the productivity of workers increases then it may be more profitable to pay a wage higher than the market-clearing rate, the balance between supply and demand. At least two of these propositions are applicable to fifteenth-century England. The Ordnance and Statute of Labourers was a direct intervention in the labour market while life cycle-servanthood – that is, annual contracts by which young men and women agreed to work for an employer for a specified wage which could be re-negotiated at the end of the year – were a feature of the late medieval labour market.[28]

'Wage stickiness'

Munro has used this theory in his analysis of wage-price movements in England and the Low Countries between 1360 and 1500. He argues that in the two decades after the Black Death, when there was still a large stock of money in circulation and the population had been halved, there was rampant monetary inflation. It was made worse by 'dishoarding', a fatalistic, hedonistic spending spree, facilitated all the more by suddenly inherited cash balances. England may have escaped the chronic effects of frequent debasements in France and Flanders but prices and wages still soared. In the long run, prices responded to monetary deflation caused by the shortage of silver coin but wages stuck at their previous high levels. Any unemployment would have been voluntary while increases in productivity were unlikely. Wage stickiness in England was institutional, as rates paid to labourers took on that immoveable force of medieval custom. It had little to do with depopulation which did not lead to any positive qualitative changes in the composition, structure and institutional utilisation of the surviving labour force.[29]

In fact none of the current economic theories for the causes of wage stickiness can satisfactorily explain what happened in the fifteenth century. The price of manufactured goods was actually lower in the late thirteenth century, when money was abundant, than it was in the fifteenth, when it was supposedly tight. Conversely, wages for unskilled and semi-skilled workers in the fifteenth century were two or three times higher than in the thirteenth, and their purchasing power much greater. An excess in demand over supply in the labour market would seem to be the only answer to this conundrum but it is not one beloved of economic modellers. This empirical explanation still leaves some questions unanswered, however. If there was such a shortage of coin and notably of silver coin, how could wages be paid or the market operate at the lower level so that artisans and day labourers could enjoy their new-found purchasing powers? As Penn and Dyer have pointed out, at least one-third of the population made all or part of their livelihood from wage labour, a statement amply supported by Poos's subsequent study of Essex after the Black Death.[30]

Credit and the money supply

The traditional answer to cases where confusion reigns is that 'more research is needed', but given the surviving sources, it is difficult to see how it could be undertaken. It has to be admitted that, at present, the only reasonable cause of fifteenth-century wage stickiness seems to be demographic decline. Where monetarist historians have a much stronger case, however, is in their argument that the availability of credit is strongly linked to the money supply. This is an important issue since some historians, including the present author, have argued that the increased use of credit would *extend* the money supply and so lessen the difficulties caused by shortages of coin. It is an accepted fact of late medieval English history that from high to low the economy ran on credit and that men and women could be both creditor and debtor to each other at one and the same time. Did this allow the economy to function with a much lower reduced money supply, in terms of silver? The monetarist historians argue that it did not. Rather, credit expanded or contracted in line with the money supply because debts had to be repaid in coin. If, because of lack of coin, **A** could not repay his debt to **B**, then **B** would not be in a position to repay his own creditors or extend credit to other parties. Illiquidity, shortage of money, meant that lenders became reluctant to lend at all, for fear that they would not be able to meet their own obligations. Money was saved, even hoarded, to ensure that rents and other compulsory payments could be made on time, and this in itself encouraged illiquidity by keeping coin out of circulation for months or even years. As Nightingale has it, 'credit in medieval England expanded, contracted and then expanded [again] with the supply of new bullion brought to the mints by overseas trade', but for long periods in the fifteenth century little gold or silver was being brought to the mints.[31]

The other reason why monetarists argue that credit should not be added to the money supply in medieval England is that written credit instruments were, apparently, not negotiable. By the late fourteenth and early fifteenth centuries, as has already been seen, such instruments usually took the form of bonds, short documents in which **A** acknowledged that he owed **B** a certain sum of money which had to be repaid on a specified date. Increasingly, these bonds contained a penalty clause which said that if the principal sum was not repaid on the due date, then the debtor would become liable for the payment of an extra 'fine', often twice the amount of the principal debt. It is argued that these instruments were not negotiable – that is, they could not be converted into cash or goods or be offered to a third party, **C**, in place of cash, so that the debt would now be repayable by **A** to **C** and not to **B**. If this was the case, then credit instruments could not be used effectively to augment the money supply, as a form of paper or fiduciary money.[32]

This question of the negotiability of written instruments will be discussed again later. For the moment, if the monetarist historians are to be believed, then the acute lack of bullion meant shortage of coin, restricted credit and monetary price deflation. The anonymous author of 'A Trade Policy', possibly someone working in the cloth industry, complained of a lack of silver so severe that manufacturers paid their workers half in money and half in goods at inflated prices, which they were then supposed to sell to make up their earnings. The poem was probably written in the years immediately before Edward IV's recoinage of 1464 and it certainly reflected widespread unease at the shortage of coin. In the parliament of 1463-65 ordinances were issued forbidding manufacturers from making their workers take part of their wages in merchandise. Instead, they were to be paid in full in lawful money for their true wages.[33] Polemical poetry can rarely be taken at its face value: these verses may have been written for propaganda purposes, to influence decisions in parliament, yet as has and will be seen, lack of money is a constant complaint in fifteenth-century England. Does it offer us the best explanation for the economic problems of the age?

The shortage of coin

At first sight, the evidence for shortages of silver coin does seem to be overwhelming. The figures for mint production have already been given but they do not represent the actual amounts in circulation. Losses, wear and tear and hoarding all took coins out of circulation. Hoarding cannot at present be quantified. The case of Richard Fitzalan, earl of Arundel and Surrey, who died in 1376, is possibly quite exceptional. He left £39,987 in gold and silver coins in what must have been a very large chest in the tower of his castle at Arundel. In London there was a further £11,433 kept for him in various chests at St Paul's, in his various castles in the Welsh Marches another £12,954, while his son John, who helped manage his business affairs in his later years had £5,657 in his hands. With the £208 held by various of his agents, this all amounted to the staggering sum of £60,240 in cash alone, or some 6 to 7 per cent of England's circulating medium. Earl Richard was not a hoarder. He used his vast wealth to buy land and marriages for his children and to make substantial public and private loans, yet all the time he retained large cash reserves, ready for immediate use, the disposable wealth so dear to the heart of the lay nobility and gentry. There were others like him. John Beaufort, earl of Somerset, was worth £20,000 in cash and moveable goods at his death in 1410 while his brother Henry, bishop of Winchester and Cardinal Eusebio, was even wealthier, with a treasure of coin, plate and bullion worth £50,000-60,000 at the height of his career.[34]

Arundel and Beaufort were exceptional only in the level of their wealth. That outstanding warrior and grumpy old man Sir John Fastolf had only £2,643 10s 0d in cash on deposit at the abbey of St Benet of Hulme (Norfolk) and plate worth another £2,456 at the time of his death, but during his lifetime he had spent no less than £23,350 on the purchase of land and on building works. Much of his cash came from the profits of war and he and his contemporaries seem to have had no worries about a sagging land market. They spent chiefly on conspicuous consumption, and spend they did, throughout the century, while at all times keeping substantial sums of cash to hand, on deposit at cathedrals and abbeys or with London or provincial merchants.[35] Those merchants would themselves need cash on hand to meet their obligations and the Londoners seem to have been able to raise quite large sums of money fairly quickly. When Sir Thomas Rempston was desperately seeking funds to pay the second instalment of his ransom to Tanneguy du Chastel in 1436, he was able to borrow £882 from a group of London merchants acting either individually or as heads of syndicates. The money was paid in cash into the account Rempston had opened with Filippo Borromei and Company of London, the Milanese bank that was organising the transfer of the ransom to Avignon. How he managed this, since he had little to offer by way of security, remains as much a mystery as how Sir John Arundell, a Cornish knight, was able to raise the money to pay the huge fine of 8,000 marks (£5,333 6s 8d) for the recovery of his estates after he fought on the losing Lancastrian side at the battle of Tewkesbury in 1471.[36] The point of all these examples is not to argue the case for a thriving economy. Great and not-so-great men and women usually had access to considerable cash reserves but in the late fourteenth and in the fifteenth century that meant removing coin, albeit temporarily, from general circulation.[37] If any or even part of these cash balances were of silver coins, then that must have made a serious problem even worse.

Archaeological evidence also supports the argument that there were shortages of small change in later medieval England. Dyer's study of the use of money by individual peasants between 1200 and 1500 – that is, those engaged in small-scale cultivation – is of great importance here. He based his analysis on the published details from 31 excavated village sites across England and Wales, with a bias towards the Midlands and the south-west. The results are striking. All show a sharp fall in coin finds on these sites after 1351, entirely in line with the evidence from Rigold's lists of single finds and of coins deposited at the Ashmolean Museum in Oxford. The denomination of the coins also tells a familiar story, with the numbers of

C: THE MONEY ECONOMY CHALLENGED, 1351-1489

halfpence and farthings, whole and cut, far outweighing the pennies. There was only one find of gold, significantly of a quarter noble, along with some foreign coins such as Scottish halfpennies and jettons or counters which may have been used for keeping accounts of purchases and then converted into real money at a later date.[38]

Dyer goes on to suggest that peasants had little need of coins in the late Middle Ages, however. Royal taxes were high between 1371 and 1381 and then again in Henry V's reign, but charges that had to be paid to the manorial lord in cash dwindled as serfdom collapsed, marriage fines were abandoned and entry fines fell in response to the low demand for land. He concludes that the amount of cash paid by each peasant in rents, taxes and Church dues fell by about 30 per cent in the century and a half after the Black Death and also points to payments by instalments and in kind, and to barter, as ways of coping with the shortages of coin.[39] Nor do the ups and downs in the rural economy fit well with the changes in the money supply. During the first bullion famine in the late fourteenth and early fifteenth centuries peasant farmers were throwing off the burdens of villeinage, enlarging their holdings and enjoying better standards of living, while the landless labourers at last began to see a rise in their real wages.[40] That still leaves most of the fifteenth century, however, when coin shortages were most severe, and Dyer's examples in this case all show how peasants 'coped with a crisis' rather than answering the question 'Was there a crisis?' in the first place. He argues that peasants were still able to engage in the market as both sellers and buyers, especially of cheap manufactured goods, a sign of a rising standard of living. The difficulty is that while shortages of coin can be quantified, in however limited terms, the volume of mutual debt cancellations, of 'hidden trade' in the fields and of payments in kind cannot. One side of the balance is markedly heavier than the other.

Taxation and the coinage

Another indicator of coin shortages that has not yet been fully explored is difficulties in raising lay taxation in the fourteenth and fifteenth centuries. From 1350 to 1500 the overall burden of lay taxation actually seems to have declined but in some ways this is an illusion. The rapid decline in wool exports and thus in the yield of wool customs and subsidies led to a crisis in royal revenues, since rising cloth exports were not taxed as heavily. The crown realised this and tried many experiments to make up for resulting shortfall in its income. There were land taxes, income taxes, parish taxes and, of course, the notorious poll taxes of 1377, 1379 and 1380-81. The surest way to raise income was still through the taxation on moveables usually known as fifteenths and tenths, however. From 1334 onward the practice of making a new assessment each time a lay subsidy was levied was abandoned. Indeed, the yield was fixed at about £37,500, reduced by £4,000 in 1433 and by £6,000 in 1446. Each vill, township and town was made responsible for raising a fixed sum, and how they did this was left entirely to them. It has been argued that the poor, who had paid the crippling burden of taxation in the late thirteenth and early fourteenth centuries, now found their burden eased, but taxation seems to have become more regressive – that is, it fell heaviest on the section of society the least able to pay it.[41] There were periods of heavy taxation in the 1370s, when £250,000 was granted for the war with France, with no obvious results. Curiously, and perhaps not coincidentally, this period of heavy taxation coincides with the first wave of complaints by the Commons in 1379 about the poor state of the coinage as a result of bullion shortages.[42] Was this the first sign of difficulties in finding the money with which to pay these taxes? Considerable amounts of coin had been temporarily taken out of circulation right at the beginning of the first bullion famine. Taxation had to be paid in coin which the collectors were bound to deliver, physically, to the Exchequer, less any allowances due to them or assignments already made on the revenues.[43]

By 1410, signs of difficulties in making payments were becoming all too obvious. The grant of one and a half a fifteenth and tenths in that year was to be paid in three equal instalments, at Michaelmas (29 September) 1410, 1411 and 1412. The usual reason given for this parsimonious grant is the Commons's dissatisfaction with Henry IV's increasingly bankrupt and strife-ridden government, but it should also be seen in the context of complaints about the shortage of coin just before the major recoinage of the following year. Collecting a whole fifteenth and tenth in one year could have proved difficult, as those who came to Parliament would have known. Spreading the collection of taxes over periods of up to three years became commonplace between 1429 and 1446 but after that grants of lay taxation became far less frequent as the country slid towards civil war. The petition in the parliament of 1445–46 already quoted is certainly worth noting again in this context, however. If there were real difficulties in buying and selling goods because of the shortages of pennies, halfpennies and farthings, then there would have been similar difficulties in paying taxes.[44]

Lack of coin for everyday use could potentially have had more serious consequences for the economy than lack of people. The argument here will be that it did not, or, as Dyer and others have suggested, that all the prob-

C: THE MONEY ECONOMY CHALLENGED, 1351-1489

lems raised by shortages of silver and gold were essentially soluble, that the money economy was sufficiently strong to cope with the new demands made upon it. This is very much 'Robinson Crusoe' economics, that hard work and inventiveness conquer all, and although this seems a simplistic approach, it's as well to remember that Defoe was much admired in the late seventeenth and early eighteenth centuries for his economic writings. In his perceptive analysis of the condition of Britain, published between 1724 and 1729, he saw a thriving economy at what is now known to have been a time of low prices for agricultural products and slow population growth, conditions not unlike those in fifteenth-century England. Modern writers have seen the early eighteenth century as a period when low prices forced landlords to look more closely at their profit margins. They increased them by greater investment in agriculture, by more specialisation and more intensive use of land to increase yields per acre at a time when labour costs (wages) were not falling as fast as commodity prices. Periods of acute depression do seem to encourage investment rather than disinvestment in agriculture.[45]

The credit market

The general case for agrarian change in fifteenth-century England in the sense of the emergence of a proto-capitalist society has already been discussed earlier in this chapter.[46] One of the essential underpinnings of such a society was the availability of credit for buying, selling and investment at all levels in society, and while at times credit may have been squeezed by the bullion famines, it did not vanish into thin air. There seems to be general agreement that the intricate networks of debit and credit still functioned throughout the economy and were used by London and provincial merchants and by landlords and their tenants, at least in England below the Humber. Successive studies, first of the manor court at Writtle, Essex, then of Willingham, Cambridgeshire, and of Colchester and Exeter have shown how extensive, indeed all pervading, those networks could be. In Writtle there was no one class of 'lenders' and another of 'borrowers'. Credit and debt flowed across the social scale – that is, horizontally – among persons of the same social grouping, rather than vertically, from rich to poor. What seemed to matter in all cases was the perceived creditworthiness of the borrower to the lender. Paradoxically, but also sensibly, most creditors were also debtors, because there were cycles of borrowing and repayment. One peasant might borrow from another to tide his family over until the harvest was in. Conversely, the lender, or creditor, might need tools or equipment to get his harvest in or complete his ploughing and might borrow them, in return for a money payment, from the same person to whom he had extended credit.[47]

Willingham in Cambridgeshire had fewer trades and industries than Writtle and there was less need for credit for craft production. Nevertheless, Briggs's study shows that *c.*1400 credit was being used in the provision of a surprisingly wide range of goods and services and confirms Clark's findings that credit was horizontal rather than vertical. Interestingly, he also argues that there had been substantial changes in the role credit played in the peasant economy and in the social relations entailed by local credit networks, compared with what is known about credit structures in other villages before 1300. Then debts in grain and other goods were more common, whereas about 88 per cent of all the 395 debts recorded in the Willingham manorial court between 1377 and 1458 were for sums of money, perhaps as a result of a change from arable to pastoral farming and more cash dealings with cattle drovers and butchers. Even more interestingly, there was a virtual cessation of manorial debt litigation at Willingham around the middle of the fifteenth century. The automatic reaction would be that this was the result of the second bullion crisis, but Briggs sees it in terms of the growing ineffectiveness and therefore the attractiveness of the manor court as a forum within which to present actions of debt, a phenomenon 'reasonably familiar from other studies'.[48]

Briggs is not the only historian to challenge the link between growth and decline in the money supply and the availability of credit. The expansion of debt at Colchester in the late fourteenth century was due to general economic expansion and thus greater availability of credit, rather than any changes in the money supply, according to Britnell, while commercial growth in Exeter during the prosperous decades after the Black Death made it easier to extend credit at all levels in the wholesale and retail trades, so that 65 per cent of all pleas held before the mayor's and the provosts' courts concerned debt.[49] Some eighty or more years ago Postan argued that previous historians had underestimated the volume of medieval credit and its multiplicity of forms, from sale credits to partnerships and loans. All subsequent investigations of its use in local, regional, national and international trade have proved him overwhelmingly right, so that Britnell could write in his survey of the economy of British towns 1350–1500 that 'the use of credit expanded in those towns that developed a stronger commercial economy in the course of the fourteenth century, helped in part by the improved institutional infrastructure created during the century before'. However, he added one important caveat, that the development of credit

C: THE MONEY ECONOMY CHALLENGED, 1351–1489

did not, and could not, offset the contraction in the money supply. Here he is adopting the strict monetarist argument that, at any time, the availability of credit is directly linked to the amount of coin in circulation.[50]

As we have seen, the most rigorous proponent of this thesis is Nightingale, who bases her arguments on evidence drawn from the debts of more than 800 London grocers, spicers and apothecaries, members of the Grocers' Company of the City of London between 1350 and 1440. They included some of the richest merchants in the capital who imported and exported on a large scale and who incurred debts of up to £2,500, as well as small retailers and shopkeepers. The surviving records chiefly refer to the transactions of the more prosperous merchants with higher levels of credit, ranging from an average £31 per head in the period 1400–1409 to £99 in the 1420s, which can be compared to the average of all credit transactions in Colchester in the same period of between £36 and £61. 'These men', Nightingale argues,' were among the more important merchant capitalists, and, since their internal trading accounts extended from Yorkshire to Cornwall, their pattern of credit and debit had an influence on the whole mercantile economy of the kingdom.'[51] Nightingale uses this evidence to demonstrate that the availability of credit was directly linked to fluctuations in the supply of new bullion brought to the mint by overseas trade. When that supply was reduced, the extent to which credit could finance industrial or commercial expansion was dependent partly on the reserves of cash merchants could call upon, partly on the extent to which they were willing to invest in trade to the exclusion of other interests such as property, and partly to the degree to which they could substitute the exchange of goods for settlements in cash. Since the Grocers dealt in dyestuffs and other raw materials essential for the expanding English cloth industry, any contraction in the credit they could offer the manufacturers had serious consequences for that industry's development and for the national economy. Shortage of coin also concentrated capital and enterprise in far fewer hands, and the money supply thus provides a vital key to important structural changes in the European economy which took place in the fifteenth century.[52]

Nightingale's article has, rightly, provoked an ongoing debate about the consequences of bullion shortages for the late medieval coinage and thus for the economy. Impressive though her argument is, the evidence on which it is based is not as solid as it might seem. It is based on an analysis of the certificates of debt that have survived in the National Archives as a result of what are known as statute staple recognizances or, more simply, statutes staple. The provisions for the statutory registration of debt under the Statutes of Acton Burnell (1283) and Merchants (1285) have already been discussed.[53] They were the first stages in a system for the speedier collection of what were supposedly mercantile debts. To make both registration and collection easier, the Statute of the Staple of 1353 extended the registration of such debts beyond London to the courts at Newcastle upon Tyne, York, Lincoln, Norwich, Westminster, Canterbury, Chichester, Winchester, Exeter and Bristol. Debts were formally registered before the mayor and the clerk of the staple of the designated town and if debtors defaulted, they or their goods could be seized straight away to enforce payment. Should the debtor or his chattels not be within the town's jurisdiction, then creditors could deposit a certificate of the debt in the Chancery (effectively by this time at Westminster) which would authorise the issue of processes for the imprisonment of the debtor and the seizure of his goods and chattels anywhere within the realm.[54]

Most of the actual recognizance rolls have not survived, which is why Nightingale has to rely on the certificates of debts deposited in the Chancery. They are, however, evidence of failure to recover a debt, which made it necessary for the creditor to go to law. What proportion of total debts they represent simply cannot be known, whatever statistical methods are applied to the evidence. This may not be an overriding objection to the use of the certificates as evidence for fluctuating levels of indebtedness. Medieval historians have to use the sources that survive and accept their limitations. But there are much stronger objections to relying on statute staple certificates of debt to prove a direct link between money contraction and the extension of credit. Merchants used gold: there were no serious shortages of that metal in late medieval England, nor of the gold coins struck from it, not even during the great slump of the 1450s and 1460s. If English exports faltered, then other explanations should be sought, the most plausible being the serious overvaluation of English gold coins in terms of their bullion content until Edward IV's recoinage of 1464–71.[55]

The second and more substantial objection to Nightingale's use of this evidence is that while the purpose of Acton Burnell, Merchants and the Statute of the Staple may have been to facilitate swift recovery of mercantile debt, by the late fourteenth century the statutes staple recognizance had become the preserve of non-merchants who used them to register personal loans and penal bonds rather than straightforward commercial debts. It was Postan who first argued this in his pioneering work on private financial instruments published in 1930, where he claimed that, from the start, one of the principal uses of the recognizances was not the recovery of actual debts but the creation of a penal sum to ensure the performance of a contract such as a marriage settlement, a property transfer or the terms of a will by the executors.[56] In her edition of *The Statute Merchant Roll of Coventry for the years 1392–1416*, Alice Beardwood made much the same point, stressing that only 15 of the 243 cases on the roll actually involved debt, but Nightingale dismisses this claim. Postan, she argues, should have gone beyond the two recognizance rolls for the City of London to the records of the Westminster Court established by the Statute of the Staple of 1353 to which London merchants went to register their debts. None of the recognizance rolls for the Westminster court have survived, however, and the certificates of debt arising from actions brought before it and subsequently enrolled in the Chancery do not give the full details of the case and so are of little help in establishing whether it was commercial or not. Two more recent studies have strongly suggested that Postan was right. Kowaleski, in her analysis of the cases coming before the Exeter court in the late fourteenth century, argues that they were mainly non-mercantile in nature, while McNall has concluded that from the very beginning of statutory debt registration in 1283 to the end of Edward I's reign in 1307 the cases were never predominantly mercantile. Parties from all walks of life, religious and secular, used the recognizances as a way of guaranteeing or underpinning other types of transactions, from property transfers to marriage settlements.[57] Thus doubts continue about the use of these certificates of debt as a measure of the amount of commercial credit extended at any point.

Kowaleski raises two other important issues about these enrolled recognizances, first that the sums demanded in cases of debt often included the proceeds of a penal bond to twice the face value of the original transaction, to be levied if the debtor defaulted on his obligation and, secondly, that taking a case to Westminster was expensive when compared with the costs of settling the action in a local court. The penal bond is discussed further below, but if Kowaleski and Postan are right, then the overall values given in some of the certificates may represent the actual debt and twice its value, or £D + (£D × 2). Given that the certificates give only a general statement of the sum due, with no details as to what it represents, it is difficult to see how Nightingale's figures can be satisfactorily adjusted, but they are surely uncertain evidence on which to build a model linking the availability of credit to changes in the money supply. Kowaleski's second point raises the more serious objection. Taking a case to Westminster was expensive and was probably an extreme step aimed at forcing the debtor to go to agreed arbitration by a third party or parties and an out-of-court settlement. Only the wealthy would probably make use of this process and then after some thought. The majority of merchants and traders almost certainly took their cases to their local courts where, as at Exeter, debts of between 1d and £80 might be settled by a licence of concord costing no more than 2-3d and in a space of a few weeks rather than months or years. The staple towns were, in any case, spread thinly around the country and many areas were not covered by them. Small wonder, then, that the greatest users of statutes staple were the Londoners.[58]

Assignment of debts

Economic models involve the simplification of and abstraction from data. If the data themselves are in any way flawed, in this case in terms of the artificial nature of some of the values in the certificates of debt and the regional bias of the evidence, then the model begins to look less valid. A further difficulty with the data for the model linking availability of credit to fluctuations in the money supply is that there were practical drawbacks to the use of these enrolled recognizances in the later Middle Ages. In spite of all the initial good intentions, they did not offer a speedy way for the recovery of debts nor were the written instruments themselves either assignable or negotiable. Since an understanding of assignability and negotiability is essential to this discussion of a society trying to cope with the monetary problems of the later Middle Ages, definitions of both terms are required. **Assignment** meant passing over a debt owed to you in order to pay off a debt you owed to a third party. Put simply, **A** owes £10 to **B** and has acknowledged this in a written instrument. **B** then finds himself short of cash and is also indebted to **C** for the amount owed to him by **A**. To satisfy his creditor, **B** makes over or assigns the written instrument of debt to **C** who could then expect to collect the money from **A** on the due date. **Negotiability** takes the process one stage further. Most credit transactions were for short periods, usually for less than a year and sometimes for only a few months. When credit was extended for a longer period, then the creditor might well find himself in need of cash, to pay taxes, to fund another venture or simply to pay his own debts. One solution might be to sell the debt on to a third party for less than its face value. The amount raised would depend on various factors, notably the length of time before the debt became due and the known trustworthiness, or lack of it, of the debtor. In both cases, it would be essential for the person assigned or buying the debt to know that, if necessary, he could enforce the contract at law, that he would have the protection of the courts.

This is an important issue on which there is no general agreement but an acceptance that the practical need to pay debts to others or to raise cash for immediate purposes made assignment, at least, a common practice.[59] For the moment, however, the immediate point is whether statute staple recognizances were either assignable or negotiable and the answer is surely 'No'. As Postan long ago argued, the easiest way of assigning a debt is to transfer the original instrument. An entry on a roll could not be transferred except by a new and similar entry. This might not matter where large sums and long terms of repayment were involved but for ordinary transactions a more informal and transferable instrument was needed. Statutes staple were used for what might be called investments and securities where legal protection was vital. For everyday use and increasingly in the fifteenth century the short, written bond, less secure than the staple recognizance but assignable, provided the answer to most contractual needs and not just those concerning debt.[60]

The bond obligatory and the question of 'paper' money

We must now move on from discussing Nightingale's arguments and consider how, practically, late medieval English society coped with the problems of shortages of coin. Credit was still essential to the economy generally and to all forms of trade and industry particularly. What was needed was some way of circumventing the restrictions imposed upon it by shortages of coin, accepting Nightingale's important point that debts eventually have to be repaid in cash. The solution was to be found in the use of written instruments as forms of paper money, with the most widely used of those written instruments being the bond obligatory. It is not difficult to see why it emerged as the most practical way of recording contractual obligations in the later Middle Ages. Bonds were short and completely to the point. In their first form the debtor, A, simply acknowledged that he or she was bound to repay the creditor an agreed sum either in full on a specified day or by instalments on other named days. There is no mention of interest because by canon or Church law the taking of interest was illegal. However, it is quite possible that the sum to be repaid was greater than the sum actually owed, making it very difficult for us to calculate interest rates. In any case, they would certainly have varied according to circumstances that would have included the length of the loan, the perceived ability of the debtor to make the payment when it fell due and the 'tightness' of the money market when the loan was made, that is, the strength of the demand for credit. In years of bad harvests, distress borrowing might push interest rates up to 25 per cent per annum, even on small loans of less than 20s. In and around Romford, Essex, less than twenty miles from London, interest rates seem generally to have been around 10 per cent throughout the late medieval and early modern periods and this, interestingly, was the upper limit for what was considered non-usurious in the statutes of 1545 and 1571. International commercial rates seem to have been lower, however. Thomas Cannings, a wealthy London grocer, borrowed the equivalent of £110 sterling in the Low Countries in September 1438 for which he repaid £115 14s 9d seven months later in London, an annual rate of 5.2 per cent.[61] These are only random examples, and calculating true interest rates in the fifteenth century would be difficult if not impossible. All that can be said is that interest was certainly charged in most cases and indeed was licit (allowed) by canon law if the lender suffered damages or incurred expenses as a result of making the loan, terms which were subject to broad interpretation.[62]

As with statutory recognizances, bonds were used for many purposes from their very beginnings, to enforce the settlement of disputes, agreements over tithe payments, marriage contracts, the transfer of title to land and the performance of services or contracts, as well as acknowledgment of debt. It was therefore a logical development to attach penalty clauses to them either in a separate document or with what is called a conditional defeasance (the penalty to be levied if the terms of the bond were not met) endorsed on the back of the document or included within the document itself. Eventually it became the standard practice for the penalty to be twice the value of the original bond, £20 for a £10 bond, for example. What turned a bond into a 'specialty' was a seal, that guarantor of the legal probity of a document in the Middle Ages. It gave the instrument authenticity in a court of law where discussions centred around whether the documents in the case were genuine rather than whether **A** actually owed the sum of money claimed by **B**.

When these bonds were first widely used is not clear. Palmer argues that the Black Death represented a significant turning point and a catalyst for legal change. There was a transformation in English law between 1348 and the Peasants' Revolt of 1381 as crown and parliament sought to persuade the 'upper orders' to stand by their own obligations to society while coercing the 'lower orders' to honour theirs. Cooperation between the lords and the commons in parliament led to the state using the law as a means of social control. Contracts had to be enforced, whether they resulted from the wage and employment regulations contained in the Ordinance and Statute of Labourers or from credit transactions. It was this new legal emphasis on coercion, now favouring the creditor over the debtor, that explains why the bond, hitherto a simple form of written contract, acquired its penal performance clauses. This interpretation has recently been revised by

C: THE MONEY ECONOMY CHALLENGED, 1351-1489

Biancalana who points out that clauses providing for money penalties in the case of defeasance first appear in English contracts and conveyances in the first decade of the thirteenth century and thereafter quickly came to be used in wide range of other documents. At first the penalty clauses were contained within the written agreement, but around the middle of the thirteenth century the practice began of having them recorded separately as recognizances on the plea rolls, the Exchequer rolls and the Chancery rolls. By 1348 the penal bond with the endorsed conditional defeasance was already in use.[63]

These two arguments are not incompatible. The penal bond may well have emerged before the Black Death but all the evidence points to its refinement and wider use from the 1360s onward, at a time of social and economic upheaval. For our immediate purposes, the question is whether use of the bond could help merchants and others work their way around the problems posed by increasing shortages of coin. There were, at all times, those who would lend: other members of the family, neighbours, business partners, clergymen, knights, ecclesiastical houses, syndicates of merchants and nobles, with members of exactly the same groups also needing to borrow. Lines of vertical and horizontal obligation, of credit and debt, ran through society. Land could be mortgaged and for merchants and others borrowing could be secured by what are known as gifts of goods and chattels. They became common in London from about the 1430s and by them, the donor made a gift of all his personal property to a group of two or three friends or associates, often to secure a loan or an advance of credit. In case of default, they would be able to recover their assets quickly and easily. The drawback was that such gifts were usually enrolled, in the case of London either in the mayor's court or in the Chancery, where they were entered on the close rolls. It was not a particularly safe way of borrowing. The creditors might claim more of the goods and chattels than was due and enrolment was a time-consuming and, in the case of the Chancery, an expensive business.[64]

It was the bond, either in its simplest form or, more securely, sealed and with a penal clause that showed the way forward, as Nightingale admits in her study of the London Grocers' company. Although gifts of goods and chattels might be the easiest way for young men or those of doubtful financial standing to raise credit, the shortage of coin obliged merchants to seek more flexibility than was offered to them by the recognizances of debt they were accustomed to register at the borough and staple courts. What the new monetary circumstances demanded was the means of transferring debts to third parties with full legal protection and therefore an alternative to payment in coin, always remembering that the majority of bonds were not concerned with credit but with the performance of other covenants or contracts.[65] Nevertheless, this is an important admission by a leading monetarist historian that the assignable bond could at least mitigate the shortage of credit caused by lack of coin.

The law of debt

If bonds were to circulate as a form of 'paper' money, so easing the shortages of coin caused by the bullion famines, they had to be assignable, that is transferable from one party to another in payment of debts. The key issue here is whether the third- or fourth-party assignee was given the protection of the courts in the recovery of debt. In real life, bonds were assigned by one party to pay debts to another. Postan produced ample and convincing evidence of the practice and there is no need to re-rehearse it here.[66] The critical question is whether the assignee – that is, C in the example given above – was given protection at law, and the answer has to be a qualified 'No'. The English common law courts did not recognise assignment, unless it was formally done by a clause in the document saying that payment could be made to a third party, an 'attorney'. Such clauses often had to be accompanied by a separate letter appointing such an attorney. The notion that a bond might be paid to the bearer or to other parties not mentioned in the original document received no support at common law.[67] Courts where the law merchant was practised, such as the mayor's court at London, other city and borough courts and fair courts, do seem to have protected assignment, however. There has been much discussion of the relative merits of the royal common law and the law merchant and whether the one did not recognise the other. The debate does seem to be something of a waste of effort, however, since common law courts often referred cases to be heard before juries of merchants because they were better placed to decide the facts in the case while, conversely, cases brought before borough courts could be transferred to common law courts, so that they worked happily side-by-side. There has also been much debate about the decision in the mayor's court of London in the case of Burton v. Davy in 1437 and whether it gave full legal protection to third parties, making bills or bonds fully negotiable. That it did not do so is strongly suggested by the complete lack of other evidence for the practice before 1500. Negotiability seems a red herring: assignability is certainly not.[68]

If the common law courts and the law merchant offered little protection to third- or even fourth-party assignees, since in practice bonds did change hands many times, where might it be found? In the late fourteenth and fifteenth centuries the Chancery was emerging as a court of reason and conscience that dealt with cases brought as a result of a petition to the Lord Chancellor, often stating that the petitioner had no remedy at the common law. It is sometimes described as a court of equity but this implies a rapid development of precedent and that probably did not occur until the sixteenth and seventeenth centuries. In the fifteenth century it was still very much a matter of looking at both sides of the case and, having heard all the evidence, delivering a judgment or decree based on common sense.[69] Had the records of this court survived in a continuous and complete series, then the question of assignability might be solved once and for all. Alas, they have not, but what is left of them suggests strongly that Chancery did offer protection to the assignee and to the debtor who claimed that he had repaid the principal sum owed or performed the services required but had failed to ensure that the bill or bond was then destroyed. That was essential. If the original document was not slashed through or completely destroyed then another claim might be made upon the debtor.[70]

'The development of negotiable bills made credit more flexible', Nightingale argues, 'but could not prevent it from contracting in line with the falling supply of money.'[71] Again, this may or may not be true because the total volume of credit offered through bonds cannot be measured, since most of them were destroyed when the debt had been paid. It is worth considering here what Kerridge wrote in his study of trade and banking in early modern England: 'Englishmen habitually made or set over [assigned] their debts; creditors regularly assigned bills obligatory ... to settle counter debts, enabling *payment without coin* [my italics]. Men went on settling debts one against the other until they found someone able and willing to pay cash and so end the credit chain.' What Kerridge describes here is a form of paper money and he echoes Postan's words of nearly half a century earlier: 'A financial instrument which could change hands so many times, and apparently without formalities or additional documents, almost deserves the name of "currency".'[72]

Banks and bankers: credit in overseas trade

If we accept, as we should, that written transferable instruments were an additional form of currency in the later Middle Ages, additional that is to the coinage in circulation, then we enter a world where the term 'money' takes on a new meaning. Payments could be made without coin having to change hands, and bonds of debt with or without specialty formed part of many a merchant's estate in the late Middle Ages.[73] Their one limitation was that the transactions recorded were essentially personal, between named individuals or between a named individual and a group of creditors, sometimes members of the same family or business partners. There were apparently no banks or bankers to act as institutional guarantors for payment or to make the loans themselves. Everything depended on the personal assessment of debtor's creditworthiness so that credit was linked to personal rather than institutional networks.

Banks did actually exist in fifteenth-century England but they were run by Italians – the Alberti, Bardi, Borromei, Contarini, Medici, Salviaiti and others – whose international and financial connections allowed them to transfer money from one country to another by way of exchange. This made it possible to borrow money in one country in one currency and to repay in another in the local currency. So Robert Elmham, the attorney or

Table 9.1 Borrowing by way of exchange, 1438–9

£55 *flemish* is borrowed in cash, at Bergen-op-Zoom and is repaid in London at an exchange rate of 88 groschen per English noble of 6s 8d, which yields **£50 *sterling*.**

At Bergen-op-Zoom

Date:	22 November 1438
Deliverer:	Filippo Borromei and company of Bruges, who pay over £55 *flemish* in cash to:
Taker:	Robert Elmham, attorney (factor) of John Derham of London, mercer

In London

Date:	20 December 1438
Payor:	John Derham of London, mercer
Payee:	Filippo Borromei and company of London

Actual repayments in London through Derham's account with the Borromei London

10 December 1438:	£10 *sterling*, in cash
27 December 1438:	£18 *sterling*, in cash
7 January 1439:	£12 *sterling*, in cash
22 January 1439:	£10 *sterling*, in cash

Sources: ABIB, BBr, ff. 147.1, 348.2; BLon, ff. 260.1, 292.4

C: THE MONEY ECONOMY CHALLENGED, 1351–1489

agent in the Low Countries of John Derham, mercer, was the taker in a bill for £55 *flemish* on 22 November 1438.

The money, in cash, was delivered to him by the Borromei of Bruges through their cash account at Bergen-op-Zoom and was to be repaid in London by Derham to the Borromei company in London at usance of one month, the settlement date being the following 22 December. The exchange rate was 88 groschen per English noble of 6s 8d which would mean that Derham had to pay the Borromei in London £50 *sterling*. Derham's account in the London ledger records the arrival of this bill on 27 December when he promised to pay them the agreed sum. In fact he had already started his payments on 10 December and by 31 December had paid over all but £22 *sterling*. This sum was carried forward to his account for 1439 and settled in cash on 7 January (£12) and 22 January (£10). Effectively he had had a loan of £55 *flemish* in the Low Countries from 22 November 1438, with the last instalment being repaid in London on 22 January 1439 over two months later. No gold or silver coins were transported across the North Sea to settle the debt. Everything was done by transfers between accounts in the ledgers of the Borromei banks in Bruges and London, with cash repayment of the loan being made in sterling in London.[74]

Exchange banking, as it is called, avoided both the Church's laws against usury and the ever-growing body of legislation prohibiting the export of bullion, which Munro has studied in detail.[75] Received wisdom has it that there were no English banks keeping current accounts for their clients and then making payments for them to other clients by book-transfers across accounts or by paying cash on legitimate demand. London appears to stand in sharp contrast to Bruges and Antwerp where moneychangers and hostellers (inn-keepers) accepted deposits from clients, made payments for them to other clients and engaged in exchange transactions across Europe.[76] It is often argued that such banking services, operating on the fractional reserve principle, were not to be found in England until the London goldsmiths started taking money on deposit in the late seventeenth century.[77]

Received wisdom should always be treated with caution, even if it is often proved right. The Borromei bank in London did offer its London clients, all 180 or more of them, drawn chiefly from those engaged in the export trade but also from leading wholesalers and retailers, the ability to settle their debts across accounts by book transfers, as well as exchange loans and transfers between the capital and Bruges, Antwerp, Middleburg and even Venice. The English clients could settle their debts to the bank by making payments on its behalf to other clients, mainly Italians, to whom the Borromei owed money. More than this, the bank also helped finance their trade by allowing them credit, in most cases for less than a year but sometimes over two, three or four years. This could all be done in the 1430s at a time of growing coin shortages when the grocers of London, some of them major clients of the bank, were apparently suffering from the effects of a severe credit squeeze.[78]

The Borromei were only one of four or five Italian banks with branches in London. They certainly seem to have given the capital's merchants an edge over their provincial rivals when it came to access to credit, as Kermode has argued.[79] But was that actually the case? The term 'English backwardness' is often used in relation to the commercial and financial practices used at all levels in society, from the gentleman keeping his estate accounts to the wealthy merchant from London or one of the major provincial towns, the woolmen in the Cotswolds, the clothiers in Essex and Suffolk. If that was the case, then credit would have been more closely tied to the money supply, since few settlements could be made in 'paper' or 'book' money. The obvious example of the advantages of such payments comes from the ledger of Filippo Borromei and company of London for 1436. The bank opened for business in the early March of that year with a capital of £1,431 13s 4d *sterling*, transferred from the Bruges branch. Between March and 31 December 1436 the turnover of all the accounts amounted to £28,630. Most of this was book money, since the turnover in the cash account for that period was only £2,189.[80] It is true that the Borromei could draw on money markets across Europe from Venice to Cologne for funds, which gave them a distinct advantage over their English rivals who traded mainly to the Baltic, where credit and exchange were strictly controlled, or to the Low Countries and the Iberian peninsula, where they were not. But all English merchants taking wool to the Staple at Calais or cloth to the fairs in Brabant, whether they came from London or not, were fully capable of writing their own bills of exchange, of borrowing in the local currency from a English merchant with funds in Antwerp, Bergen-op-Zoom or Middleburg and then repaying the money on a specified date in sterling in England, and of making debts over at Antwerp.[81] This is little more than the use of the bond for exchange transactions and we should perhaps be a little more wary of talking about 'English backwardness' in the absence of any English mercantile accounts. There are no signs in the Borromei ledgers that such bills were assignable or negotiable, but for once that is of no matter. London merchants were able to use the Italian banks for money transfers to and from the Low Countries to finance their trade, but they and presumably merchants from other towns engaged in the export and import trade with the Low Countries were also quite capable of managing without their services and writing their own bills of exchange, drawn either on a correspondent or on their own servants resident in Brabant and Flanders.

Credit in internal trade

The value of English exports to the Low Countries and elsewhere was only a fraction of the value of all English trade, however. Most production was for the internal market which was probably more highly integrated in the fifteenth century than it had been in the thirteenth.[82] Manufactured goods that could not be produced in England or those for which demand outran supply, as well as dyestuffs, spices and Mediterranean fruits, expensive and inexpensive cloth from Italy, south Germany and the Low Countries, were imported and redistributed from London, Southampton and, until the late fifteenth century, Sandwich, along with a host of other ports whose trade across the Channel and the North Sea may be difficult to estimate but should never be overlooked.[83] Towns also had to be fed and supplied with raw materials, even if total urban demand did fall in line with the halving of the population by the mid-fifteenth century. Lines of credit and debit ran across England, from the ports to the provincial markets and fairs, from town to countryside and back again. Some have now been studied in depth, such as those created by the grocers and mercers of London and the merchants of York, Beverley and Hull in the north-east and Exeter in the south-west. Others are currently being investigated but, as yet, there is no overall analysis of how internal credit worked, in the sense of how dependent it was on the use of coin.[84]

Looking forward to what happened next can sometimes provide the historian, as well as the reader of detective stories, with clues as to what had happened earlier. In this case, we should consider the model provided for us by Kerridge in his study of early modern inland trade. He argues that by the mid-seventeenth century hybrid bills and bonds had come into use, combining the promise to pay of the bill or bond obligatory with an order to pay. It was no more than a bill of exchange here used for inland rather than overseas trade. A factor or agent might give a receipt for payment in which he undertook to pay the money over to a third party, so that **A** delivered a certain sum in sterling to **B** who undertook to repay it on a certain date to **D** through **C**. This was a combined receipt, promissory note and inland bill of exchange and was much used by 'country' suppliers who built up credit balances with factors or merchants in London and used them to buy raw materials and other goods, paying for them by deductions from their accounts. As early as 1576 current accounts were also being provided by London scriveners who received payments on behalf of their clients, distributed moneys as authorised, paid interest on deposits and occasionally allowed overdrafts. These men were bankers in all but contemporary name which was still reserved for those who dealt in foreign exchange.

This was the banking system used in sixteenth- and seventeenth-century England by merchants, traders, manufacturers and suppliers as their principal means of payment. All held accounts in London and they paid one another by transfer from one account to another by what became known as the bill on London. Funds could be transferred from London to provincial towns using the same system, through the banking facilities offered by merchants in various commercial centres. Not all payments could be made through this credit system. Some balances were settled by the transfer of specie and not everyone participated in the network. Only a minority held bank accounts but debts could be discharged by making payment in coin to the creditor's banker, to the use of the creditor. Another shortcoming of this and every other credit network based on bills of exchange was that because each increase in the amount in circulation by bill diminished the resources of the market, the negotiation of further bills was made more difficult. Cyclical shortages of bills were inevitable, given seasonal fluctuations in trade and payments. Nevertheless, English internal trade between 1560 and 1660 was mainly conducted by credit and the financial instruments chiefly employed were the old established bills obligatory and the newly invented inland bills of exchange, the majority of both being informal until the legal developments of the second half of the seventeenth century.[85]

The question that must now be asked is whether all or any part of this inland banking system, as described by Kerridge, existed in later medieval England and the answer must be 'Yes'. There are some limitations to the argument that follows, the most important of them being that it is a view from the top, demonstrating only what happened at national and regional levels of trade and ignoring the most important local level, where informality and oral contracts often prevailed.[86] But the debate on the use of written instruments of credit is conducted at this level, and there are some useful comparisons to be made between the late medieval and early modern periods. Most historians now accept Nightingale's argument that by the fifteenth century London had assumed its full role as the economic driving force in the English economy. The city, with its outports at Southampton and Sandwich, handled most of the country's overseas trade. Its merchants redistributed imports or sold them to provincial chapmen who

C: THE MONEY ECONOMY CHALLENGED, 1351-1489

then re-sold them to local communities. Wool exports were bought directly from the woolmen in the countryside while the main market for cloth for export was at Blackwell Hall in London, although direct contracts with provincial clothiers were also important. Britnell suggests that one of the most lasting consequences of the 'Great Slump' of the 1450s and 1460s was to starve out provincial towns from access to funding and to consolidate the Londoners' hold over credit networks. However, Keene's survey of debt cases brought before the Court of Common Pleas shows that, as early, as 1424 London's commercial links had extended far beyond the south-east, into the Midlands and the north, and that the city was already the hub of the main internal credit network.[87]

This is a tentative argument, but there is other evidence to support it. As in the sixteenth and seventeenth centuries, it was not necessary to be an account holder to participate in the system. The Borromei bank in London was only too happy to sell fustian and silk cloth to any Londoner who was prepared to pay cash and sometimes allowed them short-term credit of a few weeks. In much the same way, those who did not keep accounts with the bank could pay in cash to settle their debts with those who did. Clients could pay cash from their accounts to settle debts to third parties and one of the most surprising aspects of the current research into the activities of the Borromei banks in both Bruges and London has been the large number of 'outsiders' who had dealings with them.[88] This may be atypical evidence, but making over debts to cancel other debts and local credit networks were to be found everywhere.[89] At Romford, some 15 miles from London and thus near enough to the capital to be influenced by its pull but sufficiently far away to have an economic life of its own,

> any two people might build up a number of outstanding debts to each other. As long as goodwill between the individuals remained firm the balances could go uncollected for years. When the parties chose to settle on an amicable basis, they normally named auditors who totalled all the current unpaid debts and detinues and determined the sum which had to be paid to clear the slate. If trust between the parties broke down, the complainant could bring suit in the Havering court, which had jurisdiction over all agreements made within the manor.[90]

Mutual cancellation of debts meant far less reliance on coin and these simple but effective methods were all part of the largely unrecorded credit networks that ran through town and countryside alike.[91]

Much did depend on the written record and the written account, however. As far as accounting is concerned, the difficulties of the evidence, or rather the lack of it, make any judgment as to whether there were significant advances in this area nigh impossible. There is nothing to suggest that the double-entry system[92] was widely adopted, or even adopted at all. The Southampton town accounts were briefly kept in this way, but the first surviving ledgers of English merchants from the late fifteenth and early sixteenth centuries show double entry being used in a very simple or, perhaps better, a very crude way.[93] Too much can be made of this apparent lack of progress. Double entry suited the Italian merchants trading from the Mediterranean to northern Europe who needed to keep track of multiple business ventures and, in the case of banks, to report back their profits to the partners in the enterprise. It was not necessarily as useful to a small merchant in midland or northern England, or in London for that matter, whose trade was local and usually with a known circle of contacts. Here the charge/discharge method, best described as a list of credits and debits which could be resolved in ways already described, was more than adequate.

The ability to read and write and to number or to have access to someone with these skills became more essential at all levels of society as the use of the written instrument increased. There has been much discussion of the growth in the number of schools and thus of literacy in late medieval England. In London there was possibly a 50 per cent literacy rate although whether that means the ability to both read and write is uncertain. It was probably not as high in provincial towns or in the countryside generally. For the wealthy, a business education was available at Oxford in the late fourteenth and early fifteenth centuries. Young men would be taught the arts of estate management, how to keep a manorial court and draw up accounts. Wealthy peasants were keen to send their children to school and merchants were required to teach their apprentices to read and write, and if they did not so could be sued for a return of the apprenticeship fees paid to them. During the fifteenth century English finally emerged as the national spoken and written language, although there were still wide regional variations in pronunciation, spelling and grammar. This made communication easier across all levels of society which in turn made internal trade much easier. Nevertheless, Orme has warned us against over-exaggerating the extent of education and therefore of literacy. There were some who made their lack of reading clear: in a Chancery case in 1448 over a penal bond for £10 Walter Parkes of Liskeard (Cornwall) said that he was a man *'minime literatus'*, scarcely literate, and that the obligation was read to him and had been expanded (explained) in English. It was only when that had been done that he sealed the bond.[94]

C: THE MONEY ECONOMY CHALLENGED, 1351-1489

This illustrates an important point about late medieval English society. There was always someone, somewhere who could read and write and who, either professionally or from friendship or kinship, could draw up deeds, bills or accounts and read them back to the 'scarcely literate'. Sometimes reading a contract aloud was part of the final process of confirming it. This was certainly the case in 1443 when William Styfford, notary imperial of Lombard Street, read the contract establishing the second Borromei bank in London out loud to Alessandro Palastrello of Piacenza, one of the partners in the company, 'with a distinct voice ... word for word' and Palastrello had to acknowledge that he had fully understood it.[95] The role of scriveners, notaries and notaries imperial in English commercial life has not yet been fully investigated. It should be. There were at least thirty to forty scriveners working in London in each decade of the fifteenth century, in addition to the clerks employed in the royal administration who undertook a great deal of 'private' work for cash. A very preliminary survey suggests that there were scriveners in most towns of any size so that there would easy access to a professional scribe for country dwellers. These men were not lawyers but they knew the correct formulae for bonds, wills and countless other documents. They could draw up a bill obligatory from either written or, more importantly, oral instructions and then read it back to the parties involved to confirm that is was what they wanted. Very little is known about their formal training except that they would have usually served an apprenticeship with another scrivener. A clause in the new ordinances drawn up for the Scriveners of London in 1497 stated that all new apprentices were to be examined by the Wardens of the Company and if it was found that their Latin was inadequate, then they were to be sent to a grammar school to be made 'competently erudite in the books of pervula (Latin grammar), genders, declensions, preterites, supynes Equivox and synonyms with other petty books'.[96]

Competence was essential since the written document carried the weight of proof in the law courts. A mistake in drafting could prove fatal, especially after the Statute of Additions of 1413 which required the correct recording of the personal status of the parties involved in any action. If it could be shown that this was incorrect, then the action failed. It is also possible that scriveners kept copies of the documents they produced, similar to the protocolla of the southern European notaries. In Italy and southern France it was the entry in the protocolla that had the force of law and would be produced in a court of law as evidence. That was never the case in England, except that in a wide-ranging enquiry as to who had sold goods to aliens on credit rather than for ready cash contrary to the statute of 8 Henry VI cap. 24, two registers of debts contracted between 1457 and 1459 were used as evidence in the Exchequer court. One dealt with Italian merchants and was kept by none other than the notary imperial William Styfford who had acted for the Borromei bank in the 1430s and 1440s. The other, concerning the debts of north-European merchants, including some Hansards, was the register of John Thorpe, another well-known London notary.[97] Whether they represent a type of document otherwise unknown to us is a matter of speculation. If so, the scriveners were more highly organised than has previously been thought and this leads to a further piece of speculation that, as in the seventeenth century, they may also have been moneylenders and bankers. It is noticeable how often they appear in the gifts of goods and chattels recorded in the mayor's court of the City of London and on the Chancery Close Rolls. Perhaps it was because they drew up the necessary deeds of gift but they may also have been involved in the transactions themselves. Lawyers, also a growing class in the late Middle Ages, may also have performed much the same functions as scriveners and this uncertainty makes the debate on the use of the written credit instrument as an alternative to coin all the more interesting.

Comparisons between the early modern banking system described by Kerridge and what is known of the credit market in fifteenth-century England should not be overdrawn, however. Too much had changed between the two periods in both monetary and economic terms to allow that. Yet it has been a worthwhile exercise because it has pointed us towards a series of interrelated conclusions: namely that the totality of the credit market can never be satisfactorily measured; that using statute staple certificates to link fluctuations in the availability of credit firmly to the money supply may be misleading; and that a society in an age of transition or structural change used all its resources to try to find ways round the problems created by shortages of bullion and most notably of silver. At times, for the majority of the population, there must have been great difficulties in buying and selling, especially in the 1450s and 1460s, but this was not in the main a society held back by an inadequate money supply.

Debasement: the advice of 1379 ignored

There remains one important unanswered question: why was there no debasement in late medieval England, which would or could have increased substantially the amount of coin in circulation? The two major recoinages of 1411–12 and 1464–70 saw adjustments to the bullion content of the coinage to correct an unacceptable ratio between gold and silver and

C: THE MONEY ECONOMY CHALLENGED, 1351-1489

to bring the value of the coins in terms of their bullion content into line with the price of precious metal on the international market.[98] The fineness of the coins was not altered and the drain of good English money abroad to be replaced by poor imitations was as much of a problem in Henry VII's reign as it had been in Henry IV's.[99] Why then did the crown not take the advice given to it in 1379 and debase or devalue the coins? Devaluation would have made English exports cheaper abroad but at some cost to the economy. In modern terms, devaluation is undertaken as part of a series of steps to stabilise an economy. These include controlling the rate of growth of the money supply to stem inflationary pressures; a reduction in government spending to control the fiscal deficit and restore the balance between the public and the private sectors' role in the economy and so further reduce inflationary pressures; and a reduction in real wages (that is, of inflation-adjusted wage payments) in order to make exports more-attractive and so increase industrial profits, which would attract inward (foreign) industrial investment, leading to import substitution and more exports.[100]

In the twenty-first century this is generally known as The International Monetary Fund austerity package and it contains two elements that might apply to the fifteenth-century English economy: a decline in imports and a rise in exports, to close the hypothetical trade gap. But for most of the later Middle Ages, except perhaps for the 1450s and 1460s, England did not have a trade gap. The country could actually afford an extensive import trade which was, in any case, mostly composed of raw materials and cheap manufactured goods for a wide market, not of worthless luxuries as the *Libelle* alleges.[101] There was hardly likely to be any substantial foreign investment in English industry when the country was usually at war, physically or economically, with its immediate neighbours. If there was no devaluation, then this was probably because it suited the vociferous merchant class, which was well represented in the Commons in Parliament, to keep the over-valued gold coinage as it was.[102] They may have sold less by the way of exports but they were able to buy imports relatively cheaply and then sell them on for a profit in England. It seems to have been their view that prevailed, given that the crown had accepted the notion that there could be no changes to the coinage without the assent of the Commons in Parliament. Sound money, that rallying cry of the political classes, meant ample supplies of gold in the late Middle Ages and that goal was achieved. The lack of silver did not seem to matter, except in parliamentary petitions and political verse where much was said but little consequently done.

Conclusion

That might have had serious consequences for the population at large, had not a more literate and numerate society found its own ways around the problem. Mayhew's figures for GDP and **per capita** GDP prove this point. They are, of course, partly based on estimates of the volume of coinage in circulation and take no account of the argument here that credit was not as firmly tied to the money supply as has been argued and that written instruments of debt could act as forms of money. Allowance also has to be made for the sharp decline in the size of the population but, nonetheless, the size of both GDP and per capita **GDP** in 1470, as compared with 1086 and 1300, is of the greatest interest, as Table 9.2 shows.

Table 9.2 Estimates of population, GDP and Per capita GDP, 1086–1470

Date	1086	1300	1470
Population	2.25 million	6 million	2.3 million
GDP	£0.4 million	£4.66 million	£3.5 million
Per capita GDP	£0.18	£0.78	£1.52

Source: N.J. Mayhew, 'Money and coinage in England, 1086–*c*.1500', in D. Wood (ed.), *Medieval Money Matters* (Oxford: Oxbow books, 2004), pp. 79, 81–3.

In spite of bullion crises, supposed credit restrictions and a great slump lasting two decades, per capita **GDP** in 1470 was twice what it had been in 1300, and when silver coinage per head had fallen to two-thirds of the levels at the end of the thirteenth century. Fifteenth-century society understood only too well that money was a vital tool:

> Penny is a hardy knight;
> Penny is mickle of might
> Penny, if wrong he maketh right
> In every country where he goes.

It also understood that if 'for lack of money it could not speed', then invention was the child of necessity.[103]

Notes

1 The most recent study of this problem is in Dyer, *An Age of Transition?*, Chapter iii, and especially pp. 97-111; see also Bailey, *The English Manor*, pp. 18-43, 104-16, 167-92 for a full discussion of the sources and their limitations.

2 D. Youngs, 'Estate management, investment and the gentleman landlord in late medieval England', *HR*, 73 (2000), pp. 125-41; Dyer, *An Age of Transition?*, pp. 97-111.

3 Nightingale, 'Monetary contraction', 563-4, using M.K. James, 'A London merchant of the fourteenth century', *EcHR*, 2nd series (1956), 364-76. This refers to him by his correct forename, Gilbert, rather than Thomas, as used by Nightingale.

4 In 'The Pastons and their Norfolk', *AgHR*, 36 (1988), 132-44, R.H. Britnell uses the letters to comment on gentry estate management and the agricultural depression in Norfolk in the 1460s. C.F. Richmond has written the standard life of the family in three volumes: *The Paston Family in the Fifteenth Century: The First Phase* (Cambridge: Cambridge University Press, 1990); *The Paston Family in the Fifteenth Century: Faastolf's Will* (Cambridge: Cambridge University Press, 1996); *The Paston Family in the Fifteenth Century: Endings* (Manchester: Manchester University Press, 2000).

5 For the Celys see A. Hanham, *The Cely Letters*, Early English Text Society, Original Series (London: Oxford University Press, 1975) and Hanham, *The Celys and their World: An English Merchant Family of the Fifteenth Century* (Cambridge: Cambridge University Press, 1985).

6 Nightingale, *A Medieval Mercantile Community*; A.F. Sutton, *The Mercery of London: Trade, Goods and People, 1130-1578* (Aldershot: Ashgate, 2005); for various printed customs records see the publications of the London Records Society and the Southampton Records Series.

7 Harold Wilson, BBC TV and Radio broadcast, 19 November 1967.

8 This is the most common translation of the moral drawn from the fable of the crow and the pitcher, but whether it is an accurate translation or the use of an English idiom is not clear. Jowett's translation of *The Republic*, Book II, 369c is '... let us begin and create the idea of a state and yet the true creator is necessity, who is the mother of our invention'.

9 M.M. Postan, 'Revisions in economic history IX, The fifteenth century', *EcHR*, 1st series, 9 (1939), 160-7. This summary of his argument is taken from Hatcher and Bailey, *Modelling the Middle Ages*, pp. 51-2; W. Abel, *Agricultural Fluctuations in Europe: From the Thirteenth to the Twentieth Centuries* (London: Methuen, 1980), pp. 49-95.

10 W.C. Robinson, 'Money, population and economic change in late medieval Europe', *EcHR*, 2nd Series, 12 (1959), 63-75; Postan's reply was carried in the same issue, 77-82. For his discussion on the rise of the money economy, see M.M. Postan, 'The rise of a money economy', *EcHR*, 1st series, 14 (1944), 122-34.

11 A.R. Bridbury, *Economic Growth: England in the Later Middle Ages* (London: Allen & Unwin, 1962).

12 R. Brenner, 'Agrarian class structure and economic development in pre-industrial England', *P&P*, 70 (1976), 30-75 and 'The agrarian roots of European capitalism',

P&P, 97 (1982), 16–113, both reprinted in T.H. Aston and C.H.E. Philpin (eds), *The Brenner Debate: Agrarian Class Structure and Economic Development in Pre-industrial England* (Cambridge: Cambridge University Press, 1985); Kosminsky, *Studies in the Agrarian History of England in the Thirteenth Century*, pp. 152–96, 283–359 *passim*; Rigby, *English Society*, pp. 127–44; Hatcher and Bailey, *Modelling the Middle Ages*, pp. 121–73 and the associated bibliographical note, pp. 244–6.

13 See for example M.E. Mate, 'The east-Sussex land market and agrarian class structure in the later Middle Ages', *P&P*, 139 (1993), 46–65, and J. Whittle, *The Development of Agrarian Capitalism: Land and Labour in Norfolk, 1440–1580* (Oxford, 2000).

14 J-H. von Thünen, *The Isolated State*, trs. C.M. Wartenberg, ed. P. Hall (Oxford; Pergamon Press, 1966).

15 In the sense that discrete and autonomous markets were converted into an interdependent and unified whole.

16 Dyer, *An Age of Transition?*, pp. 3–6 for a summary of his arguments. F.R.H. Du Boulay had already written in much the same terms in his *An Age of Ambition: English Society in the Late Middle Ages* (London: Nelson, 1970) and J.L. Bolton attempted a similar approach in '"The World Upside Down"', pp. 49–77.

17 Dyer, *An Age of Transition?*, pp. 175–8. He had already examined low use of coins by the peasantry in his Howard Linecar lecture 'Peasants and coins: the uses of money in the Middle Ages', printed in the *BNJ*, 67 (1998), 30–47.

18 Ecclesiastes 9:19.

19 Hatcher, 'The great slump of the mid-fifteenth century', pp. 237–72 and especially p. 244.

20 C.H. Feinstein, P. Temin and G. Toniolo, *The World Economy between the World Wars* (Oxford: Oxford University Press, 2008), pp. 170–3; J. Stevenson and C. Cook, *Britain in the Depression: Society and Politics, 1929–29* (Harlow: Longman, 1994), pp. 10–13.

21 A.J. Pollard, 'The North eastern economy and the agrarian crisis of 1438–40', *Northern History*, 15 (1989), 88–105; Pollard, *North-eastern England during the Wars of the Roses: Lay Society, War and Politics* (Oxford: Clarendon Press, 1990), pp. 50–2; B. Dodds, 'Estimating arable output using Durham Priory tithe receipts 1341–1450', *EcHR*, 2nd series, 57 (2004), pp. 245–85; Dodds, *Peasants and Production in the Medieval North-east: The Evidence of Tithes, 1270–1536* (Woodbridge: Boydell Press, 2007), pp. 71–131; 'The Battle of Towton' in R.H. Robbins (ed.), *Historical Poems of the Fourteenth and Fifteenth Centuries* (New York: Columbia University Press, 1959), p. 216, lines 11–25. In a recent (2010) article Nightingale sees the decline of York in terms of bullion shortages and lack of credit. Since her argument much depends on Statute Staple certificates of debt for evidence it should be viewed with some caution: P. Nightingale, 'The rise and decline of medieval York: a reassessment', *P&P*, 206 (2010), 3–42.

22 Kermode, *Medieval Merchants*, pp. 223–47.

23 J. Hatcher, 'England in the aftermath of the Black Death', *P&P*, 144 (1994), 6–25; S.K. Cohn examines labour legislation across western Europe in 'After the Black Death: labour legislation and attitudes towards labour in late-medieval western Europe', *EcHR*, 2nd series, 60 (2007), 457–85; S. Penn and C. Dyer, 'Wages and

earnings in late medieval England: evidence from the enforcement of the labour laws', *EcHR*, 2nd series, 43 (1990), 356-76; Munro, 'Wage stickiness, monetary changes, and real incomes in late-medieval England and the Low Countries', pp. 185-295 and especially pp. 186-95.
24 E.H. Phelps Brown and S.V. Hopkins, 'Seven centuries of the prices of consumables compared with builders' wage rates', *Economia*, 22 (1956), 296-314 and *A Perspective of Wages and Prices* (London: Methuen, 1981), pp. 1-59; J.E. Thorold Rogers, *Six Centuries of Work and Wages: The History of English Labour*, 2 vols (London: Swan Sonnenschein, 1884) and *A History of Agriculture and Prices in England from 1259 to 1793*, 6 vols (Oxford: Clarendon Press, 1866-1902); for methodology see Dyer, *Standards of Living*, pp. 217-20.
25 Munro, 'Wage stickiness', 186-95.
26 Munro, 'Wage stickiness', 195-204.
27 For a review of the current debate on this issue see S.H. Rigby, 'Gendering the Black Death: women in late medieval England', *Gender and history*, 12 (2000), 745-54.
28 Munro, 'Wage stickiness', 204-6.
29 Munro, 'Wage stickiness', 194-5, 210-13 where he rejects Hatcher's arguments about wages in 'Aftermath of the Black Death' 6-8, 19-20, while accepting the general tenor of his case; Rigby, *English Society*, 80-7, 114-15.
30 Penn and Dyer, 'Wages', 356; L. Poos, *A Rural Society after the Black Death: Essex 1350-1525* (Cambridge, 1991), pp. 207-28.
31 P. Nightingale, 'Monetary contraction', 574. See also Mayhew, 'Money and prices in England from Henry II to Edward III', 121; P. Spufford, *Handbook of Medieval Exchange* (London: Boydell and Brewer, 1986), pp. 346-8; Munro, 'Wage stickiness', 216-17.
32 See above, pp. 9-10, 73-4, 124, 204 for earlier discussion of bonds; Munro, 'Wage stickiness', 217, although here he seems to be arguing against his own case for the negotiability of instruments in '"English backwardness" and financial innovation in commerce with the Low Countries, 14th to 16th centuries' in P. Stabel, B. Blondé and A. Greve (eds), *International Trade in the Low Countries (14th-16th Centuries): Merchants, Organisation, Infrastructure* (Leuven-Apeldoorn: Garant, 2000), pp. 105-67.
33 'A Trade Policy', Robbins, *Historical Poems of the Fourteenth and Fifteenth Centuries*, p. 171, lines 81-96; *RP, vol. v*, p. 502.
34 C. Given-Wilson, 'Wealth and credit, public and private: the earls of Arundel 1306-1397', *EHR*, 106 (1991), 1-26 at 1-2, 26; G.L. Harriss, *Cardinal Beaufort: A Study of Lancastrian Ascendancy and Decline* (Oxford: Clarendon Press, 1988), p. 411.
35 K.B. McFarlane, 'The investment of Sir John Fastolf's profits of war', *TRHS*, 5th series, 7 (1957), 91-116 at 103-5, 109.
36 J.L. Bolton, 'How Sir Thomas Rempston paid his ransom: or, the mistakes of an Italian bank', in L. Clark (ed.), *The Fifteenth Century*, VII (2007), pp. 111-13; N. Kingwell, 'The Arundells of Langherne and the cost of civil war', unpublished paper given to the Late Medieval Seminar at the Institute of Historical Research, University of London, 2007. I am grateful to the author for his permission to use this material.

37 See for example the discussion of the wealth of the higher clergy by D. Lepine, where he concludes that while few were as fabulously wealthy as Walter Sherrington, chancellor of the duchy of Lancaster, who had over £3,200 in cash at the time of his death in 1449, estates of between £300 and £1,300 were not uncommon. Richard Ravenser, archdeacon of Lincoln, had an annual income of c.£900 from 1371 to his death in 1386 and in one year alone, 1358, was able to make 14 loans totalling over £400: D. Lepine, 'The noiseless tenor of their ways', in J. Boffey and V.G. Davis (eds), *Recording Medieval Lives, Harlaxton Medieval Studies, vol. xvii* (Donington: Shaun Tyas, 2009), 29, 37-8.

38 Dyer, 'Peasants and coins', pp. 3-36 for methodology, pp. 36-40 for the coin finds.

39 Dyer, 'Peasants and coins', pp. 40-4; Dyer, *An Age of Transition?*, pp. 174-5.

40 Dyer, 'Peasants and coins', pp. 46-7.

41 Maddicott, *The English Peasantry and the Demands of the Crown*, pp. 6-15 (lay taxation), 15-34 (purveyance); Dyer, 'Taxation and communities', pp. 168-90; G.L. Harriss, *Shaping the Nation: England 1360-1461* (Oxford: Oxford University Press, 2005), p. 60.

42 *RP, vol. iii*, p. 64.

43 Harriss, *Shaping the Nation*, pp. 437-40, 456-7. The collectors were allowed reasonable expenses. Royal debts could also be assigned – that is, repaid from specific revenues before they reached the Exchequer.

44 Jurkowski et al., *Lay Taxes*, pp. 86-99; *RP, v*, pp. 108-9; see above, pp. 34-5.

45 B.A. Holderness, *Pre-Industrial England: Economy and Society from 1500 to 1750* (London: Dent, 1976), pp. 118-19; E.H. Hunt and S.J. Pam, 'Responding to agricultural depression, 1873-96', *AgHR*, 50 (2002), 225-52.

46 See above, pp. 262-3.

47 Clark, 'Debt litigation in a late medieval English vill', pp. 265-71.

48 C. Briggs, 'Manor court procedures, debt level litigations levels, and rural credit provision in England, c.1290-c.1380', *LHR*, 24 (2006), 555-6; Briggs, 'The availability of credit in the English countryside, 1400-80', *AgHR*, 56 (2008), 1-24; Briggs, 'Seignorial control of villagers' litigation beyond the manor in later medieval England', *HR*, 81 (2008), 410-22; Briggs, *Credit and Village Society*, deals in depth with all these issues.

49 Britnell, *Growth and Decline in Colchester*, pp. 98-108, 206-7; Kowaleski, *Local Markets and Regional Trade*, pp. 202-20.

50 Postan, 'Credit in medieval trade' p. 27; R.H. Britnell, 'The economy of British towns 1300-1540', in Palliser (ed.), *Cambridge Urban History, vol. i*, p. 324.

51 Nightingale, 'Monetary contraction', 564-5; Britnell, *Growth and Decline in Colchester*, pp. 107-8.

52 Nightingale, 'Monetary contraction', p. 574; another statement of her argument can be found in 'England and the European depression of the mid-fifteenth century', *JEEH*, 26 (1997), 631-56.

53 See above, pp. 73, 199, 202-3.

54 Postan, 'Private financial instruments', pp. 37-8; Kowaleski, *Local Markets and Regional Trade*, pp. 212-13.

55 See above, pp. 238-9, 245-6, 248.

56 Kowaleski, *Local Markets and Regional Trade*, pp. 213-14; Postan, 'Private finan-

cial instruments', pp. 35-7.
57 Kowaleski, *Local Markets and Regional Trade*, pp. 212-14; McNall, 'The business of statutory debt registries, 1283-1307', pp. 68-88, at p. 82.
58 Kowaleski, *Local Markets and Regional Trade*, pp. 212-20; M. McIntosh, 'Money lending on the periphery of London, 1300-1600', *Albion*, 20 (1988), 557-71, shows a similar pattern of debt recovery in a local court near London; also, McIntosh, *Autonomy and Community*, pp. 166-70.
59 See above, pp. 283-4.
60 Postan, 'Private financial instruments', pp. 29-54.
61 Kowaleski, *Local Markets and Regional Trade*, p 208; McIntosh, 'Money lending', 562-3, 566; A[rchivio] B[orromeo] dell' I[sola] B[ella], libro mastro no. 8, Filippo Borromei e compagni di Bruggia, ff. 80.6, 117.2; ABIB, libro mastro no. 7, Filippo Borromei e compagni di Londra, ff. 156.4, 272.4, discussed in the author's forthcoming article, 'London merchants and the Borromei Bank in the 1430s: the role of local credit networks'.
62 De Roover, *Medici Bank*, pp. 9-14; R.A. Goldthwaite, 'The Medici bank and the world of Florentine capitalism', *P&P*, 114 (1987), 3, 4, 12; Spufford, *Power and Profit*, pp. 43-6; 'Banks and banking', in C. Kleinhenz (ed.), *Medieval Italy: an Encylclopedia, vol. i A-K* (London: Routledge, 2004), pp. 90-1; S. Homer and R. Sylla, *A History of Interest Rates* (New Jersey: Wiley, 4th edn, 2005), pp. 67-70.
63 R.C. Palmer, *English Law in the Age of the Black Death: A Transformation of Governance and Law* (Chapel Hill, NC: University of North Carolina Press, 1993), pp. 9-13, 62-91; J. Biancalana, 'Contractual penalties in the king's courts 1260-1360', *Cambridge Law Journal*, 64 (2005), 212-42.
64 P.E. Jones (ed.), *Calendar of Plea and Memoranda Rolls of the City of London 1437-57* (Cambridge: Cambridge University Press, 1954), Introduction, pp. xxii-xxviii; P. Tucker, *Law Courts and Lawyers in the City of London 1300-1550* (Cambridge: Cambridge University Press, 2007), pp. 67-70. In this valuable study Tucker shows that it is impossible to determine how much private business was done in the Mayor's Court after 1307 because of selectiveness in enrolment (p. 150). It is another powerful argument against quantification of credit.
65 Nightingale, *A Medieval Mercantile Community*, p. 476.
66 Postan, 'Private financial instruments', pp. 40-54 where he also discusses other assignable instruments such as debentures of the Company of the Staple at Calais and bills of the mint at Calais.
67 The important AHRC-funded project 'Londoners and the Law in the later Middle Ages' has sampled cases in the Court of Common Pleas (TNA: PRO CP 40) in the fifteenth century. Many involved bonds but there is so far little evidence of assignment of debt. Ex inf. Dr M. Davis and Dr H. Kleineke, Institute of Historical Research, School of Advanced Study, University of London.
68 J.H. Munro, 'The international law merchant and the evolution of negotiable credit in late medieval England and the Low Countries', in D. Puncuh (ed.), *Banchi pubblici, banchi private e monte di pietà Nell-Europa preindustriale, Atti della Società Ligure di storia patria, nuova serie*, 31 (1991), pp. 63-71; J.S. Rogers, *The Early History of the Law of Bills and Notes: A Study of Anglo-American Commercial Law* (Cambridge: Cambridge University Press, 1995), pp. 32-51.

69 The most recent discussions of the emergence of this court are T.S. Haskett, 'The medieval English court of chancery', *LHR*, 14 (1996), 245–313 and for bonds see especially pp. 302, 307; P. Tucker, 'The early history of the court of chancery: a comparative study, *EHR*, 115 (2000), 719–811, which draws comparisons between the chancery and the courts in the city of London.
70 The surviving records of the medieval Court of Chancery are to be found in The National Archives: Public Record Office, Class C 1. Haskett, 'Medieval English court of chancery', p. 281, explains that as the Chancery was not a court of record, there was no need for any of the evidence brought before it to be kept. Nor are there any surviving books of decrees (decisions) made by the Chancellor.
71 Nightingale, *A Medieval Mercantile Community*, p. 477.
72 E. Kerridge, *Trade and Banking in Early Modern England* (Manchester: Manchester University Press, 1988), pp. 40–1; Postan, 'Private financial instruments', p. 49.
73 S. Thrupp, *The Merchant Class of Medieval London* (Michigan: Ann Arbor, 1962), p. 109. Collecting debts without specialty was often difficult.
74 ABIB, BBr f. 348.2; BLon ff. 260.1, 292.4.
75 De Roover, *Medici Bank*, pp. 11–14; Munro, 'Bullionism and the Bill of Exchange', pp. 131–239, *passim*.
76 J.M. Murray, *Bruges, Cradle of Capitalism, 1280–1390* (Cambridge: Cambridge University Press, 2005), pp. 121–3; J.L. Bolton and F. Guidi Bruscoli, 'When did Antwerp replace Bruges as the commercial and financial centre of north-western Europe? The evidence of the Borromei ledger for 1438', *EcHR*, 2nd series, 61 (2008), 374–8.
77 In fractional reserve banking, the bank holds a liquid asset such as cash in just sufficient quantities to cover likely withdrawals. It then lends out the rest of cash, at interest, to borrowers, thus creating credit. Credit creation in this way is held to add to the money supply in all but its narrowest definition, M (0). The London goldsmith accepted deposits and issued the depositors with notes which then circulated as a form of paper money: F.T. Melton, 'Deposit banking in London, 1700–90', *Business History*, 28 (1986), 41–2.
78 Nightingale, 'Monetary contraction', Table 3, p. 567; Bolton, 'London merchants and the Borromei bank in the 1430s', forthcoming. Thomas Cannings, grocer, was granted £806 credit over three years by the bank and Thomas Hawkyn £448 over two years. These figures should be compared with those in Nightingale's table. They may give pause for thought.
79 See Kermode's conclusions in *Medieval Merchants*, pp. 274–5.
80 Calculated from ABIB libro mastro no. 7, ledger of Filippo Borromei and company of London, March–December 1436 by Dr F. Guidi Bruscoli. Munro uses the term in the title of one of his working papers (1998) which appeared in revised terms as above fn. 66, 'International law merchant and the evolution of credit'.
81 E. Power, 'The English wool trade in the fifteenth century', in E. Power and M.M. Postan (eds), *Studies in English Trade in the Fifteenth Century* (London: Routledge, 1933), pp. 68–9; Sutton, *The Mercery of London*, pp. 302–11, shows in detail how the London mercers who had factors or attorneys resident in the Low Countries secured credit through exchange.

C: THE MONEY ECONOMY CHALLENGED, 1351-1489

82 Britnell, 'Urban demand in the English economy', pp. 11-16; Britnell, 'The economy of British towns 1300-1540', pp. 313-33, for a very balanced survey of a period usually characterised by urban decline; market integration is explained above, p. 262, n. 15.
83 A point well made in M.E. Mate, *Trade and Economic Development, 1450-1550: The Experience of Kent, Surrey and Sussex* (Woodbridge: Boydell, 2006), pp. 81-101.
84 84 Nightingale, *Medieval Mercantile Community*, pp. 432-89, *passim*; Sutton, *The Mercery of London*, pp. 310-11; Kermode, *Medieval Merchants*, pp. 223-47; Kowaleski, *Local Markets and Regional Trade*, pp. 222-324; C.M. Barron, *London in the Later Middle Ages: Government and People 1200-1500* (Oxford: Oxford University Press, 2004), pp. 76-83; Palliser (ed.), *Cambridge Urban History, vol. i*, pp. 313-34, 412-26, 517-26, 576-82, 631-8, D. Keene, 'Changes in England's economic hinterland as indicated by debt cases in the court of common pleas', in Galloway (ed.), *Trade, Urban Hinterlands and Market Integration*, pp. 59-81; Britnell, 'Urban demand in the English economy', pp. 1-21.
85 Kerridge, *Trade and Banking*, pp. 45-50, 75.
86 Dyer, *An Age of Transition?*, chapter five, 'Subsistence and markets', pp. 173-210, *passim*; Dyer also argues that access to credit became ever more crucial for the emerging class of farmers managing their own estates and seeking to enlarge their holdings, ibid., pp. 122, 189-90, 200.
87 Dyer, *An Age of Transition?*, pp. 192-3; Nightingale, 'The growth of London in the medieval English economy', pp. 89-106; Keene, 'Changes in London's economic hinterland as indicated by debt cases in the court of common pleas', pp. 57-81 and especially Figure 4.1 (p. 60) and Figure 4.4 (p. 70).
88 The Borromei Bank Research Project is based in the School of History at Queen Mary, University of London. The ledger of Filippo Borromei and company of Bruges for 1438 is now online at www.queenmaryhistoricalresearch.org. The corresponding ledger of the London branch for 1436-39 will also be made available online at this site.
89 See for example Dyer, *An Age of Transition?*, pp. 193-4 and Dyer, 'The hidden trade of the Middle Ages', 149-53.
90 McIntosh, 'Money lending', p. 561.
91 Dyer, *An Age of Transition?*, pp. 180-90.
92 The workings of the double entry bookkeeping system are described in detail in the Introduction to The ledger of Filippo Borromei and co. of Bruges at www.queenmaryhistoricalresearch.org.
93 See for example the ledger of Thomas Howell, 1517-28, in the archives of the Drapers' Company of London and the ledger of Sir Thomas Kytson, Hengrave Hall MSS., Cambridge University Library.
94 N. Orme, *Medieval Schools: From Roman Britain to Renaissance England* (New Haven and London: Yale University Press, 2006), pp. 253-4, 339-43; TNA: PRO CP40/740, rot. 119. For a similar instance of man claiming to be 'minime literatus' see TNA: PRO CP40/781 rot. 329. I owe these references from CP40 to the kindness of Dr Hannes Kleineke of the History of Parliament, along with the pleasure of long conversations about debt in late medieval England.

95 ABIB Box File 1051 (c). The document is in Latin and the translation is mine.
96 F.W. Steer (ed.), *The Scriveners' Company Common Paper 1357–1628: With a Continuation to 1678*, London Record Society 4 (London, 1968), pp. 49–52.
97 The registers are TNA: PRO E101/128/35 (Thorpe) and E101/128/36 (Styfford). They have been analysed by S. Jenks, 'Das Schreiberbuch des John Thorpe und der Hansische Handel in London 1457–59', *Hansische Geschichtsblatter*, 101 (1983), 67–113 and by W. Childs, '"To our losse and hindraunce"': English credit to Alien Merchants in the Mid-Fifteenth Century', in J. Kermode (ed.), *Enterprise and Individuals in Fifteenth-Century England* (Stroud: Sutton, 1991), pp. 68–98. The author gave a paper on 'Notaries Imperial, scriveners and the recording of debt in fifteenth-century London' to the Late Medieval Seminar at the Institute of Historical Research on 16 March 2007 and much of the material in this section of the chapter is taken from it.
98 For a discussion of both topics, see above, pp. 48, 70–1.
99 *RP, vol. vi*, pp. 355b, 403a, 542a; S.B. Chrimes, *Henry VII* (London: Eyre Methuen, 1974), pp. 176, 225.
100 J.M. Cypher and J.L. Dietz, *The Process of Economic Development*, 2nd edn. (London, 2004), pp. 504–5.
101 Bolton, *The Medieval English Economy*, pp. 306–7. The figures for the balance of trade given there are used again by Hatcher in 'The Great Slump', p. 243.
102 For mercantile representation in the parliaments of Henry VI's reign, see Bolton, 'Alien Merchants', pp. 236–61.
103 Fifteenth-century carol, cited in J.A. Yunck, 'Dan Denarius: the almighty penny and the fifteenth-century poets', *American Journal of Economics and Sociology*, 20 (1961), 217; 'London Lickpenny', ibid., 212–14.

10

Conclusions

Writing the history of one's own country has its peculiar dangers. As Herbert Butterfield said, historians often have a tendency to see history as a story of progress, leading ultimately to the glorification of the present. It would certainly be wrong to see in this study of money in the English economy between the late tenth and the late fifteenth centuries a triumphant 500-year march of progress from the constrictive bonds placed upon a society without a money economy to 'the broad, sunlit uplands' of a money economy meeting all the challenges thrown at it and laying the foundations of the credit and banking systems of the future.[1] Such has not been the intention here. The inhabitants of medieval England may have been materially better off, better fed and better housed in 1500 than in 1100 or 1300, as the estimated figures for per capita GDP suggest, but life expectancy seems to have fallen in the second half of the fifteenth century, poverty was rife, links between land and people had been broken and the new class of landless labourers would only benefit from high wages while population levels remained low, as a consequence of endemic plague. The purpose of this book has been neither to praise nor to condemn such changes but rather to present as vigorous a case as possible for the money supply being accepted as one of the most important variables in the workings of the economy and for its role being much more important than has heretofore been allowed.

However, even if we accept this case, problems remain. For example, we need much more exploration of regional differences in the availability and use of coin. The assumption has been that from the mid-thirteenth century onward, as the money supply grew, money was spread evenly across the realm. That is what the coin-hoard evidence appears to tell us, but it may be misleading. Until such time as a more thoroughgoing investigation of the use of coin in the northern and far south-western economies has been undertaken, however, any account of the role of money in medieval England must be biased towards what happened in the south, the centre and in East Anglia.

'Never apologise and never explain – it's a sign of weakness' says Captain Nathan Brittles to his junior officers in *She Wore a Yellow Ribbon*.[2] That is sound advice, but it is now time to draw some conclusions about the role of money in the economy of medieval England. The first is that the driving force behind the economic expansion of the twelfth and thirteenth centuries was, without question, sustained population growth. The approximate doubling of the population over the course of the two centuries created the demand in the economy that was served by the growing number of markets and fairs, the expansion of existing towns and the foundation of new ones and by increasing local, regional, national and international trade. At the same time the money supply increased tenfold between 1180 and 1300 and much more if the comparison is drawn between 1100 and 1300. In other words, the economy could not have expanded in the way it did had the increase in population not been matched by an even greater growth in the money supply and in the use of coin as the main medium of exchange. This last is important. Expansion could not have been based on barter, nor on the use of money as a standard of value in exchange which is, after all, only one stage on from barter. That is why comparisons have been drawn here between the 'monetarised' economy of the Anglo-Saxon and Anglo-Norman period from 973 to 1158 and the 'money economy' that developed between 1158 and 1351. For all the emphasis on the glories and sophistication of the Anglo-Saxon and Anglo-Norman world it was, economically, a cramped society. The amount of coin in circulation was so small as to have caused basic difficulties in exchange. In such a context, payment of money rents on a large scale would surely have been impossible and it is perhaps time for a thorough reassessment of the pre- and post-Conquest economy in the light of what numismatists now tell about the size of the money supply.

Of equal and parallel importance in the centuries of economic expansion was the growth in the credit market. The rise and fall in the number of cases of debt being brought before the courts can tell us something about stress in the economy and, more importantly, about commercial links between a town or market, its immediate hinterland and with the wider regional or national economy. What cannot be determined from this evidence, however, is the totality of the credit market, and that is another important conclusion to be drawn from this study. Nevertheless, it is still possible to ask some serious questions about the role of credit in the medieval economy. The first is about whether the outcomes of the crises of the late thirteenth and early fourteenth centuries would have been worse than they were if credit had not been widely available. It is worth remembering here the depth of these crises. Population pressure and monetary instability had led to wildly fluctuating prices in the early fourteenth century, making life hard for those with insufficient land to feed themselves. Then, between 1315 and 1317, there was harvest failure and serious famine across the whole of northern Europe followed by a cattle plague that killed a quarter of the plough and draught oxen in England and murrains that severely reduced the sheep flocks vital for manuring the arable and producing the cash crop, wool.

The cumulative crisis struck at the heart of both the arable and the pastoral economy and the consequences for the peasantry in general and smallholders in particular were catastrophic. Recent studies of the credit market by Schofield and Briggs have suggested that it helped the rich get rich and the poor get poorer[3] in the sense that those who had money were only prepared to lend to those who had something to offer by way of surety, most notably land. Wealthier peasants were also able to buy small parcels of land to enlarge their own holdings from those desperate for cash to buy food. Schofield, Briggs and others are almost certainly right, since smallholders were ill-equipped to withstand three bad harvests in a row, but the availability of credit at village level may well have offered them the chance of survival in all but the most extreme circumstance. The ability to borrow could have meant the difference between life and death at times of harvest crises. If the emergence of a money economy in which widely available credit played a key part mainly benefited the better-off in society, it also offered some protection to the poor, however fragile that protection may have been. Thus, growth in the money supply and in the availability of credit underpinned the expansion of the twelfth and thirteenth centuries. They did not cause it nor did they iron out all the inequalities that expansion created but, nonetheless, by 1300 a robust money economy had emerged.

The next of our questions must be about whether this economy was sufficiently robust to withstand the shock of a sharp reduction in the money supply combined with, as some monetarist historians argue, a contraction in the availability of credit in the late fourteenth and fifteenth centuries. In fact, as Chapter 9 argued, a more literate and numerate society found its own ways around these monetary difficulties. More generally, long-term changes in late medieval English society were not held back by either the contraction in the money supply or a growing shortage of credit. Indeed,

CONCLUSIONS

it is probably more useful to turn the question around and to ask whether a very real crisis, a long-lasting depression, was not staved off precisely because of the resiliency of the money economy.

Arguing about what might have happened in history rather than what actually happened is a highly speculative business, but often worthwhile. The great slump or depression of 1450–70 had no one main cause, according to Hatcher, but resulted from a confluence of long-term trends. Depopulation and stagnant prices combined with a decline in earnings from overseas trade, a fall in the money supply, high wages and declining manufacturing output worked together to produce a recession and a sharp fall in GDP. Today recession is seen as only one part of a longer business cycle which has five main stages: growth or expansion, peak, recession, trough or depression and recovery. It could be argued that the economy went through such a cycle between c.1370 and 1500, with the last quarter of the fourteenth century experiencing growth, the peak being reached between 1400 and 1420, recession setting in between 1420 and 1450 followed by depression between 1450 and 1470 and then a return to growth in the late fifteenth century.

In practice, however, there are considerable difficulties with such an interpretation. The period between 1450 and 1550 is one of the least studied in English economic history and there is no certain way as yet of establishing whether renewed recovery did follow the great slump. Figures for cloth exports are often seen as evidence for economic revival after 1470 but they should be used with some caution. There are no signs of population recovery before the 1520s at the earliest and outside London perhaps not before the 1540s. The very steep rise in cloth exports after 1500 – and not much before then – is often taken as indicating a return to prosperity but how, then, should the evidence from the same source for the 1430s and 1440s be interpreted? Cloth exports in these years ran at levels they were not to reach again until the last decades of the fifteenth century, and that, surely, is not a sign of a recession before the depression of the 1450s and 1460s. What the long-run figures also disguise is a fundamental shift in England's export trade which now passed more and more through London, to the supposed detriment of English regional ports and their hinterlands. Much of London's success, according to Nightingale, was due to monetary shortages which gave Londoners – with their access to the capital's superior credit facilities and greater supplies of capital – a major advantage over their provincial rivals. In theory, however, credit should have dried up everywhere in line with decline in the money supply, perhaps the more so in London because there the money economy was more developed than anywhere else in England. Again, it could be argued that it was the wool trade upon which England relied for its wealth and its supplies of bullion and that was in sharp decline. Yet the real decline in the wool trade came in the fourteenth century, between 1360 and 1390 at a time when cloth exports were only just beginning to increase. After 1400, taking into account fluctuations caused by diplomacy and warfare, the two being inextricably linked, average annual exports were fairly stable until about 1450, again, right on the eve of the great slump.[4]

The first half of the fifteenth century does not fit neatly into the business cycle model and there is as yet insufficient evidence to show that the last decade of the century and the first two decades of the sixteenth saw the period of revival that should have followed the slump. What all the discernible trends in agriculture and land use, landholding, urban decline and growth with some markets failing and others thriving, and in overseas trade, indicate is that England was coping with a significant shift in its economic and social structure. As Dyer has argued, times were hard but that gave some the opportunity to prosper in what was an age of economic and social transition. In our case, changes in the quantity of coin in circulation and its composition, with more gold than silver, did not lead to an inexorable economic downturn but to new ways of solving old problems which had significant implications for the early modern period. The money economy was tested but it survived. Had it not done so then we might still be discussing an age of stagnation tinged with gloom.

Our main focus here has been on the coinage and the economy and on how coins were made, how they circulated and from where the precious metals from which they were struck came. Fluctuations in the money supply, it has been argued, can best be understood in the light of the rise and fall in mining output in Europe and Africa; of trade balances with the near and far East; and of the monetary problems of England's immediate neighbours in northern Europe. In the monetary sense, England appears to be firmly part of a much wider European, African and Asian world. Yet, in its insistence that only one coinage should circulate within the realm and its refusal to debase that coinage, England was also in a monetary world of its own: it is the debasement-ridden monetary histories of Flanders and the Low Countries and France and Germany which represent the historic norm.[5] What should make the medieval English currency interesting to historians is that it can be seen as something unique and worthy of study both in its own right and for its role as one of the main variables in the workings of the economy. The still anonymous author of *The libelle of Englyshe polycye* hoped that his little book would

Go furthe ... and mekely shewe thy face,
Apperynge ever wyth humble contynaunce
And pray my lordes thee to take in grace.[6]

Five hundred and seventy five years later the present author has much the same hopes.

Notes

1 H. Butterfield, *The Whig Interpretation of History* (London: Bell, 1931), p. 2; W.S. Churchill most notably used the phrase in his speech to the House of Commons, 18 June 1940.
2 Directed by John Ford for RKO Radio Pictures, 1949. Brittles was played by John Wayne.
3 With apologies to the estates of Gus Kahn and Raymond B. Egan, authors of the lyrics for 'Ain't we got fun', 1920–1.
4 Carus-Wilson and Coleman, *England's Export Trade*, pp. 122–3, 138–9; Nightingale, 'Growth of London', 89–106; Sutton, *The Mercery of London*, pp. 290–3.
5 J.H.A. Munro, ' Coinage and monetary policies in Burgundian Flanders during the late-medieval 'bullion famines', 1384–1482', http://ideas.repec.org/p/tecipa/tecipa-361.html, appendix a, 26–33. In fact there is no mention of Parliamentary consent to changes in the coinage in either the Commons' petition in parliament or in the Statute of Purveyors: *R.P., vol. ii*, p. 160; *Statutes of the Realm, vol. i*, 25 Edward III, statute 5, cap. xiii, p. 322. See also above, pp. 11, 30, 106.
6 *Libelle*, lines 1142–3.

BIBLIOGRAPHY

For bibliography for this book please refer to: http://www.history.qmul.ac.uk/bolton/

INDEX

Aaron of Lincoln 196, 205
abacus computation 32, 122, 133
accounting systems 29–33, 290–1
Acton Burnell, Statute of
    (1283) 202–4, 208, 211,
    276–7
Æthelræd II Unræd 12, 34, 66
Alexander III of Scotland 157–8
Allen, M. 15, 24–5, 61, 92, 104, 107–8,
    125, 141, 146, 154, 157–8, 162–3,
    241–3, 250–1
Angevin Empire 149
Anglo-Saxon Chronicle 4, 87, 91–2,
    98–9, 103–4
Aquinas, Thomas 36
Archibald, M.M. 153–4
Arundell, Sir John 271
Ashtor, E. 233
assaying 54–6
assignment of debts 73–4, 279–80,
    283–4
    definition of 279
Athelstan, King 30, 88–9
Aylesbury, Richard 245–6, 248

Bacon, Sir Francis 3, 188
Bailey, M. 5, 213
balance of payments, monetary
    approach to 93, 249
Baldwin IX of Flanders 151
banking 8, 156, 161, 164, 166, 195–8,
    271, 285–9
    fractional reserve principle 211–12,
    286
Barratt, N. 178

barter 11, 15, 22, 28, 117, 129, 132,
    134, 305
Beardwood, Alice 278
Beaufort, John 270–1
bezants 88, 154
Biancalana, J. 281–2
bills of exchange 287–9
bi-metallic currencies 48, 51, 68–71,
    76, 159, 168
bi-metallic flows 70, 165, 167, 233–4
Black Death 175, 184, 281
'black' money 239
Blackburn, M.A.S. 94, 102, 105
Blanchard, I. 67, 104, 142
'blanched' money 46
Bompaire, M. 249
bonds 9–10, 27, 30–1, 73–4, 269,
    278–84
    penal 278, 281–2
Borromei banks 246, 285–7, 290–3
Bowers, R.H. 207
Bradenham, Sir Lionel de 201
Brand, J.D. 55, 61, 94
Brenner, R. (and 'Brenner
    debate') 261–2
Bridbury, A.R. 127–8, 185, 261
Briggs, C.D. 210–11, 275, 306
Britnell, R.H. 117, 129, 131, 175, 209,
    262, 275–6, 290
Brown, I.D. 62
Bruce, Robert 164
Bullion Ordinance of the Staple
    (1429) 246, 248
bullion supplies 8, 11, 18, 36–9, 48,
    65–71, 74–6, 98–9, 103–4, 107,

INDEX

134, 165, 228–35, 245–8, 263, 308
Burgundy, dukes of 230, 241, 246–8
Buridan, Jean 35
business cycle 307–8
Butterfield, Herbert 304

Cade, William 205
Calais mint 240–2
Cambio, Philip de 157
Campbell, B.M.S. 15, 188–9, 210
Cannings, Thomas 281
capital investment 212
capitalism 37–9
Carpenter, D.A. 154, 186
Castagnolo, Paolo da 237
Cely family 258–9
Charlemagne 30
Charles V 236
Chaucer, Geoffrey 37
chirograph chests 197
Clanchy, M.T. 33
Clark, E. 275
clipping of coins 46, 147, 156–7, 177, 237–8, 245–6
Cnut, King 92
Codere, H. 31
Coggeshall, Ralph of 177
coinage 3–4, 7
    attributes and advantages of 19–21, 34–5
    changes in weight and fineness of 48–9, 53–5, 96–102
    face value and *intrinsic* value of 45–7, 239, 245–6
    foreign 11–12, 103, 157–8, 245–6
    per head of population 25–7, 107–8, 128, 149, 159, 174, 181–4, 243–4
    and the rural economy 188–91
    shipped abroad 12–14, 149–50, 158, 162–3, 181

    shortages of 270–3, 276, 280–3
    wear and tear on 45–7, 153
    see also clipping of coins; gold coinage; recoinages; silver coinage; weighing of coins
Colchester 274–6
commercialisation of society 14–15, 58, 96, 117, 134, 145, 157, 175–6, 187, 213, 262
Company of the Staple 73
conditional defeasances 281
contracts, enforcement of 203
Cook, B.J. 154
Copernicus, Nicolaus 12
Coss, P.R. 186
counterfeiting 34, 36, 104
Craig, J. 54–5
credit 8–10, 30, 71–3, 76, 108, 113, 122–4, 133–4, 187, 191, 264, 269, 274–6, 305–6
    forms of 192–5
    in internal trade 288–93
    in kind 193
    sources of 196–8, 207–11
    at village level 209–11, 306
'crisis of the knights' 185–6
crockards 12, 69, 143, 158–62, 240
Crowther, G. 20
currency
    estimation of volume in circulation 57–65, 108, 158–9, 163, 241–5
    exchange of 57–8, 143–6
    see also debasement; devaluation; revaluation

Dampierre, Guy of 160
David I of Scotland 103
Day, J. 231, 234, 249, 263
debasement of currency 36, 104, 163, 166, 236, 293–4, 308
debts, registration and recovery

INDEX

of 124, 197–9, 202–4, 208–9, 276–8; *see also* assign-ment of debts
deferred payments 194
deflation, monetary 7–8, 12–13, 39, 71, 76, 160, 163, 179, 181, 184, 249, 259, 264, 266
Defoe, Daniel 274
demesnes 115–16, 125, 129, 175, 185–6, 189, 258
de moneta tax 101
depopulation 71, 75–6, 175, 184, 231–2, 259–68, 307
Derham, John 285–6
devaluation of currency 67, 93, 236, 259–60, 294
dies used to produce coinage, analysis of 59–65, 251
di Giovanni, Niccolò 73
Dodds, B. 263
Dolley, Michael 55, 61, 88–94, 99, 107–8, 125
Domesday Book 15, 32–3, 46, 52, 91, 101, 113–20, 125–9, 134
Durham Cathedral 130
Dyer, Christopher 15, 37–8, 128, 188–91, 251, 258, 262, 268, 271–4, 308

Eadmer 104
Edgar, King 30, 50, 52, 87–9, 100, 106, 141
Edward I 35–6, 54, 58, 69, 143, 156–8, 161, 174, 208
Edward II 208
Edward III 36, 51, 69–70, 166, 174–5, 196, 208
Edward IV 243–5
efficiency wage theory 267
Elmham, Robert 285–6
equation of exchange 6–8, 13–15, 39, 71, 74–5, 179–83, 264

erratic spending 130–1
estate management 185–6, 201
Eusebio, Cardinal 270
exchange banking 286
exchange rates 166
  mint parity theory of 49
Exchequer of the Jews 124, 197
Exchequer practices 32, 46–7, 121, 178, 200
Exeter 274–5
expansion, economic 174–6, 260, 305
exports 49, 67, 92–3, 160, 164–8, 194, 230, 307–8

famine 231–2, 306
Farmer, D.L. 176, 264
Fastolf, Sir John 271
Faulkner, K. 186
feudalism 38, 118
  'bastard' form of 212
Fisher, Irwin 6, 13
Fisher identity *see* equation of exchange
Fitzalan, Edmund 206–7
Fitzalan, Richard 270–1
Fitznigel, Richard 32
fitzRobert, William 209
Florence 234
Flores Historiarum 87
Fossard, William 196
free trade 262
Frescobaldi family 195–6
Friemar, Henry of 19–20
'full money economy' 133

Garner, Richard 238
geld levies 34–5, 64, 66, 87, 91–3, 96–9, 103–4, 118–19
Glanvill treatise 193, 199
Gloucester, Miles (sheriff) of 120–1
gold, value of 18, 20, 70, 155, 166–9

313

gold coinage 21, 51–3, 154–5, 165–9, 234, 243, 248–51, 294
Goldbeter, Bartholomew 250
Goldstone, J.A. 180–2
Gough map 23
government, growth of 31–7
Gregory, William 238
Gresham's Law 12
Grierson, P. 60
groats 70, 157
Grocers' Company 276
gross domestic product (GDP) 15, 125–8
  per capita 295, 304
Grossesteste, Robert 201

Harlewyn, William de 157
Harold II, King 100
Harthacnut, King 92
harvest failures 4, 7, 30, 45, 76, 105, 174, 177, 184, 213, 231–2, 280, 306
Harvey, Paul 175, 177, 185, 201
Hatcher, J. 5, 129, 263–4, 307
Henley, Walter of 201
Henry I 46, 92, 104–7
Henry II 32, 143–7, 186, 193, 200, 205
Henry III 51, 88, 149, 151, 154–5, 165
Henry IV 244, 273
Hinderclay (Suffolk) 210
hoards of coin 59–65, 93–4, 177, 181, 249, 251, 304
  in royal treasuries 152–5, 178–9
Hoccleve, Thomas 237
Hodges, R. 34, 67
Hoo, John 245–6
Hopkins, S.V. 266
Hosting Statute 246–7
Hume, David 3
Hyams, P.R. 209–10

imitation coinage 158–61, 169, 240, 294; *see also* counterfeiting
imports and import substitution 49, 67, 92–3, 164–5, 230
inflation
  monetary 7, 39, 148, 177, 182–7, 249, 268, 270
  in wages 175–6
ingots, use of 44
Innocent III, Pope 36
interest 38, 72, 193–8, 280–1
International Monetary Fund 294
Irish coinage 157
Italian bankers 198, 285–7

Jean I of Brabant 160
Jevons, W.S. 19
Jewish communities and businesses 123–4, 147, 154–7, 178, 186–7, 196–8, 205, 209–12
John, King 147–51, 178–9, 193, 212
John of Gaunt 245
Joliffe, J.E.A. 178
Jones, S.R.H. 93
Jonnson, K. 97

Keene, D. 290
Kermode, J. 259, 287
Kerridge, E. 284, 288–9, 293
King, E. 118, 134
Kitsikopoulos, H. 190, 202
knighthhood, status of 185–7
Knighton, Henry 163
Kosminsky, E.A. 189, 201
Kowaleski, M. 278

Langdon, J. 14, 117, 134–5
Langton, Walter 203, 207
Latimer, P. 146, 149, 154, 176–7
leases 31, 115–16, 185–6, 258
legal tender 44
Leycester, Richard 245, 248
life-expectancy 76, 304

314

INDEX

literacy 33, 133–4, 186, 188, 199–200, 213, 291–2, 295, 306
Lloyd, T.H. 151, 162, 198
London 118, 189
Louis IX of France 165
lushbournes 169
luxury goods, import of 164–5, 230

Macleod, H.D. 12
McNall, C. 278
Maddicott, J.R. 210
Maghfeld, Gilbert 258
Malthus, Thomas 261
manorial structures 126–7
markets and the market economy 37, 117, 175, 183, 191, 213
Marx, Karl 37–8
Masschaele, J. 14, 117, 134–5
Mate, M.E. 156, 206
Mayhew, Nicholas 14–15, 124–8, 144–7, 153, 158, 162–3, 180, 183, 190, 243
McDonald, J. 125
Melton, William de 206–7, 212
Merchants, Statute of (1285) 202–4, 208, 211, 276–7
Metcalf, Michael 59–63, 88–99, 107–8, 146
mintage 69, 156, 158
mints and minting 13, 55–8, 68–71, 88–91, 94–7, 100–6, 131, 141–8, 153, 157–63, 166, 169, 234–41, 248–51
Miskimin, H.A. 180–2
modelling of an economy 259–62, 268, 279
monetagium commune tax 101
monetary policies 99
monetisation 15, 22, 58, 75, 119, 125, 128, 134, 180
 definition of 14
money
 definition of 19–21

flowing to the countryside 130–1
 primitive forms of 19
 regional variations in use of 131–2
 use as a medium of
 exchange 114–17
 see also paper money; purchasing
 power of money; 'sound
 money'
'money economy', emergence
 of 21–4, 28–33, 38–9, 75–6, 93, 113–34, 141, 145, 159, 176, 181–3, 187–8, 213, 260, 274, 304–8
 case against 124–32
 case for 114–24
money markets 211–14
money supply 5–11, 23–8, 39, 72–6, 125, 134, 148–54, 158, 162, 174–91, 205, 212–14, 249, 261–4, 269, 272, 293, 304–6
 definition of 8–11
moneylending 205–10
moneys of account 52
mortgages 193
Multon, Thomas de 206–7
Mun, Thomas 227–8
Mundill, R.R. 210
Munro, J.H.A. 68, 229–30, 240, 248–9, 268, 286
Murray, A. 24, 133

negotiable financial
 instruments 269, 279, 283
Newton, Humphrey 258
Nightingale, P. 52, 90, 101, 122, 146, 231, 269, 276–84, 289, 307
numeracy 33, 133–4, 186, 188, 200, 213, 295, 306

Offa, King 50
Oresme, Nicholas of 35–6, 248
Orme, N. 291

Palastrello, Alessandro 292

315

INDEX

Palmer, R.C. 281
paper money 73–4, 214, 280, 283–4
Paris, Matthew 153
Parkes, Walter 291
parliamentary activity 36–7, 244–8, 270, 273, 294
partnerships 194
Paston letters 258–9
payments in kind 46, 115–16, 128–9, 132
peasant farming 189–91
Penn, S. 268
pennies, use of 50–2
Petersson, H.B.A. 96–7
Phelps Brown, E.H. 266
Philip IV of France 35, 160, 165
Philip VI of France 166
pipe rolls 32–3, 46, 58, 103, 113, 122–3, 129, 134, 144, 185, 205
Piron, S. 34
plague 231–2, 264, 304
plate, holdings of 10–11, 66, 92
Pollard, A.J. 263
pollards 12, 69, 143, 158–62, 240
Poos, L. 268
'population and resources' model of the economy 5, 7–8, 75, 261
population growth 22–4, 117, 134, 145, 174–5, 181–4, 187, 213, 305
Porche, Percival de 167
Postan, M.M. 194, 205, 231, 260–1, 275–80, 283–4
Postan-Abel thesis 266
pounds
    Troy and *Tower* 53–4, 146
    use of 52
poverty 174–5
Prestwich, M. 166
price indexes 266
prices 4–7, 45–9, 156, 161, 175–84, 260–8, 306–7
Ptolemy of Lucca 29–30

purchasing power of money 44–50, 71
purveyance 189

Razi, Z. 201
recognizances 277–82
recoinages 47–8, 53, 57, 59, 66, 69, 87–94, 99–102, 105–6, 131, 141–8, 152–3, 156–8, 161–2, 167–9, 177, 182, 227, 236–9, 247, 293–4
Rectitudines Singularum Personarum 114–15
Rempston, Sir Thomas 271
renforcements de la monnaie 236; *see also* revaluation of currency
renovatio monetae 87, 90, 93, 102, 146
    end of 106
rent payments 115
revaluation of currency 67, 236
Ricardo, David 261
Riccardi family of Lucca 156
Richard I 149, 151
Rigby, S.H. 6–7, 261
Rigold, S.E. 64–5, 190, 271
Robert of Normandy 103–4
Robinson, W.C. 261
Romford (Essex) 280–1, 290
royal officials 207

Salamon de Ripple 47
Sawyer, P.H. 93
Schofield, P.R. 210, 306
Scottish coinage 103, 157–8, 245–6
scriveners 292–3
scutage 118
seignorage 69, 146, 155–8, 161, 168, 189–90
shillings, use of 52
silver, value of 18, 20, 49, 70, 162–3, 167–8
silver coinage 21, 50–1, 87–8, 167–9, 243–4

316

silver mining 48–9, 53, 66–8, 74–5, 103–4, 141–2, 160, 164, 167, 232–4, 308
small change 51, 65, 71, 76, 105, 128, 157, 239, 243–6, 251, 271
Smith, Adam 262
Smith, R. 201
Smith, R.M. 210
Snooks, G.D. 125–8
Sombart, Werner 37
'sound money' 35, 39, 49–50, 133, 247, 294
Spufford, P. 234–5, 249, 263
Stacey, R.C. 123
Statute of Additions (1413) 292
Statute of the Staple (1353) 277–8
Statute of Treasons (1352) 34
statute staple certificates 276–8, 293
Stephen, King 103
Stratton, Adam de 207
stray finds of coins 64–5, 93–4, 131, 190–1
Styfford, William 292–3
subsistence economy 125–7, 132–4, 188–90
Sussman, N. 249
Swanland, Simon 206

tallies, use of 32–3, 121
taxation 35, 58, 118, 122, 159–60, 174–5, 189, 272–3
    on minting 101
    see also geld levies
Tealby coinage 145–7
Terricus of Cologne 209–10
Thorold Rogers, J., M.P. 266
Thorpe, John 293
Thünen, Johann-Heinrich von 262
Tidenham (Gloucestershire) 31, 114
Titow, J.Z. 190
touchstones 55

trade balances 67–8, 92–3, 98, 142, 149–51, 164–5, 181, 233–5, 245–7, 294, 308
trading relations 151
transaction costs 24, 181, 230
transaction volumes 13
Trentegeruns, William 205
trial plates 54–5
'turneys' 163

unemployment 267–8
usury 195–6, 206–7

valets, manorial 125–7
velocity of circulation 6–7, 13–15, 74, 124–8, 132, 180–4
vifgage 193
village-level credit 209–11, 306
Vincent, N. 200

Wade, Henry 210, 212
wages 175, 179–83
    index of 266
    real 264–5, 272
    stickiness of 266–9
war and its consequences 229–30
Watson, A.M. 233
Weber, Max 37
weighing of coins 237–8
weights and measures, standardisation of 29–30, 133–4
Wendover, Roger of 87–8
'white' money 239
William I 12, 52, 91–2, 100–8, 123
William II 92
Willingham (Cambridgeshire) 274–5
Wilson, Harold 260
Worcester, John of 62
Writtle (Essex) 274
Wykes, Thomas 35

317